Goddess and Grail

ALSO BY JEFFREY JOHN DIXON

The Glory of Arthur: The Legendary King in Epic Poems of Layamon, Spenser and Blake (McFarland, 2014)

Goddess and Grail

The Battle for King Arthur's Promised Land

Jeffrey John Dixon

McFarland & Company, Inc., Publishers
Jefferson, North Carolina

LIBRARY OF CONGRESS CATALOGUING-IN-PUBLICATION DATA

Names: Dixon, Jeffrey John, author.
Title: Goddess and grail : the battle for King Arthur's promised land / Jeffrey John Dixon.
Description: Jefferson, North Carolina : McFarland & Company, Inc., Publishers, 2017. | Includes bibliographical references and index.
Identifiers: LCCN 2017024471 | ISBN 9781476668666 (softcover : acid free paper) ∞
Subjects: LCSH: Great Britain—Religion. | Grail. | Goddesses. | Wisdom.
Classification: LCC BL980.G7 D59 2017 | DDC 809/.93351—dc23
LC record available at https://lccn.loc.gov/2017024471

BRITISH LIBRARY CATALOGUING DATA ARE AVAILABLE

ISBN (print) 978-1-4766-6866-6
ISBN (ebook) 978-1-4766-2928-5

© 2017 Jeffrey Dixon. All rights reserved

No part of this book may be reproduced or transmitted in any form or by any means, electronic or mechanical, including photocopying or recording, or by any information storage and retrieval system, without permission in writing from the publisher.

Front cover: *How Sir Galahad, Sir Bors and Sir Percival Were Fed with the Sanct Grael; but Sir Percival's Sister Died by the Way*, 1864, Dante Gabriel Rossetti (1828–1881) (© Tate, London 2017)

Printed in the United States of America

McFarland & Company, Inc., Publishers
 Box 611, Jefferson, North Carolina 28640
 www.mcfarlandpub.com

In memory of
my father Joseph Dixon (1923–2002)
and my friends
Anthony Mark Tuffin (1961–2000)
Anthony Maurice Tuffin (1937–2016)
and Stan Pollard (1951–2016)

Acknowledgments

I couldn't have done it without the support of my family and of friends, including: the Penwauners (Steve, Jenny, Skye and Ben); Sharrisimo; Jill; Derek and Sumie; and the Tuffin clan (Sass, Dan, Chris and the new generation).

Special thanks also to Judy McCallum and the staff at Llandrindod Wells Library, for invaluable help in obtaining research materials; as well as to Martin Williams for insightful comments at an early stage.

Table of Contents

Preface   1
Introduction—The Other World of the Gods   5
Prologue—From Eden to Albion   15

Part 1. Mythological Roots   19

ONE: A Mighty Goddess   20
TWO: The Lady of the Rings   31
THREE: The Otherworld Bride   44
FOUR: Fate and Faerie   58
FIVE: A Woman's Wiles   69
SIX: The View from Fortune's Wheel   87

Interlude • The Deceitful Savior   98

Part 2. Realms of Symbolism   123

SEVEN: By This Sign, Conquer   124
EIGHT: The Prophet of the Grail   137
NINE: Moon Magic   153
TEN: The Marvels of the Holy Grail   171
ELEVEN: Mountains of Heresy   186
TWELVE: An End to Adventures?   203

Epilogue—From Albion to Avalon 223

Appendix—Tolkien's Lonely Isle 231

Chapter Notes 239

Bibliography 247

Index 253

Preface

In this, my third book, I return to the subject of the Grail legend, which was also the focus of my first book, *Gawain and the Grail Quest*, published in 2012. In that work, however, I primarily concentrated on the Grail poets, from Chrétien de Troyes and his continuators in France to Wolfram von Eschenbach and Heinrich von dem Türlin in Germany, contrasting the imaginative creativity and sense of wonder evoked by these writers with the heavily theological sermonizing characteristic of the later prose romances, in which mystery gives way to miracle.

In this new work I revisit the prose tradition, focusing on the last two great cycles, known to scholars as the Vulgate and the Post-Vulgate, which effectively brought to an end the creative outpouring that transformed the literary landscape of twelfth- and thirteenth-century Europe. My reason for doing so is to explore the contrasts between the Vulgate and its successor, the Post-Vulgate, in order to bring to the surface what I see as a tension between two very different concepts of Britain.

The first concept is that of Britain as the Promised Land of the Goddess, which is established by the early Arthurian chroniclers Geoffrey of Monmouth and Wace. Echoes of this idea, as I show in Part One, survive in the Vulgate Cycle, embodied by powerful women endowed with supernatural powers, such as the Lady of the Lake and Morgan the Fay, or of arguably supernatural origin, such as Guenevere. Here, for good or for bad, Britain is an island of fays, or dethroned pagan goddesses—for, as the visionary artist and poet William Blake (1757–1827) puts it: the fairies of Albion are the gods of the heathen.

The second concept is that of Britain as the Promised Land of the Grail, which is established in the course of development of the Vulgate Cycle and reaches its apogee in the Post-Vulgate Cycle. Here, as I show in Part Two, the process of demonization of Faerie (along with women in general) is accentuated; for the Grail Quest is one in which only chaste men can be successful. Nevertheless, our understanding of these cycles has been considerably enriched by the work of two female scholars, on which I have very much relied.

The first is Lucy Allen Paton (1865–1951), whose explorations of the fairy mythology that underlies much of Arthurian romance deserves to be better known. Without accepting all her conclusions, I have found her work inspirational. The second is Fanni Bogdanow (1928–2013), whose studies of the development of the prose cycles has cast great light on a previously obscure part of Arthurian literary history. She has enabled us to see more clearly how, as the Vulgate was reworked into the Post-Vulgate, the Island of the Goddess was disenchanted by the missionary zeal of the Company of the Grail, for whom only one experience of the sacred was permitted.

As with my previous books, my approach to the Arthurian and Grail legends has been informed by the imaginative poetry of Blake, who transformed the figure of the Maimed King into the fallen Albion in the epic cosmogony of his prophetic books; and by the philosophy of the imagination of the French scholar Henry Corbin (1903–78). While primarily focusing on the study of Islamic mysticism, Corbin devoted his life to revealing the lost continent that lies submerged between the dualism of mind and matter, a continent which he named the *imaginal world*. Although most of Corbin's major works are now available in English translation, the complexity of his thought means that we can benefit enormously from the work of Thomas Cheetham, a poet and scholar who has elucidated the ideas of the French philosopher in five books, the latest of which was published in 2015.

Although Blake believed it was necessary to create his own system so as not be enslaved by anyone else's, his belief in the creative power of the imagination was shared by other Romantic poets such as Wordsworth and Coleridge, who argued that the imagination is a reflection in the human mind of the divine creative power. This belief was also championed by the great twentieth century fantasy writer J.R.R. Tolkien (1892–1973) who, like Blake (though much more successfully, at least in his ability to communicate to a wider audience), created his own mythology through a process that he called *mythopoeia*, or "sub-creation." According to Corbin, Tolkien has given us a prelude to the Grail Quest, in which the will to power must be renounced in order to be worthy. Anyone who wishes to gain an insight into the toils and travails of the creation of the myths of Middle-earth will find invaluable help in the twelve volumes that Tolkien's son Christopher has devoted to detailing the creative processes of his father. Equally essential are Humphrey Burton's biography and selection of Tolkien's letters, in many of which the author discusses the development of what he called his *legendarium*.

Whereas Blake's creative process was a lonely one, Tolkien benefited from the intellectual companionship of a group of Oxford-based writers and thinkers known as the Inklings, who followed and for the most part encouraged his discovery (for such he understood it to be) of Middle-earth. Corbin also, from the 1950s to the 1970s, was part of what has justifiably been termed the "alternative intellectual history of the twentieth century" unfolding at the annual Eranos conferences held on the shores of Lake Maggiore in Switzerland. The story of Eranos has at last been given the in-depth treatment it deserves by the German scholar Hans Thomas Hakl, whose exhaustive worked has only been available in English translation since 2013. Consequently, it is only now that we can begin to assess the true significance of the Eranos phenomenon.

The guiding spirit of Eranos in its early years was the Swiss psychiatrist and founder of the school of analytical psychology, C.G. Jung (1875–1961). But the role-call of lecturers includes the German Indologist Heinrich Zimmer (1890–1943), the Hungarian classical scholar Carl Kerényi (1897–1973) and the Romanian historian of religion Mircea Eliade (1907–86); as well as Corbin, who lectured there from 1949 to the year he died, and the American James Hillman (1926–2011), the founder of the Post-Jungian school of archetypal psychology, who gave his first lecture in 1966. The fact that the names of all these thinkers will recur in the course of this book testifies to the influence that Eranos has had on my understanding of the importance of myths and symbols to modern life. More generally, they help us to understand the continuing relevance of Arthurian legend and the Grail Quest to our twenty-first century preoccupation with religious fundamentalism and ecological destruction.

While it seems likely that there was direct transmission of pagan mythological material into the Arthurian romances at an early stage—and while it is even possible, as Jessie L. Weston (1850–1928) argued, that there was direct transmission of ancient Gnostic heretical ideas—I believe that the pagan and gnostic themes and images that scholars have detected in the stories come above all from the artistic imagination, expressed especially in the poetry of the first romances. As the eminent Arthurian scholar Richard Barber has stated, the Grail is neither the creation of pagan religion nor of Christian mysticism, but of poets working with imagination through these traditions. But I would add that, as Blake and Corbin have shown us, by "imagination" we must understand an active intelligence, part of the divinity that shapes our ends.

Whatever ancient pagan myths may have been drawn on and whatever Gnostic heresies may have been rekindled, the stories constitute a mythology in their own right. The Grail Mythos contains its own gnosis, poetic and therefore heterodox at first, but becoming, as the literature developed, increasingly orthodox and mystical at best, or prosaic and didactic at worst.

Nor, Barber adds, is the Grail the creation of the scholars; but there is no doubt that, alongside modern writers of historical and fantasy fiction, they have contributed to the developing mythology. What the scholars have done is precisely to re-open the gnostic Grail Quest, the search for knowledge of the symbol uncovered; by (in Jung's phrase) dreaming the myth onwards. It is my hope that this book will become part of that dream.

Introduction—The Other World of the Gods

> How and where shall we find our entrance from the world of romance into that Other World of the gods?[1]
> —Roger Sherman Loomis

Of all the medieval products of Western European literature, none continue to exert such a hold on the popular imagination as the Arthurian legends. Who has not heard of Lancelot and Guenevere, Galahad and the Holy Grail, Merlin the Magician and the Lady of the Lake? Their names, if not their stories, are known to those who have never encountered the vast literature in Welsh, French and German, to mention only those living languages in which the most important original texts were written, or retold to reach a wider audience. The stories themselves met with great success, since they quickly spread to the edges of the continent, with versions appearing in the Italian and Iberian languages, in those of eastern Europe, in Norse and Dutch and, of course, in English, the vernacular language of the country where so many of the stories are set (although they purport to take place at a time when the English had not yet come to dominate the east, center and south of the island of Britain).

The rapid spread and long-lasting popularity of the stories is even more remarkable when we consider that the core texts which establish the legends were all written in a period of about a hundred years following the appearance, in Latin prose, of the first complete account of the birth, life and doubtful death of the Once and Future King whose reign, according to its chroniclers, was the glorious culmination of a long line of British monarchs: King Arthur. His story is not, however, history as we know it; while the long line of his predecessors is also composed for the most part of legendary characters, purportedly the heirs of a Trojan exile. Brutus, who gave his name to the island of Albion when he conquered it from the giants, was believed to be the great-grandson of Prince Aeneas, who fled the burning city of Troy and whose descendants would also found Rome, the Eternal City.

Classical myths (including the story of Troy) and the British legends (including the story of Arthur) would in fact constitute two of the three great subject matters of medieval literature. The Matter of Rome and the Matter of Britain were complemented by the Matter of France, a cycle of romances recounting the adventures of Charlemagne's paladins, of whom Roland is today the best known. Classical mythology has a continuing hold on western cultural life, but this has little to do with the medieval Matter of Rome; while the Matter of France had a powerful influence on later poets such as Ariosto and Spenser, but its influence has declined since then.

By contrast, the Matter of Britain continued to produce masterpieces in the English language long after the medieval flow of great, original material had trickled out. Sir Thomas Malory translated mainly French romances to produce his "whole book" of King Arthur in the late fifteenth century, giving us in *Le Morte Darthur* a compilation of adventures that would become the basis for all later exploration of the legends in the English language. Spenser's *Faerie Queene* successfully fused elements of the Matter of Britain, particularly its fairy mythology, with the epic verse style of Ariosto, to produce an allegory of Magnificence and Glory in the late sixteenth century. Shakespeare also incorporated British legend into some of his plays, most notably in *King Lear*. But the seventeenth century lacked a great Arthurian epic primarily because John Milton, looking for a suitable subject, rejected Arthur in favor of the Biblical Adam, ironically (to our eyes), because he was never sure that King Arthur had ever really existed.

But it was in the nineteenth century that the English-speaking world really rediscovered Arthur. William Blake incorporated elements of the Matter of Britain into his great prophetic books, but he drew mainly on Welsh traditions; his epic poems never became part of the mainstream of English literature. It was a new edition of Malory, with a scholarly preface by the Poet Laureate Robert Southey, which inspired the imagination of the Pre-Raphaelites and led to the writing of the great Victorian verse cycle, Tennyson's *The Idylls of the King*.

Since then, Arthur has never been far away. His legends have been reinvented for every generation, recycled in every possible form: from bowdlerized retellings for the young with magic and moral fables to uncensored retellings for grown-ups with lashings of sex and violence; in illustrated children's books and adult graphic novels; in paintings, photographs and films; in operas from composers as diverse as Richard Wagner, Ernest Chausson and Harrison Birtwistle.

And alongside the creative retellings comes the scholarly work. From the nineteenth century onwards, we have seen the publication of printed editions of all the important texts—the ones on which popular knowledge of the stories is based—so that now, in the early twenty first century, we have both annotated editions and modern English translations of almost the entire Arthurian corpus.

With the establishment of the texts comes the attempt to interpret them; inevitably so, for meaning is not the preserve of the academy. Speculation is the mirror image of scholarship and the borderline between them is frequently contested. Morgan the Fay has been claimed as a champion of paganism against Christianity; the Grail as a symbol of heretical gnosis rather than orthodox faith; Arthur as a Celtic god…

* * *

And here perhaps we begin to see the answer to the question that must be asked: Why, of the three medieval "matters," is it only the Matter of Britain that continues to have such an important cultural impact?

The answer cannot be simply that the Arthurian legends are full of action and adventure, although these continue to be the staple subject matter of books, comics and films. After all, the *chansons de geste*, the epic poems that recounted the Holy War of Charlemagne against the infidel, are full of both.

Nor can it be simply that there is a mythic quality to the stories: legends are, after all, where history meets myth. But the Matter of Rome was full of myths; yet we turn for our classical mythology to translations of the original texts or to modern retellings and scholarship, not to the medieval versions.

The answer, I believe, is that the stories of King Arthur and his Knights of the Round Table are set only partly in our world; they live, love, fight and die as we all must, but they sometimes wander (for they are *knights errant*), as if by accident (*peradventure*), into *another* world, one which casts a powerful glamour over them and us. It may be the single most important reason why the Matter of Britain has put a spell on Western culture.

Medieval Christendom, of course, always believed in another world; some of us still do. This other world is the Kingdom of Heaven, ruled by the Trinity. Its subjects include the mother of Jesus (the Blessed Virgin Mary) along with the angels (God's messengers) and saints (the souls of the blessed dead). Opposed to this realm and ruled by the fallen angel, Satan, is the Kingdom of Hell, whose subjects include demons, devils and the souls of the damned. Between these two kingdoms is a third world, Purgatory, where dwell souls awaiting redemption.

All three realms were explored in the famous poem of Dante, the *Divine Comedy*. The action of this supposedly took place in 1300 and, therefore, after the creative heyday of the less theologically sound Matter of Britain, to which Dante makes few references (the most famous being a passage in which he warns against the effects of reading about the illicit love of Lancelot and Guenevere). Moreover, the Matter of Britain is rooted in a different triad of worlds, all of which are to be found *on* Earth, though they are not necessarily *of* it.

The first of these three worlds is King Arthur's Kingdom of Logres, whose name is derived from the Welsh word for what is now England (*Lloegr*). It is here that the adventures always begin and end; it is hither that the knights return, if they have survived their quests. It is the British earth in which the Matter is rooted.

Contrasting the court of the Fisher King with the court of King Arthur, the Table of the Grail with the Round Table, we find a kingdom that houses the goal of the highest quest to which Arthur's knights can aspire. But although the Kingdom of the Grail appears to be somewhere in Britain, perhaps between Logres and Wales, it cannot be securely located; not all seekers can find it. Corbenic, the Castle of the Grail, is to Camelot as spirit is to matter: an inspiration to achieve perfection in mortal life in order to go beyond it; as the Grail itself ultimately leaves Corbenic for the eastern city of Sarras (whence Joseph of Arimathea had originally brought it) before being taken up to Heaven. If Logres is where Western chivalry flourishes, then the Kingdom of the Grail re-orients us to the spiritual source of life.

But there is a third world in the Matter of Britain, albeit one that is never as clearly defined as the other two. In fact, this lack of definition is part of its character, which is ever shifting and transforming. This is the Kingdom of Faerie, called Annwfn in Welsh, whose denizens are the fays or elven women and other supernatural beings who share the land with us, albeit often disguised as mere mortals, for illusion is their métier. Nor are they peripheral to the medieval conception of Logres. In a sense, they are at its very heart. One might say they are the soul of the Matter of Britain.

Arthur is conceived in the fairy castle of Tintagel. Fays bless him at his birth. Spenser portrays him as a young prince searching for his ideal love, the fairy queen whom he has seen in a vision. At his end, Arthur goes to dwell with his sister, the ruler of the fairy island of Avalon, whence it is believed he will one day return. During his reign, Arthur's knights fight giants, dragons and other supernatural menaces; but fays are more ambiguous. Knights love them and father heroes on them; but they can also be seen as perilous seductresses, especially in the later Grail romances with their focus on spiritual purity. Their supernatural powers begin to be explained away as the products of arcane arts and sciences practiced by women who have taken up the dangerous craft of book learning.

This intermediate, fairy world lies (not geographically but metaphysically) between the earthly Kingdom of Logres and the spiritual Kingdom of the Grail. It is unearthly, yet not heavenly; nor, despite its eventual denigration as such, is it intrinsically hellish, though its fays come to be seen as devil women. As an in-between world, it is best understood as an *imagined* world, rather than the concrete one seen with the physical senses or the abstract one perceived with the intellect. As such, it corresponds in the microcosm of medieval literature and folklore with what, in the macrocosm, is a universe that can only be perceived by the imagination but which is far from being merely *imaginary*. Seen with what Blake calls the Imaginative Eye, it is a world of vision that only appears when the doors of perception are cleansed, glimpsed in a grain of sand or a wildflower. The French philosopher Henry Corbin calls this the *imaginal* world and argues that it is as objectively real as the universes of mind and matter that are acknowledged in our modern worldview. Yet it has largely been forgotten as the threefold structure of being that it implies has been replaced by a cultural dualism.

This reduction of the trichotomy of mind, image and matter to a dichotomy is paralleled in the western religious concept of the human being, where an ancient threefold structure (body, soul and spirit) has been replaced by the dualism of body and soul. In doing so, soul has been displaced from its role at the heart of the human being, deprived of its traditional function of holding the tension of the opposites. Without this soul bridge, the *contraries* become *negations* (to use Blake's language): matter and spirit, science and religion pull apart; for, as Yeats warned, *things fall apart* when *the centre cannot hold*.

But it is not just that science and religion have come to negate each other. A similar process occurred centuries earlier within the religious worldview itself, when Christianity replaced the Romano-Celtic paganism of Western Europe and the polytheistic pantheons were rejected in favor of a Trinitarian monotheism. Polytheism and monotheism need not negate each other: they can be seen as two different ways of perceiving the same ultimate reality, which is always filtered through the lens of culture and history. But when the Christian Church became the official religion of the Roman Empire, it soon claimed exclusive rights on the soul. The indigenous pagan religions were outlawed, their gods and goddesses demonized.

Yet the ancient deities did not vanish completely. Although there is no evidence for the continuance of worship of the old gods in the British Isles after the eleventh century, medieval Christendom incorporated many elements of the ancient paganism: high ritual magic among the elite; village charms and folk customs among the lowly; images in art. And, in literature, we find the curious presence of supernatural, sometimes immortal, beings in Irish, Welsh and Breton stories: beings that are neither devils nor angels. Medieval Celtic literature was written by Christians so there are no gods and goddesses acknowledged in these stories; but there are many indications that these supernatural beings were once part of pagan religion. Sometimes the names of characters are cognate with those of Romano-Celtic deities known from inscriptions and place names. More often, their attributes and stories read as "fragments of a faith forgotten."

These beings, whom the Irish know collectively as the People of the Síde (pronounced "shee," whence the English "banshee" or "fairy woman"), were once the Tribes of the Gods who ruled Ireland until the coming of the Gael. They were then banished underground, into the hills (*síde*) and caves. In contemporary folklore they dwell in the wild places, in forests, by or beneath lakes, even overseas. Because their domain is *other* than ours, though always close by, it has become known simply as the Otherworld.

Medieval Welsh literature is also full of supernatural beings who may once have been gods. The giant Brân, for example, possessor of a cauldron of rebirth, who has long been seen as the precursor of the Fisher King of the Grail legends, is probably the most important. But we could also mention Lludd Silver Hand (who gave his name to London) and his father Beli, revered as the ancestor of important Welsh dynasties. These, along with several others, have often been suspected of reincarnating as Arthurian knights.

Although we cannot be sure how stories of the Celtic Otherworld and its denizens found their way into Continental Arthurian romance, it seems likely that many of them were transmitted originally from Ireland to Wales, where a poetic tradition associated with the name of the bard Taliesin would have been fertile ground for re-invigorating pagan vestiges. Taliesin was actually a historical, sixth century praise poet but poems of great obscurity containing arcane and frequently anti-clerical material began to circulate in Wales in the centuries after his death, purporting to be by him. These apocryphal, pseudo–Taliesinic poems include one in which he journeys with Arthur to Annwfn, which is also called Caer Sidi (the Fortress of the Síde): thus neatly encapsulating the interweaving of Irish, Welsh and Arthurian elements in the presentation of the Otherworld in medieval literature.

The events of 1066 must have provided fertile ground for the encounter of Breton and French storytellers with the insular material; for, less than a hundred years after the Norman Conquest, a Welsh cleric called Geoffrey of Monmouth wrote the first complete "history" of the Kings of Britain up to the Anglo-Saxon invasion. This incorporated material from an early ninth century Welsh account that presented Arthur as a victorious warlord, but also included much material of a more mythic nature along with a sprinkling of what we would accept as historical facts.

*   *   *

At this point I should also clarify what I mean by "myth," to avoid much possible misunderstanding. Throughout this book, I will call a myth any story about God or the gods, angels and demons, semi-divine heroes and other supernatural beings, regardless of the religious context of the story. Myths are not fictions, though their truth is symbolic and not necessarily literal; while the most inspired fiction aims at a mythical status. Myths are as true on their level of reality (the imaginal) as historical facts are on theirs (the material). It is only by recognizing this that we can escape what Corbin has called the "banal dualism" of myth and history, as Geoffrey of Monmouth did when he combined the two to produce the legends that are the foundation of the Matter of Britain.

Nor should we think of myth-making as the prerogative of archaic or "primitive" cultures. As the Eranos scholars have shown us, mythical thinking is as much a part of the medieval and modern mind-set as it was of those ancient peoples whose mythologies have entered into world literature; or as it is of contemporary hunter gatherers and shamans. Although there is much to be said for the work of those scholars who have attempted to trace elements in the Arthurian stories back to ancient myths, it must be recognized that the Matter of Britain constitutes a feat of myth-making in its own right. It is a medieval mythology loosely interwoven with history to produce legend, a mythology that has continued to develop as it has been added to by poets and writers of fiction up to the present day.

Moreover, there is a fatal flaw in our attempts to trace Arthurian motifs back to ancient originals. For, unfortunately, the Celtic myths of pagan Ireland and Wales have not survived in the way that those of the ancient Greeks and Romans have; or, for that matter, those of the monotheistic religions, which were written down by and for people of the faith. By contrast, the medieval Celtic stories were all written down by people of the new faith, Christianity; so pagan themes survive as elements of marvel and wonder, rather than belief. It is precisely this that guaranteed their continuing appeal. It is the element of the *marvelous* associated with the Otherworld and its inhabitants that enabled originally pagan characters and themes to cross over from Ireland into Wales and thence into continental Europe, where they were absorbed into a burgeoning literature that began when the Jersey cleric Wace translated Geoffrey of Monmouth's Latin *Historia* into French.

Over the next few decades, another French poet, Chrétien de Troyes, made a "beautiful conjunction" out of oral tales and courtly verse, writing the first adventures of King Arthur's knights in a series of poems that would inspire many other, lesser, poets to add to the canon. These, along with Breton *lais* (poems written in French but of continental Celtic provenance), established the *fées* as an almost indispensable feature of Arthurian romance. Supernatural women would both initiate a knight's adventuring and be the goal of his quest, especially in the earliest stories.

As if this was an insufficient achievement, Chrétien went on to write the unfinished story of the Grail, thus introducing that most numinous of symbols into western literature. Furthermore, precisely by leaving the story incomplete with many of its mysteries unexplained, he inspired the next generation of creative artists to write poems that claimed either to continue and finish what he had started, or to put it in an explanatory context. Unfortunately, most of these attempts at "elucidation" served only to complicate a seemingly never-ending story, whose proliferating variations became increasingly difficult to reconcile with each other. Eventually an attempt was made to bring some sort of satisfactory order into the corpus, in the form of vast prose cycles which effectively brought to an end the creative outpouring of original material.

In Chrétien's original poem, we know nothing of the Grail's origins; only that the hero must ask a question about its purpose if the kingdom is to be saved. In the prose romances the story of the Grail starts at the Crucifixion and ends in Heaven. It is identified as a vessel containing the Holy Blood of Jesus and its purpose on Earth seems primarily to inspire the conversion, forced or otherwise, of pagans into Christians; while leading the most Christ-like to another, better world.

The indigenous pagans of Britain (whither the Grail is brought from the Holy Land by Joseph of Arimathea) are worshippers of the seven celestial bodies of traditional cosmology; but their most important deity is the moon goddess, known by her classical name of Diana (or as Tervagant, the Thrice Wandering, since she rules in Heaven, on Earth and in the Underworld). It is Diana who originally guides a group of Trojan exiles to the giant-infested island of Albion in the West, where they become the founders of British civilization, having promised that they and their descendants will worship her in perpetuity. But the arrival of the company bearing the Holy Vessel on these shores in the late first or early second century A.D. means that the Britons will betray that promise, thus setting the scene for a protracted battle between the adherents of the Goddess and the adherents of the Grail.

But this conflict is not just a battle for supremacy between two different religions: it becomes a battle between the theology of a male-dominated Grail cult, focused on the heavenly afterlife (on one hand) and the life of the imagination, embodied in the supernatural women or fays who are the heirs of the old pantheon (on the other) for the soul of Britain. Central to this conflict is the figure of Merlin, for he is the Prophet of the Grail, but he loves a fay who ultimately makes away with him. Whether his disappearance is a retreat into love and nature or a cruel entombment in the earth depends upon who is telling the story.

Once Merlin departs this world, the Quest of the Holy Grail finally brings to a close the story begun about fifty years earlier by Chrétien. The sacred vessel inspires a knight who is pure in thought and deed to set out to find it and, having done so, be helped to leave an Earth which he is clearly too good for! The afterlife, it would appear, has won out; the fays fade from view. Deprived of its central, mediating role, the imagination is co-opted by the two opposing negations: buried in the Earth, it succumbs to literalism; or carried off to Heaven, it is exalted into unworldly abstraction. Either way, Logres is disenchanted.

* * *

But that is not the end of the story; for it was continued primarily in English—perhaps surprisingly, since that is the language of the conquerors of Britain whom King Arthur had resisted so successfully during his lifetime. English poets in the fourteenth century adopted Gawain rather than Lancelot as their favorite hero and, although this trend was partly reversed by Malory (reworking mainly French texts into his *Morte Darthur*), he also mitigated the anti-cosmic mysticism of the Grail story in a work that celebrates earthly chivalry. At the same time, he made the goal of the quest the Sangreal, the Royal Blood of Jesus, rather than the vessel that contained it; so effectively bringing us back down to Earth with blood, instead of exalting us to Heaven with grace.

But it was Spenser who re-introduced the fairy mythology that connects us both with the natural world (whose domain is that of the elves and fays as much as it is ours) and with the other world of the gods, thus beginning the process of re-enchanting Logres. In doing so, he paved the way for the great work of William Blake, who substituted inspired vision for Spenser's allegorizing, re-imagining Britain as the domain of the fallen giant Albion: Divine Humanity shrunken and divided against itself when war breaks out in Heaven.

It is Blake who can be seen as discovering, or restoring, the inner meaning of the Arthurian legends, at the same time as providing a prequel to the medieval stories of the Matter of Britain. It is therefore with Blake—whose epic poems take us from before the Creation to the Last Judgment—that we will begin, as we will end.

Prologue—From Eden to Albion

> Arthur was a name for the constellation Arcturus, or Boötes, the keeper of the North Pole. And all the fables of Arthur and his round table; of the warlike naked Britons; of Merlin; of Arthur's conquest of the whole world; of his death, or sleep, and promise to return again ... of the Giants of Ireland and Britain; of the elemental beings called by us by the general name of fairies.... All these things were written in Eden.[1]
> —William Blake

In the great epic poems that he wrote at the beginning of the nineteenth century, most of which he produced as illuminated books, William Blake was drawn to the medieval stories which constitute the Matter of Britain as much as he was to those of the Bible. In fact, he tried to combine the two in a unique synthesis that makes of Albion (the poetical name for Britain) and Canaan (the Biblical Promised Land) one united Holy Land before the Fall: this is Blake's Eden.

In doing so, Blake also reconciled other opposites, as part of his task of transforming *negations* into *contraries* without which (he stated) there can be *no progression* (BCW 149). For example, in his day the Matter of Britain was understood as profane history, as opposed to the sacred history of the Bible; but the legendary figures that he chose for his personal, idiosyncratic mythology were rediscovered as (or reworked into) metaphysical entities who exist before the foundation of Britain as a historical identity.

In so doing, he managed to avoid two related pitfalls which bedeviled all the histories of Britain written up to that date, including that of Milton whom he so admired. The first was the pitfall of factual inaccuracy, principally caused by the reliance of historians on untrustworthy sources and by their lacking the critical tools to separate the wheat from the chaff. The second was the pitfall of confusing history with myth, principally caused by a theological tradition of crediting the Bible with historical accuracy as well as divine revelation, since then only other cultures' religions could be dismissed as being based on myths.

By transforming what he thought of as history into myth—by, that is, tracing the external events back to their spiritual archetypes—Blake no longer had to concern himself unduly with the accuracy of the historical material he had inherited. He could avoid what Henry Corbin (1995, 12) has called the "fatal" choice between history and myth, thus pointing the way to overcome our modern dualism through the creative imagination. Hence Blake's creation story begins in Eden, before the separation of myth and history, where the Giant Albion dwells in harmony with his female counterpart (daughter or "emanation"), Jerusalem, in whom we can see the ancient figure of Divine Wisdom. But when the four Living Beings (whom he calls Zoas, from the Greek word for "life") who are the component parts of Albion start to vie with each other for supremacy—notably the Zoas of Imagination and Reason—there is War in Eden.

Creating his own mythological system, Blake re-visions Albion as the Eternal or Ancient Man who once held the Starry Heavens in his mighty limbs but who is now shrunken to an island in the Atlantic, "a Rocky fragment from Eternity" (*BCW* 685). The fairies he sees as air elementals fallen into materialization, who would be worshipped as gods by the heathen. Arthur is the Giant Albion himself, fallen into time and space, incarnated as a Prince of the Dark Ages; while Guenevere, Arthur's wife, is the incarnation of one of the Daughters of Albion.

Beautiful but destructive because divided from their source and from each other, the Daughters are really aspects of the False Female, the shadow of Jerusalem, who is exiled into the East when Albion falls. But if Jerusalem is only a shadow of her former self, so Albion, bereft of Wisdom, is reduced to a Spectre, suspended between Heaven and the Abyss in a deathlike sleep. So it is that, although there is no Grail in Blake's Mythos, Albion is in effect a Maimed King and the story of his healing is Blake's equivalent of the Grail Quest.

The enormous task Blake was inspired to undertake was not just to show the consequences of the division of Albion (West) and Jerusalem (East), which created both the shadowy False Female and an equally dangerous male Spectre with seemingly endless subdivisions. He also sought to show how they could be re-integrated through the Immortal Imagination, so that East and West could become again one planet able to contain all things in Heaven and Earth: "the Human Existence itself" (522). This planet seen through Blake's Imaginative Eye is the materialization of the primordial Human Being from whose limbs the Starry Heavens are now fled, for Albion has fallen into division and sleep. The awakening of Albion, which is also the return of Arthur, will re-unite not just East and West, Woman and Man, but also Heaven and Earth.

The unfolding of this vision was explored through the thousands of lines of verse and hundreds of illuminated pages of Blake's prophetic books. While we must each decide to what extent he was able to succeed in painting, in words and images, things un-attempted yet, I would suggest that one of his greatest achievements was to locate the story of Arthur within the myth of Albion for, in doing so, Blake bids us begin the process of re-enchanting the landscape, which is littered with evocations of the Sleeping Lord. But Arthur will return with tenfold splendor and, though the medieval stories always portray this event as occurring in the future in linear time, for Blake the awakening is a Last Judgment which is always happening here, now, in vision.

Before creation Albion, his wife Britannia and their daughter Jerusalem dwell together in Eternity but, when Albion falls into Chaos, creation begins: The Holy Land, which once encompassed the whole Earth, is divided between Canaan (East) and Albion (West). The story of Britannia, when Albion and Jerusalem become separated, is that creative struggle which we know as the Matter of Britain and which Blake calls the British Antiquities. But Blake does not retell any of the stories of Merlin and Arthur with which we are familiar. Rather, he presents us with the archetypal reality behind the king and his prophet. Thus Arthur is described as the Spectre of Rational Power and Merlin as the personification of Immortal Imagination. And so it is that when, in the Dark Ages, Merlin acts as a spiritual guide to King Arthur, this is a blest moment in time when Reason and the Imagination work together in harmony.

It will not last. But, at the point where Albion has reached the nadir of his descent from Eternity into Chaos, we are presented with a vision of redemption: The Heavenly Canaan is seen above Albion's Land but since, for Blake, "What is Above is Within" (709), we must understand that the heavenly Canaan is also *within* the earthly Albion. It is the spiritual substance that animates it, its soul. Here Albion's island becomes revealed, like the Biblical Canaan, as a Promised Land—the promise being the restoration of the state of wholeness to which his divided self aspires and to which his soul will lead him, until the earthly Isle of Albion and the heavenly Canaan can become one, when the Sleeping Lord awakes.

Thus what Blake effectively does in his epic poems is to provide us with a Prologue in Heaven to the events on Earth: For the mythical War in Eden is reflected in the legendary history of the invasion of Albion's Land, with which the Matter of Britain commences.

The chronicles tell us that before the civilizing of the island, it is inhabited only by giants—for Blake, primeval powers which have become dehumanized through the fall of Albion. Brutus, a Trojan exile who will give the island its new name of Britain, is guided to the western Paradise by a threefold goddess whose role is as ambiguous as any of Blake's Daughters. Like every earthly Paradise, this other world of the Goddess is guarded by supernatural beings. As the giants of Canaan bar the way to the Israelites, so the giants of Albion bar the way to the Trojans; but they must be overcome for the land to fulfil its promise.

For, if Canaan is the Promised Land of the Israelites (the children of Jacob), Albion is the Promised Land of the Britons (the children of Brutus) and if the kingdom of Israel which will be created after the exodus from Egypt is the Promised Land of Yahweh, the kingdom of Britain which will be created after the exodus from Troy is the Promised Land of the Goddess. It is this Goddess and her transformations in the Arthurian legends that we will encounter in the following chapters.

Part 1.
Mythological Roots

"The marvellous adventures were not invented by any one artist, however cunning, at any particular time or place. Their roots are in the mythology, the religion … of a whole people. Men of literary skill have from time to time retouched and renewed the Grail story, but its source is far back in ages gone by. It is a brook of clear water proceeding out of the impenetrable forest of the past … the great imaginative legend of the western world…."

—A.C.L. Brown[1]

One

A Mighty Goddess

"Mighty goddess of the forest, terror of woodland boars,
  you who can travel through celestial orbits
and through the halls of death...."[1]
—Geoffrey of Monmouth

The Matter of Britain shares with another popular medieval cycle, the Matter of Rome, the tragic events of the Fall of Troy as the foundational cataclysm out of which new empires would be born in a mythic pattern of destruction and rebirth.

The two cycles also share an ancestral hero, Aeneas (the son of the goddess Venus); whose descendants would build both the Roman and the British empires, competing against each other, at least according to the British chronicles, for world domination. But although Venus is the divine ancestress of the Britons it is another goddess, Diana, who is responsible for guiding Brutus, the great-grandson of Aeneas, to the island that will henceforth bear his name and where she will be worshipped forever.

Brutus and the last of the free Trojans are wandering the Mediterranean in search of a land where they can make their home when they come to the uninhabited island of Leogetia, two days' sail from the Grecian mainland. This island, which has been devastated and depopulated by pirates, is sacred to Diana: for, in the ruins of a once mighty city, the exiles find her temple and, within its precincts, an oracular statue of the goddess herself.

This Brutus consults by sacrificing a white hind—an animal which is especially sacred to Diana—and mixing its blood with wine in a goblet. Raising the sacrificial goblet in his right hand, he asks the powerful goddess, who can travel through "the airy heavens and the halls of hell" (*HKB* 65), to grant him a home where he can dedicate temples to her and worship her forever. He repeats this prayer nine times before casting the wine and blood onto a fire he has built in front of a make-shift altar and then lying down on the skin of the hind to sleep.

During the night Brutus dreams that the goddess appears to him in a vision and bids him seek a sea-girt island in the western ocean where dwell only giants.[2] This will be their new home—a second Troy—and from it his descendants will make themselves the masters of the world.

From the Goddess of Wild Animals to the Mysteries of Holy Night

Who is this mighty goddess (*diua potens*) who promises an island to Brutus and his progeny so that it will forever be sacred to her?

Diana is the Latin name for the moon goddess whom the Greeks worshipped as Artemis. Her brother is Apollo and their mother is a Titaness who was born in the land of the Hyperboreans, "at the back of the North Wind." This legendary northern Paradise has been identified by some scholars with Britain.[3]

The stories about Artemis in Greek mythology have been exhaustively explored by Anne Baring and Jules Cashford, two contemporary Jungian analysts who are concerned to trace both the historical evolution of the image of the Goddess[4] in human culture and its mythical evolution in the human psyche; for, as they point out: "Myths are not history, yet they manifest in time and create history and so are clothed in the language of becoming and change" (305).

Baring and Cashford show how the image of the Goddess can be traced back to the sculpted figurines that have survived from the Paleolithic (Old Stone) Age and they explore the way in which people at the end of the last Ice Age, before the development of solar calendars, would have used the moon to measure time and change. From this, they imaginatively reconstruct the way in which Paleolithic people would have experienced the phases of the moon—its waxing and waning, its apparent death and rebirth—as an image of their own existence. This, they consider, is the birth of the power to see and experience life *imaginally*, out of which arises "the inexhaustible creativity of humanity. Myth was the expression of this primordial experience" (19).

If mythical thinking arises from our experience of the moon, it is fitting that the moon should be "the central image of the sacred" for the earliest peoples and that it should remain "one of the supreme images of the Goddess" right up to the classical mythology with which we are today most familiar, as well as in poetry and metaphorical speech. The moon goddess could be seen as embodying in her divine person the breaking asunder of the primordial unity and its ultimate restoration: "Duality, imaged as the waxing and waning moon, was contained and transcended in her totality" (21).

One of the enduring images of the Goddess of the Old Stone Age is that of the Lady of the Wild Animals. Baring and Cashford suggest that the Paleolithic myth of the goddess, expressed as sculptures made out of "the enduring substances" of stone and bone, contains within itself the myth of the hunter, expressed as cave paintings that dramatize the rupturing of the unity of "the goddess as the eternal image of the whole" by an act of killing that is necessary for survival in time.

Just as, in the person of the moon goddess, life and death can be understood as contraries, rather than negations, so, when the cave is understood as "the womb of the goddess," hunter and hunted can participate in "a continuum of relationship" and be "contained in one vision." But this unified vision, though it persisted through the invention of agriculture in the Neolithic era (or New Stone Age), was apparently lost in Old Europe when the new myth of the warrior hero arose in the Bronze Age, about four thousand years ago[5]; for his story can negate rather than complement that of the Goddess. "When this happens, the connection with the invisible dimension out of which both life and death come, and which confers sanctity on both, is lost.... Life in time came to be separated from the vision of eternity as the part broke away from the whole" (39f). Baring and Cashford argue that both the pagan mystery cults and Christianity were attempts in the western psyche to restore that lost connection.

Along with the Bible, it is classical mythology which provides modern Western culture with its deepest and richest literary images, reflecting the archetypal human experiences of life and death, of sexuality and spirituality, of ecstasy and tragedy; as well as of the possibility of transformation. The Mysteries even offered the hope of transcending death through initiatory rebirth (an offer that Christianity would extend to the community of the faithful and not just to the "gnostic" elite). But, because initiates were vowed to silence on pain of death, we know very little about these cults.

The spread of Christianity throughout the Roman Empire in the second century (a development alluded to in the legend of the conversion of Britain during the reign of King Lucius) would mean the discovery of a new moral vision. But at the same time and perhaps to some extent in response to the challenge of the new religion, classical paganism underwent something of a renaissance. In particular, an empire that had reached the greatest extent of its worldly conquests began to turn inwards on itself, searching for something more than the material wealth and physical fecundity that the exoteric religious cults offered. In consequence there was a rise in interest in the mystery cults that, wherever they originated, would now be transported to the far-flung reaches of the empire by soldiers and traders. Their appeal was, above all, that they restored the lost "vision of eternity" and, in some cases, they restored the unified image of the Goddess as "the central image of the sacred."

This can be illustrated by a famous passage in a work of Roman literature, *The Golden Ass*, written in what is now Algeria by a lawyer called Lucius Apuleius around the middle of the second century. He would thus have been contemporary with the British Lucius, if the latter had any historical reality; but, where the legendary king is believed to have found Christ, the North African Lucius was initiated into a series of Mystery cults (including those of Dionysus, whose mystical association with wine would be absorbed into early Christianity).

We do not know if Lucius Apuleius ever found what he was looking for, but he has left a remarkable account of his spiritual odyssey in his only surviving novel, an early example of what we now call "magical realism." Towards the end of the book the eponymous narrator, whose magical transformation into an ass is only one of his misfortunes, tells us how he falls asleep on a secluded beach, praying for release from his cursed condition, only to awaken to the sight of the full moon rising from the sea. He invokes her as the Supreme Goddess, the Blessed Queen of Heaven and Mother of the Harvest, as celestial Venus and as dread Proserpina (Persephone), who was lost and found (*TL* 268–9).

Falling back asleep, Lucius has a "transcendent vision" of the shining goddess, who tells Lucius: "I am Nature, the universal Mother, mistress of all the elements, primordial child of time, sovereign of all things spiritual, queen of the dead, queen also of the immortals, the single manifestation of all gods and goddesses that are.... Though I am worshipped in many aspects, known by countless names, and propitiated with all manner of different rites, yet the whole round earth venerates me" (271).

The Goddess tells him that, in the course of her festival the next day, at which she will be invoked as the Daughter of the Stars, Mother of the Seasons and Mistress of the Universe, she will effect his transformation back into a human being. In return, he must dedicate the rest of his days to her service. He will be rewarded by her favor in this world and the next.

The Mistress has made him an offer he can't refuse and so, the next day, his miraculous transformation completed, Lucius enters the service of the Almighty Goddess, a service which is perfect freedom and which culminates in his initiation "into the mysteries of the holy night" (283). Concerning this initiation, he can tell us only that he set foot on the threshold of Proserpina, saw the sun at midnight and experienced the gods of both the lower and the upper-world as presences (286).

Though the author himself humorously suggests that we will be none the wiser for this "inside story," we can nevertheless see an important pattern shining, like the midnight sun, through the allusive words. In the images of death and rebirth, of midnight and sunshine, of upper-world and underworld, we can see the paradoxical coming together of opposites and their overcoming—and know that this is the transcendental experience of the Goddess.

That Untamed Region

The paradoxical transcendence of opposites is also implicit in the Greek stories of Artemis, one of the "thousand names" of the Great Goddess according to Apuleius. Whereas Diana, in British legend, presides over the founding of a great civilization, in the earlier Greek myths Artemis is a goddess of wild places and is often found hunting "where the wild things are." As such, she inherits the mantle of the Paleolithic Goddess of the Wild Animals of the Hunt, embodying, according to Baring and Cashford, the lost wisdom "both of outer nature and of that untamed region of human nature, and of the necessary relation between them" (323). This relation needs her mediation, insofar as, in the classical world, the Stone Age myth of the hunter has been replaced by the Bronze Age myth of the warrior-hero and the "primal unity" of the myth of the goddess has been shattered.

Artemis therefore presents herself to the Greek consciousness, paradoxically, as "both hunter and hunted, since the wild animals are the goddess herself incarnate in animal form" (324). The animals she is especially associated with are the deer and the bear.

One of her most famous myths concerns the hunter Actaeon, who accidentally surprises her while she is bathing; the ever-virgin goddess, jealous of her privacy, transforms him into a stag and his own hounds tear him to pieces. The image of the goddess bathing naked may remind us of those medieval lays in which the hero discovers a fay bathing in a fountain—a prelude to his amorous stay in the Otherworld—and, whenever we witness the hunt of a white stag in the Arthurian romances, we can be sure that we will soon find ourselves in Faerie. As we will see in Chapter Nine, it is as a huntress of deer that the Arthurian court first encounters the Lady of the Lake.

The bear also has Arthurian connections, since it gives the king his name ("bear" is *arth* in modern Welsh), while Blake followed scholars of his time in identifying Arthur with Arcturus, the star that guards the Pole in the constellation of the Bear (*Arktos*). Artemis' handmaidens are "little bears" (*arktoi* in Greek), dedicated to lifelong chastity in her honor. But when one of them, Callisto ("the beautiful") grows up and becomes pregnant, the goddess transforms her into a bear and would have hunted her to death, had Zeus not transformed Callisto into a constellation, the Great Bear. The classical scholar Carl Kerényi suggests that, in the earliest form of this myth, Callisto herself was "the beautiful" Artemis and that she and Zeus coupled in the form of bears (146). Their son is Arcas, whose name, like that of Arthur, means "bear." In this reading, Artemis is the Great Bear goddess and Arthur, the Son of the Bear.

Another animal association of Artemis is with the cat, in the version of her myth preserved by early mythographers and reprised by the Roman poet Ovid. Here we are told that when the monstrous Typhon, the youngest son of Mother Earth, attacks the Olympian gods, they flee to Egypt where they disguise themselves as animals. Artemis takes the form of a cat (*MO* 124f), thus revealing her identity with the Egyptian cat-goddess, the Eye of the Moon.

However, the identification of Artemis with the cat-goddess goes back to at least the fifth century BCE, in the writings of the Greek historian Herodotus (*HH* 176). In Egyptian mythology the cat goddess can be as ferocious as a lioness and it is this ferocity that we see in the curious British myth of a giant supernatural cat that finds its way from the Welsh Triads to Arthurian romance in the early thirteenth century.

The Devil Cat

According to the Triads, Coll, one of the Three Enchanters of the Island of Britain, is tending swine in Cornwall when it is prophesied that an Old White Sow in his care is pregnant with offspring that will be burdensome for the island. Hearing of this, King Arthur assembles his armies and sets off to destroy her. She escapes and travels round Wales giving birth at different places to grains of wheat and barley and to honey bees.[6] These three gifts to the people of Wales are matched by the births of three creatures of prey: an eaglet, a wolf cub and a kitten.[7]

It is under the Black Stone of Llanfair, near the ancient Roman fortress of Segontium, that the kitten is born; but Coll, the Powerful Swineherd, who has been chasing the Old White Sow throughout her itinerary, throws it into the Menai Straits (which separate the Isle of Anglesey from the mainland). The supernatural creature does not drown, however. On the contrary, it is rescued by the sons of Palug, growing up on Anglesey (Môn) to become one of the Three Great Oppressions of that island (*TYP* 52). This monstrous cat kills its rescuers eventually, but is in turn killed by Cei (Sir Kay) in Welsh legend (473f).

However, it turns up again in the thirteenth-century *Estoire de Merlin* (part of that cycle of French prose romances known, because of their popularity, as the Vulgate) where it is called the Devil Cat of the Lake of Lausanne. King Arthur has just achieved his greatest victory—the defeat of the Romans and their allies—and is considering whether to march on Rome itself, to add the Eternal City to his continental empire, or to return to Gaul to consolidate his victory. As usual, he turns to Merlin for advice; but the prophet reveals that destiny has another life-and-death struggle in store for him: Arthur must neither go back to Gaul, nor on to Rome, but across the Lake of Lausanne in what is now Switzerland. There he must fight a devil who has laid waste the countryside, killing and maiming everyone it encounters—a devil, not in human form, but in the shape of a huge cat.

The origin of the monster is then revealed by Merlin, who has been given knowledge of all past events by his own demonic father: It was on the Feast of the Ascension, four years earlier, that a fisherman on the lake, seeking divine help, promised to sacrifice to God the first fish he caught. In the event, however, the fisherman hooked such an enormous, beautiful and valuable pike that, believing his need to be greater than the Lord's, he decided it would be better to keep it and sacrifice his second catch instead. But when this turns out to be worth even more than the first, the fisherman decides that it should be third time lucky for God. His third catch, though, is not a fish at all, but a black kitten. This, also, the poor man feels unable to sacrifice, since it would be useful to free his house of vermin. Consequently, he takes it home; but the creature grows to such a size that it is big enough to strangle him, along with his wife and children. Thence it escapes to a mountain on the far side of the Lake of Lausanne and there it lies in wait for anyone or anything that passes, killing everything it touches.

It is this creature, Merlin tells Arthur, which the king must destroy before he can reach Rome; for its lair lies directly in his path. Accordingly, accompanied only by his trusted advisor and a handful of loyal warriors, King Arthur sets out through a landscape deserted by its people, who have all fled to escape the beast. At last Merlin guides him to a cave on the mountaintop where the cat dwells. At Merlin's whistle, the monstrous creature emerges. A ferocious battle ensues, in which the king barely escapes with his life. But the cat, whose claws are so sharp that they penetrate his armor, cannot withdraw them; so Arthur lops them off, splitting the cat in two with his sword as it tries to hop back to its cave.

The cat's giant paws are brought to Arthur's court as a trophy and the mountain where it was killed is henceforth known as the Hill of the Cat.

The Cult of Tervagant

On one level, this story can be seen as a simple fable of the consequences of not rendering to God what is God's. But, when we take into account its roots in Welsh legend (perhaps deriving from pagan Celtic mythology) and explore its associations with the symbolism of the moon goddess, we can see that it is emblematic of a conflict that, for hundreds of years, existed between the followers of the indigenous religion of this island and those who were exclusive in their embrace of the good news of Christ.

We do not know when the first Christian missionaries arrived on British soil, but we do know that, by the end of the fourth century, the Emperor Theodosius declared the Catholic faith as promulgated in the Nicene Creed to be the official state religion of the empire. The Edicts of Theodosius thus put an end to the pagan imperial religion that, in Britain as elsewhere in Europe, encouraged the identification of native with Roman deities. However, if there was a Celtic moon goddess whom the Romans identified with Diana, we do not know her name.[8]

Where history and archaeology are inconclusive, the legends of the Matter of Britain can provide us with an imaginative theology and metahistory that tell us more about the soul of its people than science.

We have already seen that it is Diana who leads Brutus and his Trojan exiles to the island of Albion, promising the country to him and his descendants on condition that she is worshipped there forever. No trace remains of whatever temples Brutus might have built in her honor; but there is no question that a goddess as popular as Diana would have had her cult in Roman Britain.[9] In fact, we get a fictional glimpse of her worship in an episode from another part of the Vulgate Cycle, the *Estoire del Saint Graal*.

Here Joseph of Arimathea, having brought the sacred vessel to Britain, is travelling in the Forest of Broceliande[10] when he encounters a Saracen—that is to say, not a Moslem, as the term was generally meant to indicate in the Middle Ages, but a follower of an astral cult whose sacred center had once been the Middle Eastern city of Sarras. Joseph and the Company of the Grail had travelled from Jerusalem to Sarras, where they converted the king and his people to Christianity; but, when they arrive in Britain, they find that the cult of the Saracens has long been firmly established there. Joseph is told that the British Saracens worship a trio of deities: Jupiter, Apollo and Tervagant.[11]

This last name, sometimes written "Termagant," is believed to be a corruption of *Trivagante*, "thrice wandering," a title of the moon as it travels through the three worlds of heaven, earth and underworld.[12] In this reading Tervagant is none other than Diana who, as Geoffrey of Monmouth points out, is as much at home above or below the earth as she is hunting in its forests. The British Saracens therefore worship a triad consisting of the Father God (Jupiter) and his children the Sun (Apollo) and the Moon (Diana).

The Saracen, whose name is Argon, tells Joseph that his brother Matagran has lain sick for over a year with a head wound and that neither his people's doctors, nor their gods, have been able to help him. Joseph offers to come with Argon to the Castle of the Rock, where his brother lies, in order to heal the injured man with the help of Him who is the Way and the Life. As they approach the castle, however, Argon is killed by an escaped lion—a creature who we might suspect of being an agent of the lunar cat-goddess. The Saracen moon goddess, it would appear, is ferocious in defense of her cult against the newcomer—but to no avail.

Joseph is brought before the injured brother and he challenges Matagran to invoke the power of his gods, through their images, to bring the dead man back to life. Needless to say, they are unable to do so and furthermore, when Joseph prays to God the Father to glorify His faith by demonstrating the powerlessness of the pagan deities, a thunderstorm rends the sky and shakes the earth. Lightning (traditionally the weapon of Jupiter, now recuperated by a higher deity) strikes the images, burning them to the ground.

Impressed at the sight of the images of his gods in ashes, Matagran agrees to worship only the Christian God if He can restore his dead brother to life. Joseph then prays to the God who created both sun and moon but who nevertheless "deigned to be born of the Virgin maiden" (*LG* I, 142). This maiden is, of course, the Virgin Mary, whose cult was to no small degree inherited from that of the virgin goddess, Diana or Artemis.[13]

Joseph asks God to bring Argon back to life, just as He Himself rose from the dead. When the dead man arises, hale and whole, everyone in the castle is baptized. Their goddess Tervagant (in the form of a lion) could kill, but she could not restore the dead to life. The extent to which even her theriomorphic forms will be taken over by the new religion is made clear shortly afterwards, when Joseph of Arimathea's son, Josephus, the first Christian bishop, has a vision of a white stag protected by four lions.

When the companions of Josephus ask him what the creatures signify, he tells them that they symbolize the High Master, "who sometimes shows Himself obscurely to his disciples" (144). The white stag, he then explains, symbolizes the virgin Jesus and the four lions, the evangelists.

We can thus see that, even during the initial missionary work of the Company of the Grail, the animal symbols of the moon goddess have been taken over by the newly revealed god. Combined with the burning of her images, this is to add insult to injury. No wonder the goddess shows her dark, destructive face when she reappears!

ONE: *A Mighty Goddess*

The conversion of Britain to Christianity is, according to legend, completed during the reign of the good King Lucius. So it is that, from around the middle of the second century after Christ (when Lucius is believed to have died), pagan worship is ended among the native Britons and the temples of the gods transformed into churches. Some three hundred years later, however, there is an attempt to reintroduce the pagan gods into Britain by the Anglo-Saxons, who are allowed to settle in this island by the treacherous King Vortigern. According to the Worcestershire clergyman Layamon (or Lawman), who translated the Matter of Britain into vernacular English for the first time, Tervagant was the name of one of the powerful deities served by the incomers (*Brut* l.6942).

However, the attempt by the Anglo-Saxons to colonize Britain and return it to paganism would be thwarted, temporarily, by a succession of Christian monarchs: Aurelius Ambrosius and Uther Pendragon, the sons of the last Roman Emperor of Britain (the usurper Constantine III) and, most famously, by King Arthur, the son of Uther. Arthur, having unified the island under his rule and driven out the pagan invaders, goes on to conquer most of Western Europe and achieves a (literally) fabulous victory over the Romans. It is after the death of the Roman Emperor that Arthur encounters the Devil Cat of Lausanne: a devil which we can now see as the angry, disinherited moon goddess, whose worship the Britons had once sworn to maintain forever, in return for her guiding them to the Promised Land.

The Dream of Flualis

If Diana appears in her destructive, feline form during the Arthurian period, it may be because her worship has not just been effectively outlawed by Christianity, but that it has been violently suppressed: an event that is depicted in the Vulgate Cycle in the curious story of the dream of King Flualis.

Shortly before the war with Rome and Arthur's battle with the moon cat, Merlin makes an impromptu visit to Jerusalem, travelling at supernatural speeds until he arrives at the court of the pagan Flualis, a worthy man within the context of his beliefs and religious laws, but nevertheless a Saracen. Flualis has gathered together the wise men of many lands in order to consult them about the meaning of a nightmare he has had:

He dreams that he and his wife are attacked during the night by fire-breathing serpents, which set fire to their palace and tear off their limbs. Carrying their limbs up to the top of the Temple of Diana, where the royal couple's followers have fled for safety, the dragons rip them to pieces. Finally they burn what remains of the king and queen to ashes, which the wind scatters towards the sea.

King Flualis is sufficiently worried by the dream to offer his daughter and his kingdom to whoever can interpret it for him. Merlin does so: the dragons are neighboring Christian kings who have set the pagan kingdom ablaze; their dismembered limbs signify their pagan children, who will be cut to pieces inside the Temple of Diana; the burning to ashes of the royal couple means that they will be purified of their sins through holy baptism; while the scattering of their ashes signifies that they will have Christian children to replace the dead ones, worthy knights who will be honored throughout the world.

With that Merlin vanishes, leaving King Flualis deeply distraught at what he has heard. Shortly thereafter it all comes true: his children are killed in the Temple of Diana, which is torn down and its sanctum violated; his land is laid waste, his palace burnt and he and his wife are taken prisoner and converted—or, as our text has it, "washed and cleansed from the filth of misbelief" (*LG* I, 414). The newly christened couple have numerous progeny who believe that it is their divinely appointed mission to exalt Christianity and they swear that they will not die until they have subjected all of heathendom to the law of God.

Accordingly, they invade Greece, Cyprus, Constantinople, the Barbary Coast and Spain; while some even make their way to the Kingdom of Logres to serve that most Christian king, Arthur. But, if the story of Flualis' dream shows the violent destruction of the worship of Diana and the other pagan gods throughout the Mediterranean, it does not mean that the moon goddess ceases to be active. In fact, we are given strong indications that, while all this destruction is going on abroad, she is still manifesting, albeit in disguised form, in Britain. There she will reappear as the beloved of Merlin, a fay who is best known as the Lady of the Lake.

It is her story, which represents the continuing story of the moon goddess in Britain, which we will begin to explore in the next chapter.

Two

The Lady of the Rings

> [T]he fay of Arthurian romance is essentially a supernatural woman, always more beautiful than the imagination can possibly fancy her, untouched by time ... altogether unlimited in her power. Insistent love is a fundamental part of her nature....[1]
> —Lucy A. Paton

The first known reference to the Lady of the Lake in Arthurian literature is in Chrétien de Troyes' poem *Le Chevalier de la Charrette* where its hero Lancelot, the eponymous Knight of the Cart, calls upon the help of the woman who raised him, whenever he encounters malign magic. This woman is a fay (*une fée*) and she has given him a magic ring: all he has to do is hold it in front of his eyes and call on her name. If he is menaced by enchantment, she will come to his aid wherever he is (*CC* ll.2335–50).

We hear no more of this mysterious lady from Chrétien. The main narrative thrust of the poem is the story of Lancelot's rescue of Guenevere, the woman he loves, from the Prince of Gorre (Meleagant), a story that would be reworked into prose as part of the Vulgate Cycle. The enormous romance known as the Prose *Lancelot*, which constitutes the bulk of that cycle, also gives us an account of the abduction of the young Lancelot by the Lady of the Lake. But the first surviving account of the childhood of Lancelot is actually found in a German poem, although it may be based on a French original which also influenced the Vulgate version: Ulrich von Zatzikhoven's *Lanzelet*, which probably dates from the end of the twelfth century (*UZL* 6, 10–13). Here we discover that the woman who raised him is a mermaid or Water Fay who lives on a paradisiacal Island of Maidens, where time stands still and flowers bloom all year round. We also discover that she abducted him as a child, carrying him from the war-torn human kingdom of his parents to her elf realm, where he is raised in safety but ignorant of his true name and inheritance.

Von Zatzikhoven's story begins with the killing of a tyrannical king when his nobles rise up against him. The terrified queen, who has escaped with her young child, takes refuge under a tree by a spring, situated between the royal castle and a lake. It is at this moment that there comes "a water fairy, as in a mist driven by the wind," who takes the child and carries him into her realm, the Land of Maidens. This fairy, "a wise mermaid," is the queen of a magical island in the sea where dwell ten thousand women, but no men! The island is enclosed by a wall with a diamond gate. Those who dwell in the castle atop a crystal mountain will never grow old, nor ever know sorrow, anger or envy; even those who leave will thereafter know only happiness.

Here the child is taught manners and music by the ladies, the arts of combat, sport and hunting by "mermen"—although he doesn't yet know his name, nor anything about his royal lineage. When he reaches the age of fifteen he requests leave to depart in order to gain glory and the Water Fay entrusts to him a mission that will enable him to achieve this: by avenging an injury done to her by one whose manly prowess surpasses all others (29–31). Consequently Lanzelet slays the malefactor but not before winning the love of his beautiful daughter, whom he marries.

Meanwhile a messenger from the Water Fay arrives to reveal to Lanzelet his name and lineage. It is made clear that his abduction had the noblest of motives: to keep the young prince safe from his father's murderers and give him an education that will enable him to fulfil his destiny. Many more adventures await the hero but, as befitting one who has dwelt in the Land of Maidens, he will assuredly live happily ever after.

There is here neither the angst of the lover of his liege's wife nor the tragic ending in which his adultery will help to bring down Arthur's kingdom. Lanzelet is never depicted as the lover of the queen, although he does rescue her from an abductor. As for the Water Fay, she is clearly both a supernatural being and one whose magic is wholly benign, two characteristics which will both be questioned in later versions of her story.

Neither in Chrétien nor von Zatzikhoven is there any direct link between the Lady of the Lake and Diana but, in the German poem, the Lady's aquatic connections (as mermaid, ruler of an island in the sea and as one who dwells in or can emerge from a lake) links her with a wider lunar symbolism, that of the moon as ruler of the waters.[2]

It is not until the composition of the great prose romance cycles of the first decades of the thirteenth century that these elements are woven together into a complete whole and we are given a complex picture of a supernatural being (or at least a person with magical powers): who has a special relationship with the goddess Diana; who lives in or under a lake; who will be a steadfast ally of Arthur (although she will do nothing to prevent her protégé Lancelot from carrying on an adulterous affair with the king's wife) and whose love for Merlin will bring about the enchanter's undoing.

The Fate of Endymion

The story of the seduction of the wise prophet, who can see everything to come apart from the manner of his own death, who becomes a fool for love and whose end comes when his own magic is turned against him, must surely count as one of the great tragic love stories of the Middle Ages. It is not surprising that it merited several retellings.

The first version that has come down to us is fairly brief and will later be considerably elaborated. It comes early on in the first great prose romance of Lancelot, which in turn constitutes only one segment of the enormous Vulgate Cycle.[3] Here the abduction of Lancelot is recounted in similar terms to the German version, with a mysterious young woman carrying him off into a lake after the death of his father (King Ban of Benoic, on the Breton border) during a war.

We are told that this body of water, which borders a small forest, has been known as the Lake of Diana since pagan times. But the Diana who gave it her name was not a goddess, as the foolish superstition of the time would have it, but a Sicilian queen who reigned in the time of the poet Virgil and who loved hunting so much that the local "miscreants" thought she was the Goddess of the Woods.[4] We also find out who the mysterious kidnapper is: she is indeed *une fée*, but in those days the term was used to describe any woman who knew about magic and divination (*d'anchantement et de charaies*). There were more of them in Britain in Merlin's time than anywhere else in the world.

Merlin himself was a prophet possessed of demonic knowledge because his mother conceived him as the result of a liaison with a fallen angel, a very devil (*deiable*). He taught Ninienne, the beautiful and highly intelligent Breton lady who will replace him as Arthur's magical protector, everything she knows about sorcery, or *nigromance*: which, as Carolyne Larrington has pointed out, is not so much *necromancy* ("the literal raising of the dead for divinatory purposes") as the "black" (*niger*) arts (16).

When the magician first encounters Ninienne, he soon falls head-over-heels in love with her. She leads him to believe that he will be able to have his way with her if in exchange he shares with her part of his great knowledge. Ninienne is particularly interested in a spell to seal someone up and another that will put someone to sleep for as long as she wishes; a sleep from which only she can awaken them. Merlin teaches her both these spells for, so she tells him, she will use them to stop her father accidentally finding them together. But what he doesn't know (and here it is his mortal part, inherited from his mother, rather than the demonic part inherited from his father, that lets him down) is that she will use them against him.

Ninienne also places a spell on her private parts, so that her virginity is protected. Whenever Merlin spends time with her she sends him to sleep but, when he wakes up, he thinks that they have made love. In the end, when Ninienne has learnt all she can from him, she seals Merlin in a cave in the Perilous Forest of Darnantes (near the Cornish Sea) and he is never heard from again.

Lucy Allen Paton, who wrote the first scholarly study of the Arthurian fairy mythology, points us here to the "evident association" between Ninienne and the goddess Diana, in the classical myth of Endymion, whose obsessive love for the moon goddess causes her to cast him into an endless sleep in a cave. The moon goddess wins for Endymion from Jupiter the gift of eternal youth, so that she can gaze upon his beauty forever. "The fate of Endymion," Paton comments, "had left an impression upon the literature of mediaeval Europe" (217).

Bewitched, Beguiled and Bewildered

This, then, is the back-story of the maiden who, as in the German version, abducts the young Prince Lancelot after his father dies during a rebellion. But unlike the Water Fay, there is nothing supernatural about Ninienne: she has learnt the magic arts from a master and even the lake into which she carries the boy is an illusion (*sanblance*). Beneath what appears to be a lake is, in reality, an estate in a valley with a river running through it. It is here that the Handsome Foundling or Precious Orphan, as he is known, is brought up.

But the figure of the Lady of the Lake was beginning to cast a spell on writers of romance. This succinct account of the death of Merlin, presented as explanatory back-story to the abduction of Lancelot, is considerably fleshed out in another romance within the Vulgate Cycle, the *Estoire de Merlin*, which also contains the story of the Devil Cat of Lausanne. Here we learn that the magician first encounters the girl who will be his undoing, when she is only twelve years of age. With his God-given knowledge of the future, he knows already what his fate will be, in the broadest terms, while, with his demonic knowledge of the past, he also knows her origin.

Her father, we learn, was a high-born vavasour (a baronial vassal) who was godson to Diana. The Goddess of the Woods gave him a gift of great worth, asking the God of the moon and stars to grant that, after the goddess' death, his daughter will inherit Her gift: to hold sway over the wisest man on earth and learn all she wishes from him. Paton points out the similarity between her role "as the giver of a 'destiny' to a child" and that of the earlier Parcae (the Roman goddesses of Fate) and the fays who would come later (276). But this Diana, though described as a goddess, is clearly mortal—unless the reference to her death means the end of her worship in the world, which is the only way a god can truly die. She herself, though a moon goddess, recognizes a deity above her who rules the moon and stars—which also constitutes an implicit recognition that the old pagan religion has given way to monotheism.

When the vavasour's daughter is born, he christens her Viviane (one of a confusing profusion of variations on the name Ninienne). When she is grown, she lives in a castle beneath a mountain on the edge of the Forest of Briosque and frequently disports herself by a fountain that feeds a lake. It is there that Merlin finds her and quickly becomes besotted with the girl, despite knowing it is unwise "to fall asleep in sin and lose his mind and his knowledge just to know the delights of a young lady, to shame her and to lose God" (*LG* I, 282). Nevertheless he shows off to her, demonstrating magic tricks. Impressed, she promises to be his lady love if he will teach her how to do them.

They meet again on Midsummer's Day. By now, Viviane has discovered that Merlin is the son of the Devil, so she is naturally afraid of him and his intentions towards her: for this reason she gets him to teach her a spell that can put a man to sleep, pretending that it is to use on her father, so that he will not find out about their liaison. She also gets him to teach her a spell that will prevent anyone from having sex with her, as though she were one of the maidens of Diana, vowed to perpetual virginity. Despite this, she grows to love Merlin deeply, because of the nobility that she discovers in his character.

It is at this time that Merlin goes to Jerusalem to predict the destruction of the Temple of Diana and the overthrow of the pagan religion throughout the Mediterranean. It is after this that he accompanies King Arthur on his Roman war and helps him to destroy the Devil Cat, which we can now see as the theriomorphic form of the angry goddess. It is almost as if Merlin's imprisonment is an act of revenge by the moon goddess for his role in the crushing of her worship. But if this is so, it is presented more as a way of gaining his perpetual devotion than of engineering his death. The wisest man in the world becomes a fool for love.

When next they meet, Viviane asks Merlin to complete her magical education with one last spell: "I beseech you to teach me how I might keep a man imprisoned without a tower or walls or irons, but through wizardry, so that he could never get away but through me" (416).

Merlin knows what she will do; but he also knows that she will do it because she loves him so much that she fears losing him. He gladly shows her how to make a magical stronghold that can never be undone, so that they can stay together there in endless joy and delight. At last, walking hand-in-hand in the Forest of Broceliande, they stop to rest in the shade of a hawthorn bush. Merlin falls asleep and the Lady casts the spells that he has taught her, using her wimple to draw a magic circle.

When he awakens, Merlin's immediate fear is that she will leave him there alone, in bed in the tower she has fashioned; but she promises to stay with him. She is as good as her word: although she can come and go as she pleases, she spends most of her time with him. To paraphrase a popular song, Merlin is bewitched and bewildered; but he is not bothered, because he has been beguiled.

When the Hawthorn Buds

This powerful story was the subject of one of the most famous paintings of the late Victorian era, "The Beguiling of Merlin" (1874) by the Pre-Raphaelite artist Edward Burne-Jones, who used as his model for the Lady of the Lake a woman with whom he was having an affair. It is possible to see in this painting an illustration of the quality of obsessive love that dooms a wise man to become ensnared in his own magic (as his body is ensnared by the hawthorn in the painting) and live out the rest of his days in a make-believe world, a fool's paradise: "I was being turned into a hawthorn bush," Burne-Jones wrote about his affair. But he seems to have also seen in the story a metaphor for artistic struggle as a battle against time and mortality, for "every year," he adds, "when the hawthorn buds it is the soul of Merlin trying to live again in the world for he left so much unsaid."[5] By the time he created this late masterpiece, Burne-Jones had already twice visited the story, which obviously had deep personal resonance. The first time was when, as a young recruit to the Pre-Raphaelite Brotherhood, he, along with his friend William Morris and others, painted a fresco on the walls of the Debating Hall of the Oxford Union building, at the instigation of their older "brother," Dante Gabriel Rossetti. Burne-Jones was given as his subject "Merlin lured into the Pit by the Lady of the Lake"—and here the manner of the beguiling reveals that the prime Arthurian inspiration for the Brotherhood was Caxton's edition of Malory's *Morte Darthur*, which had been re-issued in 1817 with a preface and notes by Robert Southey, the Poet Laureate. Burne-Jones had been beguiled by Malory's Arthurian world ever since he caught sight of Southey's edition in a bookshop at the age of twenty-three; unable to afford it, he was reduced to reading it in the shop every day until Morris bought it for him. They were both hooked from then on (Larrington, 162).

In Book Four of *Le Morte Darthur*, Malory presents a succinct account of the ruthless dispatching of Merlin by *the damesell of the Lake* whom he calls Nenyve or, in Caxton's edition, Nimue. Merlin becomes besotted with her and follows her everywhere she goes until she, fearing for her maidenhead, buries him under a Cornish megalith. Malory's is a very different lady to the one we encounter in the Vulgate: Nimue is certainly not in love with Merlin and she only puts up with his harassment as long as it suits her purpose, which is to learn as much as possible about his spell-craft so that, once she has had enough of the game, she can use his own magic against him. The difference in characterization can be accounted for by the fact that Malory in turn was basing his account not on the Vulgate, but rather on the later prose cycle known as the Post-Vulgate, which we will explore in Part Two.

Yet another influence on Burne-Jones' image of the Lady of the Lake was Tennyson's poem *Nimuë* (1857), which the artist read when it was privately circulated. Even more than Malory's, Tennyson's Nimuë is archetypically "false," a serpent in Merlin's garden, woman as harlot. In fact, so far from the medieval original was Tennyson's thoroughly modern temptress—a "stunner" whose malign gossip sows discord among the brothers of the Table Round—that Burne-Jones, shortly after completing his mural in 1858, prevailed upon the poet to change the name of his anti-heroine to Vivien, in order to distance her from Malory's damsel (Larrington, 151-9).

Despite the difficulty he encountered in working in fresco, Burne-Jones' Oxford mural was highly praised and he returned to the subject in 1861 with a watercolor, a medium in which he was more comfortable. Here the influence of Malory is explicit in the stone tomb which the artist places in the forefront of the picture. But also implicit is the influence of the Vulgate version of Merlin's disappearance (which Southey summarized and partly translated in the notes to his Preface to Malory[6]); for Burne-Jones depicts Nimuë reading from her book of transcriptions of Merlin's spells, a detail which Malory omits but which is included in the Vulgate and quoted by Southey.

There is even less of Malory in the great 1874 oil painting, where Nimuë is shown with a snake entwined in her hair, a detail borrowed from Tennyson.[7] She is holding her book of spells and gazing down at the beguiled enchanter (who also seems to be "being turned into a hawthorn bush") with an expression, as Carolyn Larrington puts it, that is "not triumphant, but wistful" (164) and, therefore, more in keeping with the Vulgate version as transmitted by Southey.

The Fairy God-Mother

Apart from looking after her captive lover, the main claim on the Lady of the Lake's time is as foster-mother (we might rather say, fairy godmother) to young heroes. The first and greatest of these is Lancelot, whom she loves more than anyone else ever could a child who was not her own flesh and blood. He is soon joined, however, by his cousins, whom a member of the Lady's entourage rescues from imprisonment through a magic trick—she casts a spell (*anchantement*) that transforms them into the likeness of greyhounds so that she can lead them to safety.

The three boys now live together under the guardianship of the Lady of the Lake, who provides for them a garland of fresh roses every morning apart from on Fridays, on the eve of the great feast days and throughout Lent. It is not natural for roses to be fresh all year round—but whatever magic the Lady is using, it is constrained by the Christian religion: the day starts with Mass under the Lake, as in the world above. When Lancelot is eighteen years old and the Lady knows from having cast lots (*par sa sort*) that he will leave her for King Arthur's court, she teaches him some of the traits of true knighthood, including defense of the people and of Holy Church.

The Lady does not just prepare Lancelot intellectually. She also equips him with silvery white armor (the color of the moon): a white hauberk, a silvery helmet, a white shield with a raised center of silver. She further provides him with a well-used sword and a spear with a white shaft and point, white robes for his knighting and a snow-white horse to ride. In fact, the Lady herself and the entire party—which includes, we discover, her new lover (*ami*), whose identity remains a mystery—are dressed in white, riding white horses.

In fact, she insists that Lancelot is made a knight wearing no other clothes and bearing no other arms. King Arthur goes along with this unusual request, so struck is he by the noble bearing of the young man. But, in the event, Lancelot will arrange things so that his knighting ceremony is only concluded when Guenevere sends him a sword, as if to symbolize that his lady is no longer the Lady of the Lake, but the Lady of Camelot. He has left the illusory, lunar realm of the Lake for the solid earth of Arthur's kingdom; but he carries an important relic of his former life in the shape of a ring that the Lady gives him before she departs: a ring that can uncover and dispel all forms of enchantment.

From now on the Lady of the Lake is still present in his life, but for the most part in the background: except for the most extreme cases, she intervenes at one remove, through the maidens who act as her messengers. Thus one maiden from the Lake helps Lancelot to achieve the Adventure of the Dolorous Guard, providing him with three shields (each of silver with one, two and three red bands) which increase his strength. It is in the course of this adventure that he also finds out who he is for the first time.

Another message from the Lady bids him devote his love only to one who will bring out the best in him. The identity of this worthy object of his devotion is made explicit when the Lady of the Lake sends a broken shield to the Lady of Camelot. On it is a design showing two lovers embracing: the knight has his arms around the lady's neck but the split in the shield prevents their lips from touching; when their love has been consummated, the shield will be made whole. On the day that happens, the queen will be delivered from her greatest sorrow and know her greatest happiness. Guenevere thinks she knows who the lovers are meant to be. The reader is in no doubt.

The shield's true worth is demonstrated when Lancelot suffers what will turn out to be only the first of three bouts of madness in his life, for it is only when it is hung around his neck that his sanity is restored; until such time as the Lady of the Lake herself arrives and heals him completely with a precious unguent. It is at this time that Ninienne meets Guenevere for the first time and the Lady of the Lake reassures the queen that her own love for Lancelot is purely maternal. She also encourages Guenevere to hold fast to her love for Lancelot, even if it seems foolish and sinful; for it is also honorable and glorious to love the best knight in the world.

The Lady of the Lake intervenes to save Lancelot's sanity again after the death of his best friend, Galehaut; but it is not the death of his friend that causes Lancelot's breakdown (since he only finds out about that later). Rather, it is his belief that he has lost the love of the woman who inspires him to his great deeds of chivalry. There is thus an opposition between Guenevere and Ninienne—the one drives him mad, the other cures him— that is part of a wider complementarity and polarity. It is not just that Guenevere takes over from Ninienne as the most important female figure in his life: their roles are also curiously conflated by the image of a magic ring which, at different times, is attributed to both of them. Or, to put it another way, when both ladies are said to give Lancelot a magic ring, we might wonder whether it is not just the rings but the ladies themselves who share a hidden identity.

In the Valley of False Lovers

As I said at the beginning of this chapter, the first mention of Lancelot's possessing a magic ring is made by Chrétien de Troyes, who states that it is given to him by the Lady of the Lake. She is introduced for the first time in the same passage; so that the fairy lady and her magic ring would appear to be linked indissolubly (an important characteristic in an underwater world!) in our, as well as in Lancelot's, mind. And, indeed, when Chrétien's story is reworked as part of the Vulgate *Lancelot*, the gift of the ring is made a part of the Lady's handing over of the young prince to King Arthur. She tells Lancelot that the ring has the power to uncover and make visible all spells: *il a tel force qu'il descuevre toz anchantemanz et fait veoir* (LdL 430).

The first opportunity Lancelot has to test the magic power of the ring is when he goes to the Valley of No Return in order to liberate the "false lovers" imprisoned there by Morgan the Fay. The sister of King Arthur, Morgan knows more about sorcery and spells (*d'encantemens et de carnins*) than any other woman, having been taught by Merlin himself. Seventeen years ago she was madly in love with a knight who loved another and, as a result, she placed a spell upon the valley where she caught them *in flagrante delicto*. No one who had ever been unfaithful to his beloved in any way, even in thought, would ever be able to leave the valley, once entered. The enchantment would only be broken when a knight arrived who had never betrayed his lover either in thought, desire or act.

Such a knight is, of course, Lancelot: he has only ever loved Guenevere. Entering the valley while engaged in a quest to find his friend Gawain, Lancelot kills two dragons and then uses the magic ring to dispel other, illusory dangers. He fights his way to a palace in the valley where he encounters, for the first time, Morgan, who conceals her deviousness with charm.

Morgan assures Lancelot that all the imprisoned knights (some two hundred and fifty three—there seems to be an epidemic of infidelity in Logres!) are now free to leave whenever they wish, but she persuades Lancelot to stay for a celebratory feast before resuming his quest for Gawain. Lancelot stays the night at the palace but, while he is asleep, Morgan comes into his bedroom and slips a ring on his finger, which prevents him from ever waking up. She has the sleeping Lancelot carried from her palace to nearby woods where he is imprisoned in a dark hole, then takes from off his finger the ring with which she enchanted him, so that he wakes up.

Morgan offers to release him so that he can complete his quest, on condition that he reveals the identity of the woman to whom he bears such faithful love. Lancelot refuses, even if it means dying in prison. Eventually Morgan agrees to let him go for as long as it takes to free Gawain, her nephew, on condition that he gives his word to return straight afterwards.

As pledge of his return, Lancelot should hand over to her a magic ring[8] that she has noticed on his finger; but the knight replies that no one will ever have the ring from him as long as he lives. Such a strong reaction on his part makes Morgan think that the queen has given the ring to him. She now regrets that she didn't examine it more closely when she had the opportunity, while he slept his enchanted sleep. In fact, the queen had given the ring in question to him on the day that she granted him her love and, although she cannot know this, Morgan is now convinced of what she already suspected: that it is the queen, her brother's unfaithful wife, who is the object of Lancelot's faithful love. Equally, what Lancelot does not know is that Morgan hates the queen because she stood in the way of Morgan's first great love affair. As a consequence, Morgan resents Guenevere's having the love she herself is denied.

Not wishing her nephew's deliverance to be hindered by her actions, Morgan agrees to let Lancelot go, on condition that he swears to return once his mission is accomplished. True to his word, Lancelot does just that. Once more, Morgan tries to get him to relinquish the ring that the queen gave him, but to no avail. When neither prayers nor menaces will get him to shift, she tries magic (*encantement*); but Lancelot's ring is protected by two odd figures (*figures divierses*) set in its emerald stone, barely visible, whose meaning is indecipherable.

It is at this point that yet a third ring is introduced (*LG* II, 323). Also once belonging to the queen, it looks the same as the one that Guenevere gave to Lancelot, but it has one important difference: that it has no power against sorcery. Morgan decides that her only option is to swap the two rings in the hope that Lancelot won't notice the difference until it's too late. She gives the knight a bedtime drink of strong wine laced with an herbal soporific which puts him out like a light and, while he is in a deep sleep, she slips the magic ring off his finger and replaces it with her own one.

Morgan sends a messenger bearing the magic ring to the court, with a message purportedly from Lancelot: He has brought shame upon the king and queen, but can no longer continue such disloyal behavior. Henceforth he will wear rough woolens and go around barefoot. Moreover, he wants to return the ring the queen had given him. With that, she hands it over and the queen, recognizing it to be her own, nearly faints.

The effect is, however, only partly what Morgan hoped for. King Arthur dismisses the whole thing as a lie, believing his wife when she says that there has never been anything to be guilty about in her love for Lancelot; but secretly the queen is furious. Guenevere tells her closest friends that Lancelot has betrayed her and will nevermore have her love. Morgan is disappointed that the queen has not been publicly disgraced and is upset to realize just how much Guenevere and Lancelot loved each other. But she is pleased to have put a wedge between them and hopes to drive the queen to despair.

Consequently Morgan tries to get Lancelot to swear that, if she releases him, he will stay away from the queen until Christmas. But she can only persuade him to do so by lacing his drinks with poisons fortified by magic spells (*confites a conjuremens et a carnins*) which induce him to hallucinate that he has found Guenevere in bed with another knight. Lancelot goes mad (again) and has to be cured by the Lady of the Lake.

The lovers will only be reconciled when Guenevere is abducted by Meleagant and carried off to his realm of Gorre. Lancelot sets off in pursuit, suffering the indignity of travelling in a peasant's cart when his horse is killed and being nearly cut to ribbons by the razor-sharp Sword Bridge that protects Meleagant's realm. Notwithstanding, when he finally reaches the queen, she gives him the cold shoulder.

Where is my ring? she coolly demands. *It's here, my lady*, he replies, innocently showing her Morgan's ring. *You're a liar!* she exclaims. *Look, this is my ring!* And she shows him the ring she is wearing. It is only when she explains about the messenger who came to Camelot that Lancelot realizes he has been duped by Morgan. He throws the false ring out the window and tells Guenevere about his hallucination; but she reassures him that she would rather die than let anyone else but him share her body. They end up in bed together.

We might be forgiven for thinking that the magic ring that the Lady of the Lake gave Lancelot has been forgotten about; that it has effectively been replaced in the narrative by the magic ring that Guenevere has given him and which causes him so much grief: but we would be wrong. Sometime later, when Lancelot has gone missing and is feared dead, Guenevere sends a messenger to the Lady of the Lake and, while awaiting her return, she looks at the ring that the Lady gave Lancelot when she first brought him to court, but which the queen now wears on her hand. She kisses it as if it were a holy relic, saying that the sight of something that her knight loved and guarded so closely will comfort her in his absence.

The affair of the magic ring has effectively brought together the three most important women of power in Arthur's kingdom. It would appear that the Lady of the Lake and Guenevere have both given Lancelot a magic ring and that Morgan possesses an un-magical ring that once belonged to Guenevere. Lancelot has evidently at some point given the queen the Lady's ring. Morgan has stolen the ring Guenevere gave to Lancelot in order to set them at loggerheads and, in this, she is temporarily successful. But her ruse is eventually uncovered, the un-magical ring that she somehow obtained from Guenevere and then used as a substitute is unceremoniously defenestrated and, since we never hear of Lancelot using a magical ring again, it is probably safe to infer that Guenevere ends up keeping her own magical ring as well as that of the Lady of the Lake.

Morgan the Fay, as her name suggests, is skilled in magic and therefore has no need of an enchanted ring in order to work her spells; whereas the Lady of the Lake, whose magic is benign by comparison with Morgan's, has given a magic ring to Lancelot for his protection. This is the first time that the magic knowledge these two fays possess is seen to be used for conflicting purposes. As their story develops, in the Post-Vulgate Cycle and in Malory's English reduction, it will turn into something of a magical battle (see below, Chapter Nine).

But the most surprising element of this affair of the rings (especially for readers who are mostly familiar with the story of Lancelot and Guenevere from Malory's version, where it does not appear) is the association of the queen directly with magic. After all, she is a beautiful and loving if capricious and untrustworthy mortal, who has nothing supernatural about her.... Or has she?

In fact, there are several indications that Guenevere is not all she seems and, if she is the owner of a magic ring that she gives to the man she loves, this may be a survival of an earlier incarnation of the queen as a denizen of Faerie who becomes King Arthur's Otherworld bride—as we will see in the next chapter.

Three

The Otherworld Bride

> Arthur's queen brought him the Round Table and was probably originally the sovereignty.[1]
>
> —A.C.L. Brown

King Arthur first meets Guenevere when he travels with his allies to the land of Cameliard, which borders on Logres, to assist its elderly monarch King Leodagan who is being attacked by the giant Rion. Merlin predicts that, if Cameliard falls, Arthur will be unable to hold Logres in peace; but he is also aware that Leodagan has a daughter called Guenevere, his only legitimate child, who will therefore inherit her father's kingdom, making her a worthy match for the unmarried king. It is while Arthur's army is rescuing her father from his enemies that Guenevere first sees her future husband wielding Excalibur and is suitably impressed. Merlin approaches Leodagan and the King of Cameliard is only too pleased to have his daughter betrothed to the son of Uther Pendragon. Guenevere herself is equally happy with the match.

On Whitsunday, King Leodagan holds court in honor of his rescuers. It is now that Arthur discovers that there are, in fact, two Gueneveres; something that will later prove to be the cause of much trouble. The second Guenevere is the illegitimate daughter of Leodagan: he fathered her on the wife of his seneschal, on the very night that his legitimate daughter was conceived.

The Queen of Cameliard, it transpires, was a very devout lady who would always go to matins if at all possible. So, on the night that her daughter Guenevere was conceived, she got up early and went to church as usual. Her husband the king, not content with having just made love with his wife, takes the opportunity to sneak into the bed of his seneschal's wife, a woman whom he had always fancied and whose husband he had sent away on business. She also conceives and the two daughters are born on the same day, both called Guenevere and nursed together. They are nearly identical except that the queen's daughter has a birthmark on the small of her back that resembles a crown but, of course, this is not visible to the company who are sat at the head of the table during Leodagan's Whitsun feast. What they do notice is that the betrothed of King Arthur is a bit taller and darker than her half-sister and better-spoken; otherwise only a lucky guess could distinguish them

The next day, Arthur and Leodagan take the field once more against Rion but, before Arthur sallies forth, Guenevere puts his armor on him and girds his sword on his side, sending him off with a passionate kiss. They are young and very much in love.

An Excursion to the Castle of Carousal

At this point it might be useful to step back and ask the meaning of this curious situation, which makes little narrative sense, in which a father gives the same name to two daughters who are born on the same day to two different mothers. The answer, I believe, can be found in the hidden mythological origins of Guenevere, which are concealed in her name.

Geoffrey of Monmouth calls Arthur's wife Ganhumara, a name which is derived from the Welsh Gwenhwyfar. If we find it odd that there are two Gueneveres, it is even odder to discover that (according to the Welsh Triads) there are three Gwenhwyfars, described collectively as the Three Great Queens of Arthur's Court (*TYP* 161).

Rachel Bromwich points out that there is a Celtic literary convention in which a group of three "seems to be no more than a multiplication of a single personage." She argues that this appears to have "a mythological basis, since in both Irish and Gaulish mythology there are various instances in which deities are portrayed alternately either in a single or in a triple form in which the members are incompletely differentiated. In Wales, as in Ireland, multiple personality may be a literary convention ultimately descended from what is undoubtedly a widespread Celtic mythological concept" (163). The three Gwenhwyfars have three different fathers but, it may be, the same mother; or, at least, that possibility presents itself when we explore her origins in Irish mythology: when we realize that the name Gwenhwyfar is the transliteration of an Irish name, Findabhair, meaning "White Phantom."

Findabhair is the daughter of Medhbh or Maeve, euhemerised[2] as the Queen of Connacht but in origin a Fairy Queen, best known through Shakespeare and Shelley as Queen Mab. But the fays were once goddesses, driven into the fairy hills to become banshees, issuing out to lure Christian men to an unknown, but distinctly heathen, fate.

One aspect of this fate is contained in the etymology of Maeve, whose name means "The Intoxicating One" (Mac Cana, 119). We are familiar with the stories of the hapless wanderer who, having drunk of the elven liquor, is condemned to live forever in the Land of Women among the Undying Ones and thereby denied his transition to the Christian Heaven; some may think it is a price worth paying! But the intoxicating drink, which the wanderer is offered, was once reserved for heroes and was offered only by the goddess of sovereignty to her chosen ones. That Maeve was once understood to be the Sovereignty of Ireland is implicit in the story of her having nine husbands, all of whom were kings.

The number nine may be significant precisely because it is the sacred number three multiplied by itself. According to Geoffrey of Monmouth nine sisters rule Avalon but we may also think of the nine maidens who, in the early medieval Welsh poem "The Spoils of Annwfn," warm with their breath the cauldron of the Lord of the Otherworld. In this poem Annwfn is depicted as an island that can only be reached by Arthur's travelling in his enchanted ship Pridwen: one of its titles is the Island of the Strong Door, suggesting that it is not easy of access, that it is the place where is guarded "the treasure hard to attain."

In his journey through Annwfn, King Arthur must traverse eight castles or fortresses (*caerau* in Welsh), some of which have names that reveal, others that seem rather to conceal, the true nature of the island. For example, one of these names is Caer Wydyr, "the Fortress of Glass," which suggests a connection with Ynys Witrin, "the Isle of Glass," an early name for Glastonbury (Sims-Williams, 60). As with much of the legendary lore connected with Glastonbury, we can see the truth only through a glass, darkly. What we do know, however, is that both Glastonbury and the mythical Glass Island were believed to be the place of imprisonment of Guenevere, as we will see later.

Another fortress that Arthur must pass through is Caer Sidi, which means something like the Fairy Fortress or the Castle of the Elves. What is particularly striking about this name, however, is that it is a transliteration of the Irish word *síde*, meaning the "fairy mounds" or ancient barrows into which the old gods of Ireland were believed to have retreated with the triumph of Christianity. As a result, they have themselves become known as the People of the Síde and the women of the Síde, the former goddesses of Ireland, as banshees.

This is the same process of reduction of the power of the old pagan deities that Blake noted in the way ancient goddesses of Destiny became Shakespeare's Weird Sisters (*BCW* 569–70). If Guenevere herself was once Findabhair, she is the daughter of a goddess. In fact, the name of Guenevere's mother seems to be concealed in that of one of the fortresses of Annwfn: Caer Vedwit, "the Castle of Carousal" or "the Fortress of Intoxication." This Welsh name is derived from the same Celtic word that gives us the Irish name Maeve; so who else is the mother of Guenevere than Queen Mab, once a powerful goddess of sovereignty, now remembered only in English poetry as a fairy queen?

If her mother is the Lady of Caer Vedwit, then it seems likely that Guenevere was originally one of the maidens who guard the Cauldron of the Head of Annwfn. Despite the obscurity of the "Spoils of Annwfn," it is usually assumed that the purpose of Arthur's expedition was to win the cauldron and/or free a prisoner. We now have a third motive for the king: to gain an Otherworld bride, one of the Maidens of the Cauldron (Green, 152). And if her mother is, like Maeve, the ancient goddess of the sovereignty of the land, then we can see that this is the gift that Guenevere confers through her marriage to Arthur: a gift that is dramatized in the romances by the scene in which she girds on Arthur his armor and sword so that he can go out and fight for her against the giants who threaten her land. Through his victory, Arthur demonstrates his worthiness to be her husband and she, in turn, confers on him the sovereignty that is in her gift.

The mythological origins of Guenevere help us to understand the way in which she is seen as sometimes threefold, sometimes twofold. Gwenhwyfar's name reveals her lunar nature: the moon flits across the sky like a white phantom and the visible moon, the Queen of Heaven, has three phases—waxing, full and waning—reflected in the three queens of Arthur's court. But the moon is also dual: it can be waxing or waning, new or old, full or dark, visible or invisible. These opposites give us the twin Gueneveres, who are in every way opposed to each other, as we will see.

Thus Arthur has not just got himself a princess bride: he has won the love of the daughter of the goddess of sovereignty and he has brought her back from the Castle of Carousal in the Otherworld to be his queen.

The Golden Cup of Sovereignty

Returning to the Vulgate *Estoire*, we discover that Guenevere travels from Cameliard to Logres for the wedding. With her she brings the greatest dowry anyone could confer: the Round Table.

Merlin made the table for Uther Pendragon but, in the chaos that followed the death of that king, it was transferred to the court of King Leodagan. As his heir, Guenevere inherits the table and therefore can bestow it, along with the land, on her husband. But it is not just the table itself that is the dowry Guenevere brings. There is also the fellowship that attends it: fifty knights when the Round Table is first instituted, later growing to one hundred and fifty.

At the time the Round Table is brought from Cameliard, there are only one hundred knights, the rest having died in battle with King Rion. It will be the first task of King Arthur, as the new head of the institution, to bring the fellowship up to its full count. It will be the jewel in his crown; ironically, or perhaps I should say fatally, it will be Guenevere who is the key to its destruction. The Lady of Sovereignty giveth and she taketh away...

The marriage of Arthur and Guenevere takes place in St. Stephen's Church in Camelot; but their wedding night is somewhat marred by a kidnap attempt. The intention of the traitors is to substitute one sister for the other, putting the seneschal's wife's daughter on the throne of Logres. But the plot is foiled—although this, as it turns out, is only the first of several abductions that befall the queen—and the king and his bride spend a passionate night of love together. As for the false Guenevere: Arthur is merciful and, resisting cries to have her burnt, merely banishes her from his kingdom. His mercy will be ill repaid later on.

After their honeymoon, King Arthur turns again to the affairs of the realm. He announces that he will hold a lavish, plenary court in mid-August, on the Feast of Our Lady, at which he and the queen will sit in state. His choice of date is significant: what is now celebrated as the day on which the Blessed Virgin Mary was bodily assumed into Heaven was once the Feast of the Nemoralia, held in honor of the goddess Diana[3] whose earthly representative is the lunar "white phantom," Guenevere.

When the day comes, everyone who is anyone is there. It is at this feast that one of the most famous customs of the Arthurian court—that the king will not sit down to eat until an adventure is announced—is established, as well as the commitment of the Knights of the Round Table to defend the rights of maidens against all wrongdoing. Not to be outdone, a group of warriors led by the king's nephew Gawain declare themselves to be the Knights of the Queen. Arthur is delighted and endows his wife with all his treasure, to hand it out as she pleases.

Exactly one year later, on the Feast of the Assumption, another plenary court is held at Camelot. It is now that King Arthur faces one of his most fearsome personal challenges, in the form of Rion of the Isles, who has taken the beards of nine kings and wants Arthur's to complete a cloak he is making. The issue is only resolved when the two kings come face to face and Arthur takes the head of Rion: a battle that establishes his supremacy over the descendants of the indigenous occupants of Albion, the giants.

Although the episode is not recounted in the Vulgate Cycle, other romances have preserved an important scene that occurs just after Arthur's victory over Rion, in which Guenevere's symbolic status is revealed. Arthur has retired to the seaside, holding court at Carduel, in Wales,[4] where the Fellowship of the Round Table was instituted. Although he is pleased to be finally rid of one of his most intractable enemies, he is sad because so many of his barons have returned home and it is now, with his strength depleted, that he faces yet another threat to his sovereignty and to the woman who embodies it.

Into the court rides a Red Knight, going right up to the king's table, demanding of him his lands and grabbing Arthur's golden drinking cup from before him. In doing so, he spills the wine it contains on the distraught queen. It is the young Perceval who, having only just arrived at the court for the first time, kills the Red Knight and returns the cup to the rightful king. The queen has been avenged and Arthur's honor restored.

This scene—from Chrétien's *Conte du Graal*—is significant for introducing the image of the golden cup of wine as a symbol of Sovereignty, which connects us with Celtic paganism: for there is an Irish story in which the goddess who personifies the realm gives a drink of red ale from a golden cup to the man who is destined to become the king (Mac Cana, 115). The Red Knight's stealing of the cup therefore symbolizes his claim to Sovereignty; his insult to the queen (who personifies the sovereignty of Logres) in front of her husband, is intended to demonstrate that Arthur is no longer fit to rule. By killing the Red Knight and returning the cup to Arthur, Perceval establishes himself as the King's Champion, the upholder of sovereignty; but it is in another court that he will encounter his true destiny and the golden cup will give place to another golden vessel, the Grail.

While Perceval is diverted from courtly life by a spiritual quest, it is the more this-worldly knight Lancelot who comes to the fore as the King's Champion. Notwithstanding, he will betray his liege lord by conducting an affair with the queen and it is this sin of adultery which will make him unworthy to achieve the Grail Quest. But the adultery of the queen may be rooted, not just in a capricious personality, but in an archetypal duality.

When King Arthur is bewitched by a Saxon enchantress and spends the night with her in the castle of his country's traditional enemies, it is as if Sovereignty turns on him her hostile face. Arthur is imprisoned by the Saxons and his queen gives her body, for the first time, to his younger champion. The symbolic importance of this act is underlined when a friend of the queen comments that Lancelot only lacks a crown to be a king.

Sovereignty is smiling on Lancelot, not on Arthur and, although the King's Champion rescues his lord from the Saxons and the wiles of the sorceress, Arthur will soon fall victim to yet another ruse.

The Sovereignty Variations

One day a messenger arrives at Camelot bringing alarming news: the queen has just escaped from prison and wants her husband and her kingdom back. She was kidnapped, it appears, only a day and a night after being married to Arthur and crowned Queen of Logres: she was taken from her bed during the night, while the king was in the privy! Her maidservant, a lookalike, has taken her place in the king's bed and rules what should be Guenevere's. The king must restore the true queen to her throne or else return to Cameliard the Round Table, which was Guenevere's wedding dowry.

The king is dumbfounded but, to be fair to the messenger, he agrees to hear in full the accusation from the woman who claims to be the true queen. The hearing will be held at Candlemas in Cameliard, whose barons should at least be able to recognize their king's only daughter. What is not widely known, however, is that, not only has the King of Cameliard fathered an illegitimate daughter on the wife of his seneschal, but he has also made this lady (who so resembles her half-sister) Guenevere's maidservant and sent her with the queen to Logres after the royal marriage. Here, with the aid of an embittered murderer, Berthelay the Old, she has planned a scheme to seize the throne and gain the king's love.

Arriving at Cameliard, the former maidservant is acknowledged as the true Guenevere by its barons and the king feels he has no option but to allow the matter to be resolved through trial-by-combat. However, fearing that he will lose the combat, Berthelay persuades the false Guenevere, the Lady of Cameliard, to kidnap and drug the king, keeping him in a state of blissful ignorance in the Castle of Enchantments. Arthur sleeps with the false Guenevere every night, falling in love with her and becoming convinced that she is his true wife. Once she is sure that the king is completely under her sway, the Lady of Cameliard tells the king to reveal his whereabouts and summon his barons to assemble in the capital city.

On the Feast of the Ascension, the hearing is held but, in the event, the barons of Cameliard continue to support the claim of the false Guenevere; while the king, whose mind is already made up, pronounces that the woman whom he had for so long believed was his queen is, in fact, an imposter. Her punishment will be: that the hair of her head, on which sat the crown to which she was not entitled, should be cut off; that the skin of her hands, on which she received the regal ointment at her coronation, should be scraped off and that she should be sent into perpetual exile.

The knights of Logres are outraged at both the verdict and the sentence and an angry Lancelot renounces his seat at the Round Table so that he is free to challenge the king himself to mortal combat; or, failing that, to take on three opponents, one after the other. The king reluctantly agrees and the date of the combat is set for a week after Pentecost. In the event, Lancelot has no trouble dispatching two of his opponents. The life of the third is only spared because Guenevere intervenes on his behalf.

Thus the queen is vindicated, but the damage has already been done. Arthur is still bewitched by the Lady of Cameliard and will not take back his real wife. Lancelot and Guenevere (who believes that she is being punished for her adultery) leave for Surluse (the kingdom of his friend Galehaut), despite the king's last-minute attempt to buy back his champion's loyalty with half his kingdom. To cap it all, Gawain announces that a shame has come to the Round Table that it has never known before.

Things cannot go on like this indefinitely, although the false Guenevere keeps Arthur under her evil sway through the use of drugs. The Pope, incensed that the King of Britain should cast aside his lawful wife, places the kingdom under interdict and the false queen falls prey to a mysterious illness, which paralyses her and causes her body to rot from the feet up. But it is not just the usurper who rots, but the land itself,[5] in a form of mythical identification between the realm and its Sovereignty figure. Here the disappearance of Guenevere from the throne recalls that of great goddesses of antiquity such as the Sumerian Inanna, the Babylonian Ishtar and the Greek Persephone, whose descent into the Underworld blights the land.

The king himself, who is at one with the land when he is endowed with Sovereignty, becomes ill in the absence of the true queen. He is in danger of becoming, like the Fisher King in the Grail romances, the Maimed King of a Waste Land; but fortunately he is saved by the intervention of a hermit, who has known the real Guenevere from an early age and who causes Arthur to see sense. The hermit gets the Lady of Cameliard to confess her sins and Berthelay the Old, who is now dying, also owns up to his crimes. While the two waste away to death, a chastened King Arthur is reconciled with his wife and her lover. Lancelot takes his rightful place once more at the Round Table.

But the Sovereignty of Logres requires eternal vigilance: it is not long before Guenevere is once more lost to Arthur and has to be returned by Lancelot from a mysterious kingdom that appears to be a region of the Otherworld. This is the story of the abduction of Guenevere by the Prince of Gorre, which is taken up by Malory in Book XIX of *Le Morte Darthur*; but it is first recorded in a Latin version of a Welsh tale, where the rescuer is Arthur himself.

Across the Sword Bridge

Caradog of Llancarfan, a cleric from South Wales, wrote a *Life of St Gildas* (the sixth-century church historian) in which Melwas, the King of the Summer Region, carries Guenevere off to his stronghold of Glastonbury, here glossed as meaning "the Glass Island" (*Ynys Wydrin*)—an etymology which suggests that we are not so very far from Caer Wydyr, the Glass Fortress of Annwfn. We should not be surprised to see the boundaries between Glastonbury and a mythical island becoming blurred: from the twelfth century onwards, Glastonbury was frequently identified with Avalon, an island that also has mythical status. Geoffrey of Monmouth describes it as a Fortunate Isle where plants grow without labor (*VM* 101). These elements are all merged in Chrétien de Troyes' picture of the mighty baron Maheloas, Lord of an idyllic Isle of Glass (*l'Isle de Voirre*) "where thunder is not heard, no lightning strikes or tempest blows, no toads or snakes stay, and it is never too hot or too cold" (*AR* 26). If the Welsh Melwas has become the French Maheloas, his Glass Island is clearly located not in South West Britain but in the Otherworld, which is not found on any map.

In another poem by Chrétien, Voirre becomes Gorre, an equally mysterious realm, but one which the poet attempts to link to *this* world. Its capital, Bath (*Bade*), locates it in Somerset (Melwas' Summer Country); but the name of its king, Bademagu, evokes the mythical founder of the city, Bladud, as the "magus of Bath." In the name of the king's son—Meleagant, Prince of Gorre—we can see yet another transformation of Melwas/Maheloas. This powerful prince rides into Camelot and carries off the queen, before her husband's very eyes, to his realm "from which no stranger returns, but is forced to stay in that land in servitude and exile" (193). The poet also tells us that Gorre can only be reached by crossing a deep and treacherous river. This in turn can only be done in two ways, both of which are highly dangerous: the first is by an underwater bridge; the second, even more deadly, is via a bridge as sharp as a sword.

Gawain sets off to rescue the queen and narrowly escapes drowning on the Water Bridge; only to find that Lancelot has beaten him to it, crossing the Sword Bridge. Lancelot gets cut to ribbons crossing the sharp steel and gets a cold reception from Guenevere when he eventually finds her—either because, in Chrétien's version, he hesitated before mounting a cart to rescue her; or, in the later Vulgate version, because (as we saw in the last chapter) he has lost the magic ring that she gave him. Either way, he still ends up bedding Guenevere and beheading Meleagant!

In the meantime, however, Chrétien reveals a striking characteristic of this Kingdom of No Return: it only requires one prisoner to be released for them all to be able to leave (*CC* ll. 3899–901). And here we move away from the Celtic Otherworld, with its paradisiacal Glass Island, to the infernal regions that Christ harrowed. By descending into Hell and then being resurrected, Christ freed all those good men whose souls were exiled there because they died before they could receive the good news that saves; just as Christ, by His death and resurrection, saves all us sons of Adam, exiled from Eden. It is as if, by crossing the Sword Bridge and overcoming the Prince of That World, Lancelot has undergone an initiatory death and rebirth and, by doing so, enables not just Guenevere but all the prisoners to begin their exodus from that realm which is no longer what Hamlet calls that *undiscover'd country/ From whose bourn no traveller returns.*

This subtle Christianization of originally pagan material is not unique to the Romance of Lancelot. In his last poem, the *Conte du Graal*, Chrétien would also introduce a hermit to suggest that the mysterious vessel that Perceval has seen in the Fisher King's castle is such a holy thing (*tante sainte cose*) that it can feed the "spiritual" (*espiritaus*) man (the Fisher King's elderly father) with a single host; although up to that point there has been nothing in the narrative to associate the Grail with the Mass or the miracle of transubstantiation. If, as has been argued,[6] the Grail Quest has its origins in Arthur's quest for the Cauldron of Annwfn, Chrétien's continuators would develop his hints at Christian associations for the vessel into a full-bodied transformation of it into a relic of the Passion. This process would reach its apogee in the great prose cycles of the thirteenth century, where the mysterious Otherworld and its supernatural fays are increasingly demonized and their role as generators of adventure is taken over by the spiritual Kingdom of the Grail and its sacred vessel.

Thus it is that, when Chrétien's Romance of Lancelot is incorporated into the Vulgate Cycle, it is subtly altered to make it one of the adventures that herald the Grail Quest. We have already been told that Guenevere's beauty can only be matched by two women in Britain, one of whom is Elaine, the daughter of King Pelles (the last of the Fisher Kings). Now we are further told that Elaine will bear a son who will sit in the Siege Perilous and bring to an end the adventures of Logres. If Guenevere is associated with the fairy magic of the Lady of the Lake, Elaine points us to the miracles of the Holy Grail to come.

But if the Lady of the Lake originates in an earlier, pagan world, her magic is never presented as anti-Christian. On the contrary, when she takes Lancelot to Camelot to be knighted, she praises King Pelles and earlier exemplars of Christian chivalry—Joseph of Arimathea and his son Galahad, the first Christian King of Wales, to whom Pelles is related—as well as the pre-Christian but God-fearing Israelite King David, from whom Lancelot is descended through his mother. She wants him to be knighted on the feast of the Nativity of John the Baptist (the old pagan Midsummer festival) because she hopes that, just as Saint John surpassed all men conceived of woman's flesh, so Lancelot will surpass in excellence all other knights in his time. As she knows much of his fate, she is probably aware, not just that her hope will come true, but that he will unite the lineage of King David with that of Joseph of Arimathea by fathering a child on King Pelles' daughter—and that the child will be named Galahad.

Even before he met the Lady of the Lake, Merlin had prophesied "that from the prideful leopard and the line of Jerusalem would come the lion feared above all other animals." The lion is the emblem of Galahad who will surpass the leopard (the emblem of Lancelot) because he will remain "from birth to death, so utterly virginal and chaste as never to feel love for a woman, married or not." Lancelot is unfit to sit in the Siege Perilous and complete the Adventures of the Grail, not because he is an adulterer who has betrayed his liege, but because he has felt love for a woman! In the brave new world of the Grail Quest, human love is a disqualification: Galahad will have a heart of steel (*LG* II, 253).

Lancelot only learns about his unworthiness when he is on his way to Gorre to rescue the queen and comes upon the Church of the Holy Cemetery, so named because of two sepulchers it contains: one is in a meadow, the other deep underground in a cave. The tomb in the meadow holds the body of Galahad of Wales and is the subject of another prophecy from Merlin: whoever is able to raise its lid is destined to free all the prisoners of Gorre. Lancelot does so with ease, the lid remaining upright even when he lets go of it. There emerges from the tomb the odor of sanctity and, at that moment, a crowd of Welsh monks arrive. They had learned in a vision that the tomb would be opened and have come to take the body of their first Christian king back to the land he converted.

Buoyed by his success, Lancelot determines to try the other adventure at the Holy Cemetery: the Tomb of the Black Chamber. But, deep underground, things work out very differently: Lancelot penetrates through pitch black smoke and a hideous stench but is unable to lift the lid of the tomb. Worse, he is scorched by the hell-fire that envelops it. He bursts into tears because he knows that he is afraid and he believes that he cannot be the best of all knights. A voice from the tomb concurs: for the virtuous Good Knight, who will extinguish the flames, has not yet come, although his advent is very close. The voice is that of Simeon, nephew of Joseph of Arimathea (who brought the Grail to Britain from the Holy Land), but a sinner. Simeon is tormented by flames that ravage both body and soul, which he must endure until the day God sends his deliverer.

Saddened at his failure to be that deliverer, Lancelot turns his attention to his primary task: the rescue of the woman he loves. His fame precedes him and the exiles flock to his side as to their redeemer. But the messianic role that Lancelot assumed in Chrétien's narrative is tainted in the Vulgate: the Sovereignty that Guenevere represents is that of emotional and temporal power but not of spiritual authority. The Otherworld from which she emerged will be rejected by the seekers of the Grail in favor of the Kingdom of Heaven.

The later Grail poets tend to demonize fays but, in the Vulgate Cycle, they are as likely to be rationalized away. Thus, after her rescue, Guenevere finds herself at a place called the Fairies' Fountain (*la Fontainne as Fées*); but it is only so called because the local forest-dwellers had spotted beautiful women there and, knowing nothing about them, had assumed that they were fays. The implication is that we are dealing with superstition rather than the supernatural and Lancelot will soon have to deal with the true source of supernatural power, a spiritual destiny hidden in a name he does not even know he possesses.

Galahad by Any Other Name

The fact that Lancelot is destined to have an affair with a woman other than Guenevere is heralded rather curiously in the Prose *Lancelot* by the device of giving the two lovers forgotten baptismal names. We have seen that the daughter of King Pelles is the only maiden who can match Guenevere's beauty. We are also told that, for reasons that are not at first apparent, she was baptized with one name (Helizabel) but known by another (Amite in the Vulgate or Elaine in the Post-Vulgate and Malory).

She is destined to mother the Best Knight in the World, who is called Galahad; but this, curiously, is also the baptismal name of her son's father, better known as Lancelot. He has, in effect, "lost" it because of "the flame of desire"; but that same desire will lead him, through the workings of divine providence, to father a son who will be worthy of the name: "Galahad, the virginal, the most excellent knight" (*LG* III, 165).

Lancelot's fathering of Galahad and his unintentional betrayal of Guenevere will come about when he arrives for the first time at the castle of Corbenic in Listenois, the Land Beyond, lured there by the promise that he will encounter the most beautiful creature in the world. On his way he is taken to another wondrous tombstone, on which is carved letters stating that it will only be lifted by the Leopard from whom will descend the Great Lion who will be born to the king's daughter. Had he thought about the inscription, he might have been wary about staying in the area after lifting the stone with ease; but his attention is taken up by a fire-breathing dragon that emerges from the tomb and that he is obliged to dispatch.

It is now that Lancelot meets for the first time the King of the Land Beyond: Pelles, the last of the Fisher Kings, a direct descendant of Joseph of Arimathea's sister and one of those (along with King David, Joseph himself and King Galahad of Wales) named by the Lady of the Lake as possessing all the great qualities of chivalry, those on whom the young knight should model himself.

Pelles takes the knight into the dining hall where a dove bearing a golden censer heralds the entrance of the Grail in the shape of a chalice, borne by a maiden whose beauty, to Lancelot's eyes, is matched only by Guenevere's. Everyone kneels before the Holy Vessel, the room is filled with the scent of spices and the tables are covered with the finest foods. The beautiful Grail Bearer is Elaine, the king's daughter, who is already at the center of a plot hatched by her father to fulfil the destiny outlined on the dragon tomb: to trick the Leopard (Lancelot) into fathering the Great Lion (Galahad). This is brought about by the arts of Elaine's tutor Brisane[7] who, that night, escorts him to a castle where he believes Guenevere is staying and then gives him a potion that befuddles his brain so that he believes he is actually sleeping with the Queen of Logres when he is really making love with the Princess of Corbenic.

Thus are two of the greatest lineages on Earth brought together to produce a Great Lion who has a noble destiny. What to the modern reader may seem like a heartless deception, little short of genetic engineering, is justified in the Vulgate as fulfilling God's plan. For the Land Beyond had been turned into a Waste Land when one of King Pelles' ancestors was killed by the sword of King David and the consequences of this Dolorous Blow, it would appear, can only be redeemed by one born to the Houses of David and of Joseph of Arimathea: one who will surpass his father as the greatest knight on Earth, a Great Lion who will take his place at the Round Table in the Siege Perilous (corresponding to the place of Jesus at the Table of the Last Supper) and who will achieve the adventures of the Holy Grail.

Although he is the deceived party, Lancelot has acted "in sin and adultery and in opposition to God and Holy Church"; whereas Elaine has sacrificed her virginity for the greater good, acting not "from lust or bodily desire, but so as to receive the fruit that would restore that entire land to its original beauty." The loss of her virginity will be more than compensated-for by the "mortification of the flesh" undergone by Galahad, who will remain "a virgin in thought and fact" (164f) until he dies in the spiritual city of Sarras.

In receiving his father's own baptismal name, Galahad is shown to be living out his father's lost potential. But Lancelot has lost more than the possibility of achieving the Grail Quest through his adultery: he will bring about the destruction of the Round Table fellowship and create the conditions for Mordred's treachery when his liaison with the queen is brought to light. Morgan the Fay, Mordred's aunt, will also play a pivotal role in the unravelling of Arthur's achievement; but, in the Vulgate Cycle, her actions are not directed against her half-brother—can, rather, be seen as trying to protect him against his wife's betrayal though complicated by her hatred of Guenevere and her desire to have Lancelot for herself.

It is time we looked more closely at this ambiguous figure whose pagan roots are as strong as those of the Lady of the Lake but who, unlike Ninienne, is never brought within the Christian fold. This might explain why her character suffers even greater degradation than does that of the Lady of the Lake as the prose cycles evolve.

Four

Fate and Faerie

> The *fée* was probably always represented as supreme.[1]
> —A.C.L. Brown

There are three women with whom King Arthur will forever be associated: the Lady of the Lake, who gives him his sword Excalibur (as we will see in Part Two); his wife Guenevere, who betrays him; and his sister Morgan, who takes him to Avalon for healing at the end of his life.

There is something deeply ambiguous about each of these women. The Lady of the Lake starts off as a supernatural Water Fay and ends up as the promoter of Christian chivalry. Guenevere has an identical twin sister with the same name who tries to take her place in the king's bed while the true queen is sleeping with his greatest knight, thus proving herself to be as false as the Lady of Cameliard. Arthur's sister Morgan also veers wildly in the stories that have come down to us between being a wise healer and a treacherous sorceress. To understand these contradictions we need to understand her origins.

Geoffrey of Monmouth gave us the first comprehensive account of the mysterious birth, noble life and tragic death of King Arthur, which was published around 1138. A few years later, he produced a Latin poem on the life of Merlin (*Vita Merlini*) which revisits his account of Arthur's death. Here a brief reference to the mortally wounded king being taken away to the Isle of Avalon for the tending of his wounds is developed into a full episode concerning that Fortunate Isle and the nine sisters who rule it.

Geoffrey here explains that Avalon is the Island of Apples, an etymology that reveals its origin in Celtic mythology: the Welsh word for apple is *afal*, plural *afalau*; while in Irish myth we have Emain Ablach, a paradisiacal Island of Apples that is also a Land of Promise and, like the home of the Water Fay who abducts Lanzelet, a Land of Women.

Geoffrey's Avalon is "fortunate" because all things grow there spontaneously. It is also a Land of Women: more specifically, of nine sisters of whom the most beautiful (and the most skilled in healing) is called Morgen—a Welsh and Breton name for a Water Fay possibly related to the Irish Muirgen, "the sea-born" (Rhys, 22f). She is a shape-shifter and has the gift of flight on "strange wings"; she teaches astrology (*mathematicum*) to her sisters and together they exercise a benign rule over all those who come to dwell in their island. Foremost among these is King Arthur, following the Last Battle.

Arthur's arrival is described by the bard Taliesin, who has already accompanied the king on a journey to an Otherworld island to gain the Cauldron of the Head of Annwfn and who now, in the company of Merlin, escorts him to Avalon. Taliesin afterwards relates how Morgen received them: "she put the king in her chamber on a golden bed, uncovered his wound with her noble hand and looked long at it. At length she said he could be cured if only he stayed with her a long while and accepted her treatment. We therefore happily committed the king to her care…" (*VM* 103).

Our first encounter with the Lady of the Isle of Avalon is therefore as a healer, a teacher and a woman of knowledge, albeit one possessed of the supernatural powers of shape-shifting and flight. Most readers will, however, be more familiar with Malory's Morgan Le Fay who, in addition to being an enemy of the queen and an attempted seducer of Lancelot, acts murderously towards the king and in opposition to his protector, the Lady of the Lake. Before joining with the Lady to welcome Arthur into the barge that will take him to Avalon, Morgan expresses the utmost solicitation for his welfare. It is these apparent contradictions in her character that we must now explain—and what soon becomes clear is that Malory was struggling to reconcile disparate source materials in his English Arthuriad, not always successfully.

She Was a Goddess

The first mention of Morgen after Geoffrey's poem is in one by Chrétien de Troyes, who translates the Brittonic name into French as *Morgain, la fée*: which we immediately recognize as Malory's Morgan Le Fay. Chrétien's Morgain has a lover called Guigomar, who is the Lord of the Isle of Avalon: a title that he presumably inherited from Morgain. This brief reference in Chrétien's early poem *Erec et Enide* (ll.1954-8) is supplemented by another reference to a sister of Arthur called *Morgue* who possesses an ointment that can heal wounds (ll.4218-28). In the later *Le Chevalier au Lion* (l.2953) we hear about *Margue la sage*, a wise woman who possesses an ointment that can cure madness.

Thus far, two elements have survived from Geoffrey—that she is a healer and is connected with Avalon—and two new elements have been introduced: that she is a fay and that she has a lover called Guigomar. It is these new elements that will determine her future literary evolution.

Both of Chrétien's poems had been translated into German by Hartmann von Aue, a poet from the upper Rhine region, by the beginning of the thirteenth century. But Hartman's references to the fay, unlike those of the French poet, also reveal a familiarity with the *Vita Merlini*.

Hartmann talks of the great good fortune of the Lord of Avalon to be loved by the fay Marguel. She can fly round the world at great speed; live in the air, under water, or in fire; turn a man into a bird or an animal and restore his original shape. She is the mistress of the birds and wild animals, of dragons and fish. She commands the demons of hell and knows the power of all the herbs in the earth. Or, at least, she did when she was alive: for, according to Hartmann, she dies before Arthur. "What great arts and strange knowledge perished with her!" he laments: "she was a goddess" (*HvA* 112).

This is the first time that she has been called a goddess and it is not altogether clear what Hartmann means by this—especially when he describes her as dying. But we have already seen that the goddess Diana has been reduced to the status of a mortal huntress (who, as we will see in Chapter Nine, ends up beheaded by her lover), so I would suggest that what we are witnessing here is a stage in the process of euhemerization of pagan deities by Christian authors.

This process is perhaps at its clearest in Irish mythology, where the ancient Celtic beings known as the People of the Goddess were believed to have been supernaturally endowed but mortal, insofar as they could die in battle. They once ruled Ireland but, with the coming of the Gaels, they were driven into the hills to make their new, underground home in the barrows, the prehistoric tombs that the Irish continued to see as places of enchantment, long after their conversion to Christianity: these are the People of the Síde. That this development also occurred in mainland Britain is suggested by the fact that one of the names of the Otherworld in Welsh medieval poetry is Caer Sidi, one of several significant linguistic borrowings from Irish that remind us that the Brittonic and Goidelic languages contain the traces of a prehistoric shared mythology.

With the Anglo-Saxon conquest, the denizens of Caer Sidi became known to the English as "elves," a name that is today very familiar through its use by Tolkien and thence its spread into modern fantasy literature. But, although the word "elves" (*aluen*) is used by the Middle English poet Layamon, the word *fées* is used by the French writers and from them comes into the English language the words "fay" and "fairy"; while Faerie (or Elvenhome, as Tolkien calls it) more properly denotes the realm of the fays, "fairyland" as it is known in children's stories. What is less well known is that behind the little sprites of popular fiction stands a very ancient and very powerful goddess: Fate.

The Fatal Sisters

The medieval western conception of Fate can be traced back to the classical period. In Greece, the goddess Moira, whose name refers to the "share" that each of us is bestowed of life and achievement, most often appears in threefold form. Kerényi tells us that this corresponds to the three divisions of the Greek month and the three aspects of the moon: "as the waxing, the full and the waning sign of a divine presence in the sky" (31).

This lunar association is strengthened when we learn that, in one version given by the early Greek poet Hesiod, the three Moirai are the daughters of the goddess Night. This genealogy was also adopted by the mystery cult founded by the poet Orpheus, which later became associated with the highest mystical philosophy. The moon, which, as we saw in the first chapter, is the central image of the sacred for prehistoric peoples, becomes the image of human mutability, personified by the Moirai (32). Among the Romans, this lunar, threefold Moira becomes *Fatum* ("that which has been spoken"), a concept that is also personified as the three Fates: who are, in turn, assimilated to the Parcae, goddesses of birth, since they bestow on the newborn child his or her destiny.

This aspect of the Fates is perhaps best illustrated by the "fairytale" of Briar-Rose, better known as the Sleeping Beauty, where wise women attend the birth celebrations of the newborn princess in order to bless or curse. Less well known are accounts of the Fates visiting Arthur at his birth. Layamon, in his English language chronicle, tells us how elves took charge of the child as soon as he appeared on earth, using powerful enchantment to bestow on him magical gifts: enormous strength, great longevity and the destiny to be a most mighty and liberal king (*Brut*, l.9608–15).

We do not know whether Layamon intended us to understand that there were three Fates, one for each gift; but this is made explicit in the Second Continuation to the Story of the Grail, where three ladies are present at Arthur's birth to confer on him "esteem and valour and wisdom and prowess and great honor, and greater courage and worth than any man of woman born" (*PSG* 186). The fifteenth century English poet John Lydgate names the sisters who spin his fate as the Parcae.[2] Elsewhere in English literature they are known as the Fatal Sisters, but Shakespeare will give them the name by which they are best remembered: the Weird Sisters.[3]

Arthur's Weird Sisters

Given the presence of the Fatal Sisters at Arthur's birth, we should not be surprised to learn that in the romances he has three older sisters, one of whom is explicitly described as a fay.

The earliest mention of this is found in the Prose *Merlin*, attributed to Robert de Boron. Here we learn that when Uther Pendragon married Igerna, she already had three daughters by her first husband, the Duke of Tintagel: the eldest of the three is married to King Loth and she will bear him Gawain as well as other mighty heroes; the second, who is illegitimate, is married to the King of Garlot; while the third is sent to a nunnery, where she learns so much about the "secret arts" that she becomes known as Morgan the Fay (*MG* 103).

We can see at once that the process of euhemerization is at work. Robert de Boron was a Burgundian knight who wrote a prequel to Chrétien de Troyes' Story of the Grail in which, for the first time, it is made explicit that the Grail is a Christian artefact, a relic of the Last Supper that was used at the Crucifixion to catch the Holy Blood. De Boron may have been concerned about the worrying ambiguity of the symbol as it appears in Chrétien's unfinished poem and he wrote an account of its early history attempting to distance the symbol from its pagan origins and to exorcise the heterodox elements in its theology (Carey 2007, 149). The reduction of the status of Morgan from a Goddess of Fate to a practitioner of the secret arts follows a similar trajectory.

Either de Boron himself or another scribe made a prose redaction of his poem and then added two more sections to form a trilogy, which I refer to as the "De Boron Cycle" since it was the first attempt to absorb the burgeoning Grail mythos into the Arthurian framework established by Geoffrey of Monmouth and Wace. In the thirteenth century, the De Boron Cycle was itself absorbed into the vast Vulgate Cycle, which continued the process he began: of thoroughly Christianizing the Grail and transforming Morgan from a goddess turned fay into a misunderstood wise woman (*boine clergesse*), whose powers only seem supernatural to those who do not have her learning.

The Vulgate *Estoire de Merlin* reveals that, in addition to the arts she learns in the nunnery, she is briefly apprenticed to Merlin, from whom she learns "many wonders in astrology and necromancy" (*LG* I, 307). She is also described as "the most lustful woman in all Great Britain and the lewdest," qualities that mitigate her undoubted beauty and "wondrous learning" (354). In fact, it is her sexuality that will prove to be her undoing: for she falls in love with Guiomar, a knight of Cameliard who is the queen's nephew; but their love will be forbidden at the order of Guenevere. From this, much trouble will ensue.

The Wounded Healer

Guiomar first comes across Morgan when she is spinning golden thread to make a headpiece for her sister, the wife of King Loth. We may have here an echo of the moon goddess as spinster for, as Mircea Eliade puts it: "It is the Moon that spins the Time, she who 'weaves' the lives of humanity; the goddesses of fate are spinners" (1960, 211). But, while we are all familiar with the spinster who casts a weird upon Briar-Rose, Guiomar falls not asleep but into love when Morgan casts her spell upon him. Caught in her web, he flirtatiously handles her golden thread until they end up playing "the game everyone plays" (354).

Unfortunately Queen Guenevere eventually finds out about it and the two lovers are separated. Morgan can never forgive the queen for ruining her first love affair and hates her for it ever afterwards. All the trouble she causes her stems from this moment.

To the modern reader, Morgan's only crime is to make love with a man who loves her; for the medieval reader, no blame would attach to Guiomar, who is only following man's nature. How hypocritical, then, of Guenevere, to destroy the love of two young people, while she herself goes on to have an affair with her husband's best friend and, in so doing, brings down the kingdom! If Morgan plays a part in the discovery of the infidelity, her vengeance is at least understandable.

The story of the thwarted love of Morgan for Guiomar has curious parallels with—and may ultimately be derived from—the legend found in two "lays," verse narratives based on songs, dating from the late twelfth or early thirteenth centuries, in which the hero is called either Guigemar or (what may be the earliest version of his name) Guingamor.

The Lay of Guigemar[4] was written by the earliest known French-language poetess, Marie de France, writing in the late twelfth century. It gives us a relatively straightforward tale of adultery, with a few supernatural elements. Guigemar, the Prince of Brittany, is a most eligible bachelor but he shows no interest in affairs of the heart until he is wounded while hunting. He shoots a white hind with an arrow and hits it, but the arrow rebounds and pierces his thigh. The dying animal curses him, prophesying that he will get no relief for his wound until he suffers the pain of love for a woman, who will suffer in her turn for his love.

A deserted ship carries him away, with no one to steer it but, as if with a mind of its own, taking him to an ancient city where a decrepit old king keeps his young and beautiful wife locked up in a walled garden, terrified of losing her—and with good reason for, as soon as Guigemar's ship arrives, it is love at first sight. They carry on an illicit affair for a year and a half, until they are found out and Guigemar banished. The magic ship carries him back to Brittany, where he continues to refuse all offers of marriage.

Now both Guigemar and the lady fulfil the hind's curse by suffering the pangs of thwarted love, although his thigh wound is completely healed. The lady manages to escape in the helpful ship, which carries her to Brittany; but she is captured by a lord who also wants her body, since she is "as lovely as a fairy" (*LMF* 52). Fortunately, Guigemar finds her and kills her captor; their trials and tribulations are over.

If Guigemar finds happiness in an adulterous affair with a fay-like lady, the anonymous Lay of Guingamor[5] leads us into an even more fantastic realm where there can be no doubt about the supernatural character of its mistress. Here, the eponymous hero is the nephew and heir of the King of Brittany.

Trying to avoid the unwanted attentions of his uncle's wife, who has become infatuated with him, Guingamor allows himself to be taunted by her into undertaking the perilous hunt, in the depths of the forest, of a wild white boar—whose color, Rachel Bromwich suggests (*TYP* 397), is a clue to its magical nature and Otherworldly origin, as with the Old White Sow of the Welsh Triads that we encountered in Chapter One. Separated from his companions, Guingamor comes upon a fay bathing in a spring and falls instantly in love at the sight of her naked body.

She returns his love and invites Guingamor to her palace of green marble, where he spends a wonderful night amid feasting and music. He decides to stay a couple more days before returning home to the king with the head of the boar, which his mistress has bestowed on him. With his quest honorably achieved, he can then come back to his ladylove. She grants him permission to leave, but warns him not to eat or drink anything while he is in his own country.

Things are not that simple, however: in this palace in the forest, three days are the same as three hundred years in the outer world. As the maiden tries to explain to him, the royal dynasty he had known is now extinct, its cities in ruin, although there are still people around who tell of the king's brave nephew, who went hunting and never came back. Realizing that they are talking about him, Guingamor is overcome with emotion and forgets his mistress' warning. Feeling hungry, he eats some apples growing in the side of the road; but barely has he tasted the fruit when his body becomes so old and decrepit that he falls off his horse. At that moment two maidens arrive. They reproach Guingamor for disobeying his mistress' instructions, place him back on his horse and transfer him to a boat on a nearby river.

We are not told the name of the elven maiden nor of her enchanted realm where time stands still but, despite the euhemerizations and rationalizations that abound in the Vulgate romances, we can see that the elements of the Lay survive in the story of Guingamor and Morgan, the Lady of the Isle of Avalon: Firstly, we have the jealousy of a queen, who conceives an adulterous passion for one of her husband's knights. Secondly, we have the love of a fay for a mortal knight, from whom she becomes separated. Thirdly, we have the great harm which befalls the realm or its champions. When two ladies arrive to carry the apparently dying knight in a boat back to the land of the fay, it is impossible not to think of the two ladies holding hands (one of whom is Morgan[6]), who arrive in a ship to carry the apparently dying Arthur off to Avalon, at the end of the Vulgate Cycle.

It is as if these different versions are so many variations on a mythic tale in which a mortal knight is loved by the Queen of Faerie but rejects the adulterous passion of the wife of his earthly liege—and who escapes this impossible dilemma by rejecting the complications of mortal life and going to live in the Island of Immortals with his elven bride. By the time Chrétien wrote down the oral tales he heard, the knight is called Guingamor and the Queen of Faerie, Morgan. Her paradisiacal island, where no mortals dwell, is called Avalon and Guingamor becomes its lord.

As the story becomes increasingly integrated into the Arthurian mythos, Morgan is identified as Arthur's sister and the queen whom the knight rejects is named as Guenevere. Or, at least, this is the case in a similar lay, also attributed to Marie de France: the Lay of Lanval.[7]

As so often in these "fairytales" (*lais féeriques*), the hero meets, apparently by chance, a beautiful fay, who showers him with riches as well as love. She will never be far from him, she promises, as long as he never discloses their relationship to anyone else. Generous with his newfound riches, Lanval becomes the center of attention at court, where he also attracts a less welcome interest, that of Guenevere. She tells him that she fancies him and is mortified when he rejects her, claiming that he must be homosexual. To defend his manly reputation, Lanval confesses that the truth is quite otherwise: he has a lover who is so beautiful that even her handmaidens put the queen to shame.

Guenevere complains to the king that he tried to force himself on her and, in addition, insulted her beauty. Arthur commands Lanval to produce this mysterious beauty, which of course he cannot do. But on the day of his trial the handmaidens of the fay appear, confirming his description, followed by the fay herself, who whisks him off to her home in Avalon, the beautiful island.

Modern readers will inevitably find some amusement in a story in which a man attacked for being gay by a "queen" is defended by a "fairy." But the serious point is that at last all the elements are in place to explain the early hostility between Guenevere and Morgan. The Lady of the Isle of Avalon loves a Knight of the Round Table. The queen attempts to thwart their relationship, because she loves the knight herself, but the knight rejects the queen and goes to live with his fairy bride in Avalon.

As the Vulgate Cycle develops, we will see that this pattern undergoes some subtle alterations: The Lady of the Isle of Avalon loves a Knight of the Round Table, but he has eyes only for the queen. The knight rejects the fay and goes to live with his liege lord's queen, while the king goes to live with the fay (no longer his fairy bride but his sister) in Avalon.

Much Pleasure in Carduel

The Vulgate Cycle also provides us with one further twist, in which Arthur fathers a child on the eldest of the Fatal Sisters. Morgause (as Malory calls her, Morcadés in the French versions) is the only one of the three sisters whose death is described, so we know she is mortal.[8] Nevertheless, she is *fated* to bring into this world, through a monstrous act, the architect of the death of Arthur and the downfall of his Adventurous Kingdom.

Morgause is the eldest of the three daughters of Gorlois, the Duke of Tintagel. She is married to King Loth of Orkney at the same time as Uther marries Igerna, as part of the peace settlement that follows the death of Gorlois. From their union will come four mighty warriors, of whom the eldest is Gawain and the youngest Gaheriet (Gareth). But Morgause will also bear a son to her own half-brother through an unwitting act of incest, which Arthur commits while he is still a squire.

It happens like this: When the barons of Logres are summoned to Carduel in Wales to discuss the future of the kingdom following the death of Uther, King Loth brings his wife with him. They are lodged in the same hall as Sir Antor, Arthur's foster-father and Sir Kay, the newly-knighted son of Antor. Arthur, Kay's foster-brother who acts as his squire, sleeps in a corner next to Loth's bedroom. He can't help fancying Loth's wife, who is so "beautiful and plump"; but she is too faithful to take any notice of the handsome boy.

Nevertheless, as an enterprising young teenager with an important destiny, Arthur is already learning to seize every opportunity that comes his way. Consequently, when Loth leaves the hall for a midnight rendezvous with his barons, Arthur sneaks into his bed; although, once next to the beautiful lady, who he assumes is still asleep, he does not dare to go any further. But he does not need to: Morgause, waking up and thinking her husband has returned, puts her arms around the lad and gives him "much pleasure," as the story says (*LG* I, 237).

Arthur must have thought that Christmas had come early—although in fact, Christmas would have something even more momentous in store for him, for he would draw the Sword in the Stone that would make him rightful King of Britain. Nevertheless, even as he is divinely elected to become an anointed king, he has sown the seeds of his own destruction: for Morgause is pregnant with the bad seed that is Mordred.

As for the lady, she appears not to have noticed the difference between a teenage boy and a grizzled veteran of the Saxon wars. At least, that's her story—and she sticks to it, even when Arthur owns up to the deception. They both agree that it's in no-one's interest to tell anyone and it never happens again. It is only when Merlin reveals to the world that Arthur is the son of Uther Pendragon that Morgause realizes that she has slept with her half-brother; but, even so, she is rather pleased to have conceived a son to the rightful King of Britain.

Although their husbands rebel against Uther's bastard, none of Arthur's three sisters ever show any hostility to him in the Vulgate Cycle: Morgan's animus is wholly directed against Guenevere, for the reasons we have seen. But her resentment at the queen's interference in her affair with Guiomar is later caught up with her own infatuation with Lancelot and this, in turn, gets caught up with her outrage over the insult done to Arthur by the adultery of his wife—as becomes clear in the episode of the prison paintings.

The Dullest of Knights

Lancelot has already had two run-ins with Morgan—in the Val Sans Retour (or Valley of False Lovers) and in the affair of the magic rings—when he finds himself once again her prisoner and love object. After freeing Guenevere and the other exiles from Gorre and unintentionally betraying the Queen of Logres by sleeping with the Princess of Corbenic, the hapless lover is lured into Morgan's clutches by a maiden who promises to lead him to a marvelous adventure in a forest, one that only he can accomplish. What he does not realize is that Morgan has built a mansion in the forest, where she hopes to detain Lancelot at her pleasure. The maiden is one of twelve who have been sent to scour the world in search of him.

Made more than welcome in the mansion, Lancelot is soon under the influence of one of Morgan's potions: his strength leaves him and he can't stay awake. When he comes round, still sick and giddy, he is locked in a room with an iron-barred window that looks out on a garden. There Morgan hopes to wear down his resistance to her love.

Deaf to her pleadings, Lancelot is so befuddled by the drugs with which she has doped him that he does not even realize he is a prisoner until he has been there a month. Then, as autumn turns to winter, Lancelot sees a man in the garden painting a mural depicting the flight of Aeneas from Troy, an event that would lead to the foundation of both Rome and Britain. Lancelot decides to have a go at painting his lady so that he can be comforted by her image and when Morgan, on one of her regular midnight visits, sees what he has done, with such artistic skill, she is impressed that love can so inspire "the dullest of knights" (*LG* III, 218). Clearly it is his body rather than his mind that she is attracted to.

But when she studies the subject matter, Morgan gets an idea: Lancelot has depicted his arrival at Camelot as the White Knight and his early adventures, which he achieved through the overwhelming power of his love for Guenevere. Morgan, who is certainly not dull, realizes that, if she lets him carry on, he will paint a damning indictment of his adulterous affair. All she will have to do then is show the mural to her brother for the queen to be utterly condemned. Revenge will be sweet.

But, before her triumph, she and all the supernatural women of Britain will take second place to the adventures of the Grail, which are about to transform the kingdom.

Five

A Woman's Wiles

> ... amidst them beam'd
> A False Feminine Counterpart, of Lovely Delusive Beauty
> Dividing & Uniting at will in the Cruelties of Holiness
> ... female forms, beautiful thro' poisons hidden in secret
> Which give a tincture to false beauty....[1]
>
> —William Blake

As a child, Lancelot was submerged by the Lady of the Lake. As a young man, he falls under the spell of Arthur's Otherworld bride, Guenevere—but, as he grows up, he is bewitched by the Grail Bearer and must face the challenge of fatherhood, eventually seeing that his son will surpass him. Lancelot will learn that there is a spiritual dimension to life beyond the magical and emotional realms opened up to him by the Ladies of the Lake and of Camelot. This spiritual dimension is located in Corbenic and it is from there that will emerge his son, who bears his own lost spiritual (baptismal) name.

The spiritual dimension will always prove challenging for Lancelot and, in fact, as it spreads out of the Land Beyond into more familiar territory, it will provoke yet another spell of madness in the hero. The first two times, it was the Lady of the Lake who cured him. This time it will require something more than magic: nothing less than the miraculous power of the most holy relic in Arthur's Adventurous Kingdom. And she who causes the madness, she who was once the bearer of the Holy Vessel, is she who must bring about his cure.

The Isle of Joy

In the last chapter, we left Lancelot painting images of his love for Guenevere in Morgan's forest prison, images that she will make very good use of for her own purposes at the appropriate time. He languishes there for two winters and a summer but, at Eastertide, love gives him the strength to escape. He sees in the garden a rose bush in bloom—and one newly opened rose that is more beautiful than all the others reminds him of his lady, whose beauty surpasses all others. The painted images no longer suffice: he must have the rose. But he cannot reach it through the window, so he shatters the iron bars and climbs out. And now nothing can stop him from leaving the mansion, refraining from having his revenge on "a disloyal and traitorous woman" only because she is the king's sister (*LG* III, 225).

Years pass, during which Lancelot regains the territories that he lost when his father died prematurely and is reunited with his mother. King Arthur, who had supported him in his re-conquest of his ancestral lands, celebrates by holding at Camelot the most splendid court of his reign, to which all his subject nobles are invited. Elaine of Corbenic attends on behalf of her father King Pelles and she brings with her young Galahad. The queen, knowing nothing of what has transpired, makes much of her, even offering to share her room with her.

But Elaine, though originally acting on her father's instructions, now has her sights set on the father of her child, so she gets Brisane to trick him once again. This time, though, no drugs are needed. The queen has made a secret arrangement for Lancelot to come to her bed but Brisane, overhearing, intervenes and leads Lancelot to the right room but the wrong bed. By the time either Lancelot or the queen realize what has happened, it is too late: Lancelot has sex with Elaine and they fall asleep "in joy and delight" (320). The queen is furious and banishes Lancelot from the court. He has a nervous breakdown while Elaine returns to Corbenic. And it is there that Lancelot, barefoot and in rags, eventually turns up in the middle of winter, having spent the best part of a year wandering, out of his mind with grief.

The madman is rescued from the insults of children and servants and looked after in the court. It is not until Easter that, as he sleeps by a spring beneath a sycamore tree in the royal gardens, Elaine finds and recognizes him. Her father has him carried to the Palace of Adventures where he will encounter, for the second time, that wondrous vessel whose mysteries he is not worthy to uncover—but the presence of the Holy Vessel cures him of his madness and restores his memory.

Unwilling to return to Logres without his lady's favor, Lancelot hides himself away on a remote island with Elaine and twenty maidens, who dance joyously around a pine tree on which the hero has hung his shield. Their dancing leads to the island being named the Isle of Joy, despite the fact that every morning Lancelot goes to the headland from which he can see the Kingdom of Logres in the distance and weeps so much for what he has lost that his mourning relieves his pain and brings "great sweetness to his heart" (335).

We are not so far here from what the Celtic scholar Proinsias Mac Cana (89) has called "the happy otherworld," like the Elysian Land of Women to which the Irish Bran travels, in one of the most famous *immrama*, or heroic voyages of medieval literature. In a sense, Lancelot has returned to the joyous Land of Maidens of his childhood, the island of the Water Fay. Here he can escape from the failures of both his love life and his spiritual life, far from the woman who has hurt him emotionally and from the Christian relic which reminds him of his unworthiness. If the Grail cured him of his madness, he is still avoiding painful reality.

He cannot avoid it for long, as his warrior instincts demand that he practice his knightly skills before they grow rusty. He has a shield made for himself, on which he depicts a queen in silver (the color of the moon) and a knight kneeling before her. He then lets it be known that the Guilty Knight awaits all comers and he defeats them all, until at last he is fought to a standstill by Perceval—significantly, one of the three companions who will achieve the Grail Quest. But he has no need to continue his exile, for Guenevere has revoked his banishment.

Returning to Corbenic, Lancelot is introduced to his ten year-old son for the first time and, when the father declares his intention of returning to Camelot, young Galahad expresses the desire to be near the father he has never known. Accordingly, a place is found for him at an abbey in Camelot Forest and he stays there until he is fifteen, when he is knighted by his father. Straightaway he goes to King Arthur's court, arriving on the eve of Pentecost.

Galahad's arrival is heralded by wonders: a sword stuck in a floating stone appears on the river, with an inscription that reads that it can only be drawn by the best knight in the world. At the same time there appears on the Siege Perilous a plaque stating that it is the place of Galahad, who is announced by a hermit as the Desired Knight, of the House of David (through his grandmother, Queen Elaine of Benoic) and of the lineage of Joseph of Arimathea (through his grandfather Pelles, the Fisher King).

Unlike all those who have tried before, Galahad is not swallowed up when he sits on the Siege Perilous—which tells us much about his messianic role, since this seat is equivalent to the place of Jesus at the Table of the Last Supper. It is also relevant to note that the name Galahad is itself related to Gilead, a Biblical mountain which, for the Cistercians whose influence on the Vulgate *Quest of the Holy Grail* was very great, signified the head of the church (Barber 2003, 9).

The feat of sitting in the Siege Perilous, the ladies of Camelot declare, proves that Galahad is "the one who shall bring the adventures of Britain to their close and restore the Maimed King" (*QHG* 39). Their belief in him can only be reinforced when he draws out with ease the Sword in the Floating Stone, replicating the feat achieved by Arthur which proved him to be divinely chosen—and which also proves that Galahad has already, at the beginning of his career, surpassed his father.

That evening, an even greater marvel occurs: the Grail, previously only seen at Corbenic, appears in Arthur's court. Although it is covered with white samite, it still lights up the assembled knights as if with the grace of the Holy Spirit and, after it has gone, Gawain swears that he will never rest until he sees it uncovered.

The rest of the Round Table declare that they too will go on this quest—much to the distress of their women-folk, many of whom want to go with their men. But a message comes from Nascien, the Hermit of the Grail, explaining that it is a mortal sin for any man to take a woman with him: "For this is no search for earthly things but a seeking out of the mysteries and hidden sweets of Our Lord, and the divine secrets which the most high Master will disclose to that blessed knight whom He has chosen for His servant from among the ranks of chivalry: he to whom He will show the marvels of the Holy Grail, and reveal that which the heart of man could not conceive nor tongue relate" (47).

Lovely Delusive Beauty

But if women are banished from this chivalric quest, they will be encountered by the knights along the way in a variety of forms: some benevolent, some allegorical, some demonic. Thus, when Perceval first sets out on the quest, he soon encounters his wise aunt, the Queen of the Waste Land, who tells him how Merlin created the Round Table in honor of both the Table of the Last Supper and the Table of the Grail (see Chapter Seven). It is, she says, "a true epitome of the universe" and it is to three knights of that fellowship (two of whom will be virgins and the other chaste) that "the secrets of the Holy Grail" will be revealed (99).

The "chaste" knight is Bors, Sir Lancelot's cousin, who has fathered a child, but only after being tricked by a princess with (yet another) magic ring (much to the chagrin of the Lady of the Lake, who thought that Bors would remain a virgin all his days); but he never strays again. The two life-long virgins are Galahad and Perceval—but the latter will have to resist temptation so that he will arrive "pure and unsullied before the

Holy Grail, and without stain of lechery." Otherwise he will forfeit the quest (102).

Such temptation is not long in coming. When his horse is killed, the Enemy (Satan) appears in the form of a woman who offers him a huge black charger if he will do her bidding when she calls him. He readily assents, but the horse would have drowned him in a river if he had not made the sign of the cross for protection. The horse itself is swept away amid flames that make the water appear to burn.

Later he has a dream in which a young lady riding a lion (symbolizing the New Law of Christianity) and another, older one riding a serpent (symbolizing those Jews who rejected Christ and still cling to the Old Law) appear to him. The young lady warns him that on the morrow he will have to fight "the most dreaded champion in all the world" (117) and, sure enough, the next day a maiden who claims to have been driven out of her exalted home asks for his aid against her dispossessor. He feels honor-bound to rescue a damsel in distress. She takes him to her ship where she gets him drunk on strong wine and, not unnaturally, his feelings for her grow "unduly warm" (128). She offers him her body as long as he will do her will in all things henceforward and the hapless hero nearly loses his much-vaunted virginity which, in his befuddled state, seems like a small price to pay.

But divine providence intervenes: as he gets into bed with the fiend, he sees a red cross which is inlaid in the hilt of his sword and the sight of it brings him to his senses. He makes the sign of the cross and the "maiden" vanishes in a pall of thick smoke, while a foul stench pervades everything so that he thinks he must be in hell. This time even the sea bursts into flame.

Yearning for death, Perceval sticks his sword into his left thigh (in a curious echo of the wound that, in the first Grail poem, killed his father and maimed the Fisher King[2]), declaring: "I have been vile and wicked beyond measure, to let myself be brought so swiftly to the brink of losing what is irredeemable, namely virginity, which cannot be recovered since it is lost but once" (*QHG* 130). The pain, however, brings him to his senses and he boards a white ship that will bring him closer to his goal.

A Model of Holy Living

But Perceval is not alone in having troubles with women. While he is narrowly saving his virginity, his entrance-ticket to the Grail Kingdom, Sir Bors (Lancelot's cousin) is also obliged to defend his chaste status. Having opted to rescue a damsel in distress rather than free his brother Lionel from capture by brigands, Bors is then led to believe that his brother is dead by a man dressed as a monk on a black horse. The "monk" bids him bring the "body" to a tower adjacent to a building which resembles a chapel apart from the fact that it lacks any Christian symbols.

Claiming to be able to interpret Bors' dreams (a gift that has been vouchsafed only to the true Grail Hermits), the false monk tells him that a woman who is "aflame with desire" for him will shortly invite him to be her lover (191). If he rejects her she will die of grief and her family will kill Lancelot in revenge—thus Bors will be responsible for two more murders, in addition to that of Lionel. And after all, he argues, which is better: that the damsel had been "deflowered" or that "one of the finest knights on earth" should have been killed? "It were better for sure," he concludes, "that every maiden in the world lost her virginity than he his life."

We might imagine that, by now, Bors is wondering whether the apparent monk is truly "a model of holy living" (192); but he allows himself to be led to meet the lady of the tower who offers him great wealth and power if he will plight his love to her. When he refuses, she threatens to kill herself and twelve of her maidens threaten to throw themselves off the battlements rather than witness their lady's demise.

To this, Bors replies that it is better that they should all lose their souls (through suicide) rather than that he should lose his (by having sex outside marriage)—an attitude which the late Victorian scholar Alfred Nutt considered to exemplify the "unhuman realm"[3] in which the successful questers must operate and, by implication, the inhuman character of the questers themselves, or of their author[4]—although it should be said that Nutt's strongest criticism is reserved for the character of Galahad, whom he sees as "wholly remote from the life of man on earth."[5] Bors has at least known the touch of a woman (though scarcely reciprocal love) and he feels pity mixed with horror when the maidens cast themselves off the tower. But, when he makes the Sign of the Cross, the tower, the lady and his brother's body vanish. He realizes that he has fought and vanquished the Enemy. Escaping to the shore, he finds a white ship in which he teams up with Perceval.

The White Ship takes them to a shore where they encounter Galahad in the company of a maiden who, refreshingly, is not in fact a devil in disguise, but she does seem to be imbued with prophetic powers. She has led Galahad to the spot where he would find his companions and, when the ship leads them to a rocky islet, she knows that they will find there another ship. This in turn they must board if they are to accomplish their quest, but it will destroy those of less than perfect faith: "For the ship is so sublime a thing that none who bears the taint of vice can sojourn there secure" (*QHG* 213).

She is, she now reveals, Perceval's sister but, unlike her brother, who was brought up in the Waste Forest in ignorance of his heritage, she knows something of the history of their family and how its destiny is tied up with that of the Ship of Faith. Their great-grandfather King Lambor was waging war against his neighbor King Varlan, a pagan only recently converted to Christianity, when the ship docked on the shore. King Varlan boarded the mysterious ship and found there a marvelous sword which had written on its blade a warning: that anyone who unsheathed it, unless he could outdo and out-dare all others, would find injury and death. The vainglorious king ignored the warning, drew the sword and used it to kill Lambor but, as soon as he put it back in its scabbard, he also dropped down dead. The realms of the two kings were laid to waste and have never since recovered. Thus was struck the Dolorous Blow that created the Waste Land.

But this was not the end of the family's tragedy. Their grandfather King Pellehan also came across the ship, while out hunting on the coast, tried to draw the sword and was instantly struck through the thighs by a flying lance. He is now known as the Maimed King and will never be healed until Galahad comes to him. As for the sword, it is still there amidships, lying at the foot of a sumptuous bed. It has a cheap and shoddy hempen belt that does not seem to be worthy of such a marvelous weapon; but an inscription on the scabbard warns that it can only be replaced when a royal virgin puts in its stead a belt "fashioned from that thing about her person that is most precious to her." Once equipped with its new belt, the sword will protect its bearer from all injury, as long as he doesn't take it any place "where sin and vice are found" (217).

Examining the bed on which the sword lies, the companions notice three wooden posts: one white, one red and one green, but naturally colored, not painted. A letter that Perceval finds beneath a golden crown at the head of the bed explains the origins of the ship and its mysteries, which can be traced back to the Garden of Eden and humanity's first fall.

A Sign of Our Return

The story begins with "sinful Eve, the first woman," who has been goaded by the Devil into committing the mortal sin of "concupiscence" (or "criminal desire"), which leads her to pluck the "deadly fruit" from the Tree of Knowledge (222). But, in doing so, she also breaks off a green branch of the tree, which she holds onto when she gives the apple to her husband Adam, the first man. At that moment sex and death enter into the world. God condemns man henceforth to eat by the sweat of his brow and woman, who is "of a frailer nature," to give birth in pain. He drives them both from "the garden of delight."

It is only then that Eve notices that she is still carrying the green branch of the tree that was the cause of her misery. She vows to keep it always as a memento of her loss by planting it in the ground of exile, where it becomes a sign to futurity, saying: "Be not dismayed if we are banished from our inheritance: it is not lost to us eternally; see here a sign of our return hereafter" (223).

Once the branch from the Tree of Knowledge is planted in the ground of exile, it grows into a tree of pure white hue, the color of virginity, for Adam and Eve have not yet had sexual relations. However, God has plans for them: He wants them to create a race of human beings who will take the place of the fallen angels and, accordingly, they unite for the first time as man and wife. Thus is their first son, Abel, conceived and, at the same time, the white tree turns green and produces blossom and fruit.

Later, when Abel is killed by his younger brother Cain, the Tree turns red and never fruits again but, because it is the sign of our return to Paradise, it is known as the Tree of Life and it is still growing when Solomon is king in Israel. Wise Solomon knows all about precious stones, herbs and the celestial movements.

> Nonetheless, all his sagacity could not combat the cunning of his wife, nor prevent her from deceiving him as frequently as she took pains to do so. Nor is this anything to wonder at; for without a doubt, when woman gives her mind and heart to guile, no mere man's wit can prove a match for her; and this is nothing new, but dates back to the mother of us all [230].

Distressed at his powerlessness in the face of woman's wiles, King Solomon is nevertheless comforted by the Holy Ghost, who reveals to him through dreams and waking visions that a woman of his line will bring such joy to mankind that it will more than compensate for all the sorrow women, since Eve, have inflicted on us. But this "glorious Virgin" will not be the last of his line. Rather, his lineage will end with another virgin, but a man this time, a scion rooted in "virtue and high valour" (231).

Solomon is much taken with the idea of somehow communicating to the last of his line that he had foreknowledge of this valorous virgin; but struggles with how to do it until his wife adds her ingenuity to his wisdom. She suggests that he builds a ship out of the most durable wood, so that it will last at least two thousand years. She counsels him to place in it his father King David's sword and even insists that the sword should have only a hempen belt, for she knows that a maiden at some indeterminate future time and place will provide it with a new one.

She further takes personal charge of an addition to the ship that she deems necessary: the construction of three wooden posts that will frame the bed, made from the trees descended from the branch that Eve brought out of Eden. Although the original Tree is now red, cuttings have been taken from it at the earlier stages of its transformations; so that white and green trees have survived from antediluvian times.

Solomon's wife determines to have a post of each color and is not fazed when the red Tree of Life bleeds when the carpenters cut into it. Once the posts have been erected, Solomon is very impressed with the result, but is still concerned that there is nothing to indicate to his future descendant that his coming was foretold. But once again his wife knows what is to happen next: "Leave the ship as it is," she says, "for you will have news of it yet that you did not look for" (234). And sure enough, that night the king dreams of a heavenly being leaving messages on the ship. In the morning, the ship launches itself onto the open sea, only to arrive, as we have seen, at key points in the history of the Fisher Kings.

Universal Poetic Genius

For all she is described as a creature of guile and deceit, Solomon's wife appears here as an agent of divine providence: her ingenuity has enabled her to solve a problem which, for all his wisdom, has baffled her husband. Her *sutilité* is an ambiguous quality making of her, like Morgan the Fay, a Shadowy Female. We will return to her story in the Interlude; for the legend of the Tree of Life and the Ship of Solomon, like the other flashbacks with which the Vulgate *Quest* is littered, will act as a bridge to the Post-Vulgate Cycle when they are re-presented (this time in chronological order rather than as flashbacks) in the *Estoire del Saint Graal*.

As the story is presented in the Vulgate *Quest*, however, the figure of Solomon's wife is counterpoised to that of Perceval's sister, who also remains unnamed. In neither case is an explanation given of their knowledge of what is to come.

On the very day that Galahad arrived at Camelot, the maiden cut off her hair and wove it with threads of silk and gold into a strange belt. She now offers it to Galahad in fulfilment of the ancient prophecy that only a royal virgin who had sacrificed her most precious possession could provide the Sword of David with a suitable belt. Galahad removes the sword from its scabbard without suffering any harm and Perceval's sister, after replacing the belt, girds it on him. By this act, she claims, she has truly made him a knight. And here the maiden is counterpoised to Guenevere, who made Lancelot a knight: for, where the queen's selfish love will prevent Lancelot from ever reaching the highest goal of spiritual chivalry, a virgin's selfless love will enable Galahad to fulfil his quest.

Nor is her hair all that Perceval's sister must sacrifice. But, before our three questers can dispense with her services, they must encounter a group of allegorical creatures whose Christian veneer may conceal a subtle manifestation of that virginal moon goddess whose cult that of the virginal Messiah has replaced in these islands.

In the Waste Forest, where a pagan might expect to encounter the maiden huntress, the four companions see a White Hart with four attendant lions, which appear to be guarding it. Galahad declares that this "wonderful adventure" is "from God" and leads the friends in pursuit of it. They follow it to a hermitage where the Mass of the Holy Ghost is being performed. At the consecration, they see it change into a man and the four lions into four winged creatures: one taking the shape of a man, the second that of an eagle, the third a winged lion and the fourth a bull-calf (*QHG* 243).

These four creatures, known as the Tetramorph, appear in the Book of Revelation and are usually equated with the four Evangelists. But they can be traced back to a vision of the Biblical prophet Ezekiel, which was in turn the subject of an early nineteenth century watercolor by William Blake, who transformed Ezekiel's "living creatures" into the Four "Lifes" (or *Zoas*) that make up the Ancient Man, Albion. According to Blake, Ezekiel's prophetic spirit draws on that Poetic Genius from which the Religions of All Nations are derived. Hence Blake's Ezekiel can claim, to the "wonder" of the narrator of "The Marriage of Heaven and Hell," that he learned "the first principles of human perception" from the "philosophy of the east" and follows the practice of "the North American tribes" with "the desire of raising other men into a perception of the infinite" (*BCW* 153f).

The variations between the different religious traditions reflect their "different reception" of this "universal Poetic Genius" (98); but the ancient Israelites came to believe that theirs was the only true understanding of "the first principle" and hence to despise the priests, philosophers and gods of other countries. As Blake's Ezekiel puts it, "we so loved our God, that we cursed in his name all the deities of surrounding nations, and asserted that they had rebelled" (153).

This tribal intolerance was transferred to emergent Christianity so that the ancient Gnostics, forebears of religious rebels such as Blake, were led to denounce the Father of Jealousy (who declares that no other gods exist apart from him) as a blind, ignorant Demiurge—old Nobodaddy. Blake's Ezekiel declares that we must not be subject to the code and god of the Jewish religion (154) but to the Poetic Genius from which the Jewish and Christian testaments are both derived: "As all men are alike (tho' infinitely various), So all Religions ... have one source. The true Man is the source, he being the Poetic Genius (98)." The pre-Christian, pagan traditions of Albion, the couch of the First Man, are also products of the Poetic Genius, although secondary to that "original derivation" which Blake finds in the Bible.

For Blake, the indigenous religion of Britain is based on the imaginative encounter with the Fairies of Albion, elemental beings who emanate from the Zoa of the Imagination but who are remembered as the Gods of the Heathen (264). Blake may intend us to deduce that the systematization of their worship is a product of the Trojan conquest, for he also refers to them as the Gods of Priam (who would have been brought to these shores by Brutus and his followers). These deities—among whom we must include the moon goddess Diana—are really "visions of the eternal attributes" which "appear to poets, in all ages"; they are "divine names, which, when erected into gods, become destructive to humanity" (571). Cut off from their source, these gods and the "warlike" nations who follow them are "detestable" (495); but no more so than the state-sanctioned monotheism of Blake's own day. This, the poet characterized as an intolerant Net of Religion because, in its Cruelties of Holiness, it denied that earlier beliefs could be considered to be a "different reception of the Poetic Genius, which is every where call'd the Spirit of Prophecy" (98).

As we learn from Blake and other poets, the same symbolic image can have very different meanings, depending on whether it is viewed with the Imaginative Eye or with that "single vision" that the Grail Hermits impose on the wonderful adventures of the Perilous Kingdom, interpreting everything in terms of Church doctrines and ultimately bringing the adventures to an end. So, when the four companions of the Quest follow the White Hart to the hermitage, they do not have to wait long for an explanation.

We have seen that the hart is transformed into a man and the four lions into the Tetramorph. We should not be surprised to discover that the hart symbolizes Our Lord, whose incarnation made Him live among us as a mortal man; or that the beasts represent the four Evangelists. The allegorical creatures have been manifesting to good men in many different lands, "so that those who saw might draw a lesson from it." But "no knight was ever able to penetrate this mystery or know what it could mean"—until now. And the four companions witness a further miracle: The four beasts carry the enthroned hart through a window without breaking it and they hear a voice declaiming: "In like manner did the Son of God enter the Virgin Mary, so that her virginity was left entire and perfect."

It is clear that the Grail Questers have been shown a vision which illustrates an important element of the Catholic faith—to them, as the hermit comments, Our Lord has "revealed His secrets and His hidden mysteries, in part" (244). But, as the medieval scholar Philippe Walter has shown, the white hart is a common figure in Breton fairytales where it leads the hero to its Otherworld home. There it reveals itself to be a fay in animal form and she becomes his fairy lover. While there can be no doubting the erotic nature of this Otherworld messenger in stories full of pagan marvels derived from Celtic tradition, Walter argues, this element has been effectively neutralized in the Vulgate Grail Quest. But the White Hart still retains its ancient role of psycho-pomp, or hermetic "guide of souls," insofar as it leads the companions to experience a divine vision (Walter, 48–9).

That vision was once of the divine Diana, who shares with Mary a sacred virginity—and Perceval's sister, who might once have been one of the moon goddess' maidens, is now a bride of Christ, who will, Christ-like, sacrifice herself for those she loves.

The Master's Will

The company comes to a castle with a most unusual custom: Every maiden who passes that way must donate a dishful of blood from her right arm, since only the blood of a royal virgin can cure the mistress of the castle of leprosy. The knights rightly object to such a shameful custom and start fighting the men of the castle but Perceval's sister, to prevent needless deaths, agrees to give her blood. The lady of the castle is healed but Perceval's sister does not recover from the loss of blood. Before she dies, she requests that her body be placed in a boat and set adrift on the sea. They will find her, she claims, in the city of Sarras. She would like to be buried there in the Spiritual Palace, alongside her brother and Galahad, who will also end their days there.

Like Galahad, Perceval's sister seems to have been made from whole cloth: a readymade maiden to fulfil the particular needs of the Vulgate Cycle. Whereas the Lady of the Lake and Guenevere can be seen as supernatural beings in origin, rooted in paganism, Perceval's sister is free of any such taint. As a lifelong virgin—"in fact and in intent" (255)—she is uniquely placed to play a vital role in redeeming the sin of Eve.

This process of redemption began when the All Mother planted the branch from the Tree of Knowledge in the ground of exile, to produce a post-exilic Tree of Life. It was continued when Solomon's wife used wood from the Tree and its offshoots in the Ship of Faith. It is concluded when, by sacrificing herself, Perceval's sister ends a wicked custom and enables her brother and his companions to continue their quest.

Her last words are that the companions should go their separate ways until they are re-united in the court of the Maimed King: "For such is the Master's will and that is His command to you through me" (249). She has served her purpose and the Grail Quest will have no more need of women.[6] It is therefore ironic that the first person to encounter the body of Perceval's sister in her boat is Lancelot, whose need of a woman will deny him the greatest of spiritual achievements and who has been discovering just how much he is missing by losing his "inner Galahad."

When he first stumbles across the Holy Vessel in a ruined chapel in the Waste Forest, he lies paralyzed while it heals a sick knight and he feels compelled to confess his adultery to a hermit. But, while acknowledging that he has sinned, Lancelot cannot help but thank Guenevere for enabling him to achieve the great feats of chivalry. It is only later that he discovers, in the modest hermitage of a monk who tells him that he will never find the adventures of the Grail that he seeks, that his love for the queen has been a hindrance all along.

He was born, the hermit tells him, with God-given qualities of virginity, humility, long-suffering, rectitude and charity: "The fire of the Holy Ghost burned warm and bright in you then, and you were heart and soul intent on holding fast to the yield these virtues made you." But from the time he was knighted, he joined the ranks of those with which the Bible is so familiar (Adam, Solomon, Samson, Absalom, etc.) who were brought low by "a woman's wiles" (142). The Enemy entered into Guenevere and caused her to seduce Lancelot so that the knight was possessed by the demons of lust and pride. It was the residue of the virtues with which God had endowed him and not (as he and the Lady of the Lake both believed) the love of his lady which enabled him to perform "wondrous feats in far-flung lands" (143).

Lancelot has sufficiently learnt his lesson so that, when he comes to Corbenic, he is able to witness the Mass of the Grail being celebrated, although he is forbidden to enter the room where he sees the Holy Vessel atop its silver table. In fact, when he attempts to do so, he is struck down and rendered blind and senseless for twenty-four days; a period of time recalling the twenty-four years that he has spent in sinful love of Guenevere.

When he finally opens his eyes, it is to lament the inner visions that he has been experiencing and that he now can see no more: "For this was no earthly but a spiritual vision" (264). His sorrow is only increased when King Pelles tells him that the mother of Galahad has died in the interim. There is nothing for the chastened Lancelot to do but to make his way back to the Kingdom of Logres.

Meanwhile, the three companions of the Grail Quest are also making their way to Corbenic. In the Perilous Forest, Galahad encounters the Adventure of the Tomb of the Black Chamber. His father's failure in this adventure had signaled that he was not the Knight of the Prophecy. But Galahad succeeds where Lancelot was found wanting: The fires that surrounded the tomb of Simeon die down at his approach, he raises the lid of the tomb and the Holy Ghost, working through the Good Knight, translates the tormented soul of Simeon "from earthly anguish to the joys of heaven" (271).

Returning at last to Corbenic, where he was born and spent his earliest years, Galahad rejoins the two halves of the Broken Sword, which had wounded Joseph of Arimathea. He then heals the Maimed King with the blood of Christ from the Holy Lance, the spear that pierced the side of Jesus on the Cross. Although this is not specified in the Vulgate, he also presumably restores the fertility of the Waste Land, a term denoting the two kingdoms that were destroyed when Galahad's ancestor King Lambor was struck by the Dolorous Blow.

We will return to the subject of the Grail Quest in Part Two, when we discuss the Post-Vulgate version, which goes into some of these details in more depth, in order to clear up some of the confusions still surrounding the relation between Arthur's kingdom and the Holy Vessel. For now, suffice it to say that Christ Himself informs Galahad that the Grail is to leave the Kingdom of Logres that very night and will nevermore be seen there, because it is neither served nor honored there as it deserves: The people "have lapsed into dissolute and worldly ways, despite the fact that they have ever been sustained by the grace of the Holy Vessel" (277).

The three companions are led by the Grail to the Middle Eastern city of Sarras, travelling in the Ship of Solomon. There they find the barque in which they had laid the body of Perceval's sister and they bury her in the Spiritual Palace where Josephus (the son of Joseph of Arimathea and first Christian bishop) had first performed the Mass of the Holy Grail.

As the knights proclaim, she has kept faith with the questers: Her sacrifice of her hair enabled her to provide the Sword of David with a suitable belt and, through her simple faith, cancelled out the deceitfulness of Solomon's wife; while her sacrifice of her blood foreshadowed Galahad's healing of the Maimed King, but lacked its redemptive quality (we are even told that, the day after the healing of the leper lady, her castle and presumably everyone in it were destroyed by a storm). It is also made very clear that what help she has been to the Knights of the Quest has only been made possible by her never having had sex. Women can have a role in the Grail Mysteries, as long as they are quite literally bloodless![7]

The Fullness of Divine Wisdom

It is in the city of Sarras (where the Company of the Grail had overthrown the star-worshippers) that Galahad, after achieving the ultimate goal of looking directly into the Holy Vessel, dies. Even as his soul is borne up by angels, so also the Grail and the Lance are carried up to Heaven by a disembodied hand, "to the end that no man since has ever dared to say he saw the Holy Grail" (284). Galahad's death is followed by that of Perceval and they are both buried in the Spiritual Palace of Sarras next to their female companion.

Lying in her tomb in the Spiritual Palace next to her brother and Galahad, three life-long virgins side by side in death, Perceval's sister has come as close as any woman in the Vulgate Cycle could ever come to being an image of feminine spirituality. What is most striking about her is her preternatural wisdom: her knowledge of the past and the future, her connection with the Ship of Faith and her role of spiritual guide or "soul sister" to the Grail Questers. So it would be useful at this point to contrast her with the ancient mythological personification of Divine Wisdom, who plays an important role in mainstream Judaism and Christianity, but becomes even more central to early Gnosticism, where she plays the part of a flawed redeemer.

Although there is an orthodox gnosis, very often Gnostics are seen as heretics within the monotheistic traditions because they believe that knowledge (*gnosis*), in the sense of direct personal acquaintance with the sacred, rather than mere faith, is what saves us from the prison of materialism. The Gnostic Christians who flourished in the first centuries after the death of Jesus were persecuted by their more orthodox brethren and effectively suppressed when the Roman Empire adopted Christianity as the sole state religion in the late fourth century. Nevertheless, gnostic ideas have continued to have an influence on religious thought up to the present day and have inspired maverick poets such as William Blake.

Gnosticism can be seen as an underground stream in western culture that bubbles up from time to time to take on new forms in new times, only to hide itself again when persecution becomes too intense. One reason for this persecution is that while mainstream Christianity teaches that the creation is good and that the Fall is the fault of humankind (Eve of course and, through her, womankind in general being blamed), it is fundamental to a Gnostic perspective that the Fall occurs in the spiritual world and precedes the material creation: The creation of the universe is, from this point of view, itself a fall from wholeness.

Surviving Gnostic literature, as well as the accounts of Gnostic ideas preserved in the polemical works of the heresy-hunters, contains many variants of this theme, although one of the most powerful is the myth of Sophia ("Wisdom"), which is found in its most developed form in the writings of the school of Valentinus, a second-century teacher. Holy Wisdom appears in the Old Testament and in apocryphal literature as existing before creation, in which she acts as God's agent—as Carl Jung puts it, "she realizes God's thoughts by clothing them in material form, which is the prerogative of all feminine beings" (55)—but the early Gnostics created a mythology in which her fall and redemption is the archetypal model for *ours*.

In these texts, Sophia is the female Holy Spirit, one of the eternal beings (aeons) who dwell in the Pleroma, the spiritual "fullness." Despite her wisdom Sophia falls into "error" (the sin of *hubris*) and creates a "deficiency" in the spiritual world through which her usurping son, an ignorant Demiurge based on the jealous god of the Old Testament, can create the visible cosmos.

Sophia, the lowest of the aeons and therefore the furthest from the divine source, experiences torment through her impossible desire to become acquainted (experience *gnosis*) with the unknowable Father of the Entirety, the Hidden God of Gnosticism. This torment separates itself from her and is cast outside the Pleroma into a region of shadow and emptiness, where it takes form as a being called Achamoth (from the Hebrew *Hokhmah*), the "lower Wisdom."

The passionate feelings that she experiences when she finds herself "beyond the pale," alone in the outer darkness, take on a life of their own. The four passions become the four elements of the material creation, over which the Demiurge rules. He creates human beings but they derive from her their inner spiritual being. It is she who creates the stars in the night sky, the light that shineth in the darkness, reflecting the inner spiritual light in human beings.

Achamoth dwells in the midpoint between the visible cosmos and the higher world of the Fullness. At the end of time, when all spiritually enlightened human beings have been initiated into the mysteries of Achamoth, she will lead them back into the Pleroma where she will become the bride of the Aeon Jesus the Savior.

In this Gnostic myth Achamoth is also called "Jerusalem"[8] and "the Holy Land" (*GS* 291). This identification of Jerusalem with Wisdom is also found in Blake's gnostic mythology, where the Emanation of Albion, following the Book of Revelation, also describes herself as the bride of Jesus (*BCW* 643).

In Blake's poems, the roles of Sophia and Achamoth are taken by Jerusalem and her "shadow," the False Female; but, in a late dramatic sketch, he portrays Eve as the Emanation of Adam who inspires her husband, when his faith is faltering, to trust in Spiritual Vision (780). Here again Blake is in tune with the heretical gospels, where Eve is Zoe ("Life"), the daughter of Sophia and agent of Divine Wisdom. Sophia sends Eve to be the first instructor of humankind in the knowledge that the Gnostics considered more important to salvation than faith—the knowledge of our true spiritual home, which we have forgotten. In another rewriting of the Old Testament, Eve's youngest son Seth is a savior figure who, as "transmitter of the divine power of wisdom," is the spiritual ancestor of the Gnostics (*GS* 185).

Interestingly it is Seth, the Gnostic Illuminator of Knowledge, who is the protagonist in the more common version of the apocryphal legend of the Holy Cross (of which the Grail legend of the Tree of Life is a variant). In this popular medieval story, Seth is sent by Adam back to Eden to gain from the Tree of Knowledge three seeds. These seeds will grow into the three trees from whose wood the Cross will be fashioned. According to Pauline Matarasso, the translator of the Vulgate *Queste*, the version given there appears to be unique: most importantly, the substitution of Eve for Seth means that "she who had been responsible for sin entering the world unknowingly prepares the world's redemption" (*QHG* 298).

By combining the legend of the Holy Cross with the story of the Grail, the Vulgate Cycle author makes of Eve and Solomon's wife agents of a continuing process of redemption beyond the Crucifixion. Central to this process is the role of the Ship of Faith in rescuing, testing and transporting members of the Grail Company, triggering the creation of the Waste Land and, ultimately, conveying the Grail Knights "to the climax of their spiritual journey," as the medieval scholar Anne Marie D'Arcy puts it, its course directed by Holy Wisdom (256). D'Arcy considers the Ship's function to be analogous to that of the Grail as a treasury of knowledge (255) but it is the Holy Vessel itself that, as she has shown in an exhaustive iconological exploration of the image and meaning of the Grail in the Vulgate *Queste*, is both "the objective receptacle of the fullness of divine Wisdom" and yet also its symbol in what she calls "all its polyvalent and emanatistic richness" (313).

D'Arcy is keen to place the Vulgate Grail in its "contemporary intellectual milieu" which included a strong tendency towards Emanationism (27)—the doctrine that beings are not so much created *by* God as manifested *from* God, emanating out of His divine substance. Emanationism was also an important element in the contemporary speculations of the Jewish Kabbalists, who identified Divine Wisdom with the *Shekinah*, the presence of God, "perceived by one strand of the Jewish mystical tradition as a feminine emanation of the Lord, or indeed, as the female aspect of Godhead." For the medieval Kabbalists, the *Shekinah* was the last of the emanations from the Godhead (290f), just as, for Gnostic Christians, Sophia was the last of the Aeons of the Pleroma.

Behind the medieval Jewish and Christian "emanatitive" conceptions, D'Arcy sees the remnants of an ancient myth of Wisdom who descends to the Earth but is rejected by human ignorance and returns to Heaven. D'Arcy sees a "striking parallel" to this in the withdrawal of the Grail from Britain after Galahad's return to Corbenic, because of the sinfulness of the people, prior to its final assumption into Heaven (289).

Although D'Arcy does not explore this aspect of the symbolism, it is also possible to see aspects of the Wisdom myth in the three female figures at the heart of the Grail legend of the Tree of Life. Eve, Solomon's wife and Perceval's sister can be seen as a triune manifestation of Wisdom: Eve is fallen but has carried out of Eden the hope of redemption, physically embodied in the Tree of Life. Solomon's wife, through her cunning, is able to be an agent of redemptive wisdom in her designing of the Ship of Faith. That higher wisdom once more manifests in the figure of Perceval's sister, who brings the knowledge of the Ship to the Grail Questers. We might also see in the death of Perceval's sister and the translation of her body to the Spiritual Palace in Sarras a foreshadowing of the departure of the Grail from Logres and its translation to Sarras, prior to its ascent to Heaven.

As D'Arcy puts it, the Grail's *raptus* from the Earth portends "a tragic consequence for the Arthurian world" (316): The Grail will nevermore be seen on Earth and, of the three Grail Questers, Bors alone returns to the Kingdom of Logres. But this is a kingdom bereft of Wisdom and one that is, with the death of the only female worthy of taking part in the Quest, once more bothered by the wiles of women and the machinations of a fay.

Six

The View from Fortune's Wheel

> In the fairy mythology of romance the law is invariable, that for the mortal who once has experienced the fairy control there is no true release, and that the fay is never to be thwarted in her plans to win the hero whose love she seeks.[1]
>
> —Lucy A. Paton

If the Grail is a near womanless quest, it is even more a quest bereft of fays. The Kingdom of the Grail is not fairyland: the Spiritual Palace is not found in the Otherworld, but is a stepping-stone to the Christian afterlife, as Galahad and Perceval discover.

The women the heroes encounter on their peregrinations are either saintly virgins and recluses or demons in disguise. Any supernatural powers in evidence are the grace of Heaven or the curse of Hell. There is no place for the intermediate realm that is the abode of fays. The Lady of the Lake, who initiated Lancelot into knighthood and guided him in his early adventures, is nowhere to be seen while Guenevere, Arthur's Otherworld bride, remains in the background as an obstacle to the quest. Morgan, whose attempt to supplant Ninienne and Guenevere in Lancelot's affections was symbolized by the battle for the magic rings, is equally invisible when the vision of the once-greatest knight is set on a spiritual goal that transcends mere magic.

But with the return of Bors, the only surviving successful quester, a Round Table somewhat disheartened by the abject failure of the vast majority of its members embarks on a frantic round of tournaments as a substitute for the Adventures of the Holy Grail, which have ended with the death of Galahad. The fellowship soon finds itself embroiled in the machinations of Morgan the Fay, who is determined that, if she cannot have Lancelot, then she will scupper his affair with Guenevere. What she unleashes will be a dramatic turn of the Wheel of Fortune, that fatal goddess who stands behind the magic of the fays.

Images and Letters

After presiding over a tournament in Edinburgh, King Arthur travels home to Camelot via the Lost Forest where he is lodged by his sister Morgan in her castle, although it is so long since he has seen her that he doesn't at first recognize her—he had, in fact, presumed that she was dead! And he may come to wish that she is, for she puts him up in the very room where, some years earlier, Lancelot had been a prisoner and where he had painted a series of incriminating images. Studying the pictures and reading the text accompanying them—*les ymages et les letres qui devisoient la senefiance des portretures* (MRA134)—Arthur comes across the scene made famous by Dante's *Inferno*, where Lancelot's friend Galehaut arranges for the first lover's kiss exchanged between the knight and the queen. At last the king knows that he has been dishonored. He begs Morgan to tell him the full story and she, feigning reluctance because she is scared of Lancelot's wrath, reveals all she knows about their affair.

After filling in some of the details, she urges the king to avenge his shame and he swears to inflict justice on the lovers. The Vulgate author decries her as *desloial* for her pains; but to whom, or to what, is she being disloyal? To Arthur, whose honor she could claim to be defending, were it not that her feelings for him (which remain ambiguous, at best) are tainted by her hatred of the queen? Is her disapproval of adultery any more to be criticized than that of the Grail Hermits? Yes, appears to be the answer, when she also is subject to human emotion (as even fays are wont to be); when she has never forgiven Guenevere for the damage done to her affair with Guiomar, her first love, or for gaining the love of Lancelot, whom Morgan also fancies. Arguably, Arthur would be better off not knowing that he has been deceived for decades by those closest to him and events might appear to support this view.

But it is not just her convoluted intentions that are suspect: there are also troubling indications that she has been trafficking with dark powers. The castle has been sumptuously redecorated in the short space of time that it takes for one of the king's knights, who has been sent ahead to check out the possibility of finding lodging, to report back to Arthur. He had seen nothing to indicate that the castle would be so beautifully and richly furbished but, when Arthur makes the sign of the cross in astonishment, it does not all vanish, as would have been the case if the furnishings were demonic (as Bors and Perceval had both experienced on the Grail Quest). Everything in the castle is superlative: he has never seen such a well furbished castle so intensely lit, such well-dressed nobles, such a well-adorned table laden with such rich food and with such a sweet musical accompaniment.

It is all literally out of this world, for he has strayed into the Otherworld. The castle belongs to the "lost forest" of the *mundus imaginalis*, where he will encounter the transformative power of images.

"The spirituality of the visionary Image is ... our inner paradise; yet it can also become our hell," writes Corbin (1998b, 166f). If the visionary image were not dangerous, it would not be able to transform consciousness. But that transformation requires the transcending of the literal and Lancelot's paintings are only too literal, tying him to *this world* through his love of its queen.

And if Morgan, as the king's sister, also has one foot in the earthly reality of Logres, it is elsewhere that her fairy nature finds its home. Hence, when Arthur asks her to come with him to the court, she assures him (*loialment*) that she will never go there again: "for when I leave here," she says, "I shall most certainly go to the Isle of Avalon, which is the dwelling place of the ladies who know all the magic in the world" (*DKA* 70). It is from this imaginal location that Morgan will arrive, when the time comes, to carry the king away to be healed.

And, indeed, that time appears to be hastening on, its arrival heralded by the appearance of Fortuna, the Goddess of Destiny.

The Most Faithless Thing in the World

The events that will bring about the fall of Logres have about them a tragic inevitability. This is partly, of course, because the story is so well-known but also, at least in the Vulgate version, it is because the participants in those events make frequent reference to Fortune, who ultimately casts down whomsoever she raises up. The first to do so is Bors, who says that the love between Lancelot and Guenevere has been arranged by Fortune, but that no good can come of it. He is right: as the fact of the adultery is brought home to Arthur, war breaks out between the king's family (headed by Gawain) and the kin and supporters of Lancelot. Three of Gawain's younger brothers die as a result, none lamented more than Gaheriet (Malory's Sir Gareth); while Gawain himself, after helping his uncle to defeat the Romans, succumbs to complications from a head wound received while battling Lancelot.

King Arthur, inconsolable at the death of his favorite nephew, invokes that fickle mistress who had once brought him worldly success: "Ah! Fortune, contrary and changeable, the most faithless thing in the world, why were you ever so courteous or so kind to me if you were to make me pay so dearly for it in the end? You used to be my mother[2]; now you have become my step-mother, and to make me die of grief you have brought Death with you..." (200).

Gawain may in fact have already met Fortune and her sister Death in the course of the war against Lancelot. Besieging Lancelot's fortress of Joyous Guard, Arthur receives a messenger from his wife's lover, a girl who has been instructed to offer terms for a truce. When Gawain, angry at Gaheriet's death and implacable in his hatred of his former friend, urges the king to reject Lancelot's terms, the girl utters a prophetic speech, announcing the death of both Arthur and Gawain. She goes on to remind Gawain of something he had experienced at the Grail Castle, where he encountered dishonor and disgrace even before the inauguration of the Quest in which he had been so signally unsuccessful. She also reveals details of a conversation Gawain had had afterwards with a hermit, who had partly spelt out the significance of a dream he had had—a dream which turned out to predict the death of Gawain as a result of the conflict between Lancelot and Arthur.

But, having partly explained the mysterious events Gawain experienced in the Grail Castle, the hermit made the knight swear on sacred relics that he would never speak about what he had been told to any man or woman alive—and Gawain so swore. Which leaves us wondering: how does the girl who Lancelot sends as a messenger know about these things?

The girl's prophetic knowledge is matched, later in the narrative, by that of "a very old woman, richly dressed and riding a white palfrey" who confronts King Arthur outside the city of Ganis, on the Breton border, where he intends to attack Lancelot. The old woman tells the king that his actions are ill-advised since he will never take the city. She further warns Gawain, that he is resolutely pursuing his own destruction, since he will never again see the Kingdom of Logres in good health: "Now," she adds, "you can truly say that the time has come that was promised long ago as you left the castle of the Fisher King, where you were dishonoured and disgraced" (158).

We might think here of Death, who rides a white horse in the Apocalypse; although, it is also possible that the old woman is the Lady of the Lake, trying one last time to protect her foundling (*MRA* 321*n*2). But, whether we see them as the allegorical figures of Fortune and Death or as shape-shifting fays, they prepare the way for Arthur's prophetic vision of the Wheel of Fortune.

Such Is Earthly Pride

Shortly after the death of Gawain, as Arthur sets off to confront his treacherous son Mordred, the king dreams that his nephew warns him against doing so. But the late lamented Gawain, even though he has been admitted to "the house of God," is not certain of the outcome: Arthur will either die or be mortally wounded (*DKA* 204). This uncertainty pervades the Vulgate account of the king's passing. That he will *fall*, however, is not in doubt, as a dream he has the following night makes clear.

He dreams that the most beautiful lady he has ever seen carries him to the top of a high mountain and places him on the highest point of a wheel, which she tells him is the Wheel of Fortune. From this vantage point he can see the whole world spread out below him and, as Fortune acknowledges, he has been lord of much of that world until now, his defeat of the Romans making him "the most powerful king there ever was. But such is earthly pride," she adds, "that no one is seated so high that he can avoid having to fall from power in the world" (205).

Then she unceremoniously shoves him down to the ground.

His pride will indeed come before a fall, because it will not allow him to heed the dream warnings and turn back from his path. This becomes clear when, accompanied by his archbishop (who has advised him that his dreams are telling him that, if Arthur fights Mordred, the Britons "shall suffer as long as the world lasts"!), he rides to Salisbury Plain and sees there an inscription carved long ago upon the rock. It announces that it is the site of the battle which will "orphan" the Kingdom of Logres (206f). This inscription, according to the archbishop, was written there by Merlin, who had often spoken of the great battle that would take place there—and Merlin, as everyone knows, had God-given knowledge of the future.

Dream images are ambiguous: they require interpretation; their meaning can be deceptive. We need only compare the Vulgate version with the ominous dream experienced by Arthur in the Middle English *Brut* of Layamon (ll.13982–14015), which shows Mordred and Guenevere pulling down the pillars of the king's hall, but accompanied by images that remain difficult to interpret, as in a "real" dream. Here the knight to whom Arthur recounts the dream confirms that the king has been betrayed, but insists that "one should never interpret dreams ominously" (*LA* 241).

But, in a culture that believes that God is the Logos (the Divine Word made flesh), the written word can avoid the ambiguity of the image. The pictures that Lancelot had painted on the wall might have been capable of more than one interpretation; but the explanations written next to them made his guilt only too clear. Here also it is the *letres* which provide the *ymages* with their *senefiance*. Unable to trust his dreams, Arthur has fallen into literalism. His future has become a *fait accompli*—accomplished, that is, by Fate in its less ambiguously Christian persona of Lady Fortune and her agent, the fay Morgan.

A Ship of Women

What Malory calls *thys wycked day of Desteny* (*MCW* 713), the final confrontation between King Arthur and the child of his incestuous union with his sister Morgause, ends with the destruction of the Round Table and the fall from power that Fortuna has revealed to him. As one of his knights comments, when his last-surviving nephew (Yvain) is killed, Fortune is playing her "tricks" by making Arthur pay for his previous success (*DKA* 219).

In the end, the father kills the son and the son gives his father a mortal wound. Arthur instructs his surviving knights to carry him to the Black Chapel on the coast. There follows the famous scene in which the king asks a knight (here Girflet rather than Malory's Sir Bedivere) to throw Excalibur into a lake on a hill, after saying that his "step-mother" Fortune "is making me devote the remainder of my life to grief and anger and sadness" (222).

A hand rises up out of the water to catch the sword and disappears with it. Then Girflet, watching from the hill, sees "a ship entirely occupied by women coming across the sea" and hears their Lady calling to Arthur to come aboard. When he sees that the Lady is holding his sister Morgan by the hand, the king immediately does so (224f).

The name of the Lady on the ship is not given in the Vulgate; but Malory says that *Nynyve, the chyff lady of the laake*, was aboard. It certainly seems fitting that Morgan and the Lady of the Lake, who had both in their way *done much for kynge Arthure* (*MCW* 717), should be united at the end, standing hand-in-hand on the ship that will take Arthur on the next phase of his journey. They took opposite sides over Guenevere's affair with Lancelot, but neither role is unambiguous: Ninienne was acting in Lancelot's interest (earthly if not spiritual) but hardly in Arthur's by supporting the adultery; while Morgan, though her motives were tainted, can plausibly be said to have been protecting the family honor throughout. Any reluctance Arthur might have felt about getting into the ship is overcome when he sees Morgan; a wounded man, he goes to her as a healer; to Avalon, where his sword was forged and where the ladies who know magic dwell.

Malory presents Morgan as one of three queens on the ship and it is tempting to think here of the Three Fates, who share out each man's measure of life. As we saw in Chapter Four, Layamon (writing probably before the Vulgate and certainly independently of it) describes Arthur's being born at a predestined time and having kingly virtues bestowed on him by the fays (*aluen*). At the end of his life, Arthur is away with the fairies: he announces that he is going to Argante, Queen of Avalon (presumably a variant of Morgan), whom he describes as "fairest of fairy women; and she shall make me all whole with healing draughts. And afterwards I will return to my kingdom and dwell with the Britons in great contentment" (*LA* 255).

It is important to note that, neither in Geoffrey of Monmouth's account of Arthur's going to Morgen to be healed, nor in Layamon's account of the Fairy Queen Argante, is the Lady of Avalon described as Arthur's sister. These were some of the facts which led Lucy Allen Paton to conclude that Morgan was originally Arthur's fairy mistress: "that he dwelt with her for a time, rejected her love, and thus incurred her displeasure, leading her to attempt to work him harm" (22). But nowhere in the Vulgate or, for that matter, in the earlier sources, is there any suggestion that Morgan wishes Arthur harm. To the contrary, such harm as she does can be seen as the unintended consequence of her attempt to defend his honor; or as her way of bringing him back to his fairy home.

But readers of Malory and more recent re-workings of the myth of Morgan the Fay are only too familiar with her harmful displeasure and Malory's source for this murderous figure is the late cycle known as the Post-Vulgate. Paton draws primarily on the Morgan stories in this cycle (but also on other stories about other fays and heroes) to reconstruct what she believes was the *ur*-myth of Arthur and the Fairy Queen. There is, I believe, much that is inspired and inspirational in her attempt, at the beginning of the twentieth century, to examine the way Morgan's ambiguous nature is conceived in the twelfth and thirteenth centuries sources "and to trace, if possible, the historic development of her character, in the hope of obtaining light upon the wider subject of fairy mythology" (Paton, 8).

Like the English Jessie L. Weston, a contemporary female scholar, whose unjustly neglected theories I revisited in my first book (Dixon 2012), the American Paton sailed into the *terra incognita* of Arthurian studies armed only with a formidable intellect and a penetrating vision that helped to turn that Forbidden Land into a Land of Promise (Weston 1906, vi), but she is largely forgotten today.[3]

Weston's theories of the origins of the Grail legends in the pagan Mystery Religions and Gnostic Christianity and Paton's theories about the Arthurian fairy mythology open up to the modern imagination worlds of wonder, like the marvelous islands to which Celtic heroes sailed in medieval tales. But in the Vulgate Grail Quest, these wondrous ships are replaced by a Ship of Faith and the mysterious islands to which it carries the questers in "the archipelago of the Grail" are not the Elysian realms of pagan mythology but the haunts of demons. This process of devaluing the Otherworld and all its imaginal works becomes even more exaggerated in the Post-Vulgate Cycle.

Although scholars are by no means all agreed on this, it seems likely that the enormous work now known as the Lancelot-Grail Cycle began life as a rather more modest Romance of Lancelot detailing his fairy origins and love for Queen Guenevere, following up elements provided in Chrétien's verse romance and providing its hero with his *enfances*. At some point this was added to by reworking Chrétien's poem in prose and interweaving it with early Grail adventures, including the creation of a new hero of the Quest (Galahad), who supplants the earlier hero (Perceval). The story of Galahad's birth and his arrival as a young knight at Camelot leads us into the definitive version of the Grail Quest which is followed, as we have seen, by an account of the events which lead to the death of Arthur. Lancelot, although his adulterous affair with the queen rules him out of the running for the spiritual prize that is the Grail, is nevertheless an important figure throughout what has now become a prose cycle of three romances: the Prose *Lancelot*, the *Quest of the Holy Grail* and the *Death of King Arthur*. Taking us from the birth of Lancelot and his abduction by the Lady of the Lake to his eventual death (after the passing of Arthur), these three romances constitute in effect an *Estoire de Lancelot*.

From this perspective, the last stage in the construction of what we now know as the Vulgate Cycle would have come about when it was decided (possibly by a single "architect" overseeing several writers) to add two further *estoires* which would act as prequels to the *Estoire de Lancelot*. The first to be composed, the *Estoire del Saint Graal*, begins by reworking the prehistory of the Grail developed by Robert de Boron but, at the point where the Grail leaves the Holy Land, it branches off on its own, interweaving new stories with episodes previously presented as "flashbacks" in the Grail Quest. These new stories tell of how Joseph of Arimathea and his son Josephus travel from Jerusalem to Sarras as missionaries and from there lead the Company of the Grail on a discombobulating journey—for once they leave the East they become literally "disoriented"—through an archipelago of adventurous islands, guided only by the Ship of Faith.

Apart from a reference to King Lucius, who is considered in legend to be the first Christian monarch of Britain and who, therefore, the *Estoire del Saint Graal* presents as having been converted by the Company of the Grail, there is little in this "history" to tie it firmly to the pseudo-historical events of the Matter of Britain as established by Geoffrey of Monmouth and Wace, which provide a context in time and place for the Round Table romances. What the Grail History does instead is to provide a genealogy which links the time of Joseph of Arimathea's arrival in Britain to the time of the Pendragons, the family of Arthur.

This genealogy is that of the Fisher Kings, who guard the Grail in a secret kingdom somewhere within the British Isles, though of indeterminate location. In what is even by the standards of the legendary History of the Kings of Britain a particularly confusing period, between the second and the fifth centuries AD, there is a clear descent of Grail Kings, establishing a spiritual continuity amidst the turmoil of power politics (and providing a Christian provenance for heroes such as Lancelot, Gawain and Yvain, who are all shown as being descended from members of the Company of the Grail). This period culminates with the coming of the Prophet of the Grail, Merlin, whose knowledge of events encompasses both worlds, that of Logres and that of Corbenic.

The figure of Merlin stands at the center of what would be the last of the elements of the Vulgate Cycle to be composed, linking the prehistory of the Grail with the *Estoire de Lancelot* by presenting us with the "origins" of Arthur, Guenevere, Morgan the Fay and the Lady of the Lake as well as of the leading Knights of the Round Table. The *Estoire de Merlin*, like the *Estoire del Saint Graal*, takes as its starting point the work of Robert de Boron, to whom is attributed the version of the youth of the prophet and his role in the accession of Arthur that includes the famous episode of the Sword in the Stone. But, once again, it branches off into a new direction, providing de Boron's Merlin story with a long continuation in the form of a seemingly endless series of battles between King Arthur and the lesser kings who will not accept his rule. This civil war culminates, of course, in Arthur's eventual victory: thanks in no small part to the young heroes who are, in fact, the very sons of those rebel kings and who will remain the backbone of Arthur's kingdom throughout his life.

Interweaved with the account of Arthur's glorious early career is the story of the king's romancing of Guenevere, followed by Merlin's equally fateful infatuation with Viviane (as she is there called), whose imprisonment of the sage completes his story. These events lead us neatly, in the very last chapter of the *Estoire de Merlin*, to the birth of Lancelot, whose father has been one of Arthur's principal allies in his battle against the rebel kings. We are now prepared for the beginning of the Prose *Lancelot*, in which Viviane/Ninienne will have a new role as the guardian of a hero-to-be—a career move from *femme fatale* to fairy godmother.

La Haute Escriture del Saint Graal

With the addition of the *estoires* of the Grail and of Merlin to that of Lancelot, the Vulgate architect would appear to have created a satisfactory corpus that welds the pseudo-historical Arthurian chronicles to the romances of the Round Table Knights. But, in reality, the cycle is marred both by internal contradictions and by the fact that it is dominated by the centrality that is quite literally given to the Prose *Lancelot*, which is longer than the four other sections combined and which exalts that very sinful adultery which the Grail Quest condemns.

Or, at least, this appears to have been the view of the author or authors of a radical reworking of the prose Arthurian cycle which they entitled *la Haute Escriture del Saint Graal*, but which scholars usually refer to as the Post-Vulgate *Roman du Graal*.[4] Taking as its starting-point those sections of the Vulgate which were actually the last to be written, the Post-Vulgate adopts the *Estoire del Saint Graal* wholesale, along with the first half of the *Estoire de Merlin*. But, at the point where Arthur is crowned, it branches off on its own, providing a new continuation known as the *Suite du Roman de Merlin*, focusing less on his wars against the rebel kings and more on his role as an adventurous hero battling against malign sorcery.

Compared with the Vulgate, the new cycle is much more tightly structured, being quite intentionally composed of three roughly equal parts, ending, not with the death of Lancelot, but with the total destruction of the Kingdom of Logres which follows, reflecting the emphasis throughout the Post-Vulgate on the realm and its king rather than on his wife's lover. Thus the revamped Grail Quest which follows the Merlin Suite concentrates on the affect the search for the Holy Vessel has on the kingdom as a whole rather than on the psychology of an adulterer who has lost his status. In the new version of the Death of Arthur which concludes the cycle, it is stressed that the downfall of Logres is the result of the incest that the king committed in its opening chapter.

Further, compared to the earlier cycle, the Post-Vulgate possesses a structural symmetry and internal consistency which enables the Grail to become the presiding symbol of Arthur's kingdom. Beginning with the arrival of the Holy Vessel in Britain, it presents Merlin as the Prophet of the Grail, presiding over the dramatic event which will set in motion the Adventures of Logres: the Dolorous Blow which leaves the Grail King maimed and his land devastated, providing a clear purpose for the Quest that must inevitably follow.

Furthermore, it is now Merlin who provides the link between the destruction and the healing, because after burying the ill-fated knight who struck the blow he sets a sword by magic in a stone and makes it float along the waterways until it appears on the river of Camelot on the very day that Galahad arrives there to claim it. Merlin, of course, will not live to see the fulfilment of his enchantment, for he has fallen victim to his own magic, wielded by a much more ruthless version of the Lady of the Lake. Also Ninienne, in the Post-Vulgate, is opposed to the sorcery of Morgan the Fay;

while Morgan is now depicted as the enemy of Arthur, not just of Guenevere.

In fact, Logres is no longer a realm of fays, as it was in the earlier lays and poems that bathed the Matter of Britain in an ancient glamour. It is now the land of the Grail Quest, a Perilous Kingdom whose adventures will only cease when the Quest is achieved; a realm that will self-destruct when it no longer has a spiritual purpose.

In Part Two, then, we will see how the Promised Land of the Goddess is disenchanted and turned into the Promised Land of the Grail. But first we will visit an extraordinary document that recounts how the Book of the Grail, written by Christ Himself, was given to an eighth century hermit—and discover what secrets he found therein.

• • • • • • • •

Interlude

The Deceitful Savior

> The myths that projected Jesus of Nazareth into a universe of archetypes and transcendent figures are as "true" as his acts and words; indeed, these myths confirm the strength and creativity of his original message.[1]
>
> —Mircea Eliade

The prehistory of the Grail that constitutes the first part of the Post-Vulgate Cycle of Arthurian romances begins with an extraordinary prologue that is quite unlike anything else in the corpus—something un-attempted yet in prose or rhyme, unless we compare it with the "prologue in hell" which begins the *Estoire de Merlin*, a glimpse at the pandemoniacal plotting that will produce, not the intended Antichrist, but the Prophet of the Grail.[2] The *Estoire del Saint Graal*, by contrast, gives us a "prologue on earth" in which Christ gives the true history of the sacred vessel to a hermit who writes it down so that it can be combined with the existing Grail history dictated by Merlin, the Antichrist *manqué*, to his scribe Blaise.

In the Grail Prologue we are told that a hermit, lying in his hut in a wild and remote part of Britain, has a vision of the risen Christ. It is the night between Maundy Thursday and Good Friday, 717 years after the Passion of Jesus. The hermit is struggling with doubts about the doctrine of the Trinity when Christ, in the form of a man of indescribable beauty, appears to him amid unearthly light and gives him a book that will set straight all his doubts; although later we are told that "all the adventures of the Grail will not be known by any mortal man. Many must be left in silence" (*LG* I, 76).

After being transported in spirit up to the Third Heaven, the hermit has a vision of the Trinity, which finally puts his doubts to rest. Christ then sends him on a quest to northwest Scotland where he uses the high book to cast out a devil. On his return Christ commands him to make a copy of the book, which must be finished by the Feast of the Ascension, for from that day the original will no longer be seen on earth.

The hermit then proceeds to tell the history of the Grail, beginning with the story of Joseph of Arimathea. The beginning of this version follows very closely that of Robert de Boron, but we are led to infer that the hermit's copy must be the original of the "high book" that de Boron claims to possess: "the creed of the great mystery of the Grail" (*MG* 22). In this text we are told the entire early story of the Grail—its prehistory, as it were—from the Deposition to the arrival of the Holy Vessel in Britain; a story that is only told in flashback in the *Queste*. Essentially, the *Estoire* retells de Boron's account of the origins of the Grail, but changes some of the details to conform to the Vulgate *Lancelot* and *Queste*.

For these changes to the De Boron Cycle, the author of the *Estoire* invokes the highest of all authorities: a book written by Christ Himself, which was transcribed and translated into Latin in the eighth century, a date which may be significant because it corresponds with the height of the iconoclastic controversy, of which more anon. What is particularly striking about the hermit's story, moreover, is that, in the *Estoire* Prologue, he tells it himself, in a rare instance of the first person singular in Arthurian storytelling.

Truth and Figuration

It is in the early hours of the morning of Good Friday that the hermit is awakened by a voice that calls him three times by his name and then declares that the Three are One and the One is Three.

As it happens, the hermit has been struggling with just this aspect of his faith: the doctrine, formulated in the Nicene Creed under the authority of Constantine the Great, that there are three persons in One God. And now, in answer to his prayers, the second person of the Trinity appears before him, a man of immortal beauty clothed in unearthly brightness, the Light of Lights. He reveals that He is the Great Master of Science, the fountain of all knowledge (*sapiense*), come to bring certainty where there is doubt.

He then puts into the hermit's hand a little book containing wonders unthinkable for a mortal heart, which have been written there by His own hand. They are the divine secrets that can only be shown to the pure and that can only be spoken of with the language of the heart for, if anyone spoke of them using human language, the four elements would be disturbed. The book, Christ says, confers joy to the body and the soul.

A shattering noise and a blinding light now cause the hermit to faint and, when he recovers, he is alone; but he still has the book. He starts reading from it: it tells him first about his ancestors, then about the Holy Grail, thirdly about the beginning of fears, lastly about the beginning of wonders. As he is reading, the whole world seems to be filled with signs and wonders.

When the time comes to celebrate mass, the hermit is aware that it is Good Friday: This is the day on which Jesus died on the Cross and, therefore, the sacrament does not have the same symbolic significance that it has on other days. On every other day of the year, the sacrament is the sign of His sacrifice; but on *this* unique day, it is no longer a question of signs (*il n'i a mais point de senefianche*), but of literal truth, for this is the day when He was truly sacrificed (*vraiement sacrefiés*). On this day, reality trumps imagery.

The hermit in fact presents us with a general principle which can be interpreted as a defense of religious literalism: "when the truth comes forward, its figuration must be set aside" (*LG* I, 5)—*la ou la verités vient avant, la figure doit estre arriere mise* (*ESG* 9)—which takes the opposition between letter and image that we saw in the episode of Lancelot's paintings (see Chapter Six) onto a theological level. The conflict between *la verités* and *la figure* is the conflict between literal and symbolic truth; a conflict that, for many Christians, revolved (without being easily *resolved*) around the doctrine of Transubstantiation, referred to in the Fourth Lateran Council, in whose shadow the *Estoire del Saint Graal* was written and to which we will return.

The hermit is about to take the Eucharist when an angel raises him up in spirit, not in body, to the Third Heaven. There he sees the three persons of the Trinity, each distinct yet forming one substance, one Godhead, one power. At this point the hermit expresses the concern that he may appear to be contradicting scripture: the Gospel of John, after all, says: "No man hath seen God" (1.2). But St John presumably meant that no *mortal* man can behold the majesty of the Father; whereas the hermit, having cast off his mortal body, sees God *in the spirit*. Blake put the same thing a different way: we see Eternity when we look *through*, not *with*, the perishable eye.

The angel now takes the hermit down from the Third Heaven so that his spirit can be reunited with his body and the hermit says that he has no more doubts about the Trinity: he has seen and learnt. He now finds himself back in his chapel, about to receive the Eucharist—the body and blood of his Savior, into which the bread and wine have been *truly* (and not *figuratively*) changed *in substance*, as Lateran IV asserts.

After the service the hermit locks the Book of Divine Secrets in the small chest where he keeps the Host; but is devastated to find, on Easter Sunday, that it is gone, just as the body of Jesus disappeared from the sepulcher of Joseph of Arimathea. A voice then tells him that, if he wishes to regain the book, he must go on a perilous journey past the Valley of the Dead to the Fountain of Tears, where there was once much killing. Here he will see a bizarre, composite animal, which he must follow; but it is only when he has lost it that he will enter the land he seeks: the north of Scotland, ruled by the pagan Norsemen and consequently known as Norwegia.

The hermit sets off, following the angelic instructions, until he sees the animal—which is truly bizarre, being part sheep, part dog, part fox and part lion—lying at the foot of the cross. It leads him across unknown, adventurous country until he meets a knight who invites him to his house. "But one thing went wrong for me: he recognized me because of a mark I had, and said he had seen me in the past and named the place. Nevertheless, no matter how much he questioned me, I never admitted anything, and when he saw that it displeased me to be asked, he let things be" (*LG* I, 7).

This curious episode is difficult to interpret: We have no idea why the hermit wants to keep his identity secret, nor why he should feel that things are going wrong at this point. However, we later discover that he used to be a knight called Nascien, a life-long virgin who forswore the chivalric path in order to become a hermit and take holy orders (288). It was he who forbade the Knights of the Round Table from bringing any women with them on the Grail Quest, as we saw in Chapter Five.

The whole quest the hermit undertakes does read like a weird dream, in which events from his past are jumbled with impossible creatures and places and, as so often in nightmares, he feels he is being accused of an unknown crime. We do not know, for example, what events led Nascien to give up knighthood; perhaps he has a guilty conscience. Certainly his memories of his life as a knight, triggered by the places he has passed (the Valley of the Dead, the great killing at the Fountain of Tears) do not seem to be particularly happy ones. If this is so, then it is also possible for the modern reader (approaching the story from a psychological, rather than a mythological or theological, perspective) to deduce that it is his own guilt which he is about to confront, in the form of demonic possession.

Against Nature

He stays the night with his inquisitive host before walking on, stopping only to say mass at a convent, until he finds a folded letter on a stone in the road. It contains a message from the Great Master: that night he will finish his quest. It further contains detailed instructions about what to do next and, just as he is about to set off, he realizes that the Bizarre Beast has vanished. He has reached Norwegia.

He follows a well-beaten path through a forest, emerging to see a chapel on a rocky knoll in the distance. As he approaches it, he hears a hideous shriek, which would have terrified him if the letter had not warned him in advance. Inside the chapel he finds a man in a dead faint, whose eyes reveal that he is possessed. On the altar, Nascien sees the little book Christ gave him. Taking the holy book, Nascien places it on the man's mouth and the demon that possesses the hermit is expelled through his rear end (*par desous*)!

Nascien stays with the Hermit of the Knoll for nine days, during which they are fed with sweet fruit by the Holy Spirit. Just before Nascien leaves, on the Thursday after Easter week, the hermit confesses to him the sin that had led to his demonic possession: it was "a sin that mortal flesh cannot resist committing" (8) and he had only committed it once in over thirty four years as a hermit.

Nascien prudently leaves it to the imagination of the readers to fill in the details of this sin for themselves. But his strange, dreamlike first-person narrative does seem to invite a psychological reading of the hermit's quest. In what follows, therefore, I will draw on the insights of the archetypal psychologist James Hillman, who stresses the importance of the spontaneity of image-making in dreams and fantasy. Moreover, paralleling Corbin's more theological concerns, Hillman (who shared a platform with Corbin at Eranos for over ten years) warns of the danger to psychic and cultural health of the suppression of the active imagination in organized religion. The sin committed by a hermit isolated for over thirty years is likely to be doctrinal or sexual in nature and Hillman shows how the two are intimately related.

In the beginning of the Prologue, the as-yet-unnamed hermit makes much of his concealing of his identity, but an examination of the identity of the Hermit of the Knoll may be more revealing. Can we, for example, see the Hermit of the Knoll as an aspect of Nascien himself (an early example of the literary device of the doppelganger)? It is at least suggestive in this regard that the Hermit of the Knoll is the only other person, apart from Nascien himself, who can see the bizarre, composite animal.

Nascien, we are told, is a virgin who has maintained his chastity throughout his preternaturally long life, as both knight and hermit-priest. If someone who has spent a lifetime as a celibate, rejecting the companionship and love of women, indulges in sexual fantasies (even, or especially, if only once in a lifetime), he may experience them as demonic possession: a temptation of the Devil. Sober-minded people can be shocked by the transgressive images that arise from the unconscious when the inner "censor" is allowed a night off. Perhaps the prohibition of masturbation has its origin, as Hillman has suggested, in a much more powerful and insidious prohibition, that of the spontaneous production of images. This might explain why the story of Nascien is set in the eighth century, in the age of the iconoclasts.

Hillman goes on to cite several examples of "mythical fantasies" in Jewish legend and Greek mythology that connect acts of non-reproductive sex "with a monster, with an unnatural image that is both negative and creative" (1975, 116). It would be hard at this point not to think of the bizarre, composite animal that leads Nascien to the Hermit of the Knoll. Could this creature be the psychic product of a sin irresistible to mortal flesh? If so, then this monstrous image, which leads Nascien to a new religious revelation, is the product of the two things (identified by Hillman as "individual symbolism and conscience") with which the religious authorities have the most problems.

To illustrate his point, Hillman instances the positions taken by the Church at the Fourth Lateran Council on a range of issues that can now be seen to be inter-related, in their opposition to "individual symbolism, forging nature into images." For it was at this meeting that the religious authorities "established vigorous modes of repression against individualistic fantasies," in which Hillman would include the heretical beliefs of the Cathars, against whom Pope Innocent III had launched a crusade a few years earlier. The Third Canon of the council specifically extended to crusaders against heresy the same indulgences and privileges enjoyed by those who fought in the Holy Land; while the final canon called for another crusade against the Saracens, to free the sacred Christian sites from the hands of the "ungodly." As well as promoting various measures of discrimination against Jews, affirming the miracle of transubstantiation and condemning the mystical theology of Joachim of Flora, Lateran IV, in Hillman's words, "circumscribed with dogma the activities of angels and defined demons as those spirits who became evil of their own accord through their own acts" (117) as well as strongly reconfirming the celibacy of the priesthood.

It was in the shadow of this council that the *Estoire* was written[3] and the result is something that Weston (1913, 123) described as "a curious, and not specially edifying, composition." Modern readers are likely to agree; but the sheer number of extant manuscripts testifies to its popularity in the Middle Ages (Szkilnik 2006, 280). In its description of the forcible conversion of parts of the Middle East to Christianity by armed missionaries and its obsession with the relics of Christ's Passion, it can almost be seen as a literary response to Pope Innocent's call for a crusade to save the Holy Sepulcher and other sacred sites from the infidel.

The Image and the Book

Having achieved all he set out to accomplish in Norwegia, Nascien promises to pray for the Hermit of the Knoll and then departs with the Book. The Bizarre Beast reappears to guide him home, which he reaches on the Saturday evening. That night he has a vision in which Christ instructs him to copy the contents of the Book onto parchment. He must finish before the Feast of the Ascension (the fortieth day after Easter Sunday) because, on that day, the Book will no longer be seen on Earth.

Nascien begins work on the second Monday after Easter. His Latin text is later translated into French by Robert de Boron and the result is *la Haute Estoire del Saint Graal*. It tells the story of the Grail from the Crucifixion to the murder of King Lancelot (the grandfather of Sir Lancelot of the Lake and the great-grandfather of Sir Galahad). At that point the Book joins up with another book, the one dictated by Merlin to the Master Blaise, which completes the adventures of the Grail in the Kingdom of Logres.

The son of the Devil and a virgin, Merlin is conceived in a demonic parody of the Annunciation, to be the Antichrist—and, although he renounces this role, he retains the demonic knowledge of the past he inherited from his fallen father. But, in the *Estoire*, Merlin's prophetic powers are superseded by those of Christ, whose divine knowledge will always triumph over that the Antichrist. It is He, for example, rather than Merlin, who reveals the lineages of the successful Grail Questers (Galahad, Bors and Perceval), as well as of the unsuccessful (Lancelot, Gawain and Yvain). But we also find in the prose Grail romances that arms and love are no longer celebrated, unless it be Christian love and arms in the service of the Church. This may explain why Nascien has a guilty conscience about his chivalric past.

There is also another element that differentiates the prose romances from the earlier poems: Chrétien and the first continuators appear to delight in conjuring up for us mysterious images that tweak our imagination and which are not always satisfactorily explained, as if the author himself did not fully understand the material that he was handling. This is why early scholars believed that they could detect pagan (Rhys, Nutt) and Gnostic (Weston) mythological themes in poems written for a mainstream Christian audience. The more fantastic and imaginative the subject matter, the less the story can be satisfactorily tied down to an interpretation that would furnish material for a Sunday sermon. As the continuations developed, however, it is easy to see a more didactic, moralistic tone creeping in, as though in reaction to the free play of fantasy in the earlier poems. The worst offender in this case is Chrétien's continuator Manessier, who finally brought the story of Perceval begun by Chrétien to a close—and whom there is good reason to believe was influenced by the prose writings (Busby, 246). In Manessier's Continuation to the Story of the Grail the mysterious and shifting boundary between this world and the Otherworld becomes rationalized as a spiritual battle between the Knights of the Church and the Demons of Hell. The first casualty is the storytelling, which becomes stifled by allegorizing.

The Attack of Spirit upon Soul

The *Estoire del Saint Graal* is one of the last of the important, original prose Grail romances to be written and, as I mentioned above, it was composed in the shadow of the Fourth Lateran Council. But it sets the events recounted in the Prologue in the middle of the eighth century, when the Christian Church was struggling with the distinction between idols and icons.

Christianity, like Judaism before it and Islam after it, is a religion of the Book. All three Abrahamic faiths share the prohibition on the making and worship of idols stated in Exodus (20.4–5). In Deuteronomy (5.8–9) the Second Commandment is reiterated and Israel is warned to take heed lest it corrupt itself by making graven images (4.16). In fact, the Israelites are commanded to break the images of other gods (Ex 34.13 and Deut 12.3), an injunction that we will see carried out by Joseph of Arimathea.

It is easy to see therefore, that the production and veneration of images of Jesus, Mary and the saints, which proliferated after the defeat of paganism in the West, could be seen by some as a return of idolatry in the guise of the veneration of icons. This was, in fact, precisely the view taken by some in the Eastern Roman Empire in the wake of the success of a rival religion, one which took the Second Commandment far more literally: for Islam was understood by its adherents to be not a new religion, but a new revelation of the eternal truths of the religion of Abraham, from whose observance Christianity was seen to have deviated in, among other things, the Doctrines of the Trinity and the Incarnation.

The success of the Moslem Jihad against the Byzantine Empire led some to think that divine Providence was at work and made them question whether the Christian world was not being punished for idolatry, as the Moslems claimed. It was the Emperor Leo III, known as "the Iconoclast," who took the first steps, after effectively breaking the second Siege of Constantinople by the forces of Islam, to eradicate the theological cause of their success: the veneration of images. But it was left to his son, Constantine V, nicknamed *Kopronymos* ("Whose Name is Shit") by icon-lovers, to elevate what had been imperial edicts to the status of official church policy, by convoking the Synod of Constantinople in 754, some four years after the supposed events described in the *Estoire* Prologue.

Here, the production, display and veneration of images of Christ, the Blessed Virgin and the saints were officially outlawed and condemned as heathenish practices. But the consequent persecutions in the East were not supported in the West and the reign of the Iconoclasts provoked a schism which would lead, firstly, to a political division and, ultimately, to the geographical division of the Church, between the Roman Catholic and the Eastern Orthodox branches of Christendom, which still continues today.

The immediate reaction, however, was the calling of the Seventh Ecumenical Council, which was also the second council to be held at Nicaea in Asia Minor—the first having been the first attempt to formulate official Church doctrine, called by the first Constantine because he wanted the Christian religion to unify the empire. The Second Nicene Council upheld the veneration of images, but made a clear distinction between their cult (*douleia*) and the adoration (*latreia*) of the divine reality that the image points to. For Hillman (1976, 56), this is a "devastating differentiation," for it means that the archetypal power of the image is reduced to a "subtly depotentiated" allegory: Spontaneous image-making is demonized; images are only allowed if they are "officially approved" and "illustrative of theological doctrine," *representing* but no longer *presenting* us with divine power.

In an earlier discussion of Nicaea II, Hillman notes that the "iconoclast attack upon the image" both "epitomizes the attack of spirit upon soul" and also sets men against women: For the war against images is a war both against the imagination and against *anima*, the feminine personification of soul, where images abide (1983, 70–1).

These are precisely the issues that Nascien (and, by implication, the author of the *Estoire*) is struggling with. Nascien sees his chivalric past as a guilty secret; while the author may be reacting against the suspicion of pagan survivals in the first chivalric romances and heterodox elements in the early Grail poems. Nascien accordingly banishes women from the Grail Quest, experiences sexual and/or spiritual transgression (the sin which mortal flesh finds irresistible) as demonic possession and produces a monstrous, composite animal (as in the alchemical *opus contra naturam*) to guide him away from spontaneous presentations of imagery and towards the abstract world of doctrinal representations. He turns to his (theologically orthodox) image of Christ for a Book that will help him to focus his Trinitarian obsession and cast off the old devil of doctrinal heresy.

One of many puzzling aspects of the Prologue is the disappearance of the Book and its reappearance in a bleak northern world where Nascien confronts a hermit like himself but who, unlike himself, has sinned. One way of understanding this is through seeing the Hermit of the Knoll as Nascien's rejected, "sinful" self: the work against nature leads him to a confrontation with his own inner sinner, a rejection (exorcism) of his inner demons through the power, not of images, but of the Word made visible in the Book.

So Nascien can have a vision of Christ, but the image which appears before him is singularly abstract: "a man standing in front of me, so handsome and charming that his beauty could not be described by any mortal man's tongue" (*LG* I, 3). When the early Gnostics, in the centuries before the First Nicene Council, received secret revelations from the Resurrected Christ, they were full of strange cosmologies and vivid mythological beings; but when Nascien reveals the contents of the Book, it turns out to be full of scriptural allegory. For, as Hillman has shown (1976, 56), by the time of the Second Nicene Council, the images have become allegories and, when this happens, "the iconoclasts have won."

Paintings can be slashed, statues smashed, but it is difficult to destroy stories even when the books that contain them are burned, for the oral tradition is remarkably resilient and resistant to censorship. That is why I believe that when early scholars looked for the survival of pagan and Gnostic beliefs, they would have done better not to search for evidence of rituals carried out in remote regions (as Weston did), or try to identify practitioners of the Old Religion (as Margaret Murray[4] and Robert Graves did in their writings on the witch-cult), but to look inside the stories themselves for what is hidden below the surface. It is above all in the stories being told in the remoter outposts of Christendom, such as the "Celtic fringe," that we find the celebration of an intermediate world of images, neither painted representations nor allegorical abstractions, with a life of their own. Far from the centers of religious control, the poets of Wales could escape the worst excesses of the iconoclasts by entering—in the name of Taliesin[5]— that inherited Otherworld where the treasures of a world that was old when Church and State were young, lie hidden.

It is this world that came under attack in October 869, when the Eighth Ecumenical Council met in the cathedral of Holy Wisdom in Constantinople. Following on from the Seventh Council (also known as Nicaea II), the Church Fathers reiterated their commitment to the veneration of images, but only for what they represent; thus, as Hillman has pointed out, "images were deprived of their inherent authenticity" (54). At the same time, Constantinople IV (as the eighth council is also known) reaffirmed the Church's belief in two natures in one Christ, proclaiming that the flesh of God-made-man is animated by a rational and intellectual soul, as are we. This is the theological basis of a creeping dualism of body and soul that gradually replaced the ancient threefold model and culminated in the confusion of the immaterial parts, soul and spirit, from which we suffer still today.

God is a Trinity but Man, a walking dichotomy. Where once the wholeness of being was perceived in terms of three interlinked worlds—a spiritual or *pneumatic* essence, an animate or *psychic* essence and a physical or *hylic* essence—there would now be two, opposite worlds, with no intermediate realm where, like two seas, the two natures could meet and metamorphose. It is this lost Interzone that, in the ninth century, was banished to Limbo. It became the no-man's-land of the Western imagination and remains to this day the battleground between the fundamentalists of faith and reason.

Lateran IV followed Nicaea II in affirming the union of opposites in Christ—He is both visible and invisible, limited and unlimited, etc., since He is both God and Man—but Hillman argues that such doctrinal unity, if it descends into spiritual one-sidedness, comes at the price of schism: "the more we rigidly insist upon unity the more will diversity constellate" (1975, 88f). Small wonder, therefore, that the council led to a schism between East and West in the very body, as well as the soul, of the Church.[6] We in the West, regardless of our conscious beliefs, are all schismatics now that we have become so spiritually one-sided that we confuse the "reality of our wholeness," as Hillman puts it, with the "singleness" of a "monotheistic description of totality" against which the soul, representing multiplicity and complexity, rebels (93); for it is the conflicted soul that makes us fully human.

"What the Constantinople Council did to soul," writes Hillman (1976, 54), "only culminated a long process ... of substituting and disguising, and forever after confusing, soul with spirit." When the Church Fathers decreed that spirit was not a substantial part of Man's makeup distinct from soul, soul had to take the place of that high-minded animus and deny its own shadow, its rootedness in the body, its depth of imagination. But equally, by the thirteenth century the champions of spirit (such as the followers of Joachim of Flora) were banished to the intellectual exile of heresy; or massacred, like the Cathars, as we will see in Part Two.

A Heap of Broken Images

This, then, is the background to the composition of an extraordinary text which, its author claims, is based on a heavenly book written by Christ's own hand, translated into Latin in the eighth century by a seemingly immortal hermit and finally worked into French by Robert de Boron in the thirteenth century (this last presumably being *li contes* which the *Estoire*'s author invokes on several occasions). The *Estoire* itself therefore has three authoritative sources—de Boron, Nascien and ultimately Christ Himself—in keeping with the Trinitarian theme that runs throughout the work.

What these sources reveal is that on the day that Jesus dies, Joseph of Arimathea does not simply take the Savior of the World down from the Cross in order to bury Him in his own sepulcher (as the Gospels relate) while awaiting the Resurrection, but also, having taken from the house of Simon the Leper the dish or bowl (*l'escüele*) from which the Son of God had eaten the Passover lamb at the Last Supper, he uses it to catch as much of the Holy Blood as he can. After burying Jesus, Joseph hides the *escüele* in his house in Jerusalem—and it is here that he is seized during the night by Jewish fanatics who believe he has acted contrary to their Law.

Joseph is imprisoned inside a pillar in a stronghold belonging to the High Priest Caiaphas, situated in a marsh outside the city; where he is given nothing but bread and water to eat at first and then, for forty-two years, nothing. But the risen Christ visits him regularly in prison, bringing with Him the *sainte escüele* containing the Holy Blood and comforting him with the knowledge "that he and his descendants would carry His name to foreign places" (*LG* I, 11).

Joseph is eventually liberated from prison, long after everyone assumes he must be dead, by the Roman general Vespasian who, having been cured of leprosy by the image of Jesus on the veil of Veronica, is now a believer and is determined to be the vessel of vengeance against all those who injured both the Prophet of Judaea and His disciple. Having had all those still alive who took part in the persecution burnt to death (apart from Caiaphas, now an old man, whom he sets adrift so that God can choose his fate), Vespasian follows Joseph (who, miraculously, has not aged while in prison) in receiving the sacrament of baptism from St. Philip.

Leaving Vespasian to continue his punishment of the perfidious Jews,[7] Joseph follows Christ's instruction to leave the Holy Land with the *escüele* in order to spread the faith and his seed in faraway places. Setting off in the direction of the Euphrates with his family and their disciples, Joseph arrives in a wood near the town of Bethany, where the Lord instructs him to shelter his companions for the night and to make an ark to contain the *escüele*. Only Joseph and his eldest son Josephus are permitted to open the ark, which they do whenever they wish to talk to God.

That morning the followers of Joseph pray before the ark and then set out on the road, travelling until they reach the city of Sarras, the center of a sect which worships the heavenly bodies. Entering the Temple of the Sun (the supreme deity of the sect), Joseph confronts the King of the Saracens, Evelach, who is concerned about the encroachments on his kingdom of the neighboring Egyptians. Joseph offers the king victory over his earthly enemies and eternal joy and glory through "the One who is powerful over all things" (16). But first he must commence the breaking of idols (*les ymages*) for it is not wood or stone fashioned by man's hand that will save us, but the One.

Divinely inspired, Joseph now delivers a long disquisition on redemption, incarnation and the Trinity—the essential elements of the Christian faith—and this is followed for Evelach by visions in which the doctrines are illustrated visually. Thus, a tree with three branches helps him to grasp the doctrine of the Three-in-One; while a child going in and out of a closed room without touching the door is a literal enactment of the immaculate conception of Jesus. These visions are the sort that we are familiar with from other Vulgate texts, the kind that hermits love to explicate.

After hearing about the doctrines, Evelach perceives them literally acted out as visual images; but these are the kind of "officially approved images" that Hillman (1976, 56) describes as being stipulated by the second Nicene Council, "ways of perceiving doctrine." They contrast with those other *ymages* that fill the Temple of the Sun, which are "spurious, demonic, devilish," precisely because they are not mere representations but "presences of the divine power." The "presentations" must be destroyed so that the allegories can win out.

And this is literally what happens the following morning, when the king summons Joseph and his son to the Temple of the Sun to continue their theological discussion. Josephus, who has been chosen by Christ to be His first bishop and is now accompanied by angels, takes over the disputation; but his words, far from being mere explanations of doctrine, act to exorcise from *les ymages del temple* the devils that inhabit them. In particular, the devil speaking through the statue of Mars is forced by Josephus' guardian angels to pick up a sculpted golden eagle from the altar of the sun god and use it to smash the statue of Apollo (the Saracenic god of *sapiense*) and then to break off a limb from each of the temple idols.

Josephus now gives to Evalach a white shield with a red cross on it, to bear into battle against his Egyptian enemies so that, by this sign, he conquers: At the moment of greatest danger, the king uncovers the shield to reveal *l'ymage* of a crucified man—and a mysterious White Knight bearing a red-cross shield rides to his rescue. As a result of this victory, Evalach's doubts are erased and he converts to Christianity, taking the baptismal name of Mordrain; while his brother-in-law is christened at the same time, taking the name Nascien. This Nascien, Duke of Orberica, is the revered ancestor of Lancelot, Bors and Galahad in whose honor the Hermit of the Grail will also be named.

Josephus goes on to convert the population of Sarras, taking the opportunity to knock down pagan statues and break the altars of the old gods into pieces, purifying the temples with holy water so that new altars can be set up to the One God. Travelling on to the city of Orcaut, he exorcises a demon whose image is on the main altar of the temple; but, while Josephus starts baptizing the people, the demon waits at the city gates to strike dead all those who prefer to leave rather than convert. This was not what Josephus intended so he interrupts his mass christening in order to tie up the demon but, as he does so, he is confronted with the vision of an angel bearing a lance.

Josephus has seen this angel before: on the day he was made a minister of Christ, he had a vision of five angels carrying relics of the Passion in the ark which his father had made to contain the holy dish. The third angel was holding a bloody lance. Josephus then had a vision of the Crucifixion in which he saw the lance sticking in the side of the Crucified One, blood and water flowing down its shaft into the bowl.

It is this same angel who now appears before Josephus with a face of thunder and who strikes him in the left thigh with the lance, reproaching him for having allowed concern for those who scorned his faith to get in the way of his orgy of conversion. Josephus is able to pull the lance out easily enough, but the tip remains lodged close to the bone and he is unable to stanch the bleeding.

Josephus carries the lance that wounded him back to Sarras and spends the next twenty two days bringing the rest of the kingdom to the true faith, burning and smashing the pagan images in the temples. The task completed, Mordrain and Nascien ask to see the holy dish in the ark before which the Judaean Christians who followed Joseph from the Holy Land pray. But when he sees the *escüele*, Nascien announces that it should henceforth be called the Grail, since it is the fulfilment of all desire.[8]

But not content with looking at the glorious vessel, Nascien wants to peek inside it to see *les privetés de son Signour*. Accordingly, he raises the flat plate (corresponding to the Eucharistic paten) that covers it. For his presumption he is struck blind; but not before he has seen "the beginning of the bold endeavour, the occasion of the great exploits, the search for the great knowledge, the founding of the great religion, the separation of the great sins, the proof of the great marvels, the end of goodness and true kindness, the marvel of all marvels."

Nascien says that it was worth losing his sight in order to see such wonders, things that no tongue can describe. But just at that moment the

Angel of the Bleeding Lance emerges from the ark, draws the broken spearhead from Josephus' thigh, heals the wound and then goes on to restore Nascien's sight with the divine blood. The angel announces the beginning of the marvelous adventures that will take place in Logres, the land to which God intends to lead the company of the Grail, where "earthly chivalric exploits will become heavenly."

From now on, the angel announces, the Holy Lance will cease to bleed, until such time as the adventures of Logres commence. At that time, the lance that wounded Josephus will maim a king who is of the family[9] of Joseph of Arimathea: "He will be struck between the two thighs and will never be healed until the marvels of the Holy Grail are revealed to the one who will be filled with all goodness. The one who will see these marvels will be the last man in Nascien's lineage."

We know what the Christians of Sarras cannot: that the angel is referring to Galahad, the ninth and last of Nascien's line, he who will be good to the world (because of his prowess, generosity and bravery) and to God (because of his charity, religiosity and total command of his chaste body). Just as Nascien, the first of the *precieus lignaige*, is the first person to see the marvels of the Grail, so Galahad, the last of the lineage, will be the last to see them, as prophesied by Jesus on the Cross (a detail inexplicably omitted by the Gospel writers). The Crucified One apparently went on to say that *la lanche aventureuse* would be the agent of vengeance for the divine death that it inflicted with the approval of the unbelieving Jews. The last person to be struck by the Adventurous Lance will, like Josephus, bear witness to the evil deed; while the Lance itself will start bleeding again just before the Dolorous Blow is struck.

The people of the land where the Lance will be at that time will be terrified, the angel continues. Finally, addressing Josephus, he announces "that the marvelous adventures in the land where God will lead you and guide you to settle your descendants will last as many years as the number of days you carried the tip of the lance in your thigh" (51).

It is now time, the angel concludes, for Josephus to lead his people to the new Promised Land; but, before he does so, Josephus will demonstrate once and for all the truth of Christ's words, that there is nothing hidden which shall not be made known (Mt 10.26; Lk 8.17 and 13.2). The king, he insists, has a *desloial samblanche* stashed in an underground chamber, an *ymage* of wood in the shape of a woman with which, for the past fifteen years, he has been having sex. The passion he experiences surpasses the love between a man and any mortal woman; but, now that his secret has been revealed, he can be freed from its sinful grasp.

The wooden idol and the beautiful raiment in which the king had clothed it are burnt, as the statues of the gods were smashed. The reign of the iconoclasts has begun in Sarras and, amidst the heaps of broken images, a new chastity rules. It is now time for Josephus to export his religious revolution. But first, Nascien will have a close encounter with a familiar ship.

The Grail Testament

Shortly after the departure of the Judaean Christians, Mordrain is carried away by the Holy Spirit and Nascien is accused of murdering him by one of the few Saracens who has managed to avoid being baptized. Nascien and his young son Celidoine are imprisoned, but rescued after seventeen days: Nascien by a fiery hand in a cloud, which carries him to an island in the Western Sea, thirteen days distant from Sarras.

This *mout estrange lieu* is the Turning Island, created at the beginning of the world when God separated the four elements and which turns with the rotation of the firmament. But, because it partakes of "heaven's nature," it cannot sustain earthly life (*LG* I, 75).

The day after Nascien arrives on this *laide et gaste* island he sees something approach him from the far west which he takes at first for a swan but which turns out, on closer inspection, to be a splendid ship. This, as he will discover, is that miraculous Ship of Faith which we discussed in Chapter Five, where its mysteries are explained to the Grail Questers by Perceval's sister; but its sighting by Nascien is the first time as far as we know that anyone has seen it since it left the Holy Land. For it is none other than the Ship of Solomon, which has been floating on the seas for a thousand years, awaiting the Chosen Knight, the last of the lineage of King David, who will surpass in goodness and chivalry all those who come before and after him. Boarding the ship, Nascien sees there the Sword of David and three colored spindles made from the Tree of Life. Because he doubts whether the colors are natural, his lack of faith causes him to be plunged back into the sea and he is forced to swim back to shore.

As the translator of the *Estoire* points out, the punishment meted out to Nascien may contain a veiled warning to any who doubt the veracity of the story: a story that does, after all, derive its authority from Christ Himself (Chase, 133). The narrator-poet (who claims to be Robert de Boron) does go to extraordinary lengths to stress the truth of his story in a series of authorial interventions into the narrative, taking some pains to point out that there were only two previous examples of Christ's writing in the New Testament. The author thus makes the "somewhat sacrilegious suggestion" that we now have a Trinity of Christ's own writings (127). The third text written by Christ is the *estoire des estoires*; it is the only thing that He ever wrote after the Resurrection, so it deserves to be called *le haute escripture dou Saint Graal* and, as *divine escripture*, it also completes a trinity with the other two sacred scriptures, the Old and the New Testaments. We now have a supplement to the Bible: the Testament of the Grail.

Having assured the reader that his *contes* is nothing less than the written Word of God, the narrator now recounts the origins of the ship which, as we have seen, is rooted in the apocryphal legend of the Tree of Life, a tree which grows from a twig from the Edenic Tree of Knowledge. It is Eve who breaks off the twig when she gives Adam the deadly fruit that leads to their expulsion from Paradise; but it is Eve also who carries the twig into our fallen world, so that the tree which grows from it will always remind us of Paradise. Thus out of sin is sown the seeds of redemption. At the beginning of time a pattern has been set of woman's deceitfulness towards men which, paradoxically, leads to a higher good.

An exemplar of this is the fate of King Solomon, who is gifted by God with knowledge of the precious stones that are in the Earth, the herbs that grow on it and the heavenly bodies above it. But he falls foul of the beauty of women, who lead him into a shameless life. His own wife's tricks and deceit shame and debase him, so that he comes to despise woman as "not a spiritual thing, but a true enemy" (*LG* I, 82). But even as he is busy blaming all women for his wife's deceitfulness and Eve for the failures of all women, he hears a voice proclaim that there will come a woman of his lineage who will repair the fault of Eve.

Reading the sacred scriptures, the wise Solomon is able to use his *grant science* to interpret the *devins segrez* and thus learn of the coming of the Blessed Virgin Mary who will conceive the Son of God: a woman who will bring as much good into the world as the misery our first mother brought. Nor will Solomon's line end there: rather, it will terminate with a knight who will surpass all others, before or after, in both goodness and chivalry.

Eager to let his distant descendant, the Good Knight, know that his coming has been foreseen, Solomon turns to his wife, whom he knows to be "more ingenious in evil and deception" than any man, for help.[10] It is she who oversees the construction of a wooden ship so water-tight that it will float for four thousand years and who instructs her husband to customize the Sword of David, utilizing his knowledge of precious stones to fashion a splendid new handle and scabbard for the blade.

But, when Solomon wants to equip it with an equally worthy sword-belt, his wife insists that a weak and shoddy hempen one must suffice for now: but in the future a young woman will replace it with a beautiful one, made of the thing she most values on herself.

Solomon can only marvel at the subtlety of his wife's words and wonder where they come from and so, indeed, might we. As the story of Merlin makes clear, it is only God who can vouchsafe knowledge of the future; but why would God make a prophetess of a woman who brings only *honte et vilenie* (*ESG* 281)—who is *plus soutil en mal et engin que nus hom ne peüst estre* (283)—unless it is precisely so that He can turn those qualities of subtlety and ingenuity to a higher good? Despite Eve's causing Adam to fall, she brings out of Eden the twig that will become the Tree of Life—*l'arbre d'aïde et de confort* (279)—that will bring hope to future generations; just as, despite all the shame, villainy and malice of Solomon's wife, she will fulfil his greatest desire and bring a message of faith to future generations.

Liberating Dames

In addition to her pivotal role in linking the Biblical and Grail stories, Solomon's wife can be seen as a type of the Deceitful Savior[11] like the earth goddesses of Greek mythology.

The first being to emerge from primordial Chaos, Gaia (familiar today as the hypothetical self-regulating planetary system of ecological science) brings forth the Sky to be a secure resting-place for the blessed gods. But as the children of Mother Earth and starry Heaven grow increasingly terrible and monstrous, the Sky Father takes to burying them away from the light of day in the body of their mother. Groaning with their weight, Gaia comes up with a "clever, evil plan" to free her children from their father's tyranny (*HT* 28): she places a sickle in the hands of her son (Saturn) and bids him lop off her husband's genitals when next he comes to take his pleasure From this act of emasculation is born the loving Venus, the divine ancestress of the Trojan exiles who will found Britain, so that Gaia's actions sow the seed for future greatness: the establishing of the realm that will be the home of the Grail for several hundred years. In the castrated Sky Father and the husbandless Earth Mother we can also see the classical prototypes of the Maimed King and the Widow Lady of the Grail legends.

Saturn becomes the new King of Heaven and rules over a Golden Age on Earth. But his wife Rhea is also driven to betray her husband when his rule becomes tyrannical, by concealing the birth of the son who is destined to overthrow his father, until he is old and strong enough to do so. Consequently Jupiter banishes Saturn to the Isles of the Blest at the outer edge of the world and there the Golden Age still lingers, though it has passed away from the fields we know. The Roman historian Plutarch identified this Elysium in the farthest West, where Saturn lies sleeping, with one of the near-deserted islands, inhabited only by a few religious people whom the locals held sacred, scattered around Britain (Barber 1999, xx) and, although this does not enable us to identify a particular island, it must surely be a type of Avalon, the Fortunate Isle where Arthur lies sleeping.

For her role in freeing the Earth, Rhea is hailed as the "Deceitful savior, liberating dame./Mother of Gods and men" (Taylor, 140); but, as the goddess who brings about the end of the Golden Age, she is also equivalent to Eve, the Mother of All Living, who causes our expulsion from Eden. In both cases, the Earthly Paradise survives in an impossibly remote region; but it is only in early Gnostic texts that Eve is described as a liberator.

In the heretical gospels, as we saw in Part One, Eve is both the daughter of Sophia and agent of Divine Wisdom, whose fall and redemption are models for ours; while Eve's spiritual son Seth, is a pre-Christian savior figure, "the likeness of the son of man" (*NHL* 119). Like Gaia, the Gnostic Eve is the "first virgin," whose "first offspring" is born "without a husband" and who serves as her own mid-wife (181). This offspring is a droplet of light which Eve will hide in the human race so that the seed of Seth will carry into the future the knowledge (gnosis) of the Fullness that exists beyond the boundary of the material world, a world created by the Demiurge who would keep humankind in ignorance of their true spiritual home. Similarly, Rhea hides the son who will liberate the world from the tyranny of Saturn (the planetary god who is traditionally identified with the God of Israel). This son, Jupiter, becomes the new King of Heaven; but, in the Grail myth, his rule in Sarras and Britain is overthrown by the Company of the Grail, who bring the good news that Heaven has a new king, Christ.

During the Grail Quest, the three pure Christian knights are helped and guided by Perceval's sister who—in attempting to fulfil the redemptive task begun by Eve after the Fall and continued by Solomon's wife—can be seen as the third person of a Wisdom Trinity. But Perceval's sister dies before the Quest is achieved and the Grail itself is carried up to Heaven.

It will be left to William Blake to rewrite the ending of the story to provide us with a more hopeful myth of Wisdom (Jerusalem), which is his own poetical take on the healing of the Maimed King (Albion).

For the Gnostics, Sophia is a female Holy Spirit but, as Anne Marie D'Arcy has shown, in the mainstream Church, Divine Wisdom was increasingly identified with the male Logos (226–8). Wisdom is hidden (or in exile) in this world until embodied in Christ, who reveals the glorious truth (233); but, after the Resurrection, His sacred vessel remained on Earth as a symbol of—and a receptacle for—His wisdom (313). The Grail legends show how that vessel was transported from the city of Jerusalem to the island of Albion.

As both Logos and Sophia, the Grail is a unifying symbol, a containing vessel for the *coniunctio oppositorum* of male and female manifestations of the godhead; or, as Blake would put it, for the reunion of Albion and his Emanation Jerusalem. As we will see in the Epilogue, Blake's Wisdom figure, Jerusalem, will arise from the ruins to be re-united with the giant Man who contains all things in Heaven and Earth. This reunion will take place in Eden (where Heaven and Earth meet) and will be achieved through the power of the Imagination (personified by Jesus) which is available to all who believe in vision.

But no such vision is vouchsafed to the authors of the *Queste* and *Estoire del Saint Graal*. To the contrary, Blake's poems and paintings are an extreme example of the individual symbol formation and spontaneous image-making attacked by the iconoclasts and condemned by the Church councils: his art reveals the divine presences; it is vision, not allegory and cannot be contained by religious orthodoxy. To take just one example, one that was of particular concern to the author of the *Estoire*, Blake appears to have understood the Trinity, not as Three Persons in One God, but as three aspects of One Person, leading him to rewrite the Lord's Prayer: "Jesus, our Father, who art in thy heaven call'd by thy Name the Holy Ghost..." (*BCW* 788).

By contrast, the Grail version of the legend of the Tree of Life seems designed to reinforce orthodoxy. As D'Arcy points out (262), the substitution of one tricolored Tree for the three trees of the Seth version enhances the Trinitarian symbolism which is so important to the *Estoire*. The three colors in one Tree become an image of the three persons in one God: thus illustrating allegorically an orthodox solution to the problem that Nascien the Hermit was wrestling with, before he was taken up to the Third Heaven.

But now we learn that Duke Nascien, after whom the Grail Hermit was named, is having the same problem. Looking at the white, green and red spindles that frame the bed on the Ship of Faith, Nascien finds it hard to believe that the colors can be natural: which, in the symbolism of the *Estoire*, is tantamount to doubting the Trinity. Nascien believes he has detected an element of *fauseté* amid the deceptive marvels of the bed—and is immediately plunged into the sea for his lack of faith.

But the modern reader, whether or not a Christian believer, may concur with Nascien's suspicion that there is deception at work: Our only authority for the wickedness of Solomon's wife and for the natural color of the spindles—a subject on which we might feel that the author doth protest too much[12]—is the text itself, which claims, without any scriptural support, to have been written originally by Christ Himself. This claim, like that of an alternative apostolic succession which is suggested by the dynasty of the Fisher Kings, is certainly heterodox if not actually heretical (Chase, 137 and *n*43); so that this pseudo-Christ, purporting to be the World Savior who replaces Saturn and Jupiter as King of Heaven, can be seen to be as much a Deceitful Savior as any Goddess of Earth.

The Land of Divine Promise

But whether or not we consider Duke Nascien to be the victim of deception, the *Estoire* certainly presents him as the victim of an angry, jealous god who will not only have no other gods before him (as the star-worshippers of Sarras have discovered and as the Saracens of Britain will also learn, to their cost) but who also punishes anyone who doubts the literal truth of the *haute escripture*. Thus, having been plunged into the sea for detecting "a grain of falseness" in the marvels of the Ship of Solomon, Nascien is forced to return to the Turning Isle where his faith turns on the words of a very old man who turns up in yet another ship the next day (*LG* I, 85).

The old man explains that what Nascien had encountered the day before was a sign (*une des demostrances*) from the Master and that it should be called a symbol (*senefiance*) rather than a ship. He then proceeds to explain the meaning of the symbols which turn out, like all images post–Nicaea II, to be representations of doctrine: thus the Ship of Solomon itself symbolizes Holy Church; the bed is the True Cross which is "the sign of solace and rest" that sinful humanity can take, thanks to the sacrifice of the Son of God; while the three spindles symbolize virginity (white), patience (green) and charity (red), the three qualities by which Christ vanquishes death (86–7).

His faith restored, Nascien will certainly require patience on the island, since over two years will pass before he is eventually rescued by his son Celidoine, in the Ship of Solomon. Boarding the sea-going symbol safely this time, Nascien is transported with his son to an island ruled by a giant, who attacks them. Having nothing else with which to defend them, Nascien draws the Sword of David from its scabbard—ignoring the explicit warning, written on the cloth that covers it, that the sword must only be grasped by an unsurpassable warrior—only to have it break in two near the hilt. Fortunately he finds another sword lying on the ground and with it kills the giant.

Nascien then returns to the ship, which immediately departs from the island. Looking at the broken Sword of David, Nascien laments that he was wrong to praise the thing he prized most after the Grail, which seems to have failed him in his need. Once again, he has ignored an explicit warning, this time written on the sword itself: that it would be most cruel to one who might expect it to be gracious.

However, they soon encounter another ship bearing King Mordrain, who boards the Ship of Solomon and joins the hilt and the blade of the Sword back together as easily as they were broken. Then they hear a noise as loud as thunder and a voice telling them to leave the ship; but, as he obeys, Nascien is struck in the left shoulder by a flaming sword. He hears a voice proclaiming that he has offended his Creator by drawing a sword of which he was unworthy. Vengeance is the Lord's.

Nascien is later healed by the ghost of a hermit in whose honor he had founded a church and whom he sees walking on the water. The hermit warns him not to break any of the High Master's commandments again, or worse will befall him; but goes on to assure him that the faithful followers of Joseph of Arimathea will also be able to cross the sea that very night, without a ship, passing into Great Britain, "for it pleases the Great Master that by this lineage the land shall be populated and increased." The ghost also sends Celidoine off, reassuring his father that they will be reunited "in the land God has promised you and your lineage" (112).

This is the first mention in the *Estoire* of Britain as a Promised Land: it is *la terre que Dex a pramise* (*ESG* 389). The Grail is travelling from one *Terre de Promission* to another, from the Holy Land (where it has performed one miracle) to the sacred land of a pagan goddess (where it will perform many), until the disenchantment of the Adventurous Kingdom is complete. It is the descendants of Nascien who are destined to play the central role in that process.

Meanwhile Nascien returns with Mordrain to Sarras where he is reunited with his wife, who has been searching for him, having seen him in a vision telling her to follow him to the precious western land that God has provided for them—*la precieuse terre d'Occident ke Diex a pourveüe* (245)—just as, a millennium earlier, the Goddess had provided it for the Trojan exiles. Believing their son Celidoine may be with them, Nascien and his wife send far and wide for news of Joseph of Arimathea and his companions, but they can find out nothing since they have long since left Sarras. Eventually, the duke hears a voice in a dream telling him to go straight to the seashore and enter the first ship he finds there. This, it turns out, is the symbolic Ship of Solomon, which he has already been forced to leave in dramatic circumstances on two separate occasions.

Waiting by the shore is a beautiful and elegantly dressed lady who asks him to carry her into the ship, since she is worn out from her travels. Nascien wants to oblige but, as he carries her to the vessel, it moves away from the shore. Putting her down, Nascien crosses himself and the "lady" reveals her true form,[13] as the Devil! He quickly boards the ship as terrifying voices issue from "the very mouth of hell" (*LG* I, 115).

Aboard ship he falls asleep and sees, in a dream vision, a man in a red robe who tells him that his son is in the land which was promised to them. Joseph and the Company of the Grail are also in "the land that was promised to their descendants and to you" (116).

Nascien then asks him if he will ever return to his own country. The man replies that neither he nor the Ship will ever be seen in the duke's native country except in dreams. Rather, Nascien will remain in the western Promised Land and the Ship will be nearby until the last man in his lineage enters it in order to go to Sarras with the Holy Grail.

The man then gives him a letter, which Nascien finds in his hands when he awakens. It tells him the names of the nine men who will descend from Celidoine, of whom only the last four need concern us: these are King Lancelot, his son Ban of Benoic, Ban's son Lancelot—and, finally, the last of the line, Galahad, who will be unsurpassed in goodness and chivalry and who will put an end to all the adventures he encounters.

Later Nascien is obliged to leave the Ship of Solomon for the third and last time and boards yet another ship, where he meets a very old man who claims to be from a country that Nascien has never visited and to which he can never go as long as he lives. The worthy man tells the duke that the eighth descendant of Celidoine (Lancelot) will be as hungry for sin as a dog. But the ninth (Galahad) will be like a river that is muddy at first but later runs clear, for he will be conceived in mortal sin by the eighth on an unmarried mother and therefore "vilely, as in fornication" (120). Yet out of this "mortal sin" will emerge an unsurpassable knight who will be a lifelong virgin and whose end will be marvelous. We shall not look upon his like again…

Apart from the flawed Lancelot, Celidoine's descendants will be lion-like kings; but the tone of the Post-Vulgate's depiction of women has been established by the devil-lady lying in wait for Nascien, blocking his path to the Ship of Faith. In the Vulgate Cycle, as we saw in Part One, there still lingered traces of an older, poetic tradition in which the moon goddess whose worship was established by the founders of Britain and the fays who are her mythic descendants can cast a pagan glamour on the land. These supernatural women are eerie, mysterious and powerful, sometimes destructive, sometimes beneficent, always ambivalent. Morgan loves Arthur, Ninienne loves Merlin, Guenevere loves Lancelot. Even Galahad's mother, destined to bring forth the Best Knight, can be seen as another Deceitful Savior (like Solomon's wife and the classical earth goddesses), since her tricking of Lancelot is for a higher, spiritual purpose.

But, for the most part, these same women as we encounter them in the Post-Vulgate will be depicted as devils in female form and this transformation will be clearest in those figures which are most clearly of supernatural origin. Here Ninienne will hate Merlin as much as Morgan hates Arthur and they will both be depicted as women who use their education (the source of their magic) to destroy great men.

When Duke Nascien meets up with his son and the rest of the Company of the Grail in Britain, it will be to wage war against the indigenous pagans, those who can still experience images as divine presences and not just as representations of theological doctrine. As if inverting the call of Lateran IV for a new crusade, the Company of the Grail will not liberate the Holy Land from the infidel, but carry the relics of the Passion to a new Holy Land. In the process the Promised Land of the Goddess will become the Promised Land of the Grail, as we will see in Part Two.

• • • • • • • •

Part 2.
Realms of Symbolism

All that essential and indescribable part of man that is called *imagination* dwells in realms of symbolism and still lives upon archaic myths and theologies.... To have imagination is to be able to see the world in its totality....[1]

—Mircea Eliade

Seven

By This Sign, Conquer

> Hither came Ioseph of Arimathy,
> Who brought with him the holy grayle, (they say)
> And preacht the truth; but since it greatly did decay.[1]
> —Edmund Spenser

The arrival of the Holy Grail in Britain is an event as transformative as the arrival of Brutus and the Trojans over a thousand years earlier. Brutus had been guided to Britain by the goddess Diana and, in return, he had agreed to establish her worship in the island forever, dedicating temples and choirs of virgins to her. But now a sacred vessel borne by a company of missionaries will bring to these shores the worship of a male god whose followers will allow no other deities before Him. The stage is set for a series of bloody wars and miraculous interventions that will ultimately sweep away the indigenous cult of the Goddess and replace it with an imported one that is still the established church in Britain in the twenty first century after the death of its man-god. By this sign—the sacred vessel and the Holy Blood that it contains—will the Company of the Grail conquer.

The Harrowing of Pagan Britain

After completing the conversion of Sarras to Christianity and destroying its graven images, Joseph of Arimathea and his band of iconoclasts, which has now swelled to several hundred, cross the Euphrates and make their way north and west, praying continually that God will guide them to the land that He has promised to them and to their descendants.

Eventually, on Easter Saturday, they reach the sea, but have no means of crossing. Undeterred, Josephus tells the bearers of the Grail to walk on the water, while the least sinful members of the rest of the Company will follow on a bridge that he makes from his undergarment—an unusual form of sea crossing, but one that proves remarkably effective: the only people to get a dunking are Josephus' cousin Simeon (who will also have to undergo an ordeal by fire before his soul can be saved) and Simeon's son Moses (of whom more anon), neither of whom are as holy as they like to make out. Wet and bedraggled, they will have to wait on the continental shore with the rest of the sinners while the select few complete their night-sea journey under the watchful eye of the moon goddess—for *la lune luisoit cler* (*ESG* 416)—and arrive on the shore of Great Britain at dawn on Easter Sunday.

Having put his miraculous underwear back on, Josephus announces to the chosen people that they have at last reached the land that was promised to them and to their descendants. Here they will multiply and fill the land with people who are more deserving of it than those who are there already. For, as the Biblical Chosen People found when they arrived at their Promised Land: there are already inhabitants with a prior claim. But Josephus has been told by God that the *mescreance et malvese loi* which are planted there must be uprooted and the new trees of the Christian faith cultivated in its place.

For Britain, we will learn, is at this time a hotbed of infidels (*de sarrazins et de miscreanz*). The astral cult of Sarras, it would appear, has a long reach and, although it has been all but wiped out in its Middle Eastern heartland, the cult of the deity of the moon and the other heavenly bodies, which Brutus and his Trojan exiles brought to Albion, is still going strong. The ancient Britons are Saracens. But the land that was once promised to the goddess Diana in perpetuity is destined to become the Promised Land (*la terre qui est pramise*) of the new Christian faith, symbolized by the Grail; and the first acts of conversion will soon occur when the company that brought the Holy Vessel to these shores is re-united, thanks to the arrival of Duke Nascien.

The Middle Eastern ruler, whose adventures after he was whisked away from his native land we explored in the Interlude, has been floating around the seas all winter; but now, at Easter, he arrives at the continental port where the more sinful members of the company have been left behind. Nascien transports them all across the Channel to rejoin their companions and the re-united company make their way to the town of Galafort, in the south east of the island, where they are astonished to see a red cross on a flag flying above the gate. "This surprised them, for they did not believe there was a symbol of Holy Church anywhere in the country, since they thought there were only pagans in all the land" (*LG* I, 123). As they soon discover, however, when they enter the hall of Lord Ganor, the ruler of Galafort, Nascien's son Celidoine is already there.

Since yet another miraculous ship brought him to Britain, Celidoine has spent his time discussing spiritual matters with a holy, forest-dwelling hermit, who was only too willing to hear the good news of Christ. But now Celidoine has turned his attention to the powerful so that it is to him that must go the distinction of being, not just the first Christian to set foot on these shores, but also the first evangelist. For, when his co-religionists arrive, he is busy arguing the finer points of doctrine with the doctors of the Saracenic law. In what will prove to be an unfortunate precedent, whoever loses the religious argument will also lose their lives.

The next day, Josephus, on behalf of the Christians, argues the case for the Virgin Birth against a pagan philosopher; which the Saracen loses when he pulls his own tongue out of his mouth! The master clerks of Galafort are now quick to convert, along with Lord Ganor himself, to whom Josephus demonstrates an uncanny knowledge of his lordship's youth. But many of their idolatrous townspeople refuse to give up the faith of their ancestors and are unceremoniously banished beyond the River Humber; or, at least, they would have been if it were not for the fact that the ship which was carrying them sinks with all hands. When the news of the mass drowning reaches Galafort, Josephus announces that such is the price for serving the Devil.

The King of Northumberland, however, to whom Lord Ganor owes fealty, sees things differently: he is determined to protect the indigenous faith against this alien import and marches south to bring his recalcitrant vassal into line. But Ganor now acknowledges only one lord—Jesus Christ—and denies all other authority. In the siege of Galafort that follows, the Northumbrians are massacred. "Thus the Christians won victory and honor in the first battle against the Saracens in the land of Great Britain" (130).

Buoyed up by their victory over the pagans of the north, the leaders of the Company of the Grail—Joseph of Arimathea and his son Josephus—set off to convert the west of the island, taking with them the Holy Vessel. But they soon fall foul of the King of North Wales, who has heard it rumored that the Christians are sustained by the grace of their god. The cruel pagan ruler[2] has the missionaries thrown into prison and tells the wardens not to bother feeding them, since their miraculous vessel will provide all they need. And, indeed, the Grail does just that.

Meantime, help is on its way: in the form of King Mordrain, who learns in a dream that the King of North Wales has inflicted on the Grail missionaries what is nothing less than the torture of a second crucifixion. Leaving his kingdom in the capable hands of one of his most trusted knights, the King of Sarras sets off at once for Britain; taking with him the white shield with the Red Cross which had helped him to win victory over the Egyptians. Teaming up with his brother-in-law Duke Nascien, Mordrain leads a Christian army into North Wales, burning not just the castles but also the houses of the Saracens, so that whole cities are ravaged. But the pagan king refuses to give up his prisoners, so he and all his followers are slaughtered.

The next day, the triumphant Christians gather to give thanks to God for their victory. But, while the newly-liberated Josephus is celebrating the Mass of the Grail, King Mordrain, despite being covered in wounds from the battle, attempts to get too close to the Holy Vessel. He ignores a voice telling him to back off; until a cloud descends on him, which he cannot ignore because it renders him blind and helpless. He who had inflicted divine vengeance on the Saracens is now a victim of it himself; but he takes it in good grace, considering it proof that Our Lord considers him to be His son. He asks only that he will live to see the good knight—"he who is to see the marvels of the Holy Grail" (135)—and the voice tells him that his wish will be granted. At this time, but not before, his wounds will be healed, his sight and strength of body restored.

Mordrain is thus the first of what will be several British Maimed Kings, awaiting their earthly savior. He is also the founder of the first Christian monastic community in Britain, for he goes to live in the forest with a hermit, accompanied by many of his nobles. They adopt a white habit and build an abbey where King Mordrain will live for hundreds of years, sustained by his desire to serve the Father with his words, the only power that remains to him. He will only be cured of his ills when the Good Knight comes to his abbey: Mordrain will die in Galahad's arms.

Meanwhile Celidoine has been chosen to sit on the throne so recently vacated; so that North Wales has the honor of becoming the first Christian kingdom within the British Isles. Having celebrated his marriage to a Persian princess whom he converted, Celidoine will now father a dynasty of notable "lions" which will end with the much-anticipated Grail Hero, Galahad, *cil qui doit les merveilles del Saint Graal veoir apertement* (*ESG* 474).

At the Table of the Grail

Josephus now begins the great missionary crusade that will occupy him for the next fifteen years. By his side are his father Joseph, his uncle Bron, the twelve sons of Bron and another relative of theirs called Peter; as well as some less faithful members of the company, including Simeon, his son Moses and the equally significantly-named Canaan (who has twelve brothers).

Taking with him the ark containing the Holy Grail, Josephus heads for the richest and most important of the cities of Britain, the one where the pagan kings are traditionally crowned: Camelot. We may be somewhat surprised at this point to learn that Camelot has the tallest mosque in the whole country (*ESG* 479); but then, Christian ignorance about *mahomerie* is not confined to medieval writings.

At this time the city is ruled by Agrestes, a Saracen who is as cunning as he is cruel. Seeing how eagerly his people start to embrace the new faith, he pretends to convert as well; but it is all a sham. As soon as Josephus leaves, believing that his job is done in Camelot, King Agrestes threatens all those who will not recant with death. *Pour encourager les autres*, he makes an example of the twelve faithful Christians to whom Josephus has entrusted the care of his flock: after dragging them through the streets behind horses, the apostate has them tied to a cross that Josephus had placed at the edge of the forest and has their brains bashed in with a mace. But the king does not escape divine vengeance: shortly thereafter he goes completely mad, murdering his wife, his brother and even one of his own children, before attempting to eat his hands. Shouting and screaming, he jumps into an oven and dies horribly.

Messengers are sent to Josephus by the frightened citizens and he returns to bury the martyrs. He also tries to wash the cross on which so much blood has been spilt, but it has turned black and will remain so until the adventures of the Grail are brought to an end. Josephus now orders the destruction of all the pagan temples and the burning of the idols of the Saracen gods. But this time he does not leave Camelot until all traces of the old religion have been destroyed. In their place he has built the church of St. Stephen the Martyr, where Arthur and Guenevere will later be married.

After traveling for a couple of days, the missionaries reach a local landmark called the Giant's Knoll. There they set up the tables to eat, but only the most worthy members of the company are allowed to sit at the Table of the Grail.[3] Peter notices that there is an empty seat between Josephus and Bron and suggests that there are many men who are worthy to sit there; but Josephus contradicts him. This seat, he explains, represents the place of Jesus at the Last Supper and can only be occupied by one whose worthiness exceeds all others. Therefore it must remain empty until the Second Coming, or at least until Christ sends someone to fill it in His place.

This explanation does not, however, satisfy everyone. Leading the malcontents are Simeon and his son Moses, the latter volunteering himself to fill the empty place. Josephus points out that Moses had already nearly drowned when he proved unworthy to cross the Channel on the miraculous underwear; but he concedes that Our Lord can make a worthy man out of a sinner in no time at all. Consequently he allows Moses to sit in the Seat of Danger, warning him that if he is not worthy it will mean not just that his body will be destroyed but that his soul will be plunged into eternal torment. Moses persists with his folly, despite being afraid—and his fear proves fully justified when seven fiery hands descend from Heaven and carry him off, burning like a dry bush, to a nearby forest. It will take a lot of pain to make him wise.

The carrying off of their companion leaves many feeling frightened and their unease is not helped when Josephus says that he will in due course take them to where Moses has ended up; it is only then that they will discover whether he has been saved. At this point Bron decides to change the subject by asking Josephus what plans he should make about marrying off his twelve sons. Josephus interviews the boys and agrees to find suitable matches for eleven of them; but the twelfth, known as Alan the Fat, insists that he intends to keep his virginity and serve the Holy Grail all his life.

Josephus is delighted to hear this and, in return for his keeping his flesh unsullied by "the sin of lust," he confers upon the boy a very important gift: "I grant that, after me, you be invested with the guardianship of the Holy Vessel you have requested, so that you will be its guardian after my death. And when you have passed from this world, the one you give it to and his descendants will be its lords. The grace of the Holy Vessel will be so important that if their lands are ever devastated, they will receive food in abundance as long as they live" (*LG* I, 139).

Thus is created a dynasty of Grail Lords who will act as a spiritual counterpart to the Kings of Logres; but who will also function as an alternative to the traditional apostolic succession of the bishops of Rome. This, along with the idea of a book written by Christ, is one of the most extraordinary aspects of the *Estoire* and can perhaps best be understood in terms of persistent British claims to spiritual seniority, the best known of which is the legend that Joseph of Arimathea built the first Christian church on British soil during the reign of King Arviragus. The Vulgate places the missionary activities of the Company of the Grail somewhat later than this but, even so, the success of Josephus in converting a great number of people to Christianity bespeaks a much earlier date for the wide spread of the new faith than is usually accepted by historians.[4]

In any case, we are told that the eloquence of Josephus, through whom the Holy Spirit speaks, leads the number of his Christian followers to swell; which becomes a problem when they find themselves in a barren region— *une terre gaste et deserte* (*ESG* 490)—where food is hard to come by. This waste land is a premonition of things to come; for, when they decide to rest by a large pond in a valley, only those sat at the Table of the Grail are fed by the Holy Vessel that is carried by Peter. The less worthy companions fear that they will die of hunger.

But a miracle is at hand: Josephus instructs the virginal Alan to get into a little fishing boat that has been left on the banks of the pond and to throw a net into the water. When Alan returns with only one fish, albeit a large one, the hungry sinners are dismayed and tell him to go back and catch some more. But Josephus instructs him to divide the fish into three portions and divide it among the multitude. Just as when Jesus fed many with little, after everyone's hunger has been satisfied there is more left over than there was to begin with.

Because of this miracle, Alan is forever after known as the Rich Fisherman and the title is passed down to the Keepers of the Grail who follow him.

The Broken and Bleeding Sword

At this point, Joseph of Arimathea takes his leave of the group and heads off alone to the Forest of Broceliande, which will be the scene of many marvels in the Arthurian era. It is there that he meets an armed Saracen, Argon, who is seeking help for his wounded brother. Joseph tells Argon that he will be able to heal his brother through the power of the One who has led his people here as He led the people of Israel through the Red Sea.

Argon tells Joseph that he would like to know which god Joseph is referring to and names the four deities that the Saracens of Britain worship: Tervagant (whom we know better as the goddess Diana) and a trinity of male gods: Jupiter, Apollo and a certain *Mahomet*, by whom is clearly meant the Prophet of Islam. The ignorance of the author about Christianity's principal rival, which allows the seal of the prophets to be confused with a pagan god (and which allows there to be mosques in first-century Britain), is only compounded in the passage which follows, in which Argon defends himself against the accusation that he invests supreme power in images that men have made with their own hands.

The images do not have power in themselves, Argon explains, but rather the power comes from the gods they represent. The images are merely the *semblance*; true power resides in the deity whose grace invests the form (*ESG* 495).

This is a surprisingly subtle take on pagan idolatry; but the author soon shows his true colors when Argon expresses his belief that a wooden statue of the Prophet of Islam (*ymages Mahomet*) can be efficacious in healing. For in the thirteenth century, when the *Estoire* was written, it was not the old Romano-Celtic pagans of Britain who still posed a threat to Christian hegemony in Europe and the Middle East, but the Moslems, whose victories had led to the iconoclastic movement precisely because they took the Second Commandment so much more literally. If he allows a distinction between idols and icons in pagan (and perhaps therefore in Christian) worship, the author of the *Estoire* shows no understanding of the beliefs of those who will allow no graven images either of God or of His prophets. In that sense he can be seen to be a true son of Nicaea II.

But he is also clear about the impotence of pagan gods to heal through their images and so Joseph asks Argon to take him to his castle in order that he can demonstrate the worthlessness of the Saracen deities. But if, as Joseph claims, the idols can "neither help, harm, take away, nor give by themselves" (*LG* I, 141), the god (or devil) that works through them is certainly capable of causing harm, as they discover on entering the Castle of the Rock. An unchained lion, running down the main road, jumps on Argon and strangles him, whereupon the seneschal of the castle stabs Joseph in the thighs with his sword so violently that part of the blade is left in the wound.

We have seen (in Chapter One) that the cat is one of the animal epiphanies of the moon goddess. We can imagine that it is this same lunar deity, she who looked down on the Company of the Grail as they crossed the Channel, who is now acting to defend her ancient rights in Britain: those honors accorded to her by Brutus which the Christian missionaries are equally determined to uproot.

Wounded, Joseph is tied up and dragged off to prison; but he asks to be allowed to demonstrate the healing powers of his god before Matagran, Argon's brother, claiming that He can bring back the dead. Matagran knows of no god who has such power but, at Joseph's prompting, he has the body taken to the "mosque" and laid before the idol of Mahomet. As the pagans pray to their gods, Joseph prays to his Father in Heaven, who made the sun and moon. In answer, from the skies lightning strikes with a clap of thunder, burning and shattering the images, which leave only a terrible smell.

Having disposed of the competition, Joseph demonstrates the healing power of Him who rose from the dead and who can, by the same token, raise others. Argon is brought back to life and both he and his brother declare their faith in the One God. The rest of the people of the castle follow them in being baptized.

Finally the seneschal owns up to his wounding of Joseph and produces the hilt of the offending sword. Having finally healed Matagran's head wound (which had brought him to the castle in the first place), Joseph draws the blade out of his thighs, declaring that the two halves of the sword will never be joined together until they are held by "the one who is to achieve the high adventures of the Holy Grail" (142); nor, until that day, will the blade ever stop bleeding. The people of the castle are astonished to see that Joseph's thigh is healed so perfectly that it is as if it had never been pierced but, from then on, the blade is never seen without blood coming forth from it. The broken and bleeding sword is kept at the Castle of the Rock, awaiting the coming of he who will put an end to these marvels.

Joseph now rejoins his companions on the banks of the River Celice, across the water from the Forest of Darnantes. Afraid to cross the wide and dangerous river, the company kneels down to pray; whereupon they see a white stag with a gold chain around its neck surrounded by four protective lions leap into the water and cross without danger.

Josephus understands the stag to be the virginal and humble Christ, the lions His four evangelists;, so he bids his followers to take this as a sign that they can cross without fear. And indeed they do so; all, that is, apart from Canaan, whose lack of faith prevents him from risking the crossing without a ship. In fact, when some passing fishermen ferry him across, the "pagan unbelievers" are rewarded for their charitable act by having their vessel overturned by a whirlwind. They all drown (144)! Our Lord, it appears, is displeased that Canaan should continue to be part of the Company of the Grail and we will shortly see why.

But first, the companions will discover the fate of Moses, who had so presumptuously occupied the Seat of Danger at the Table of the Grail: he has been carried to a beautiful but ruined castle in a valley in the forest, where he burns in unbearable anguish. The "ministers of hell" would have carried him to their "dark house" had not a forest-dwelling hermit leading a holy life spotted him and demanded that the demons leave him to divine mercy. He now awaits the coming of Galahad, "the good knight, the one who will put an end to the adventures of the Holy Grail and will complete the adventures of Great Britain" (145). Moses bids his former companions to continue to evangelize to the indigenous pagans and their prayers at least mitigate his torment.

But Moses' father Simeon and Canaan, who has so recently been saved from drowning, remain so steadfast in their unbelief that the Grail ceases to feed them. Hungry and resentful towards God for apparently not caring about them, they decide to take it out on their more fortunate relatives. That night, with the moonlight shining down on them, Canaan kills his twelve brothers in their sleep; while Simeon stabs his cousin Peter (who had even been entrusted with carrying the Grail) but not fatally—which is fortunate, since he will go on to found one of the most illustrious Christian dynasties in Great Britain.

The Grail Dynasties

The murderers are soon discovered and the company decides that the malefactors should be buried alive but, before the sentence can be carried out, two burning figures appear flying through the air, snatch Simeon up and transport him to Wales. Canaan is however buried alive as planned, surrounded by the twelve tombs of his brothers. The next morning, the companions find that the swords they had laid on the tombs are now standing upright and that Canaan's tomb is burning fiercely. Josephus prophesies that it will continue to do so until Lancelot extinguishes it by the power of "his knightly grace": Lancelot, that is, the begetter of the good knight who "will accomplish all of the adventures and marvels of Great Britain, where other knights will fail" (148).

Meanwhile Peter's wound starts to fester and the herbal treatments he is given only seem to make it worse; so he begs to be set in a ship that God will take to a place where he can be healed. Adrift in the sea, Peter is eventually washed up on the shores of Orkney, where he is rescued by the king's daughter. Discovering that he is a Christian, the pagan princess takes him to one of his co-religionists for healing and, by the time Peter has recovered, she has fallen completely in love with him.

Peter is both handsome and valiant, as he demonstrates when he agrees to act as the champion of the King of Orkney, who has been falsely accused of treachery. The trial-by-combat is held in London, in front of Lucius, the High King of Britain, from whom the King of Orkney holds his lands. Peter is victorious. His reward is the hand of the princess and both she and her father convert to Christianity, so impressed are they by Peter's faith. King Lucius comes to the wedding and he also agrees to become a Christian, as long as Peter agrees to be his companion-in-arms.

When Peter dies, he is buried in Orkney in the Church of St. Philip (the apostle who baptized Joseph of Arimathea) and from him descends a dynasty of Christian kings, of whom the most famous will be King Loth and his son Gawain (who can, therefore, claim to be of the lineage of the Grail Company). But at the same time that Peter is converting the ruling families of Britain, Josephus and his followers are travelling throughout the length and breadth of the British Isles, converting large groups of unbelievers.

It is thus that Josephus' younger brother, Galahad, becomes the first Christian King of Wales.[5] He was conceived when Joseph of Arimathea and his wife were travelling through a wintry forest in Europe but was born in Galafort, the first city in Britain to be converted. Galahad has grown up there in the fifteen years that his family have been carrying out their missionary activities.

Galahad's worthiness prompts his older brother to invest him with a kingdom that risked falling into ruin when its old ruler died without issue. It is on the Feast of Pentecost that the young Galahad is crowned, consecrated and anointed with holy chrism. Some three hundred or so years later, it will be on that same feast that his namesake, Galahad of Corbenic, will prove himself worthy of the spiritual kingship of Sarras when he draws the sword from the Floating Stone in Camelot.

After his coronation Galahad of Wales takes a wife and from them will descend a dynasty of Christian kings of whom the most famous will be Urien of Gorre, along with his son Yvain (a notable Knight of the Round Table). And it is on the outskirts of Gorre (which borders Wales) that King Galahad comes across his cousin Simeon, who has been deposited there by demons and who is in perpetual fiery torment because of his attack on Peter of Orkney. At Simeon's request, King Galahad has an abbey built there, where he himself will be buried and whither Sir Galahad will come on the Grail Quest to put an end to Simeon's pain: "And at that time," Simeon prophesies, "the adventures that will happen in this country through the great marvels of the Holy Grail will end" (156).

This encounter with Simeon is only one of several episodes in which the author of the *Estoire* provides us with a back-story to events in the Vulgate Cycle. Thus we learn that both Joseph of Arimathea and Josephus are buried in an abbey in the north of the island, in what is now Scotland. We further learn that, before his death, Josephus gives to blind Mordrain the White Shield with which the Egyptians were confounded and paints on it, with his own blood, a red cross: This is the sign (first raised in this island by Celidoine at Galafort) by which the Saracens of East and West have been conquered. Moreover, this Red Cross Shield is the same one that Sir Galahad will win at the beginning of his quest.

But Josephus' most important final act is the entrusting of the Grail itself to Alan (the son of Bron) whom we know as the Rich Fisher. Alan and his brothers take the Holy Vessel to the Land Beyond (*Terre Foreine*), whose king is suffering from leprosy—and promise to cure him if he becomes a Christian. The king is accordingly baptized, taking the Christian name of Alphasan and, of course, he not only abandons his Saracen faith (*la loi sarrazinoise*), but also has all the pagan temples knocked down, the idols broken and burnt. He even has all his subjects who do not want to convert, killed.

The modern reader may feel that Alphasan has somewhat misinterpreted the message of his new Lord, who in His lifetime on Earth preached compassion for sinners and the forgiveness of sin. But we should also remember (as if we could forget!) that there are many monotheists today who believe it is justified to kill people who have a different interpretation of the religion of Abraham, let alone those who are not even peoples of the Book, like the pagans of Sarras and Britain. In any case, the introduction of capital punishment for unbelievers seems to have done the trick, as far as the missionaries are concerned, since the conversion of the Land Beyond takes less than a week. Moreover, Alphasan himself is cured of his leprosy merely by looking at the Grail, leading him to declare that the vessel is truly holy and blest (*seintismes et beneoiz*).

So pleased is the king with the Holy Grail, in fact, that he creates a beautiful stronghold for it on the banks of a river. When the construction is finished, an inscription appears on one of the gates, written in the Chaldean language, saying that the castle should be called Corbenic, meaning the Place of the Holy Vessel (*liu a seintisme vessel*). This building, of course, is the Grail Castle that has appeared in so many stories, since Chrétien de Troyes first wrote his *Conte du Graal*—and the kings who rule there, after Alphasan, will constitute a dynasty of Rich Fishers, so named in honor of Alan.

Alphasan gives his daughter in marriage to Joshua (Alan's brother) and, when Alphasan and Alan die on the same day, Joshua becomes both King of Corbenic and also the first of the Fisher Kings who will guard the Grail in the following centuries. Thus Joshua is succeeded by his son Aminadap, who marries one of the daughters of Lucius (the High King of Britain converted to the Christian faith by Peter of Orkney); so that, in a sense, the royal bloodline of Britain merges with the spiritual lineage of the Grail.

Aminadap is succeeded by his son Carcelois, who fathers the next king, Manuel. He in turn fathers Lambor who, in addition to being the fifth of the Fisher Kings, will also become the first King of the Land Beyond to receive a Dolorous Blow. In his case it proves fatal and it comes about when the Ship of Faith first arrives on the shores of Britain.

This ship, originally set adrift by King Solomon, has spent a long time wandering through the seas, testing the faith of any who board it. The last we heard of it was when it ditched Duke Nascien into the water for doubting the natural provenance of the colored spindles on the bed. He was also struck with a flaming sword when he dared to draw the Sword of David (also aboard the ship), which can only be handled by the worthiest man in the world. So we know the arrival of the ship can spell trouble for those who do not pay proper heed to its dangers. And so it proves.

King Varlan is a Welsh monarch whose territory borders the Land Beyond but, although he has recently abandoned his Saracen faith to embrace Christianity, this does not prevent him from waging war against his neighbor King Lambor. Their forces meet on the seashore and King

Varlan's army is destroyed. As he flees along the water's edge, Varlan comes across a "beautiful and sumptuous" ship. He leaps aboard and, finding the Sword, draws it from its scabbard. Finding his enemy has caught up with him, Varlan strikes him on the helmet. Lambor falls dead and the consequences, both for his own Kingdom of the Land Beyond and the parts of Wales ruled by Varlan (who himself drops dead as soon as he replaces the Sword in its scabbard), are devastating.

> This was the first blow of the sword in Great Britain. There resulted such persecutions to both kingdoms ... that for a long time afterwards the lands that should have been cultivated were not. Nor did wheat, oats, or anything else grow, nor did the trees bear fruit, nor were any fish to be found in the waters except very little ones. And for this reason, the land of the two kingdoms was called the Waste Land [159–60].

Fortunately King Lambor has a worthy son who succeeds him. But Pellehan, as the sixth Fisher King is called, will not escape the curse that seems now to blight the Grail dynasty, ruling as it does over *la Terre Gaste*.

It is fair to say that our sources show considerable confusion over the fate of the later Grail Kings. According to the *Estoire*, King Pellehan is "wounded in both thighs in a battle in Rome," as a result of which he is henceforth known as the Maimed King. But, as we saw in Chapter Five, the Vulgate *Queste* gives a different cause of his maiming: he is struck by a flying lance through both thighs when he attempts to unsheathe the Sword, after coming across the ship by chance while out hunting.

The best-known account of his maiming, however, is that originally given in the Post-Vulgate Cycle as it continues on from the *Estoire*, in which King Pellehan is struck a Dolorous Blow by Sir Balin the Savage; for it is this version which is taken up by Malory and reworked by Tennyson. It is this version which we will explore in the next chapters.

Eight

The Prophet of the Grail

> For Merlin had in Magick more insight,
> Than euer him before or after liuing wight...
> And sooth, men say that he was not the sonne
> Of mortall Syre, or other liuing wight,
> But wondrously begotten....[1]
>
> —Edmund Spenser

The last part of the Vulgate Cycle to be written, the *Estoire de Merlin*, follows on directly from the *Estoire del Saint Graal*.

It begins with the demons in Hell bemoaning the loss of Adam and Eve along with many others of their prisoners who have been freed by Christ, an event that is traditionally placed on Easter Saturday, between His death and resurrection. Significantly, it is on this date, sometime in the late first century AD, that the Company of the Grail cross the Channel into Britain to begin "saving" the indigenous pagans, by force if necessary—an act that can therefore also be seen as a "harrowing."

We have seen the success of its mission—culminating in the conversion of Lucius, High King of Britain—and the marriage, sometime in the second century, of Lucius' daughter to Aminadap, the second of the Fisher Kings who guard the Grail in their castle of Corbenic in the Land Beyond. From then on the Grail Kings seem to go into "occultation": it is difficult to match the lives of those who possess the most Holy Vessel of Christendom with the known events of history, as if the Land Beyond is an "inner" realm where time passes more slowly than in the outer world.

Here, after the death of Lucius in AD 156, the deeds of Roman emperors loom more largely in British affairs than do those of the indigenous kings who succeed the great dynasties which dominate the first millennium and a half of British counter-history—that hybrid of mythical narratives and historical events that constitutes the legendary Matter of Britain. Thus, even in the somewhat garbled accounts that have come down to us filtered through the imaginations of Geoffrey of Monmouth and Wace, we learn of the reigns of Septimius Severus (who died at York in 211); of his son Bassianus, better known as Caracalla (d. 217); of Carausius, who declared himself Emperor of Britain in an attempt at independence from Rome, but who was murdered by his treasurer Allectus in 293; and of Constantius Chlorus, who killed Allectus and restored Britain to the Empire in 296.

Constantius was famously married to Helena, who would later claim to have discovered the True Cross of Jesus, who founded the Church of the Holy Sepulcher in Jerusalem and died as a saint, after bearing to her husband the even greater son who would found the city of Constantinople as well as make Christianity the official religion of the Roman Empire. According to the legendary chronicles, Helena is a British princess: the daughter of Coilus, or Old King Cole, an honorable exception to the rather undistinguished and mostly anonymous succession of kings who rule in Britain during the last two centuries of the Roman occupation.

When Constantius died (like the Emperor Severus a hundred years earlier) at York in 306, his son Constantine was declared emperor; but he soon left Britain to make himself the undisputed ruler of the Roman world. A similar strategy was attempted by Magnus Maximus, a legionary of Spanish origin stationed in Britain, who usurped the Empire of the West but died in 388, his ambitions thwarted. According to Welsh legend, Maximus (Macsen) marries a British princess called Elen of the Hosts, whom he first sees in a dream and who confers on him the Sovereignty of Britain. When he leaves the island to establish his rule on the continent, he takes with him the cream of British manhood, resulting in what the Triads call one of the Three Unfortunate Levies: armies that departed from this island and never came back.

This unmanning of Britain leads almost inevitably to two of the Three Oppressions that afflicted the island and also (unfortunately, as the Welsh Triads see it) never went back: the Picts[2] and Saxons. Successive rulers, with greater or lesser support from the continental Roman Empire (itself under increasing strain from barbarian incursions), were obliged to face the threat from these pagans from the north and east. The last to do so (of those who can also be unequivocally attested in the historical record) were the western emperors Constantine III and Constans II.

The usurper Constantine was elected by the remnants of the Roman legions in Britain in 407 in order to lead their defense of this neglected outpost of empire but, like Magnus Maximus before him, he in fact led the last British legions to ignoble defeat on the continent in a vain attempt to claim the Empire of the West; dying, along with his son Constans, whom he had also elevated to the imperial purple, in 411. But native legend, we should not be surprised to learn, sees the events that led to the final severing of the links between Britain and Rome quite differently.

Between Moon and Earth

According to the chroniclers of the Matter of Britain, Constantine is the younger brother of the King of Brittany, the realm founded in Armorica by Conan Meriadoc, the cousin of Elen of the Hosts. When the Romans leave Britain undefended, it is the Breton prince who leads his troops back to their ancestral homeland to drive out the pagan invaders and who is unanimously chosen as king by an assembly of the barons.

We learn from Wace—whose French verse chronicle of the history of the British (the *Roman de Brut*) is the one most likely to have been familiar to the authors of the Grail romances—that Constantine's reign lasts only twelve years, but during that time he fathers three sons: Constans, Aurelius Ambrosius and Uther. When King Constantine is assassinated by a Pict, the Welsh Count Vortigern persuades his peers to elevate Constans to the throne, with Vortigern himself acting as regent to the boy-king.

It is not long before the scheming Vortigern wields total power, amassing to himself the wealth of the nation—and he even incites the Picts to kill Constans. Feigning outrage, Vortigern has the murderers executed and takes advantage of the state of emergency to proclaim himself king, while Constans' younger brothers are spirited away to their relatives in Brittany for safety.

Now at war with the Picts, King Vortigern is not displeased when three shiploads of Saxons arrive on the Kent coast and their leaders, Hengest and Horsa, ask for safe passage: they are looking for lands to settle and have been led to Britain by their chief god, Mercury, whom they worship as Woden, the ruler of the fourth day of the week. They also worship a goddess, Frea, who rules the sixth day of the week and who therefore corresponds to Venus, the divine ancestress of the ancient Britons. The Saxons also have three other gods, whom Wace presents by their Roman names: Phoebus (the Sun), Saturn and Jupiter.

The Saxon migrants are therefore bringing with them to these shores the very divinities of the heavenly bodies that the Grail Company had condemned as demons when they encountered them in Sarras and in Britain—and whose worship, we can assume, would have been largely eradicated from at least the south of the island when Christianity became the official religion of the empire. King Vortigern is as shocked to hear their names as Joseph of Arimathea had been when he learned about them in the Forest of Broceliande; but he believes he can make use of the newcomers. In fact, Vortigern ingratiates himself with Hengest by marrying the Saxon chief's daughter in a shockingly pagan manner:

> God, what sin! The Devil led him so far astray ... he fell in love with her in the morning and had her in the evening ... [RB 177].

It is his apparent apostasy that more than anything turns his subjects against him. As a result he is temporarily deposed by Vortimer, his son by a previous marriage; but, when Vortimer is poisoned by his wicked stepmother, Vortigern regains the throne.

King Vortigern's alliance with the Saxons is short-lived, however, as the natives once more start to become alarmed by the increasing numbers of pagan incomers. A meeting to resolve their differences on May Day on Salisbury Plain turns into a massacre when the Saxons, who have smuggled weapons in what was meant to be an unarmed discussion, turn on their hosts. This is the infamous Night of the Long Knives, which leaves Vortigern a hostage to his erstwhile allies.

Abandoning much of the south and east of the island to Hengest, Vortigern flees across the Severn into Wales where he consults his soothsayers (*sortisseürs*) about the best means of defending himself against his enemies. They advise him to build an impregnable fortress on Mount Snowdon; but whatever is constructed during the day is found to be in ruins by the next morning. Required to account for this strange anomaly, the soothsayers come up with an equally bizarre solution: the king must find and kill a fatherless boy and mix his blood with the mortar; only then will the fortress endure.

The desperate king orders a search throughout Wales and, unlikely as it seems, his messengers find, in Carmarthen, a boy who is widely believed to have no father. When they question his mother, who leads an exemplary life as a nun, she insists not only that she never saw the father but also that she could not be sure whether it was a man or a *fantosmerie*. When the mother and child are brought before the king, one of his wise men says that she could be telling the truth, since "there exists a kind of spirit between moon and earth ... partly human and partly supernatural. They are called incubus demons; their realm is the air and they frequent the earth.... They have deceived many girls and ravished them in this way" (189).

The Creed of the Great Mystery of the Grail

This is as much of an explanation of the origin of the fatherless child as we get from Wace; but the *Estoire de Merlin* confirms that the boy's father is no mere apparition or phantom—and not even a common-or-garden incubus rapist—but a demon sent to Earth by the infernal Pandemonium to redress the balance of power after the Harrowing of Hell. The Devil wants to have a prophet just as God has His, someone whose demonic knowledge of the past and future will deceive as many as the evangelists have saved. Moreover the child will be conceived in a blasphemous parody of the Immaculate Conception.

A demon which has the ability to take on the likeness of a human being and engender a child on a mortal woman therefore sets about sowing fertile soil by disrupting the lives of a Welsh family and turning them against God. Only the oldest sister keeps her faith with the support of her confessor, Blaise; but when one night she goes to bed angry and forgets to make the sign of the Cross, the Devil takes his opportunity. The incubus has sex with her while she is asleep and she conceives a son. But as soon as she wakes up she realizes that something is wrong, crosses herself and, appropriately enough, prays to the Holy Lady Mary, who also conceived from an invisible presence.

When she tells Blaise what has happened, he sets her a penance—to forswear lasciviousness for the rest of her life—and the Devil has no more power over her. When the child is born, he is extraordinarily hairy and has all the power and mental cunning of the demon that spawned him. But because his mother was the victim of deception and asked for divine mercy, when the child is baptized God grants him knowledge of the future, as well as allowing him to retain that knowledge of past events which is his demonic inheritance. Like all human beings, Merlin must choose which master to serve with these God-given powers.

Merlin is less than two-and-a-half years old when the messengers come looking for him, but already he is talking like an adult and astonishing everyone with his knowledge of secret things. Merlin, of course, knows that King Vortigern's men are coming to take him away; so, before he goes, he makes arrangements for Blaise to act as his amanuensis. He tells the clerk to write down everything that he knows about the history of the Grail and then proceeds to tell Blaise about the great voyage of Joseph of Arimathea and his companions (including the adventures of Alan and Peter) and the first Christian Kings of Britain. Blaise is to set everything down in a book and, when the king's men come for Merlin, he is to take the book with him: first of all to the forests of Northumberland, where Merlin will visit him regularly to update him on the events that he needs to include in it. Eventually, when the work is finished, he must travel on into the West—"to the place where the people are who possess the holy cup, the Grail"—and there it will be combined with the Book of Joseph to create "one beautiful book."

This is the first that we have heard of a book written by Joseph of Arimathea himself, if that is indeed what this passage indicates—a passage which, like all the opening chapters of the *Estoire de Merlin*, is closely based on the Prose *Merlin* that forms the second part of the De Boron Cycle.[3] If, as seems likely, the Book of Joseph ends with his death, then the book Merlin dictates to Blaise will pick up the story of the Grail from that point on; but it also seems to reiterate the events in Joseph's life with one important exception: Merlin will not repeat the "intimate words" that passed between Joseph and Christ in the Jerusalem prison (*LG* I, 176) and, since Robert de Boron has also refused to write them down, they are forever lost to us.

These lost words form the subject of one of the most intriguing passages in the Prose *Joseph of Arimathea* (the first part of the De Boron Cycle): "Then Jesus spoke other words to Joseph which I dare not tell you—nor could I, even if I wanted to, if I did not have the high book in which they are written: and that is the creed of the great mystery of the Grail. And I beg all those who hear this tale to ask me no more about it at this point, in God's name, for I should have to lie" (*MG* 22). This High Book may be the Book of Joseph or the "one beautiful book" into which the latter was combined with the Book of Blaise; or, indeed, the Book of Christ which the hermit Nascien copied into Latin and which Robert de Boron was credited with translating into French.

Either way, for the Christian occultist A.E. Waite (1857–1942), probably best known today for being the designer of a Tarot pack, these "other words" reflect a mystical tradition existing not in contradiction but complementary to the mainstream religion; they are at the heart of a secret tradition which he called the Hidden Church of the Grail. This idea would also be taken up by Henry Corbin, whose theology of the Lost Word seeks an esoteric ground of connection between the Abrahamic faiths, an inner connection that reaches beyond the apparent contradictions in the exoteric creeds. We will return to this in Chapter Eleven.

Merlin's words to Blaise are also the first indication of the possibility of communication between Britain and the Land Beyond since it became a Waste Land. They prepare us for the tragic encounter of an Arthurian knight with the inhabitants of the Grail Castle, an encounter whose disastrous consequences can only be redeemed by a quest which will spell the beginning of the end of the heroic age, as many set out but only few are chosen to find the elusive stronghold of Corbenic. We have a direction for it—it is in the West, near Wales—but no precise geographical location. Nor should we search for it on our terrestrial maps: it is occidental in the metaphorical way that Sarras is oriental.

Corbenic is in the archetypal Land of the Setting Sun and Blaise's journey there is a journey into mystery for, as Merlin tells him, "just as I will remain obscure except concerning those things wherein I wish to reveal myself, so will your book remain hidden." It is only after Blaise has joined the Company of the Grail that his work will be talked about and his book "gladly heard everywhere." Even then, it will not possess the authority of the gospels, because whereas the apostles put down in writing what they themselves had seen and heard, Blaise is only writing down what Merlin has told him (*LG* I, 176).

It is perhaps to establish greater authority for the story of the Grail that Christ Himself intervenes in the eighth century, supplementing the beautiful book of Joseph and Blaise with an account written in His own hand, in the language of Heaven.

The Third Table

In due course, Vortigern's emissaries arrive to take Merlin to the royal court, while Blaise sets off for Northumberland, confident that his labors will be rewarded when he has finished his book and earnt the joy that is experienced by the Grail companions.

Brought before the king, Merlin dumbfounds the royal astrologers with his knowledge of their secret divinations[4] and confounds their expectation—for they have read it in the stars—that he will be the cause of their deaths. First of all, he explains the reason for the collapsing of Vortigern's tower: there are two dragons underneath it whose movements disturb its foundations. Secondly, he obliges the astrologers to forswear their use of "the occult arts" if they want their lives to be spared. Merlin explains that his demonic father had tricked them into believing that he would be the cause of their death—which had prompted them to make up the story about the fatherless boy's blood—because Merlin has definitively chosen his Father in Heaven over his earthly father, the Devil (184f).

Thirdly, Merlin prophesies that Vortigern will be burnt to death by the sons of Constantine. This in fact proves to be the case when Aurelius and Uther, now grown to manhood, arrive from Brittany to avenge their brother's murder and reclaim the throne that is rightfully theirs. With Merlin's help Hengest is killed and the Saxons routed but Aurelius, who has become king after Vortigern, is himself killed at the great Battle of Salisbury Plain, which nevertheless marks the triumph of the Britons. During the battle a red dragon appears in the sky, disheartening the pagans, as a result of which Uther, who becomes king when his brother dies, takes Pendragon as his surname, since the appearance of the dragon was the sign of his victory.

Merlin further advises King Uther to build on Salisbury Plain a fitting monument to Aurelius and the British dead. The result is the erection of Stonehenge, an arrangement of gigantic stones brought overseas from Ireland and stood upright by the magic of Merlin. They will be there as long as the world lasts.

Merlin serves King Uther faithfully in the following years and gains his trust. Equally, Merlin decides to entrust the king with a mission even greater than the erection of Stonehenge: the creation of a table that will signify, not just a chivalric institution, but also the workings of the Holy Spirit in Britain.

First of all, Merlin explains to Uther his own twofold power: how the Devil gave him knowledge of the past, but God gave him knowledge of the future: "And thanks to that sovereign power, the devils lost me, for I will never, God willing, be subject to their will."

He then goes on to explain to Uther how Joseph of Arimathea, having taken Jesus down from the Cross, wandered with his followers in a wilderness—and how Christ instructed Joseph to create a table in the name of the Table of the Last Supper and to place on it the cup which Christ had given to Joseph in prison. This cup, the Grail, divides the good from the wicked and "perfects men's hearts." All those who are deemed worthy to sit at the Table of the Grail experience the fulfilment of their heart's desires; but there is always a place left empty to remind us of Judas, who left empty his seat at the Table of the Last Supper when he went off to betray Jesus (*LG* I, 196).

And now Uther must have a third table made, in the name of the Trinity; for the sacred cup has drawn those who guard it hither, into the West. Moreover others have been led here in search of it; so the king must form a fellowship which will be worthy of the quest. He is to summon his nobles to Carduel in Wales at Whitsuntide and there the few will be chosen.

Accordingly, on Whitsunday, Merlin selects fifty knights and tells them to take their places at the new table. But one seat he insists must be kept empty for the time being: the one who will occupy it has not yet been conceived, but it is he who will fulfil the adventures of the Grail—not in Uther's time, but in the reign of the king who is to follow.

Seated at the Round Table, the fifty knights form an instant bond of love; but some of them are suspicious of Merlin and question why no one is considered worthy enough to sit in the empty place. Consequently, while Merlin is in Northumberland relaying his latest exploits to Blaise, a very highborn and wealthy baron insists on sitting in the seat … and instantly melts away! Although Merlin refuses to be drawn on the subject of the baron's fate, we might imagine that it is not dissimilar to that of Moses, who likewise sat in the Seat of Danger at the Table of the Grail.

Thus is born the legend of the Siege Perilous.

EIGHT: The Prophet of the Grail

The Sword in the Stone

From now on, Carduel is the preferred site of three of the greatest annual British festivals—Pentecost, All Hallows and Christmas—and it is here that King Uther meets and falls in love with the Duchess of Tintagel (who is unfortunately already married) and the stage is set for some of the most famous episodes in medieval literature.

The story is well-known from Malory and numerous later retellings: when he discovers that the king is lusting after his spouse, the aggrieved duke hides his wife in the impregnable fortress of Tintagel. But if the fortress is impregnable, his wife is not, especially when the shape-shifting arts of Merlin are employed in the king's cause. With his knowledge of herbs—*Par nuvels medecinemenz*, according to Wace (*RB* l.8702) and using his *enchantemenz* (l.8727)—Merlin transforms the king into the likeness of the duke. Thus Uther is able to enter the castle and its lady's bed with no further hindrance.

Meanwhile, however, the real duke has been killed in battle and the king is now free to marry the lady whom he has made pregnant. On the day that Uther Pendragon and the Duchess of Tintagel are wed, Igerna's eldest daughter is married to King Loth—a direct descendant of Peter of Orkney, so that the British royal family is once more intermarried with that of the Company of the Grail. As for the youngest daughter, Morgan, she is sent to a nunnery where she learns to read and write and master all the arts.

> She became wonderfully skilled in an art called astrology, and she worked hard all the time and knew a great deal about the healing arts. For her mastery of knowledge, people called her Morgan the Fay [*LG* I, 208].

Meanwhile, Queen Igerna has come to term and she gives birth to a son, in the darkest hours of the night, between midnight and dawn. But her husband has made a pact with Merlin: in exchange for getting into bed with Igerna, Uther has agreed that the child who will be born of that illicit union will be handed over to the prophet for his own, undisclosed purposes—and this is done, as soon as the boy is born. Merlin in turn hands him over to Antor, one of the barons of the realm, who is instructed to have the boy christened "Arthur."

Fifteen years pass and Uther Pendragon is dying. The king, worried about leaving the kingdom without an heir, asks Merlin about the boy. Uther is reassured to learn that Arthur is "handsome and big and well fed"; whereupon Merlin adds: "And I tell you that your son will be head of your kingdom after you through the power of Jesus Christ, and he will perfect the Round Table you have founded" (211). This power will be manifested that Christmas, when Merlin instructs the nobles of the realm to gather in London, where they will witness a sign of God's plan for the future of the kingdom: a sign in the shape of a block of stone with a sword stuck in it, which appears in the courtyard of the city's main church. On the stone it is written that the one who can pull the sword out will be king by the choice of Christ.

All the barons are, of course, eager to be the first to pull out the sword from the stone, but none succeed. It is not until New Year's Day that the young Arthur, acting as squire to his foster-brother Sir Kay but ignorant of the circumstances surrounding his birth and adoption, draws the sword from the stone and finds himself proclaimed King of Britain. The barons, equally ignorant of Arthur's illustrious pedigree, are nonplussed and ask for the coronation to be delayed until the Feast of Pentecost. But finally, on Whitsun Eve, Arthur is made a knight by the archbishop and, on Whitsunday, is crowned king.

Such Strange Things

It is at this point that the Post-Vulgate Cycle branches off from the earlier Vulgate Cycle.

The *Estoire del Saint Graal* and the early chapters of the *Estoire de Merlin*, spanning a period of about four hundred and fifty years (from the Deposition of Jesus to the coronation of Arthur), will be incorporated wholesale (with only a few adjustments for consistency) into the new cycle, providing a starting-off point for an account of Arthur's reign which will stress his role as King of Adventures and minimize the love affair between Lancelot and Guenevere, while maximizing the Grail Quest as the spiritual lynchpin on which the kingdom stands and falls. The remaining chapters of the Vulgate *Merlin* (a rather tedious account of the wars between Arthur and a group of rebel kings) will be replaced and the huge Vulgate *Lancelot* (which we have explored in Part One) bypassed by a new Continuation to the *Merlin* in which the presence of the Holy Grail in Britain will become more widely known and its effects on the kingdom will ripple outwards, shattering the destinies of its inhabitants and transforming Logres into a Kingdom of Adventures. At the same time the sisters of Arthur will come to the fore, but their role will be to sow the seeds of his destruction; for there is no important part for a benevolent woman (especially one who may once have been a pagan goddess) to play in the Promised Land of the Grail.

It is therefore indicative of what is to follow that the Post-Vulgate *Merlin Continuation* begins with the arrival of his eldest half-sister in the court of the newly-crowned king, leading to the original sin which will play a crucial role in the undoing of Arthur and the fall of his kingdom. Curiously, this sister remains unnamed throughout the entirety of the Vulgate and Post-Vulgate cycles. It is only from Malory's reworking of the romances into English that we know the Queen of Orkney as Morgause. It is also important to remember that in the prose romances, unlike in the early chronicles, the mystery of Arthur's conception extends to his birth: he is whisked away by Merlin and no one else even knows that Uther Pendragon has a son.

Thus, when the beautiful Morgause comes to Arthur's court at Carduel to present herself and her children, she has no idea that the man to whom she pays homage is her half-brother. Arthur himself is equally in the dark, so what happens next is perfectly understandable, if reprehensible: they know each other "passionately" and "carnally" and, as a result, Morgause conceives the man who will betray the king and destroy the kingdom (*LG* IV, 167). The couple know that they are committing adultery; what they do not know is that they are committing an unnatural act that will lead to the equally unnatural consequence of a father and son killing each other.

However, there are soon signs that something is wrong: Arthur is haunted by a nightmare in which his kingdom is ravaged by monstrous creatures and, in an attempt to find distraction, he goes hunting. It is then that he meets Pellinor, King of the Isles, who is hunting the Questing Beast: a bizarre creature that sounds as if it has thirty baying hounds living inside it. The king is much taken with a creature that is even more marvelous on the inside than it is on the outside, declaring it the greatest wonder he has ever seen, adding: "Never before in the kingdom of Logres were such strange things found or seen" (168).

Arthur in fact wants to take up the quest himself, but King Pellinor explains that it is reserved for the best knight of his kindred. What he does not tell Arthur is that the kindred he is referring to is the Grail family: for Pellinor is the son of King Pellehan (the current Fisher King) and the grandson of King Lambor, who died when the Ship of Faith first docked in Britain. Pellinor's son Perceval will, after his father's death, be brought up in the Waste Forest in Wales (presumably one of the Welsh territories devastated by the Dolorous Blow that killed Lambor) and go on to take up the pursuit of the Questing Beast.

Shortly after Pellinor has set off again in pursuit of the bizarre creature, King Arthur meets Merlin for the first time. The prophet explains that the king's nightmare is caused by his having committed incest, however unintentionally. Furthermore, in sleeping with his half-sister, he has begotten a son from whom "great evil will come to the land" (169). As for the Questing Beast, so "grotesque and strange of form" (171), Merlin will tell him nothing save that it constitutes one of the Adventures of the Holy Grail; but he will learn the truth about it from Perceval the Welshman ("one of the best knights in the world, full of grace in the eyes of Our Lord, for he will keep his virginity surely and marvellously"[5]), who will witness the destruction of the Beast at the hands of Palomides the Saracen.

Merlin now reveals that he is *li boins devins* about whom the king has heard so much and that he knows the truth about Arthur's parentage. The king is delighted to learn that he is the son of Uther Pendragon and summons his mother to Carduel to tell her story to the court. When Igerna arrives, she brings with her Morgan, her youngest daughter, who is by far the most beautiful maiden at court that day.

> Unquestionably she was a beautiful girl up to the time she began to learn enchantments and magic charms; but once the enemy entered her and she was inspired with sensuality and the devil, she lost her beauty so completely that she became very ugly, nor did anyone think her beautiful after that, unless he was under a spell [172].

As we will see, Morgan, free from the nunnery, will be submitting several men to her charms (*charroies*), despite the fact that her brother marries her off to King Urien, a direct descendant of King Galahad of Wales and therefore also of Joseph of Arimathea. She will bear Urien a son, the noble hero Yvain, one of the most illustrious of the Arthurian knights; but the antagonism that soon develops between her and her husband may not just be a product of her roving eye.

As one of the Fatal Sisters, she is a representative of that Goddess whom the family of the Grail are intent on supplanting. In fact, the identification of Morgan the Fay as the mother of Yvain tells us something about her mythical prehistory and shows us that the description of her by Hartmann von Aue as a "goddess" is not just a throwaway remark.

Yvain is the French form of the Welsh personal name Owein—and Owein, son of Urien, is one of the few undoubtedly historical characters to be found at Arthur's court—if somewhat anachronistically, since his father was king of a northern British kingdom in the late sixth century. The memory of the historical Urien was preserved because of two famous victories, celebrated by the bard Taliesin, who was for a while his praise-poet at court. By the twelfth century, however, the historical facts are becoming blurred: Geoffrey of Monmouth makes him King of Moray (in the far north-east) and the brother of King Loth; while the romances make him king of the distinctly mythical realms of Gorre and Garlot. Moreover, in Welsh tradition, Urien's son Owein is the product of a mythical encounter.

The Welsh Triads describe Owein as the son of Modron, daughter of Afallach (*TYP* 195). An oral tale from the sixteenth century embellishes this brief statement with an account of how Urien meets a woman washing at a ford, who claims to be the daughter of the King of Annwfn. She must wait at the ford until she conceives a son on a Christian man and Urien duly obliges, fathering Owein.

Despite the lateness of the source, Rachel Bromwich sees this tale as reflecting a Celtic myth of great antiquity in which the ancestor deity Afallach has become identified with the King of Annwfn (450) and with the island of Avalon as its eponymous ruler (275). This myth became attributed to the historical ruler Urien because of his heroic status: "a myth which depicted him as mating with the locally worshipped goddess *Modron*, and which depicted his famous son Owein as a fruit of their union" (451).

But: if Morgan as the mother of Yvain can be identified with Modron as the mother of Owein, who is Modron?

Her name indicates that she is the Romano-Celtic Matrona, the divine Great Mother who gave her name to the River Marne and whose cult may be associated with that of the Three Mothers, which was attested in Roman Britain (449). Modron is primarily remembered in Welsh tradition as the mother of Mabon, a figure derived from a Celtic god whose cult is attested in North Britain: Maponos, the Great Youth or Divine Son of the mother goddess Matrona (424). From this we can begin to see Morgan and her two sisters—each of whom are associated in the prose cycles with one or more heroic sons—as survivals in Arthurian romance of the Three Mothers.

But, if the Fatal Sisters now stand revealed as the three faces of the mother goddess of British mythology, the king is about to seriously offend the Great Mother by threatening her newborn child, as we will see shortly.

The Sword of the Lake

Meanwhile, as we learn from the Post-Vulgate Merlin Continuation, when the various surviving players in the conception and fostering of Arthur have all come forth to tell their stories, the nobles of the realm know that he is king by inheritance as well as by divine selection. This is just as well, for the sign of that selection—the sword that he drew from the stone to prove his right to rule—shatters shortly afterwards in the course of a fight with King Pellinor and his life is only saved by the intervention of Merlin, who casts Pellinor into a deep sleep and hurries Arthur off to a hermitage to heal his wounds.

Arthur is naturally concerned about the loss of his sword, but Merlin reassures him that he can get a good sword from a lake where fays dwell (*un lach ou fées habitent*). Merlin himself cannot get the sword for him: he has no power over it. Clearly there is a magic here to rival Merlin's own.

Leaving the hermitage two days later, they ride until they arrive near to the sea, turn right toward a mountain and come upon a very deep lake, into which no one could go without dying, unless he had the blessing of the fays. Tantalizingly, a hand and lower arm appear above the surface of the water, clad in white silk, holding the good sword of which Merlin had spoken; but the king can see no way of getting it.

At that moment a maiden is seen riding at great speed towards them from the direction of the sea. She greets them and explains that she was in a hurry to meet them, because she alone could obtain the sword for the king and he alone could make the best use of it. In return, the king must agree to give her the first thing she asks of him.

Arthur promises to do so and the lady steps lightly over the surface of the lake, not even getting her feet wet. She seizes the sword from the hand (which disappears back beneath the water) and returns to the shore to give it to the king, omitting to tell him its name but reminding him that he now owes her a reward.

When she leaves, Merlin commends her to God and thanks her repeatedly for her kindness: an acknowledgment, perhaps, that she is his equal, if not his superior, in magical status. As far as we know, Merlin and this maiden will never meet again in this life; but Arthur will encounter her shortly afterwards in shocking circumstances—although, not as shocking as the events that follow immediately his gaining of the Sword of the Lake.

Under pressure from the king, Merlin has explained to Arthur that his kingdom will be destroyed by a man who will be born on the First of May (the old pagan feast of Beltane, when the powers of evil were believed to be at their height[6]), but he refuses to disclose the identity of the child, since he will not be complicit in its murder. The king, however, is prepared to take drastic action to secure the future of his realm: he orders that all children born on that day should be brought to him and he has them set adrift on the sea in a master-less ship, thus allowing divine Providence to decide their fate.

King Loth sends the child Mordred (whom he believes to be his own son) to Arthur, as commanded, not knowing what the king has in store for him and all the other children born at the same time. But what none of the participants in this extraordinary story know, is that Mordred never makes it to the court of the man whom everyone thinks is his uncle, but who is really his father: as the ship that carries him leaves Orkney it is caught in a violent storm and wrecked on the shore of the mainland. Only little Mordred survives, floating to safety in his cradle. He will grow up to have his revenge on the father who abandoned him to his fate. As for Morgause, she never forgives her brother for Mordred's disappearance, despite Merlin's reassurance that all the children are safe and well.

The Ill-Fated Sword of Avalon

Meanwhile, other family hatreds are about to erupt in Arthur's court, which have a convoluted relationship to the gift of the Sword of the Lake.

The king is at dinner in Camelot when a maiden arrives, bearing a sword which she cannot un-girdle from her waist. It was given to her by the Lady of the Isle of Avalon and only the most loyal of knights can draw from its scabbard. It is Balin the Savage, a poor knight from Northumberland, who succeeds in this when all others fail. He is about to leave the court, taking the sword with him despite the maiden's warning that it carries a curse (that the first man he kills with it will be the man he loves most in the world, who will kill him with it in return), when the lady who gave Excalibur to Arthur enters and, after telling the king the name of his sword for the first time, insists that he discharge his debt to her.

She demands as her gift either the head of the maiden who brought the sword or the head of Balin, leading to a string of accusations and counter-accusations concerning the deaths of family members, which is only brought to an end when Balin draws the accursed sword and strikes off the head of the Lake Lady. He insists that she was the falsest lady who ever entered Arthur's court and had killed one of his brothers. Notwithstanding, Balin is forced to leave the court because he has killed someone who, as a guest, was under the king's protection. The knight sends the head of the Maiden of the Lake of Fays to his friends in Northumberland, so that they know he has avenged his brother's death.

This is the first time that we see the fairy magic of Avalon working against that of the Lake. Our first encounter with the Lady of the Isle of Avalon in the poetry of Geoffrey of Monmouth is as a healer, a teacher and a woman of knowledge, albeit one possessed of the supernatural powers of shape-shifting and flight. In the Post-Vulgate Cycle, however, this Lady's motives appear to be altogether less beneficent and her actions set her in opposition to the Maiden of the Lake of Fays: for it is the Lady of the Isle of Avalon who has provided the accursed sword that is brought to Camelot where it ends up being used to strike off the head of the lady who gave Arthur his sword Excalibur.

The ramifications of this become even more convoluted when we remember that Excalibur is forged in Avalon: so the magic of that island can be used for good or ill. This in itself is not surprising: and if Geoffrey's Morgen, as seems likely, is the same Lady of the Isle of Avalon who created Arthur's magical sword,[7] this fits well with her role as his healer: The sword confers victory on him in life but, when he must change his life, he returns it to the Lake and puts himself in Morgen's care.

As for the Ill-Fated Sword, we have no reason to assume that its magic was ever intended to be used against Arthur. However, very soon the Post-Vulgate will show the Lady of the Isle of Avalon acting murderously towards the king and it is this transition in her character that we must endeavor to explain. But for that, we will have to await later chapters, where we will also discuss some of the other curious aspects of this story: the Northumberland connection, the theme of magical swords and their use for beheading—and, above all, the symbolism of the lake.

But, for now, we must pursue Balin the Savage on his ill-fated journey to the Castle of the Grail.

NINE

Moon Magic

> Little by little the veil is being lifted and here and there, in dim valleys, and on misty heights we discern the forms of these early Arthurian heroes, we see their movements, we hear at times their speech. The vision is not for long, the curtain falls again, but it is less impenetrable than it was of old, and we know it now for what it is, a veil merely, and no impassable barrier ... a survival of that early Fairyland which preceded the ordered and chivalric splendours of Arthur's kingdom.[1]
>
> —Jessie L. Weston

In the last chapter we saw how the demons tried to create an evil prophet, a type of Antichrist, whom they invest with knowledge of the past; but how the Devil's son, Merlin, is saved by his mother's faith and invested by God with a superior knowledge, that of the future. Merlin uses his powers to aid the Pendragon dynasty, the heirs of Christian Rome, against its pagan enemies, to create Stonehenge as a monument to pagan treachery and to inform King Arthur and the heroes of Logres about the Adventures of the Holy Grail, of which he is the prophet.

In this chapter we will see how he is destroyed by his love for a magical woman. But, if his fate can be seen as an episode in the battle between Goddess and Grail for Arthur's Promised Land, it is one in which the apparently supernatural powers of an enchantress are really the product of dangerous learning. At the same time, the virginity of the devotees of the moon goddess has become subsumed by the Christian man's fear of women's sexuality, creating a more malign Lady of the Lake than was presented in the earlier Vulgate Cycle.

We will also see the limits of Merlin's powers: the Prophet of the Grail can foresee but not prevent the Dolorous Blow that will maim the Fisher King, for the act will be carried out by a man who is cursed by an older magic than Merlin's, the magic of Avalon and its Lady.

A Man Born for Destruction

Balin the Savage, who is now known as the Knight with Two Swords, seems to be plagued by ill-luck wherever he goes: in addition to the consequences of his historic feud with the Maiden of the Lake of Fays, he now seems to have fallen foul of the Lady of the Isle of Avalon, whose sword we can perhaps see as an anti–Excalibur: for Excalibur is a weapon also forged in Avalon[2] and one that, as soon as its name is revealed, brings death to the maiden in whose gift it is. Death is also the fate of a knight who pursues Balin, intent on avenging the insult to King Arthur's honor—and of the knight's lady, who kills herself with Balin's sword when she sees her lover dead.

At that moment Merlin turns up and demands to know why Balin didn't act more quickly to stop her: "You won't be so slow," he prophesies, "when you strike the Dolorous Blow by which three kingdoms will be impoverished and wasted for twenty-two years.[3] Know that there never was nor will be so dolorous or odious a blow struck by a man as this one will be, for all misery will result from it" (190).

But, just as he ignored the warning of the messenger from the Lady of the Isle of Avalon, Balin dismisses the prophetic warning of Merlin, saying that, if he believed it, he would kill himself first and thus prove Merlin a liar. Merlin vanishes away and Balin will only see him again when the prophecy is proved true.

Meanwhile a blow, which is almost as dolorous in its consequences as the one Merlin has prophesied, will soon be struck in a war that erupts when Rion, the King of the Giants—those primordial powers of Albion, long subdued but not wiped out—leads a rebel army against Arthur. Balin, desperate to redeem himself in the eyes of King Arthur, captures Rion. He inflicts such damage on the enemy that Arthur describes him as being "a man born on earth for human destruction" (197).

It is not Balin, however, but Pellinor, the Knight of the Questing Beast, now allied with Arthur, who strikes the most important blow of the battle; for he kills King Loth who, festering at the fate of his son Mordred (lost, presumed dead), has joined the rebels. The consequences of this are twofold: on the one hand, Pellinor and his sons will become some of Arthur's most important knights; on the other hand, they will earn the undying hatred of Gawain and his brothers, the sons of Loth. Thus two great families descended from the Company of the Grail—Loth being descended from Peter of Orkney and Pellinor from Bron—will become bitter enemies

Despite his treachery, Loth is given a right royal burial at which both Morgause and Morgan are present. At this time Morgan is almost ready to give birth to Yvain; but she is by now a malicious schemer, full of evil thoughts. She observes with admiration one of Merlin's feats of magic: Arthur has ordered the making of statues to commemorate his victory over King Loth, placing in the hands of the vanquished kings lighted candles but lamenting that they cannot burn forever. Merlin says that he will make the candles last until the day of his own death: at the time that the lights go out for the magician, so will the candles be extinguished.

Impressed, Morgan decides to learn sorcery from him and, in order to get him to do what *she* wants, she promises to do whatever *he* wants. Merlin is at once besotted with this beautiful woman; but she is a clever, ingenious and eager pupil and soon learns all she wants about the theory and practice of magic (*la scienche d'ingromanchie et l'art*). As soon as she has mastered the necromantic arts, she has no more need of him: she drives him away, threatening him with torture if he doesn't leave her alone, for she now finds his attentions excessive.

But if Merlin's love for her is out of balance (*fole amour*), she knows true love (*fine amour*) with a handsome knight of the kingdom, with whom she conducts an adulterous affair after the birth of her son.

One day King Arthur, who at this stage trusts Morgan implicitly, asks her to look after his sword and scabbard, requesting she take particular care of the latter, since it prevents its bearer from losing blood in battle. Morgan of course reveals everything to her lover, who prevails upon her to make an exact copy of the scabbard and substitute it for the original, which he wants to steal. This she arranges, having the artificer killed as soon as he has fabricated the counterfeit.

Unfortunately, in an episode that takes on a farcical character, Morgan gets the two scabbards mixed up and gives her lover the false one. After he nearly dies in battle, mistakenly imagining that he will be protected by the scabbard, he turns against Morgan and reveals the truth to the king. But Merlin, who is still in love with Morgan, lies for her and manages to persuade the king that it was her lover's idea, not hers. Consequently Arthur beheads the knight, thanking Providence that he didn't have his beloved sister executed for treason.

Morgan wants nothing less than her brother's death; but the reason for Morgan's hatred is never explained. Not even her lover understands it. But Lucy Allen Paton has suggested a back-story to the relationship between the king and his sister which may shed some light on it; for, if hell hath no fury like a woman scorned, how much worse must it be when the woman is a fay?

Paton considers it probable that the story of Arthur and Morgan in the *Merlin Continuation* is based on leftover fragments of an *ur*-mythos, "an original story to the effect that the fairy queen offered her love to Arthur, that he dwelt with her for a time, rejected her love, and thus incurred her displeasure, leading her to attempt to work him harm. She may have been represented as enticing him to her by a fairy stag and boat" (22), since these are elements that recur, albeit in disjointed form, in the Post-Vulgate, as we will see.

Now Begin the Adventures...

Meanwhile, Balin's destructive trajectory continues unabated. When two knights whom he encounters and whose safety he had guaranteed are killed by an invisible assassin, he determines to avenge them, even though Merlin warns him that if he pursues this quest he will strike a blow with the Avenging Lance that will have worse effects than the blow that King Varlan struck with the Sword of David. That blow turned the Land Beyond and parts of Wales into a Waste Land. The blow Balin strikes will turn the Kingdom of Logres and many others *a dolour et a destruction*; while the author of this *grant dolour* will himself die miserably. As if to add to everyone's woe, Merlin prophesies that Gawain will avenge the death of his father by killing King Pellinor in the very cemetery where Balin buries one of the knights he was supposed to protect.

Eventually Balin tracks down the invisible killer in the Castle of the Perilous Palace (better known as Corbenic). The assassin is called Garlon the Red, he wears magical armor that enables him to strike undetected and his brother is King Pellehan of Listenois, the most honored of princes, a man much loved by Our Lord. When Balin arrives at Corbenic, the king is hosting a magnificent feast but, rather than join in the festivities, Balin sits brooding, wondering how to attack Garlon in plain view of the court. As it happens, he does not need a stratagem, for the haughty murderer slaps Balin's face to get his attention and wishes him ill-health if he does nothing but think at the king's table; whereupon Balin draws his sword and cleaves Garlon's head all the way down to his chest!

There is uproar in the feasting hall and King Pellehan, mad with fury at the death of his brother, grabs a wooden rod and swings it at Balin; who raises his sword to defend himself, only to see the blade shatter just below the hilt. Now, we know Balin as the Knight with Two Swords; but, since gaining the ill-fated Sword of Avalon, he has not used it, except to behead the Maiden of the Lake of Fays with it—perhaps because he believes the maiden from whom he gained it, who said that the first man he killed with it would be the one he loves most in the world. And so it is that, having broken one sword, he does not draw the other in the Perilous Palace, but instead runs from room to room looking for a weapon with which to defend himself against King Pellehan.

Having searched two rooms fruitlessly, Balin opens the door to a third and, despite hearing a voice which announces that he is not worthy to enter, he dashes in. His senses are hit by the smell of spices and he sees a silver table, which we recognize (although Balin cannot) as the Table of the Grail, which Joseph of Arimathea brought to Britain: for in the middle of the table is a vessel of silver and gold and, standing in it with its point facing upwards, is a lance, which we know as the *Lanche Vengeresse*. Seeing only the weapon he needs and deaf to a voice that warns him that it would be sinful to touch it, Balin seizes the lance just as Pellehan enters the room and runs the king through both his thighs with it. Pellehan falls to the floor, grievously wounded and his assailant replaces the lance in the Grail where it stands upright, as before, though unsupported.

But as Balin starts to make his way out of the palace the walls start shaking, sections of masonry collapse and the inhabitants of the castle start to drop to the floor as if dead, thinking that the Last Judgment has come. A voice is heard throughout Corbenic: "Now begin the adventures and marvels of the Kingdom of Adventures, which will not cease until a high price is paid…" (*LG* IV, 212).

Balin himself is struck unconscious and lies for two days next to the maimed King Pellehan; until Merlin, knowing that the Lance of Vengeance could not be used without great marvels happening, turns up and finds them among the ruins. The Holy Lance and Vessel are unscathed, but Merlin laments that a "wretched, unfortunate sinner" should have touched "such a noble, precious shaft" with "his soiled, low-born hands, befouled by the base venom of sexual indulgence" (213).

We already know, from the Vulgate Quest, that an active sex life debars one from intimate access to the Grail Hallows. The Post-Vulgate adds poverty to the exclusionary factors and so Balin, it would appear, despite being the best knight of Logres, free of treachery, fraud and treason, lacks the two most important qualifications for spiritual success in the Promised Land of the Grail: noble birth and virginity.

Awakened by Merlin, Balin rides off through the Kingdom of Listenois, which is so devastated that it is from now on known as *li roiames de Terre Gastee* or the Strange Land[4]; all is "laid waste and turned to mourning and destruction" (214). Everywhere he goes, the survivors curse him and he has further reason to consider himself "the most unfortunate knight alive" (217) when a desperate lover, whom Balin tries to help, ends up killing the woman he loves, her new boyfriend and, finally, himself.

But, in the end, he is himself the victim of the curse of the Ill-Fated Sword, when fate leads him to a tower on an island with a barbaric custom: he must fight to the death with a knight who guards it and whoever wins the battle will stay on as (or become the new) lover of the Lady of the Castle. Just before undergoing this battle, Balin is persuaded to try on a new shield. Fate seems to be laughing at him when a young girl gives him a message from Merlin, to the effect that he will die that very day because he no longer bears a shield that his friends would recognize, adding that this misfortune is divine vengeance for his actions in King Pellehan's castle.

And this turns out to be the case when Balin, drawing at last the Ill-Fated Sword, kills with it his opponent, who turns out to be none other than his only surviving brother (the man who he loves most in the world) and who would never have followed the custom of the castle if he had seen Balin's true shield. At their dying request, the two who came from the same womb are buried in the same tomb.

Merlin once more arrives to oversee the aftermath of a tragedy. First of all, the prophet writes on the tombstone an inscription explaining that the knight who lies there is the striker of the Dolorous Blow; then, after creating various enchantments on the island (which will lead to its being renamed the Isle of Marvels), Merlin takes the Ill-Fated Sword, replaces the pommel and writes on it: GAWAIN WILL DIE BY THIS SWORD. And so it will prove, for the sword will be taken away by Lancelot and it is with this sword that he will give Gawain the wounds that will later lead to his death.

Finally Merlin uses his magic to fix a sword into a block of marble at the water's edge, prophesying that only the best knight in the world could draw it out unscathed.

> Then he pushed the stone and put it in the water and performed so many spells that it then went floating on the water a long time and was seen in many countries; it went so from place to place until it came to Camelot after a long time and arrived at the city gate the very day Galahad first came to court [222].

It is Galahad who is destined to undo what Balin has wrought, following a ceremony that mimics the one that conferred on Arthur the Sovereignty of Britain.

The adventure of the Sword in the Stone in both cases symbolizes divine election but, as we have seen, Arthur must also seek a sword from the Lake of Fays, suggesting a connection with an older religion than that of Christ, the indigenous cult of the Goddess. Further, as his barons point out, his power must be complemented by that of a woman. For it is woman who incarnates the Sovereignty and, as we saw in Chapter Three, there is no woman who better incarnates the old powers than Guenevere, whose mother may have originally been the Lady of a fairy fortress (the Castle of Carousal) and whose father is, in Welsh tradition, a giant.

And so it is that, as the Adventures of Logres that are the result of the Dolorous Blow begin, King Arthur makes the fateful decision that (as if his sisters Morgause and Morgan were not trouble enough) he will complicate his life even further by becoming entangled with another woman, whose unfaithfulness will constitute another strand in the web of fate that will ultimately destroy him. Nevertheless, Guenevere will bring as her dowry the Round Table, the institution with which he will forever be associated and whose precepts of chivalry will never be forgotten. And it may be that, if he continued to have the wise Merlin by his side, he might have better weathered the storm to come.

But it is not to be—for Merlin also will soon be undone by a femme fatale who we have already met in the Vulgate Cycle but who, in the Post-Vulgate, takes on more sinister characteristics.

The Huntress of Wild Things

We will first encounter the lady who will destroy the Prophet of the Grail in the days that follow Arthur's marriage to Guenevere in the city of Camelot.

Although Merlin warns him that her beauty will prove to be both a help and a hindrance to him, the king has fallen in love with the Princess of Cameliard. She brings with her as her dowry the Round Table which Uther Pendragon had constructed on Merlin's advice at Carduel: for, since the old king's death, it has been in the guardianship of King Leodegan, the father of the bride-to-be. The table seats a hundred and fifty knights but fifty of them have died in the civil wars that marked the last years of Uther's reign and one of Arthur's first tasks will be to make up the number with the valiant knights of his household. This he delegates to Merlin, who arranges for all the seats but two to be occupied by the time the king is married. What is more, the name of each of the knights miraculously appears on his wooden seat.

As for the two empty seats: with regard to one, Merlin explains to Arthur (as he did to Uther) that it is the Siege Perilous and that it must remain empty until the good knight who will bring an end to the Adventures of Logres sits in it. Furthermore, the man who will bring that knight into the world is not yet two years old and Merlin himself will not see the fulfilment of the quest that he has prophesied.

As for the second seat: this is filled shortly after Arthur and Guenevere are married in St. Stephen's Church in Camelot, when Pellinor, the Knight of the Questing Beast, enters and is led by Merlin to the seat next to Arthur's; so that, as the magician explains, the Round Table begins and ends with a king. But the noble status accorded to Pellinor rankles with Gawain, who had asked his uncle to knight him at the wedding feast and who vows vengeance on the man who killed his father, King Loth.

Nevertheless, for everyone apart from the disgruntled Orcadians, the rejoicing is great in the royal palace at Camelot. The festivities are in full swing when Merlin announces that three marvelous adventures are about to befall them, the first adventures to be achieved there.

At that moment they see a pure white stag come bounding through the gardens, hotly pursued by a brachet (a female hunting hound) and, after it, a beautiful green-clad maiden equipped with an ivory hunting horn and a bow and arrows, accompanied by a pack of thirty black dogs. Thirty is traditionally a lunar number, being the average number of days in a month, so we are immediately prepared for an epiphany of the moon goddess. The stag, of course, has been associated with the Goddess of the Wild Things since prehistoric times (as we saw in the first chapter). It runs into the great hall where the knights are eating and the brachet leaps onto it, only to be grabbed by one of the knights. He rides off with it, despite the protestations of the huntress. Meanwhile, the black dogs continue to chase the stag through the gardens until they are lost sight of, all of which leads the lady to complain to the king about the fact that this has befallen her in his household.

Merlin advises that two young men who have recently been knighted should take on the adventure: Gawain, the king's nephew, should be sent to bring back the head of the stag and such of the dogs as survive; while another newly knighted companion of the Round Table should fetch back the knight and the brachet, whether dead or alive.

Just as they are arranging this, an armed knight gallops into the hall, grabs the huntress, holds her over his horse's withers and rides off with her. She calls out that the king is obliged to free her and Merlin delegates this task to King Pellinor. Thus begin the Adventures of Logres, which will only end with the completion of the Grail Quest.

King Pellinor soon tracks down the kidnapped huntress and kills her abductor. Her cousin, who had also tried to rescue her, tells the king that she is "the daughter of a king and a queen[5] and comes of a noble line." But she delights only in hunting in forests and mocks the idea of having either a lover or a husband (239).

If she is not an avatar of the moon goddess, Ninienne certainly appears to be devoted to her, like the virginal "little bears" of Artemis, the goddess of untamed nature.

On their way back to Camelot, Pellinor and the huntress overhear by chance a treasonous plot against Arthur. The lady at once demonstrates that desire to protect the king which will be a consistent aspect of her character in all the versions of her story. When Pellinor tells her not to worry because Merlin "the wise prophet" is at the royal court, she acknowledges that the king is indeed safe, "for Merlin knows whatever is done or thought." This recognition of Merlin's preternatural power is an important key to understanding her later behavior towards the wise prophet (240).

At Camelot the huntress is persuaded to stay on to serve the queen for four months and this is plenty of time for Merlin to fall passionately in love with her. But Ninienne is wise beyond her years and knows enough about Merlin to be afraid that he will use his magical powers to bring shame upon her or have sex with her while she is asleep. Accordingly, she gets him to promise that he will not use his enchantments to cause her grief but, at the same time, she hints that he might be able to win her love if he teaches her as much magic as she asks. Eager to move their relationship on to the physical level, Merlin teaches her all about the sorcerous arts (*d'ingromanchie et d'enchantement*). She keeps him at a distance, but is nevertheless an apt pupil.

Eventually Arthur receives a message from Ninienne's father, the King of Northumberland (a realm that has a reputation for wildness and uninhabited forests), to the effect that he wants her to come home. Merlin, of course, is devastated until she disingenuously suggests he accompany her—not for a moment thinking that he will get permission from the king. But he goes anyway, sneaking off with her first thing in the morning. And now her fear turns to hate.

Initially, the odd couple cross the channel to Brittany and from there travel to the neighboring realm of Benoic, the kingdom ruled by Arthur's ally Ban. These are perilous marches, for Ban is at war with his neighbor King Claudas. It is while he is at the front that his queen receives Merlin and Ninienne at her castle near the River Loire.

Elaine, Queen of Benoic, has a young son, not yet a year old, whom they have baptized Galahad, but who is known affectionately as Lancelot. Ninienne is entranced by the good-looking child. The queen, watching her kiss the boy more than a hundred times, cannot know what will later transpire between her guest and her son or, indeed, that her guest is a huntress who always gets her prey—whether the hunted be a stag, a wise prophet or a beautiful child. Merlin does know, of course, but he wisely restricts himself to predicting Lancelot's future fame and prowess, making the queen happy by reassuring her that she will live to see the total defeat of her enemy Claudas.

Merlin now takes Ninienne to a beauty spot he knows called the Wood in the Valley and asks her if she would like to see the Lake of Diana, which she has often heard about: "Anything of Diana's would please me," she replies, "and I would gladly see it, for all her life she loved the pleasures of the forest as much as I do or more."

Arriving at the banks of a wide, deep lake they see a marble tomb beside a block of stone. Ninienne cannot know the irony invested in Merlin's words when he tells her "that here lies Faunus, Diana's lover, who loved her to excess, and she was false to him and killed him by the greatest treachery in the world. Such was his reward for loving her faithfully" (246).

It was in the days of the poet Virgil that Diana walked the earth, roaming and hunting through the forests of Britain and Gaul—and she made her home by this lake in the Wood in the Valley, which delighted her above all other spots. Here she met and fell in love with a young prince called Faunus, who came to live with her by the lake. But after two years of happiness, Diana became enamored of another young man, the lowly-born Felix, whom she met one day while out hunting: her new catch, one might say.

Eager to be shot of Faunus in order to accommodate her new love, she took advantage of the situation which arose when the prince came home wounded by wild beasts. The marble tomb was at that time filled with healing water which had been enchanted by the diabolical sorcery of a magician. Unbeknownst to Faunus, Diana had the water removed, but still persuaded him to lie down in the tomb: she would close the tombstone over him and then throw healing herbs through a hole in the stone.

But it is not herbs that Diana pours over the unfortunate young man, once he has lain down under the heavy tombstone, but boiling lead. He is burnt alive: a crime so horrific that, when Felix hears what she has done, his first act is to draw his sword and cut off her head. Her body is thrown into the lake, which henceforth bears her name.

An Excursion to the Lake of the Moon

It is at this point that those familiar with the legend of the Lady of the Lake may experience a feeling of déjà vu and even begin to wonder how many lakes there are and how many ladies are associated with them. For the story that we are most familiar with, from Malory and Tennyson (and via their retellings, with the countless modern versions in literature and film—after all, who can forget Monty Python's "watery tart" and her "farcical aquatic ceremony"?) is of the lake-dwelling lady who gives King Arthur his sword Excalibur, the sword that he must return to the lake at the end of his life in order that he can be taken to Avalon for healing.

This story is in fact presented as an earlier episode in the Post-Vulgate Cycle, the events occurring before his marriage and shortly after his coronation, as we saw in the last chapter. Although it is clear that the Maiden of the Lake of Fays, who gives to Arthur his sword Excalibur and is beheaded by Balin, is not the same person as the huntress of the Lake of Diana, there are some interesting parallels between their stories:

There is, for example, the connection with Northumberland: a thickly-forested land that Merlin describes as "forbidding even to those who belong there, for there are places where no one has yet been" (*LG* I, 181). The Maiden of the Lake of Fays' disembodied head is dispatched there by Balin. Ninienne is sometimes described as the daughter of the King of Northumberland, sometimes not. One thing is clear: Northumberland is a mysterious *terra incognita* that we would not be surprised to find haunted by fays or by avatars of the Goddess of the Woods.

There is also the theme of beheading: The huntress Diana is beheaded by her lover Felix and her head is thrown into the lake which henceforth bears her name. The Maiden of the Lake of Fays demands the beheading either of the maiden who brought the Ill-Fated Sword of Avalon to Camelot, or of Balin, who won it, but in the event it is she who loses her head.

Thirdly is the theme of magical swords: Excalibur, the sword given to Arthur by the Maiden of the Lake of Fays, was, according to the chronicles, forged in Avalon. It is another, ill-fated sword connected with Avalon—perhaps forged there, certainly in the gift of its Lady—that is brought to Camelot. Excalibur confers victory on whoever wields it, whereas the Avalonian sword won by Balin carries with it a curse. The magic of the island where Arthur will ultimately dwell can clearly be used for good or ill and its power may be a match for that of Merlin himself.

Fourthly, of course, is the lake itself: although the Lake of Fays is apparently situated on the south coast of Britain and the Lake of Diana in Brittany, we might be forgiven for wondering whether lakes such as these can really be located on a terrestrial map. Moreover if fays are as much a part of the mythology of the moon goddess as is the virgin huntress, we may also wonder whether in fact we are looking at different localizations in time and space of the same, archetypal lake: the Lake of the Moon.

Another localization of the lunar lake occurs in Greek mythology, where it is situated in Thessaly, on the western side of Mount Pelion. Lake Karla, as it is now known, was once called Boibeis after Phoebe, who was the Titaness of the Moon and the grandmother of Artemis. Her myth recounts that, at the beginning of time, Phoebe came forth from the lake and took, as her lover, the god Hermes (a magician and trickster figure like Merlin). As Carl Kerényi has pointed out, when we encounter another myth in which Hermes is the lover of Artemis, we are in fact dealing with another version of the same story, the myth of the birth from a lake of the Great Goddess of the Moon and her love affair with a magical being (171): For the grand-daughter of Phoebe is the Titaness reborn, just as the daughter of the godson of Diana is the Goddess of the Woods in mortal guise.

The British myth is less kind to its euhemerized deities than is the classical myth to its divinities. It is perhaps precisely because of the pagan and diabolical origins of Ninienne and Merlin that the medieval Christian storytellers are uncomfortable with the idea of a happy ending: for the Lake of Phoebe is so named because she is born from it, whereas the Lake of Diana is so called because her dismembered head is thrown into it! Equally, the fruit of the union of Hermes and Artemis is Eros; but the fruit of the unconsummated love of Merlin for Ninienne is Thanatos: death!

Damoisele del Lac

Ninienne is very struck by the story of Diana when she hears it and is disappointed to discover that the father of Faunus, the man Diana killed, had her home by the lake destroyed; for she has determined to live there herself. Accordingly she is delighted when Merlin offers to build new halls and houses there and disguise them so thoroughly that a visitor would see nothing but water.

It is worth pointing out here that the Lake of Fays is equally illusory. When Arthur asks Merlin how the maiden who gave him the sword was able to cross the water without getting her feet wet, the magician explains that she was not walking on the water but on a wooden bridge made invisible by spells.

Thus the magic of the fays as well as that of Merlin seems to come down to nothing but trickery: magic in the modern sense of illusion, rather than supernatural powers. The magic that Merlin teaches to Ninienne also seems to be used for nothing more than games and entertainment for her household; although she does seem to have learnt how to stop him reading her thoughts before she speaks and, what is even more important for her purposes, she has used necromancy (*ingremanchie*) to partially obscure his God-given knowledge of the future. Thus Merlin knows that someone is trying to kill him, but he doesn't know who.

Shortly after he has designed her new home, Merlin addresses Ninienne for the first time as the Lady of the Lake (*Damoisele del Lac*) and warns her that King Arthur is in great danger. The source of this peril is someone he trusts, who is very close to him: in fact, Arthur's fate seems to be as closely tied to her as Merlin's is to Ninienne. The danger comes from his youngest sister Morgan, in fact, who at this time is constantly at court with the queen.

We know that Morgan's proximity to Guenevere is not due to any love she holds for the queen, due to the latter's meddling in Morgan's affair with Guiomar. The truth is that a plot is being hatched, which will pit Morgan's magic against that of the Lady of the Lake for the first time.

A Magical Battle

Tolstoy famously remarked that each unhappy family experiences its misery in a unique way and some support for this observation can be found in the rather exceptional circumstances that surround the House of Constantine.

Arthur's family relations, already fatally damaged by his incestuous relationship with his eldest sister, are not improved by how things stand with the youngest. Morgan neither loves nor respects her husband King Urien, for which reason their son Yvain, newly made a knight, has no love for her. But she also hates her brother[6] with the hatred that only "bad, false people" always have towards those who are honorable and gracious—or, at least, so the *Merlin Continuation* assures us, in a passage that suggests that she was simply born evil. At the same time, she loves Accalon, a knight from Gaul, to distraction. Her feelings are at first reciprocated, so she hatches a plot to kill her brother and put her lover on the throne of Logres, with the aid of the Devil and her own magic skills (*LG* IV, 258).

Morgan also intends to somehow bring about the death of her hated husband Urien. The opportunity to kill two birds with one stone eventually presents itself, when the three principal men in her life go hunting together in the forest of Camelot.

There is something fated about this hunt from the very beginning. Arthur, Urien and Accalon identify the strongest and swiftest stag in a herd of deer and, in pursuing it, soon get cut off from their men. After a long chase their horses die of exhaustion and they find the stag and the hounds that had pursued it also all dead by the banks of a river.

Arthur blows his horn to summon his men; but they are too far away to hear it. The summons is answered instead by a mysterious ship covered with red silk hangings.[7] From it emerge twelve maidens who insist that the royal party stay the night aboard, since the day is nearly over. The hospitality they receive there is fit for a king—so much so, in fact, that Arthur marvels greatly at it all. He is astounded but not, unfortunately, suspicious—and gets a good night's sleep in a bed as comfortable as his own one in Camelot.

Things look rather different when he wakes up. For a start, he is no longer aboard a wondrous ship but in a pitch black dungeon, where the hospitality is considerably less lavish. There are about twenty other prisoners there and they explain that Arthur's only way out is by agreeing to fight on behalf of Domas (the treacherous Lord of the Tower of Ambush) against Domas' brother, with whom Domas has been engaged in a long-running dispute.

Domas has been kidnapping Arthur's knights to try to get them to fight for him but, knowing Domas to be in the wrong, they have all begun by refusing. It is only when the rigors of prison have weakened their resolve that some have eventually offered to fight but, by then, prison life has also weakened them bodily, so that Domas no longer considers them suitable candidates. Many of the prisoners have subsequently died.

The survivors urge Arthur not to make the same mistake but, rather, to offer his services while they are still of use. The king agrees—but only on condition that the imprisoned knights are released immediately. He will do what they should have done and put himself in God's hands.

On the day of the battle, a maiden arrives with a message from his sister: she has sent him his sword and scabbard, which she has been keeping for him (despite the unfortunate mix-up we heard about in the previous chapter). What Arthur does not know, since he still trusts his sister, is that she has once more been at the counterfeiting art and that this time she has made a perfect replica of the sword as well as of the scabbard. The real Excalibur and the magical scabbard that prevents its wearer from shedding blood, Morgan has sent to Accalon: who, after sleeping on the wondrous ship, has woken up in much more congenial circumstances than his liege lord.

Accalon in fact awakes in a lovely herb meadow beside a fountain but, confused by what has happened overnight, he starts cursing both his surroundings and all women, whom he sees as the source of treachery in the world. In his mind, the maidens of the ship were clearly the Devil's ministers (*fantosmes ou dyables*). But at that moment a dwarf arrives, bearing Excalibur and its scabbard, which he presents to the knight on behalf of the lady Morgan. As for how Accalon got where he is, the dwarf can tell him nothing except that what has happened to him must constitute part of the Adventures of Britain or of the enchantments of the land. Regardless, Accalon's mistress now commands him to undertake a battle against an oppressor.

When Arthur and Accalon take to the field, they are equally in the dark: neither knows against whom he is fighting, nor the extent of Morgan's treachery. But when he starts losing blood, Arthur realizes something is wrong. He is not alone: while they are still in Brittany Merlin warns Ninienne that Arthur's trusted sister, Morgan, has swapped the king's enchanted sword and scabbard for worthless counterfeits. The magician fears that Arthur will die in the ensuing battle.

Ninienne had once trusted Merlin to keep Arthur safe but she will now take a more direct role in the care of the king. First of all, she asks Merlin if he can use his powers to delay the battle between Arthur and Accalon long enough for them both to get there in time to save the king. Merlin says that he can manage a delay of twelve days; but that he fears that he will be killed treacherously if he returns to Logres from Brittany. What Merlin does not realize is that the treachery is close to home. Like Arthur, Merlin is in danger from a woman he trusts.

Merlin and Ninienne cross the Channel. On their way to the Perilous Forest they encounter two sorcerers, who attempt to rape Ninienne; but Merlin overcomes them by his superior skills and buries them alive in what, although he doesn't realize it, will turn out to be a foreshadowing of his own fate.

Ninienne has been saved by Merlin's magic; but she still feels nothing but hatred for him because he is a demon's son. Moreover, she is determined to use the magic he has taught her against him. Her chance comes when he brings her to a secret love nest in a rocky valley. A king's son had had it built as a hideaway for himself and his lowborn lover, where they could escape his father's disapproval; here they lived and were embalmed together when they died. Ninienne pretends to be taken with this story of faithful love and suggests that she and Merlin spend the night there. He shows her where the lovers are buried, using the power of his mind to lift a stone that would normally require the strength of ten men and revealing the two bodies in the sarcophagus.

Far from being horrified by the sight of the bodies, as Merlin feared, Ninienne claims to be delighted by this memorial to their undying love and insists on having her bed made up next to the tomb. Merlin does the same; but they are in separate beds, for Ninienne is determined to keep her virginity. However, Merlin is increasingly under the spell of Ninienne's enchantments, which, thanks to his desire for her, have enabled her to cloud his mind and memory. He falls into a troubled but heavy sleep and immediately he is unconscious Ninienne casts further spells until he is completely paralyzed.

Calling her retainers, she complains to them about the Devil's son who would deflower her and they are ready to dispatch him straightaway. But

Ninienne is too squeamish to witness his murder. Instead, she has him thrown into the sarcophagus with the lovers she claimed to admire and her retainers manage to replace the stone lid. Now she starts to work her magic, sealing the tomb of the lovers with the power of her conjuring; using, that is, the power not of physical strength but of words. No one apart from she herself will ever be able to move it in order to see Merlin alive or dead.

When Merlin comes round and realizes what has happened—that "a woman's mind" has defeated his and he has been given over to death by "a woman's wiles" (*LG* IV, 261)—he utters a cry which can be heard the length and breadth of Logres; but no one knows who has made it.

With Merlin out of the way and her virginity secure, Ninienne can now devote herself to the service of Arthur, taking the prophet's place as the king's magical defender. She sets out in all haste and arrives just in time to save the king's life. Arthur is weak from loss of blood and Accalon, wielding Excalibur and wearing the enchanted scabbard, is about to deliver the killer blow. The Lady of the Lake casts a spell that immobilizes the Knight of Gaul and the Sword of Avalon falls from his frozen fingers. Seizing his opportunity, Arthur grabs the sword that is rightfully his and tears the scabbard from Accalon's side.

All the blood that Accalon should have shed now flows freely, the protection of the scabbard having been withdrawn—and the dying Knight of Gaul dishes the dirt on Morgan who, he feels, has betrayed him as much as the king, by tricking him into bearing arms against his liege lord. Arthur now discovers the extent of his sister's treachery—that she stole Excalibur in order to kill him and set her lover on the throne of Logres—and can only forgive Accalon, who didn't know whom he was fighting. The only one to blame is Arthur's "false sister." Should she ever come to Camelot again, the king will take such vengeance on her that the people of the kingdom will talk about it long after his death.

When Accalon dies a few days later, Arthur sends his body to Morgan, with the message that he has done to her lover what she would have done to her brother: "Let her know that never was a betrayal as costly as this will be, if God gives me health, however she may flee into a distant or alien land" (263ff).

Enchanted to a Stone

The object of this opprobrium, meanwhile, had thought to dispatch her husband as well as her brother. When King Urien fell asleep on the ship on the river, he awoke in his own bed next to his wife; but his surprise didn't stop him from falling back to sleep. Morgan at this stage thinks her plot is all coming together: seizing her husband's sword, she is about to behead Urien in his sleep when their son Yvain intervenes, just in time, denouncing his mother as a wretched, diabolical agent of Satan (*feme maleuree et plainne de dyable et d'anemi*). The knights of the realm are right, he says, when they complain that she is forever about the Devil's work (*ouvrés par art d'anemi*). Incorrigible, she falls on her son's mercy, thanks him for preventing her from committing murder and thereby losing her soul and persuades him not to disgrace his family by speaking of what has happened. Her poor husband eventually wakes up, none the wiser.

When the dead body of Accalon is delivered to Camelot, along with the king's message, Morgan pretends it's all a joke. But, once alone, she summons twelve of her maidens and tells them that they are leaving presently for the Kingdom of Garlot, where she will be safe from her brother. At moonrise she sets off with thirty retainers but, the next day, makes a detour to the abbey where Arthur is recovering from his wounds. She finds the king asleep, his sword clutched tightly in his hand. But the scabbard is at his feet and this she takes, before making a hasty getaway.

When Arthur awakes, he is quick to establish what has happened and sets out in hot pursuit, nearly catching up with Morgan in a valley before she can lose herself in a nearby forest. Cornered, Morgan resorts to desperate measures: she hurls the scabbard into a lake in the valley (foreshadowing the casting of Excalibur itself into the Lake of Fays) and turns herself and her retinue into stone statues. She is unable to use her magic spells on Arthur himself, she realizes, because he is under the protection of someone as powerful as herself, if not more so. This is none other than the maiden huntress who has learnt all she knows of the necromantic arts (*de ingromanchie et des enchantemens*) from the king of magicians (*li souverains des devineurs*), that is, from Merlin, the very man whom she has buried alive.

Morgan herself has learnt not a little from that same "sovereign diviner" and so, when Arthur gives up the pursuit, believing that God had punished Morgan by turning her to stone, she restores herself and her followers to life and sets off for her castle in Garlot, where she is accorded great honor as the king's sister. It is here that she has built a tomb in which she conceals an ivory box which Merlin had given her when they were an item. The box contains an inscription on which is written the way in which Arthur and Gawain will die, along with the name of their killer (Morgan's nephew Mordred, as it turns out). But Morgan has never opened the box because Merlin had warned her that no woman could live if she saw the inscription. Many men would later die in a vain attempt to discover the fate of the king.

Not knowing the hour or manner of the king's death does not stop Morgan trying from afar to hasten the event: she sends one of her maidens to Arthur's court with a silk mantle as a present for the king, ostensibly a gift from the Lady of the Enchanted Isle (*la Damoisele de l'Isle Faee*). But the Lady of the Lake turns up, once again in the nick of time, to warn Arthur that this so-called "fairy maiden" is none other than his sister Morgan and that the mantle will kill whoever wears it. The king forces the maiden who brought the mantle to try it on, despite her protests that it is designed for a high-ranking man, not a lowly woman servant—and she instantly falls down dead.

Ninienne explains to the king that she is helping him, not so much for his own sake, but for the sake of the chivalrous institutions that he upholds. Arthur would like nothing more than for her to stay with him in Logres; but Ninienne is set on returning to her own realm of Brittany. It is while there that she will enter into the most well-known phase of her life: as the abductor and "fairy godmother" of the young prince of the neighboring kingdom of Benoic: Lancelot, who will as a result of his sojourn in her magical realm forever after bear the sobriquet, "of the Lake."

Ten

The Marvels of the Holy Grail

> What the Grail was from the first, that throughout its development it has remained, the symbol and witness to unseen realities, transcending this world of sense; on whatever plane the effort be made, the attempt to penetrate from the outer to the inner, to apprehend behind the sign the thing signified, to bring the lower, and temporary, life into contact with the higher and enduring is a task worthy the highest energies of man. I do not think it matters in the least whether or not the Grail was originally Christian, if it was from the first the symbol of spiritual endeavour.[1]
>
> —Jessie L Weston

The life and career of Lancelot of the Lake, which constitute the heart of the Vulgate Cycle, are only alluded to in the Post-Vulgate. It is possible to read the later cycle as a supplement to the Vulgate, telling us what else was going on while Lancelot and Guenevere were carrying on. At the same time, the Post-Vulgate shows us how the presence of the Grail, which has been spoken of so much by the late lamented Merlin, gradually impinges on the Knights of the Round Table. For the Waste Land, with its attendant perils, is slowly spreading into Logres, as a result of the Dolorous Blow struck by Balin.

A Country of Strange Adventures

The first knight to encounter one of the marvels of the sacred vessel is Morholt, the brother of the Queen of Ireland, best known for his death at the hands of Tristan, a deed which will launch the career of that famous lover. But in the *Merlin Continuation* we encounter Morholt at an earlier and happier time, when he teams up with Gawain and his cousin Yvain, who have left their uncle's court under a cloud. Yvain has in fact been banished from the court for no other reason than that he is the son of Morgan, whose murderous intentions are now known to the king—and despite the fact that (as we saw in the last chapter) Yvain has protected his father King Urien from being killed by that same murderess, whom he denounced as a devil in human form. Gawain takes his cousin's side and leaves Arthur's court with him and, after meeting up with Morholt, they travel through North Wales.

The three heroes are making their way through the forest of Arroy, a country of strange adventures, when they come across three damsels by a spring in a valley. The youngest damsel is no more than fifteen, the middle one about thirty years of age and the oldest must be at least seventy. The three damsels offer to lead them through the adventures of this country and the knights, accordingly, each choose a companion: Yvain, as the youngest of the trio, takes the elder lady, Morholt the middle one, while Gawain picks the youngest of the three. They agree to meet up at the spring in a year's time.

After several adventures Morholt and the maiden come to a crossroads marked by a large wooden cross with a marble block right before it. There are red letters cut into the stone which read: ON THIS BLOCK MAY ONE SEE MANY OF THE MARVELS OF THE HOLY GRAIL HAPPEN. However, it continues with the warning that anyone who does so will be killed or maimed, at least until the Good Knight puts an end to the adventures.

The maiden tells him it is called the Stone of the Stag, although she doesn't know why. Despite the dire warning, Morholt determines to stay there until he has witnessed "some of the adventures of the Holy Grail that men think so marvelous" (*LG* V, 16). They sit down under two elms that are nearby and watch until nightfall. In the moonlight they see two knights arrive, fight, make up and leave. A stag then lies down on the stone; only to be killed by four beagles, which are, in turn, swallowed up by a dragon. The dragon heals the stag and vomits up the beagles, which set off in pursuit of the flying stag. The dragon flies away.

Morholt doesn't know whether he's under a spell or dreaming, but falls asleep anyway. During the night he is stricken through the thighs by a spear and his squire and the maiden are killed.

No further explanation is given for these curious events, as though anything can happen (and probably will) once the Waste Land starts encroaching on our everyday reality. But the reference to dreaming suggests one approach, since in the manner of dreams previous events (known to the reader but not to Morholt) are jumbled here in oneiric fashion: a battle between two friends (Balin and Balan); a dragon (a creature that also appeared in Arthur's dream); a fatal blow by an invisible assailant (Garlon); a spear-thrust through the thighs (the Maimed King).

But another approach would be to look at the lunar imagery of the episode. We started, after all, with the appearance by a spring (the typical abode of fays) of three maidens representing the three ages of woman and perhaps the three faces of the Goddess who rules both the visible moon (with its three phases of waxing, full and waning) and the three seasons of the Earth (growing, harvest and dying). The marvels of the Holy Grail are seen by moonlight and include the sacred stag and hounds of the lunar huntress.

It is almost as if we are witnessing a symbolic battle between the encroaching Grail Christianity and the indigenous cult of the moon goddess. If this is so, it would explain a later episode, which can be interpreted as the Goddess showing her angry face.

The Knight of the Goddess

Feeble from loss of blood, Morholt is at first befriended by a passing knight who, on hearing what has befallen him, expresses no surprise ("for these are adventures of the Holy Grail") but then attacks him when he finds out who he is (he blames Morholt for the death of his father) and leaves him for dead (17).

Fortunately Gawain, who has been deserted by the youngest maiden of the spring, happens to come that way and takes Morholt to a nearby tower to be healed. Two months later, when Morholt is fully recovered, the companions set off again on their adventures; only to encounter an apparently old woman who tries to seduce them. Thinking she is at least a hundred years old the two knights mock her, insisting that they prefer younger women.

Now, on another occasion Gawain will face a similar challenge, but will handle it quite differently. In an English poem entitled "The Wedding of Sir Gawain"[2] he agrees to marry a hideous creature who is threatening his uncle; but, when he overcomes his revulsion and kisses her on their wedding night, she turns into the most beautiful woman he has ever seen. She then offers him the choice of having her beautiful at night and ugly during the day, or vice versa. Gawain gives *her* the choice and, by doing so, he has said the magic word; for what she really wants is *sovereignty* and that is what he, in his wisdom, has bestowed upon her. Or, rather, he has returned to her what is rightfully hers. Render unto the Goddess...

But in the Post-Vulgate Cycle (and consequently also in Malory, but not in medieval English poetry) the character of Gawain is blackened. Whereas in the earliest French poems he is the model of chivalry and courtesy, an advocate of peace and love but a superb fighter when he needs to be, the prose romances increasingly denigrate his behavior. Several knights, even one of his own brothers, are better fighters than him and the charming lover becomes ruthlessly promiscuous.

What is the reason for this changing depiction?

A clue can be found in an earlier passage, where we are told that Gawain "was of such a nature that in all seasons his strength doubled around noon and grew and increased more than any other man's" (*LG* IV, 272). Variations of this characteristic are found in several poems as well as in other prose romances, leading some early scholars to see it as the survival of an old solar myth which was later Christianized. But, in the Vulgate *Mort Artu*, it is explained away as a gift from God to show how much He values the prayers of the hermit who baptizes the Orcadian prince (*SRM* 681).

Jessie Weston, in her landmark study of the Gawain legend published at the end of the nineteenth century, argued that Gawain was in origin a solar hero from "remote Celtic antiquity" (1897, 15), whose lover was the Queen of the Otherworld (45). She considered that it is these pagan characteristics that explain his "remarkable and striking change" into "a mere libertine, cruel and treacherous" in "the most highly developed and ecclesiasticised form of the Grail legend" (9) with its "strongly moralising tendencies" (10).[3]

Read this way, Chrétien de Troyes' description of Gawain and one of his many lovers (called in this instance, appropriately enough, Lunete) as the sun and the moon (*CL* ll.2398–414) becomes not just a poetic metaphor but a mythic echo. It is thus that it has been interpreted by the early twentieth century scholar R.S. Loomis (63–4), who argued that Gawain's many Otherworldly lovers are "but different manifestations, different names for the same primeval divinity, whose power is felt in the mysterious influences of the moon, and whose beauty in the golden gorse and yellow fields of wheat. She has always borne many names…. Gawain was no light of love, for in spite of his many marriages, it was the same goddess he loved" (301). This theme has been taken up more recently by the prolific contemporary writer John Matthews, who hails Gawain as the archetypal Knight of the Goddess and argues that, as Her champion, he "underwent a form of character erosion similar to that of the Goddess herself" (21–2).

Although this curious element in his legend may suggest pagan origins, the factor which is most explicit in the stories and therefore most likely to have concerned the most "ecclesiasticized" and "moralizing" of his medieval readers (and romance writers) is his close connection with the Otherworld which, as the historian Ronald Hutton has pointed out, "as a realm (apparently) separate from the terrestrial one, which is neither heaven nor hell and is populated by superhumans who are not definitively good or evil ... has no place in Christian teachings."[4] It is Gawain who, of all Arthur's heroes, seems most at home in this intermediate space and most in love with its female denizens. Indeed, the mother of his famous son, Gingalin, is a fay.

But in the Post-Vulgate, confronted with another Loathly Damsel, Gawain resorts to mockery. There is no longer any question of his acknowledging the Goddess as Old Woman or of according her the sovereignty and, consequently, he falls victim to her sorcery. Bespelled, he and Morholt start fighting each other; but are disenchanted by one of the Maidens of the Lake who has been taught magic by Merlin. She explains to them what we have probably already guessed: the centenarian is really "one of the most beautiful ladies in the world"; but she holds *this* world in disdain and uses her knowledge of spells to transform herself into an image that this world disdains, that of an aged crone. Interested only in the outward signs of beauty, Gawain rejects her even though she promises him that he would gain far more honor from loving her than from a much younger lady (*LG* V, 19f). It is a test that he has failed and it will set the tone for the rest of his career in the Post-Vulgate Cycle.

How that career will eventually conclude is shortly thereafter made known to him, when he and Morholt travel together to the Rock of the Maidens where they meet twelve sisters who divine the future. They even overhear one predicting that Gawain's death will be at the hands of a friend and that it will presage the decline of Great Britain.

Nevertheless, the knights are eager to join the ladies in their palace atop the rock, not knowing that it is really a place of imprisonment: the twelve have been banished there by Merlin, whom they had challenged in a magical contest. And now the knights are also prisoners of glamour and illusion. At first learning spells and games, waited on hand and foot by beautiful maidens, they end up lying fully clothed in bed while dreaming that they are off to foreign lands, having chivalric adventures. They no longer have any sense of who or where they are, nor of the passage of time.

It is as if they are still suffering from the curse of the Old Woman: they have experienced the dark side of Faerie. For the Otherworld is only a paradise when it is experienced in the light of consciousness, perceived with the active imagination and not with that passive imagination which is only a receiver for sensory impressions. As Henry Corbin puts it, the imaginal world can be paradise or hell. Gawain and Morholt only *believe* that they are in Heaven. They are no longer seeing outer reality with what Blake called the "perishable" eye, but nor are their Imaginative Eyes open.

The Cry of Merlin

Yvain, with whom Gawain had left the court and who has had similar experiences to Morholt at the Stone of the Stag, attempts to rescue his former companions, but to no avail. That task will be achieved by Gawain's younger brother Gaheriet. But meanwhile Yvain is welcomed back at court, his uncle regretting the way he blamed the son for the crimes of the mother. Arthur suggests that they ask Merlin to free the heroes from the Rock of the Maidens, so word is sent out to find the magician but, instead, word comes back of his death.

Yvain's cousin Bademagu, it transpires, had happened to be travelling through the Perilous Forest when he came upon the magically-sealed stone sarcophagus only four days after Merlin had been placed inside it. Bademagu tried to lift the stone lid but he heard Merlin's voice declare that no-one can free him unless it should be she herself who put him there.

At last the court knows the origin of the cry that had resounded throughout the length and breadth of Logres. Everyone agrees that the realm has been diminished by the loss of Merlin the Wise; but that loss is also ours, when we consider what it means for the prophet to be buried in the ground.

The true prophet, as Corbin has shown, is not someone who predicts the future, although the prophetic message is not bound by the constraints of linear time (1986b, 338) and may astound later generations by the accuracy of its "forecasts." Rather, the prophet is "someone of more than human inspiration, who brings a divine message which ordinary people would be incapable of attaining by themselves" (1998b, 209). If Merlin is, as he describes himself, "left and forgotten" (*LG* I, 421), it is not because no one remembers his name—that will survive the centuries—but because he personifies that active imagination which allows us to perceive a world that we in the West have left behind, with the triumph of rationalism and scientific materialism (what Blake calls "fixed" as opposed to "sweet" science). That world is what Corbin calls the *mundus imaginalis* and it is that world— on whose existence depends "the truth of the *spiritual sense* perceived in the imaginative data of prophetic revelations" (1995, 11)—which we have forgotten. It has become a Lost Continent and, with its loss, which Corbin considers to be nothing less than a metaphysical tragedy, we have forgotten the meaning of Merlin.

William Blake tried to restore the spiritual meaning of prophecy, so it is not surprising that he should have hailed Merlin as "immortal Imagination" (*BCW* 663) and lamented his unknown death. But the Prophet of Albion himself has also been largely left and forgotten—dismissed as an incomprehensible eccentric at best, or as a madman at worst—because he wanted to restore to poetry "the grandeur of Inspiration" and "clothe" Albion with Imagination (533).

Corbin was one of the most important writers in the latter half of the twentieth century to take up Blake's poetic challenge and warn about the consequences of the triumph of Rational Demonstration over Faith and Inspiration for the middle realm of the Imagination. For if this intermediate realm, he wrote (1998b, 125f), "were to disappear—if we were to lose all trace of it—then prophetic and mystical visionary experiences … would all lose their place. They would literally "no longer take place," for their place is neither of the sensory nor the intellectual world, but that of the intermediary … world where the body is spiritualized, and the spiritual is embodied.… In the absence of the imaginal world, we are reduced to mere allegory, for the active Imagination itself has been downgraded to the status of producer of the imaginary."

Blake also rejected allegory as an "inferior kind of Poetry" (*BCW* 604) while J.R.R. Tolkien (to whom we will return in the last chapter), who did so much to relocate Faerie in the English imagination, disliked "conscious and intentional allegory" (1981, 145). As Corbin explains elsewhere, "allegory is a sheathing or, rather, a disguising, of something that is already known or knowable otherwise, while the appearance of an Image having the quality of a symbol is … unconditional and irreducible, the appearance of something that cannot manifest itself otherwise to the world where we are" (1995, 18). So, whereas the symbolic image presents us with metaphors of an otherwise un-manifested reality, allegory is reductive and literal—and literalism, in both religion and science, is what plagues our contemporary world, where the imaginal has become the merely imaginary.

The fatal consequences of literalism are spelt out in an early thirteenth century prose romance which falls outside of the great cycles and which is, paradoxically, almost as full of heavy-handed allegorizing as the Vulgate *Queste* and *Estoire del Saint Graal* but, at the same time, is full of Otherworldly paganism (Williams, 264). Nevertheless, the Romance of Perlesvaus presents us with some interesting variations on familiar themes: for example, there is a unique account of the tomb of Merlin which here is not in a forest but in the castle of Tintagel; but outside rather than inside the chapel—and, moreover, empty, because, as soon as the body was placed in the tomb "it was borne away by God, or by the devil" (*HBG* 181). Thus in death, as in life, Merlin remains ambiguously situated between Heaven and Hell.

But one of the most striking episodes in this romance occurs right at the beginning. As a result of Perceval's failure to ask the Grail Question, the kingdom has fallen into decline (a variant on the theme of the Waste

Land spreading into Logres) and so, in order to restore his flagging spirits, King Arthur determines to set out on adventure. Accompanied only by a squire, a grandson of King Urien called Cahus, Arthur will seek out the fabled Chapel of St Augustine, "which stands in the White Forest and can only be found by chance" (21).

But as chance, or Fate, will have it, Arthur will make the journey alone. For that night, the squire has what at first seems like a typical anxiety dream, in which he finds that the king has gone without him. It soon becomes less typical: Saddling up, he rides through the forest until he comes to a chapel in a clearing, surrounded by a cemetery filled with tombs. In the chapel he finds a dead body on a bier lit by four candles. Surprised that he cannot see the king anywhere, he takes one of the golden candlesticks and rides off with it; only to be stopped in his tracks by "a dark and ugly man" who demands that he hand it over (22). When Cahus refuses, because he wants to give it to the king, the dark man thrusts a knife into his side and the squire wakes up, as is usually the way with dreams.

But there is an important difference to other dreams, for this one has "come true most horribly": He still possesses the golden candlestick and there is a dagger stuck in his side. When it is pulled out, he dies (23).

Jessie Weston claimed that this story had a "semi-historical character," relating events that had actually taken place in Northumberland (that forbidding *terra incognita* again!), when a young man took a "test of fitness for an initiation" into "the sources of physical life" which "would probably consist in a contact with the horrors of physical death." Weston believed that such initiation rituals, dating back to the times of the pagan mystery religions, had survived in remote, out-of-the-way parts of Britain—and that one such, which had gone "horribly" wrong, "had made a profound impression upon the popular imagination." Weston was, of course, aware that she might risk "startling" her early twentieth century readers when she declared that the Cahus episode was the story of an initiatory test *carried out on the astral plane, and reacting with fatal results upon the physical* (1920, 182); but it is also a rather literal reading.

An alternative approach would be to see the story as a commentary on the fatal consequences of literalism itself. There is a long tradition of interpreting events in the dream world as having an *inverse* relation to events in our world: thus, a dream death means a birth in the waking world and vice versa (Corbin 1983, 14*n*1). But in *Perlesvaus*, the candle-stick and knife cross over directly into our world and so, unfortunately, does the wound. The consequence is the physical death of Cahus. Rather than his initiatory death symbolizing a psychic rebirth, he *literally* dies! Or, to put it another way, *the letter killeth*...

But it is precisely the triumph of literalism that we see in the spread of a murderous "provisional wing" of religious fundamentalists as well as in the "progress" of scientific materialism, with more long term but no less fatal consequences for the environment. Thus the novelist Wilson Harris can trace in Merlin's cry a lament for all those species, "witnesses to the mystery of creation," which have been flattened by the wheel of "man-made progress" in a "man-made world" (11f) that now bears witness only to the "illiteracies of the imagination" (5).

If the letter kills, the spirit blows where it lists. But what happens when the spirit is captured, unable to blow freely across the Earth but is imprisoned inside it? If Merlin embodies the imagination, what happens when that faculty of perception is wrenched from its intermediate position in the human being where it serves as a bridge between body and mind?

The unmoored imagination can make us lose our minds as easily as we can lose touch with our bodies. Entombed in the Earth, its images are degraded: they lose their *symbolic function* and are reduced "to the level of sensory perception pure and simple." This degradation comes about because our "scientific civilization" has turned its back on "traditional culture" (Corbin 1995, 30f).

Here the perspective of Corbin, the Protestant scholar of Islamic esotericism, resonates with that of the Islamic philosopher Seyyed Hossein Nasr, who argues that solving the environmental crisis requires "a very radical transformation" in modern consciousness: nothing less than the rediscovery of "the traditional way of looking at the world of nature as sacred presence" (6). Or, as Blake put it, of recognizing that *everything that lives is holy…*

For Corbin, this radical transformation requires a re-evaluation, a recognition of the *noetic* function of the Image, that is, the power of the visionary Image to transform consciousness. But he warns that this noetic function can become hellish when the images that surround us are merely those of film or television—and for that matter, he might have added, of advertising billboards and computer screens. We live in an "image-oriented" culture, but it is one whose images "remain tenaciously bound to sense-perception" (1998b, 166f). Nor should we confuse "spiritual vision of the spiritual world with what relates to the fantasy of science fiction. There is an abyss between the two" (1995, 33*n*14).

Nevertheless, we must acknowledge that the growth of heroic fantasy literature in the twentieth century is the nearest thing that we have to the Arthurian legends and that the Otherworld of the medieval imagination finds its modern echo in the other worlds of science fiction. As the contemporary Canadian novelist Margaret Atwood, herself a writer of speculative fiction, argues, "SF stories can explore the outer reaches of the imagination," creating, in the process, "patterns that purport to depict the relationship of man to the universe, a depiction that takes us in the direction of religion and ultimately into the preoccupations of metaphysics and mythologies" (63–4). "For every question that myths address, SF has addressed also. Indeed, it's arguable that this form and its subforms have subsumed the mythic areas abandoned by literature" after Milton, Bunyan and Blake (55f). However impoverished these imagined worlds may be in comparison to those of ancient mythology, they speak to the need of the secularized soul for something that can bridge the gap between banal, everyday earthbound reality and a spiritual yearning that becomes increasingly utopian and purely *imaginary* (in the sense of *unreal*) as we lose all trace of the traditional sense of sacred reality.

Even super-hero comics (combining word and image like cut-price, mass-produced heirs of Blake's illuminated works) provide us with contemporary Knights of the Round Table, leaguing for justice or assembling to avenge injustice: avatars of ancient gods whether clothed in medieval armor or twenty first century spandex. The Thirties, the decade that began with the triumph of Nazism and ended with the outbreak of the Second World War, also witnessed the arrival of Superman from the doomed planet Krypton, the bursting of Conan the Barbarian fully-formed from the head of a writer of pulp fiction (*REH* xxi–ii) and the publication of *The Hobbit*, a prelude to what would develop into the most authentically mythic of modern fantasy worlds.[5] So we should not be surprised to learn that Corbin hailed the adult sequel to Tolkien's children's fairy-tale as a modern prequel to the Grail Quest, as we will see in the last chapter.

An Excursion into Merlin's Forest

The version of the death of Merlin presented by the Post-Vulgate became the best-known in the English-speaking world because it was taken up by Malory, who powerfully condenses the story, describing Merlin as *assotted* upon the Damsel of the Lake, who makes him swear not to use his enchantments to have his way with her. Tired of his constant attentions and *aferde of hym for cause he was a devyl's son*, she finally contrives to *be skyfte of hym … by hir subtyle worching*, entombing him *undir a grete stone* (*MCW* 76–7).

But alternative versions of Merlin's fate continued to circulate. We have seen in Part One how the Vulgate version was shared with the Pre-Raphaelites through the advocacy of Robert Southey, presenting a more benign form of magical imprisonment at the hands of a loving fay. But Merlin is even shown as surviving Arthur's passing to Avalon in the *Vita Merlini*, that Latin poem by Geoffrey of Monmouth which also contains the first mention of Morgen and her sisters on the Isle of Avalon, whither Merlin and Taliesin are supposed to have taken the wounded Arthur to be healed.

Awaiting the return of the king, Merlin is driven mad by the murderous folly of the Britons and retires to the Caledonian Forest; where he is eventually cured by a healing spring which breaks out from the foot of the mountains. Taliesin describes how God has endowed certain waters that flow through the Earth with healing powers and how sometimes, when they encounter a blockage such as a stone, they will force themselves up to the surface.

This seems a powerful metaphor for the underground stream that is the consciousness-transforming power of the imagination which can at times seem to be trapped under the Earth, like Merlin in his stone tomb; but that at other times will break out, such as in the visionary poetry of Blake or the poetic philosophy of Corbin. At other times again, it can be seen to have never really gone away, like the Golden Age; or to be all around us, if we would but see it, like the Gnostic Kingdom of Heaven; or to be close by, just beyond the fields we know, like the Kingdom of Faerie.

One scholar who was inspired by the closeness of that other world was the German Indologist Heinrich Zimmer who, in the 1930s (that seminal decade for the literary creation of the other worlds of heroic fantasy and science fiction), took a holiday from his day job to take an excursion into the Celtic forest, in order to explore the fate of Merlin. Riffing on the Vulgate story of Merlin's submission to Ninienne as well as on the accounts of Merlin's retirement to the forest, Zimmer sees Merlin's withdrawal as voluntary. The trickery of Ninienne is mere illusion whereas "Merlin's abandonment to it is knowledge" (197) and, in this knowing abandonment, he "rises to the calm heights of an Indian god who withdraws, after a period of manifestation, back into his own silence, knowing that he has no further part to play in saving or judging the world" (198).

The moral of the story of the disappearance of Merlin is not, in this reading, an example of the kind of Christian triumphalism that we find so often in the Post-Vulgate—Ninienne as a daughter of Eve seducing a man to his destruction—but rather "it is the morality of elves and fairies, of the powers of water and forest, the old nature religion and the essential mysticism of the Celtic tribes, that celebrates its victory." Merlin has renounced the will to power by abandoning his earthly kingdom, a renunciation which, according to Corbin, is the essential pre-requisite of the Grail Quest of which Merlin is the prophet: "But the whitethorn hedge blossoms imperishably," writes Zimmer, "and in it Merlin is living still" (200). In some stories, though his body is trapped behind an invisible wall, Merlin's guiding spirit continues to be active in the affairs of the Round Table.

Thus there is a romance in which a disguised Merlin (according to Zimmer) makes an important, albeit monstrous, appearance: in this tale the hero of the story is Yvain (or Owein in the Welsh version). Intrigued by accounts circulated at court, Yvain sets out to achieve the Adventure of the Fountain, which all before him have failed. But he can only find his destination with the help of the Ward of the Wood—a giant, black, deformed herdsman—the Lord of the Animals, whom he encounters in the Forest of Broceliande.

Zimmer follows Loomis (131–3) in identifying this animal-skin clad *hom sauvage* with Merlin, the shape-shifter of the romances and the *homo silvester* of Geoffrey's poem, who guides Yvain to the Castle of the Fountain. There he must overcome its guardian; only to find that whoever does so must become its guardian in turn and must marry the Lady of the Fountain; for such is the custom of the castle.

Again, Zimmer follows earlier scholars in identifying this custom with an ancient ritual made famous by Sir James Frazer in his multi-volume study, *The Golden Bough*. This notorious book is a landmark work of armchair anthropology in which Frazer explores the myth of the Dying and Resurrected God in relation to the alleged practice of killing the sacred king at the end of his allotted span and its related rituals. Frazer's myth-and-ritual theory was hugely influential in its day, being developed in the Arthurian scholarship of Jessie Weston and the poetic writings of Robert Graves, among others. Whether or not Frazer's speculations tell us anything at all about prehistoric rituals of kingship need not concern us here, for myths have a life of their own: the story he told about the ritual combat to establish the priesthood of Diana's sacred grove by Lake Nemi, just outside Rome, would itself become an important myth in the intellectual life of the twentieth century.

As the story goes, the priest of the grove of the moon goddess, known as the King of the Wood, could hold that position only until another could take it from him; so the rule of the sanctuary was serial murder. The priest-king "was regarded as an incarnation of the god consort of Diana, the goddess of the lake and grove; and their marriage-union was the source of the fruitfulness of the earth, of all animals, and of mankind." Zimmer equates the guardian of the sacred spring in the Romance of Yvain with the King of the Wood and the Lady of the Fountain with the incarnate moon goddess who symbolizes "the perennial power of life, continuous and unbounded" (105). She is a pagan goddess who becomes, in the Christian world of the romances, "the fairy mistress of the Fountain of Life" (108).

Having killed the consort of the goddess incarnate, Yvain takes his place as a Lord of Faerie and is lost to the world of the Round Table for three years; but eventually King Arthur comes looking for his nephew. The ritual combat of the sacred spring is once more undergone, but this time the king's champion Gawain fights his cousin to a standstill and the custom is broken. With the permission of his fairy mistress, the Lady of the Fountain, Yvain returns to the fields we know, supposedly for three months only. But he soon gets caught up in the everyday reality of worldly chivalry and forgets the Otherworld and its Lady.

But the Otherworld has not forgotten him and so, when three more years have passed, a messenger arrives from his Lady to denounce his faithlessness and reclaim his mistress' ring, the token of her love. Bereft, Yvain wanders the wilderness in a state of madness, until he is healed by an ointment created by the magic of his mother, Morgan the Fay. It is at this crucial juncture that he encounters his "totem animal," a lion (119), which represents "the intuitive guiding principle that conducts the hero to the sphere of supernatural power, which is at once above and beneath the social plane" (122). It is in this sphere that he at last accomplishes "his ultimate task—the difficult reunion with the Goddess of Life" (125).

For Zimmer, Yvain has undergone an initiatory death through madness and been spiritually reborn as the Knight of the Lion. It is only now that he is worthy to regain in full consciousness what he had previously stumbled upon, as if in a dream. His marriage to the Lady of the Fountain is repaired and she now accompanies him to King Arthur's court, so that Yvain no longer has to choose between Logres and Faerie. He is the master of two worlds: *this* world and the Otherworld. His dual sovereignty is the precious gift of those who brave Merlin's forest, those who listen to the guidance of the Prophet of the Grail, even in his most monstrous of transformations—and who accept healing from the fays.

We are a far cry here from the Post-Vulgate adventures of Balin, who ignored the warnings both of the messenger of the Lady of the Isle of Avalon and of Merlin—and who, wielding a destructive supernatural power, killed the Maiden of the Lake of Fays and struck the Dolorous Blow. When Balin is obliged to undergo a ritual combat against the guardian of the custom of a castle, his opponent turns out to be his own brother and the encounter results in both their deaths. The fault of Balin can only be redeemed by the sacrifice of Perceval's sister and of Galahad, virginal Christians rather than fairy lovers.

By Divers Paths

The Post-Vulgate does not give us an account of Yvain's adventures at the fountain; but the action of the second half of Chrétien's poem *Le Cheva-*

lier au Lion plays out in tandem with Lancelot's quest for Guenevere in the Kingdom of Gorre, events which themselves are described "offstage," as it were, in the Post-Vulgate (in contrast to the Vulgate Cycle, where the deeds of Lancelot are center-stage). Thus the Post-Vulgate describes in some detail the escalating feud between the House of Orkney and the Grail kindred (Gawain kills Pellinor in revenge for the death of King Loth; while Gaheriet, up till now presented as the noblest of Gawain's brothers, dirties his copybook by beheading his mother, Queen Morgause, when he discovers that she is having an affair with Pellinor's oldest son) but gives only a cursory summary of events at court:

After winning victories on the continent, King Arthur organizes a celebratory feast at Camelot. To this comes Elaine of Corbenic with her young son Galahad; leading to Lancelot's madness when he is tricked into sleeping once more with Elaine, much to the queen's displeasure. A posse of knights sets out to find the Leopard of Benoic, separating when they enter the Forest of Camelot; for they think it "shameful and cowardly" to travel other than "by divers paths" (*LG* V, 60f).

The adventures that befall the various knights in their search need not detain us here, other than to take note of a storyline which, as in the account of the death of Balin, seems to have faded echoes of the theme of ritual combat and mythic guardianship that is so developed in the Romance of Yvain. It concerns the sister of Perceval who has the dubious distinction of being the only woman allowed to play any kind of active role in the Grail Quest, thanks to her lifelong virginity, even though it ends with her sacrificing her life so that her brother and his companions can go on to greater glory.

We have seen that Perceval's father, King Pellinor, was killed by Gawain in revenge for the death of King Loth but, not content with this, the vengeful Gawain goes on to kill Pellinor's oldest sons. We are a long way here from the "sun of chivalry," as Gawain appears in Chrétien and it seems appropriate in the context of the Post-Vulgate for this most lustful of knights to be opposed by the most chaste of maidens.

Perceval's sister determines to entrap Gawain by appealing to his pride and lust for battle. She has a tower built on one of her father's islands by a forest frequented by knights errant and hangs a shield and lance in front of a tent as an invitation to single combat. She commands her posse of knights to force the first knight who crosses over to take on all comers, until his place is taken by whoever can defeat him. Thus, when Gawain eventually turns up, as he is bound to—for he is "always seeking adventures" (*LG* V, 88)—he will have a most formidable opponent and, should he be victorious, her knights will kill him anyway.

In the event, when Gawain does make his way to the island, he discovers that its champion is a fellow Knight of the Round Table; so he invokes their oath of companionship to end the battle. The two of them team up against the posse of knights and drive them off, leaving Perceval's sister distraught and wishing to join her family in death.

Meanwhile her youngest surviving brother, Perceval, has set off for King Arthur's court at Carduel, leaving their mother to die of grief. While there he is accorded an unexpected honor, being seated at the right hand of the Siege Perilous, an indication he is "worthy to be one of the chief knights in the quest for the Holy Grail" (86).

Later, while searching for the missing Lancelot, Perceval comes to a little river which runs between two mountains and on the water, near the bank, sees an elegantly equipped boat, in which is a crowned man fishing, who seems very sick. The fisherman tells Perceval that he pursues this pastime because he doesn't have the strength to ride, adding: "My baptismal name is Pellehan, but others call me the Rich Fisherman. Since I can't make use of my limbs at will or at need, others call me the Maimed King" (109).

What we know, but Perceval cannot, is that Pellehan was maimed by Balin the Savage wielding the Holy Lance and that this was the Dolorous Blow which is responsible for the enchantments of Logres. When King Pellehan learns that the knight is the son of Pellinor, he tells him that they are close kin but, because Pellehan cannot give him any news of Lancelot, Perceval rides on, in what must be considered one of the greatest missed opportunities in medieval literature. For, in the earliest version of his story, this is the moment when Perceval is invited into the castle of the Fisher King, witnesses the Grail and the Lance in a mysterious procession and famously fails to ask the all-important question which would have restored his host and the land.

It is to these conflicting versions and the possible reasons for important changes in the story that we will now turn.

Eleven

Mountains of Heresy

"Heretics of the world unite!"[1]

—Henry Corbin

Few moments in medieval literature can have had so powerful and long-lasting a resonance in western culture as the episode in which the young, naive hero Perceval first encounters the Grail in the court of the Fisher King.

Part of the appeal of the story, as originally presented by Chrétien de Troyes, is that it is so mysterious. Perceval encounters a maimed king fishing, is invited to his castle, presented with a sword that is destined to break at a crucial moment and witnesses a procession in which a bleeding lance and radiant vessel (a "grail") are carried through the hall before disappearing into a back room. Too polite to quiz his host about the meaning of what he has witnessed, Perceval retires for the night only to find, on awakening, that the castle is deserted.

Riding on, Perceval encounters his cousin, who tells him that the Fisher King was maimed in battle and roundly condemns him for maintaining his silence: he should have asked why the lance bled and where the Grail Procession was going. Had he done so, the Maimed King would have regained the use of his limbs. Later, in King Arthur's court at Caerleon, a hideous maiden again upbraids Perceval for his silence, as a result of which lands will be laid waste. Perceval swears that he will not rest until he learns who is served from the grail and why the lance bleeds.

Finally, Perceval learns from his uncle, a hermit, that the person served by the grail is the elderly father of the Maimed King: "he's served with a single consecrated wafer brought to him in that grail—that supports his life in full vigour, so holy a thing is the grail" (*AR* 459). This explanation may seem slightly anti-climactic, given what has gone before; until we realize that it actually explains very little. So many questions are left unanswered: Why, for a start, would a simple question have healed the Maimed

King's wounds? Why *does* the lance bleed? Why will the sword break? And why is the grail holy?

To cap it all—and this is another reason why the Story of the Grail has maintained its mysterious appeal—Chrétien left his poem unfinished, so we will never know how he had intended to answer these questions. Several poets attempted to complete his story, along the way providing their own answers to at least some of these questions but generally provoking new ones.

So we learn that the lance bleeds because it is the Holy Lance of Christian tradition (with which the centurion Longinus pierced the side of Jesus on the Cross) and it will bleed until the Last Judgment. The grail is holy because it is the dish with which Jesus served the Paschal lamb at the Last Supper and which Joseph of Arimathea used to collect His blood. From now on it is *the Holy Grail*. The Fisher King was maimed by a Dolorous Blow which caused the wasting of the land. The sword has already broken, being the weapon that struck the blow. It will be made whole, but will break again…

As for the Grail Question, it undergoes various transformations until being abandoned altogether in the Vulgate version. Here the Broken Sword is one which wounded Joseph of Arimathea during his conversion mission in Britain and the Holy Lance is wielded by angels to exact divine vengeance. The Holy Grail is the mystical object of a quest to find a knight who is too perfect for this world and who (having looked inside it to see what tongue cannot tell nor heart conceive) is rapt up to Heaven with the sacred vessel, which is nevermore seen on Earth. The Post-Vulgate provides the final piece of the jigsaw, explaining that the Fisher King was maimed by the Avenging Lance; except that by now we must recognize that it is a very different jigsaw from the one Chrétien originally created.

If the heirs to Chrétien seem often to have provided answers to the riddles by rewriting the story to suit their explanations, the same could be said of some of the scholars who, since the nineteenth century, have been attempting to explain its mysteries, while frequently adding to them.

The King's Highway

The first important scholarly contribution was the recognition that some of the themes and characters in the medieval stories are derived from Celtic paganism. This belief is still prevalent today, if not uncontested. Thus John Carey, a specialist in medieval Irish, has recently presented the case for the earliest Grail stories deriving from a collection of Irish tales which was transmitted, first to Wales[2] and then to France; part of the "imaginative appeal" of which was its focus on "the mysteries of the afterlife and of rebirth" (2007, 330).

Carey (15–19) follows Loomis in seeing Perceval's first encounter with the Grail as derived from an Irish Otherworld adventure in which the hero encounters the immortal Lugh, one of the leaders of the Tribes of the Gods, in the company of a female figure personifying Sovereignty. The man to whom she offers her wine cup is the rightful king. Carey further follows Proinsias Mac Cana in seeing the Irish Sovereignty figure as derived from the Celtic Rosmerta (a goddess of plenty and of prophecy, who is depicted bearing a cornucopia) and Lugh as connected with the Celtic deity whom the Romans referred to as Mercury and who is frequently paired with Rosmerta. This leads Carey to the intriguing possibility that one could imagine "that the true origin of the Grail is revealed by the cult of Rosmerta" (357). However, Carey accepts that we "will never find the Grail's ultimate source," for "mystery belongs to the very essence of the Grail, and of the traditions from which the story came" (358).

Certainly other scholars have insisted that these traditions cannot be limited to the Celtic hypothesis. For the Christian mystic A.E. Waite, the undoubted folklore elements were subsumed by an alchemical "alembic of transmutation" (172) into an alternative esoteric and Johannine tradition, hidden but not inimical to the mainstream Church. By contrast Jessie L Weston was drawn to the anti-ecclesiastical, heretical tradition. She accepted that there is "a basis of truth" for tracing various isolated features of the legend to Celtic folklore which has been "worked over by ecclesiastical writers" (1920, 2), but felt that the case had been exaggerated by its adherents. She argued that "the root of this theme is far more deeply embedded than in the shifting sands of Folk and Fairy tale…. A path that leads but into a Celtic Twilight can only be a by-path, and not the King's Highway!" (186–7).

The royal path that Weston found was one that led rather to the ancient mystery religions which, though rooted in the exoteric fertility cults of imperial paganism, also provided an esoteric ritual of personal salvation. She believed that the key to the secret of the Grail would be found not in mythology and folklore, but in *initiation*, which is the inner form of a spiritual tradition, as religion is the outer. The Grail could best be understood as the symbol of an esoteric tradition whose "final stage is the initiation into the higher Secret of the Mysteries, that of regeneration and spiritual life" (1913, 90).

Weston believed that the Gnostics of the first Christian centuries, who elevated direct experience of—or acquaintance (*gnosis*) with—the sacred over mere faith, formed a bridge between the old pagan Mysteries and the new covenant. She gives as an example of this the Naassene sect, who overtly identified Jesus with the dying-and-resurrected gods of the ancient mystery religions such as Attis, Adonis and Osiris (1920, 149–59). Thus she argued that the fusion of pagan Mystery and Christian Gnosis provided "all the elements necessary for a mystical development of the Grail tradition" (158).

Weston believed that an underground cult survived the suppression of paganism and Gnosticism and continued to satisfy "in cave or mountain-fastness, or island isolation ... those who craved for a more sensible (not necessarily sensuous) contact with the unseen Spiritual forces of Life than the orthodox development of Christianity afforded." Among such cravers, she suggests, could have been the Knights Templar, who may have come across a sect like that of the Naassenes when in the East and adopted their heresy. In this case we would have an explanation both for the condemnation and destruction of the Order by the papal and regal authorities and also for the "puzzling connection" of the Templars with the Grail (187), found especially in the German version of the Story of the Grail, Wolfram von Eschenbach's *Parzival*. Here the symbol (imagined as a stone rather than a dish or chalice) is guarded by an order of Templars (*Templeisen*) in their mountain fastness of Wildenberg (*Muntsalvæsche*).

In a lecture of 1904 the Austrian "spiritual scientist" Rudolf Steiner, founder of the school of Anthroposophy, claimed that the Templars were not just servants and messengers of the Grail, but had been *initiated by it* in a wisdom center that they built on the site of Solomon's Temple (43). In the Thirties the German scholar Otto Rahn claimed that the Grail was the sacred symbol of heretical contemporaries of the Templars—the medieval Cathars of Languedoc, whom he saw as the heirs of the ancient Druids and Gnostics. This alleged association of the Grail with Cathars and Templars, which would lead to increasingly apocalyptic conspiracy theories as the century drew to a close, is one we will return to later.

Rahn's theories about the Grail, unsurprisingly, relied principally upon the most important German text, von Eschenbach's *Parzival*; while this epic poem was also the basis for studies of the Hermetic sources of the Grail which appeared in the Fifties and Sixties. Von Eschenbach followed the main narrative thrust of the Story of the Grail as it is presented in Chrétien's poem, but also provided it with a prequel and a conclusion. Along the way, Wolfram changed so many important details that it is possible to take seriously his contention that he drew on a more authoritative source, a certain Kyot. This Kyot, Wolfram claimed, drew in turn on the wisdom of the pagan astrologer Flegetanis, who read the name of the Grail in the stars.

In their book *The Krater and the Grail*, Henry and Renée Kahane summarized and developed their researches, in which they claimed to have identified this Kyot with William of Tudela, an early thirteenth century geomancer who wrote an epic poem about the crusade against the Cathars.[3] William, they argued, had transmitted to von Eschenbach the initiatory doctrines that he found in an Arabic recension of the mystical writings attributed to the mythical Hermes Trismegistus (the Thrice Great) and known therefore as Hermeticism. Von Eschenbach had then transposed these doctrines into a narrative that could convey them to a wider public.

Hermeticism is a form of pagan gnosis that is not disfigured by the extreme "anti-cosmism," the rejection of the body and the created world that characterizes some of the dualist writings of the early Christian Gnostics (Broek and Hanegraaff, 16–7). The Hermetic way was rather "to make the world transparent toward God" (12). In support of their thesis, the Kahanes provide various points of comparison between *Parzival* and the treatises known collectively as the *Corpus Hermeticum*, some of which are inevitably more persuasive than others.

To begin with, they argue for the derivation of the word "grail" from the Greco-Latin word *crāter* ("vessel") and for the identification of Flegetanis' constellation with that known as the Crater. Furthermore, they identify Wolfram's Grail with the Krater, the mystic vessel of Hermeticism (Kahane, 2). One of the most striking divergences from Chrétien is von Eschenbach's detailed description of the Grail Procession, in which twenty four figures eventually face the Grail Bearer. This corresponds, the Kahanes claim, to the twenty four stages of the soul's ascent to the Monad, the one-and-only divine principal of Hermeticism (101–5). The name of Trevrizent, the hermit who instructs Parzival about the Grail, is derived from Trismegistus (62–3); so that Parzival is initiated by Hermes himself.

The Kahanes' thesis was taken up in the Seventies by Henry Corbin, who nevertheless shifted the focus of their exploration to his own "imaginal" philosophy. Thus, according to the Kahanes, in *Parzival* "Hermetic doctrine is transposed into concrete narrative" (70). But, Corbin argues, von Eschenbach's poem is not the literalization of an esoteric doctrine (1971, 192–3), as if the doctrine were the "inner" and the story the "outer" versions of an initiatory event. Rather, the poem should be seen as a "visionary recital" which brings us closer to a real event in the soul than does the abstract doctrine. The recital is the exoteric version of the soul-event, the doctrine the exoteric version of the recital and so, by the same token, the poem is the *esotericization*, not the concretization, of the doctrine (193–5).

We are in a world of correspondences, in which Hermetic doctrines and poems as mystical recitals represent different levels of manifestation of the Ineffable. So, for that matter, do historical events—and here we should mention not just the attempts of Rahn to identify the crusade against the Grail with the one against the Cathars in the thirteenth century, but also the localization by Rudolf Steiner and his disciple W.J. Stein of the Parzival quest in the ninth century. We can go further back in time, if we follow our sources literally, dating the revelation of the *veraie estoire* to the hermit Nascien to the eighth century, Arthur's passing to Avalon to the sixth century and the conversion of Britain by the Company of the Grail to the late first and early second century AD, during the reign of good King Lucius. We can argue that these stories bear no relation to genuine historical events and maintain them as inspired fiction or, alternatively, attempt to demythologize them, retaining only those elements that can be plausibly situated within the known historical record.

But Corbin warns against the "banal dualism" of history and myth. Historical events, Hermetic doctrines and mystical recitals all *symbolize with* each other; they are in correspondence (193). They all reflect, on their different levels, events of the soul.

So, for example, von Eschenbach tells of the Grail Bearer's journey to the East, where she gives birth to Prester John, the legendary priest-king. Albrecht, a later German poet, says that Parzival eventually brought the Grail itself to Prester John's Indian kingdom, so that the light of the sacred vessel would be preserved from the impious darkness of the West. But it would be futile to attempt to draw the boundaries of this Far Eastern kingdom any more than it would be to pin Sarras down to a location in the Middle East, or Corbenic to one in the West.

Whether we see the Grail as transported to Sarras and thence borne up to Heaven, as in the Vulgate version, or taken from Muntsalvæsche to India, as in Albrecht, we are always talking about journeys from one Otherworld location to another. The movement ever eastward, reversing the original westward journey of the Grail from the Holy Land to Britain, is a re-orientation of the soul. In the spiritual East, the Grail undergoes an *occultation mystique* (177) of which the destruction of the Cathars and the suppression of the Knights Templar are the outward, exoteric expression in the impious West. They are historical milestones marking the spread of the Waste Land in our cultural landscape.

A Poetics of Strangeness

Henry Corbin is best known as a scholar of Islamic esotericism, insofar as he is known at all.[4] But his writings also frequently refer to the corpus of Grail legends as a "bible" of Christian esotericism, although he tends to focus on the symbolism of the images in the Vulgate and German texts, which are not the earliest. But Corbin is less concerned with the chronological development of the romances than with the visionary imagination, which can break through at any point in the development of a cycle, so that we should not focus unduly on establishing a chronological priority for the texts in order to interpret their significance.

There is no doubt, however, that the *Perceval* of Chrétien de Troyes continues to be the foundational text for all that came after in the Story of the Grail—even for the Post-Vulgate version, which radically rewrites its key scene, as we saw at the end of the last chapter. It is useful, therefore, that a French medieval scholar, Pierre Gallais (1929–2001), has complemented the work of Corbin by applying the latter's imaginal philosophy to Chrétien's seminal work.

Gallais reads the poem in the light of oriental mystics and theosophers (especially of the Sufis and Ismaili gnostics researched by Corbin) and sees Perceval's quest as essentially an initiation through his love for a woman (Blancheflor, Perceval's "Beatrice"), human love leading to the love of God. Woman, for the man who seeks to know the Beloved through his beloved, is mediatrix, Psyche as the bridge between spirit and matter. She belongs to the *mundus imaginalis* (Gallais 1998a, 226), which is why Perceval will not be reunited with her in this life until he has passed through that *lieu intermédiaire* (neither Heaven nor Earth, but the place where they touch) which is the Grail Castle (56). Here he will meet that king who is the mediator between man and his soul and who therefore represents the object of his quest: that knowledge of his self which *is* knowledge of God (74).

The encounter will take place in a world that is not imaginary but imaginal; which is the product, not of Chrétien's personal imagination, but of the *Imaginatio vera* of the alchemists, which can distinguish a spiritual reality from a fantasy (93). For the Otherworld, so near to our own everyday world, is so difficult to see with our everyday eyes (1998b, 56). In order to find the Grail Castle, which exists outside of time and space, Perceval has to see with other eyes. It is therefore significant that shortly after leaving it he divines his true name, which had always been kept from him; for it is not just that the Otherworld cannot be situated on a map, but that it is what enables us to "situate" ourselves. It is the fact of having been there *and come back* that reveals to the hero his true being (and hence his true name). Therefore Perceval can now realize his love for Blancheflor, when his Imaginative Eye shows him her face in drops of blood on a snowy field (56–7).

But what is it that opens the Imaginative Eye? For Perceval, it is the experience of the supernatural light of the Grail which, as Chrétien describes it (*CG* ll.3162–7), outshines the candles in the Fisher King's hall as the dawn outshines the moon and stars. The Grail Procession, as Perceval perceives it, takes the form of an arrow—a symbol in the East of the Hindu Great Goddess, as it is the attribute in the West of the classical moon goddess—or of a cross (Gallais 1998a, 215–6).

It is the image of the Grail Procession as a cross made of living beings that is further explored by the scholar of medieval literature Francis Dubost (54). At the center of the cross, he writes, is the Grail vessel itself, suffused with intense light—a supernatural light that eclipses the natural light of the candles. The procession passes from the royal feasting hall to a secret chamber where, we later learn, the Fisher King's aged father is kept alive by being served a single Host (or consecrated wafer) from the Grail. This movement has the effect of turning our attention from the visible to the invisible, from earthly to spiritual nourishment (163).

Ultimately Dubost, having laid out many of the arguments for a Celtic, Christian or oriental origin for the Grail, argues that Chrétien has left us with a theatrical spectacle that is, in the end, unintelligible (164). But Dubost's reference to the *inintelligible* is itself significant insofar as he has already pointed out that the twin heroes of the Story of the Grail, Perceval and Gawain, are subjected in the course of their adventures to literary effects such as the doubling, mirroring and inverting of themes and images in locations touched by wonder (*la merveille*), moving between (visible) body and (invisible) spirit, between what we experience through our senses and what we perceive through the intellect: *le sensible et l'intelligible* (19).

We have already encountered these as the opposing universes of western dualism and seen how Corbin bridges them with what is *imaginable*. Dubost comes close to this perspective when he describes the episode of the blood on the snow as an initiation *au mode symbolique* which represents, at root, the fundamental principle of literature itself (127–8). Perceval's discovery of the *faculté de symbolisation* (129) is to Dubost's concern with the literary art of "sign-making" what Perceval's awakening of the active imagination is to Gallais' concern with the existential art of "soul-making."

For Dubost, Chrétien's art is a "poetics of strangeness," *une poétique de l'étrangeté* (162) in which space and time are distorted into the *merveilleux* and the *fantastique* so that for both the hero and the reader what is seen is distanced from what is known. The image is separated from its understanding, the *sensible* from the *intelligible* (95). What a contrast with the Vulgate *Quest*, in which Galahad looks into the Holy Grail and immediately is granted a vision of the ineffable mystery of mysteries, a revelation of that higher form of gnosis which is the *intelligible* (104)! For Chrétien, knowing is always subordinate to vision (96) whereas, throughout the prose versions of the quest, it is never long before a hermit explains away dreams, visions and wonders, reducing them to allegories of doctrine—the imaginable is always subordinate to the intelligible, soul to spirit.

We should not be surprised, therefore, that in the prelude to the Post-Vulgate *Quest*, all the wonder and mystery with which Chrétien has invested the meeting of Perceval with the Fisher King has been dispensed with. Above all, there is no vision of the Grail at the center of a living cross of light. Why should this be? One possibility is that, as I have pointed out in a previous work (Dixon 2012, 51–3), this image has a troubling resonance with one found in the Christian apocrypha.

An Image out of Spiritus Mundi

In the late second century text known as the Acts of John and attributed to a disciple of the evangelist, after encountering Jesus as the Lord of the Dance, John goes up to a cave in the Mount of Olives from which he can witness the Crucifixion. But instead he has a vision of a cross of light, from above which he hears the voice of the Lord (not the familiar voice of Jesus) proclaiming that the cross is also called Word, Mind, Door, Way, Resurrection, Spirit, Life, Truth, Faith, Grace … (*ANT* 320).

The Cross of Light, the Lord announces, is that which separates the Above from the Below: It must not be confused with the cross of wood below, nor should the Lord be confused with the man dying on that cross, in the darkness of the sixth hour. The suffering of which the Lord sang, in the round dance, with the apostles circling Him—"I will be pierced, and I will pierce. Amen…. Who am I? You shall know when I go away. What I am now seen to be, that I am not" (319)—is what Corbin calls an "apparitional reality." We understand our suffering through seeing His suffering; we are moved by it and are made wise by His mysterious paradoxes: "You hear that I suffered, yet I suffered not ; that I suffered not, yet I did suffer; that I was pierced, yet was I not wounded … that blood flowed from me, yet it did not flow; and, in a word, those things that they say of me I did not endure, and the things that they do not say those I suffered. Now what they are I will reveal to you for I know you will understand" (*ANT* 321).

We should therefore perceive in Him the piercing, the bleeding, the wounding, the suffering and the death—of the Logos in the first place, in the second place of the Lord and, in the third place, of the man. And so He speaks, "discarding manhood," separating it from the Word-hood, the cross of wood from the Cross of Light; in order, so Corbin argues, that we do not fall into the literalism and materialism of the official dogma of the Incarnation as it was formulated by the Church councils: For it was a Church council which in the eighth century (the century in which the hermit Nascien was supposed to have received the Book of the Grail from Christ) condemned the Acts of John as heretical.

The heresy, known as Docetism, is the belief that Jesus did not have a physical, material body, despite appearances; or, rather, that He was all appearance. But this does not necessarily mean that He was some sort of unreal phantasm. Rather, He had a psychic or spiritual body, for the early Gnostics; while Corbin speaks of a "real apparition" which differs according to the capacity of soul of the person perceiving Him (1983, 60-3).

For one of the troubling aspects of the Acts of John and other apocryphal texts is that they share with the Gnostic scriptures the idea that, even before His resurrection, Jesus could appear in different forms to different people (*ANT* 316-8) and, if we follow the verse continuations of Chrétien's *Perceval*, so can the Grail King as he appears to Perceval and Gawain. Sometimes he is maimed, sometimes not; sometimes there are two kings, sometimes only one; sometimes one is maimed, the other dead. We also learn, in the First Continuation, that the Bleeding Lance in the Grail Castle is the weapon that pierced the side of Jesus on the Cross.

We have then, in the early poems, a Grail King who reflects in striking ways the Docetic Jesus: the Lord who stands between the spiritual Word and the material Man; in whom the Grail hero perceives variously the piercing, the blood, the wound, the suffering, the death.... But the Acts of John was condemned at the Second Nicene Council (*ANT* 305)—that same ecumenical gathering at which allegory triumphed over imagination—and there is no way that a poet such as Chrétien, whose patron was a notorious heresy hunter, would have consciously intended to support Docetism or any other heterodox perspective.

Chrétien was a poet, not a theologian and, like all great artists, he allowed his poetry to speak for itself. If this means that he did not fully understand the story he was telling, he is in good company: as Mircea Eliade, himself a prolific novelist and short-story writer as well as a historian of religions, has observed: "in most cases an author does not understand all the meaning of his work. Archaic symbolisms re-appear spontaneously," even when the myths in which they find their original context have decayed. They come from the depths of the human being (1991, 25), regardless of whether we call the transcendental source of the soul's images the collective unconscious (as Jung does), the *mundus imaginalis* (as Corbin does), or the trans-conscious (as Eliade himself does).

Poetry speaks in images that cannot be reduced to mere representations. This is one reason why scholars have been able to claim the Grail poems for so many causes—pagan survivalism, Gnostic revivalism, orthodox mysticism—or reduce it to the category of "pure" entertainment. But however it began—and John Carey and earlier scholars have argued more convincingly for a Celtic origin than Weston did for an initiation ritual surviving in remote regions—the Grail legend, as it has developed, has become all these things and more.[5]

So are the advocates of a pagan, Gnostic or Hermetic Grail simply reading into the literature something that isn't there? This, I believe, is too reductive. While there is no reason to believe that the early Grail poets were anything other than orthodox, God-fearing Christians—there is no evidence, for example, to support Weston's claim (1909, 280) that de Boron was an "initiate"—this does not mean that heterodox elements could not have found their way into their work.

The most obvious path of transmission is through historical time and geographic space: cultural diffusion. Thus advocates of a Celtic background to the Grail legend can trace a convincing route from Ireland to Wales and thence to continental Europe, whereby stories that still contain mythic elements are written down by Christian monks and reworked by poets who are not themselves familiar with the pagan milieu within which the stories originally emerged, but are attracted to the air of mystery that these elements engender. Similarly, as we have seen, the Kahanes have traced a route whereby Hermetic materials could have been transmitted by Arabic writers to the West.

Henry Corbin, for his part, does not dismiss the possibility of diffusion in time and space (1971, 158). He is nevertheless more interested in spiritual transmission. From his perspective, those symbolic images in the Grail literature that we recognize from the Christian apocrypha and the Hermetic gnosis belong to the world of the soul, which knows neither past nor present (159). They are images, to borrow Yeats' phrase, out of *spiritus mundi*. The Grail poets were, above all, storytellers, architects of the imagination and it is in the poetic imagination that paganism and gnosis live on eternally.

A Rich Inheritance

"All over Europe," the historian of prehistoric religion Ronald Hutton has written, "the pre–Christian religions bequeathed a rich inheritance of beliefs, practices, remedies, stories, symbols, images, ideas and forms." Thus, we do not need to search for "evidence of the long-term persistence of paganism as an organized religion of resistance, meeting in secret" (2003, 137), or assume that the writers of the Arthurian and Grail legends were clandestine adherents of dualist heresies, let alone initiates of a hidden mystery cult, to find in this literature, from the "Spoils of Annwfn" to the Post-Vulgate Grail Quest, over a span of some four hundred years, traces of an underground stream that bubbled up, irrepressibly, as though from some subterranean blockage, whenever the times were right.

The *stories themselves* were the carriers of the counter-culture of the imagination, for they came from that middle realm which can neither be controlled by the censors of abstract theology nor denied by the ruthless purveyors of a narrow-minded realism. This is the realm of Faerie explored by the poets and celebrated by scholars such as Corbin and Hillman as the Otherworld of the Soul.

It is this world that came under attack from the iconoclasts in the eighth and ninth centuries; it is under attack still. But in the twelfth century there was a "renaissance of the imagination," the return of outlawed pagan images and gnostic themes in a new disguise: as literature. If Christian iconoclasm was a response to the success of militant Islam, the spread of the Grail literature can only be understood in the historical context of the Crusades, in which a new confidence seized the Christian world, only to be dashed by the century's end.[6]

Chrétien de Troyes began writing his romances around 1170 and the last of these, *Perceval*, was left unfinished at his death. Although we cannot date the demise of the greatest of the *romanciers*, it is assumed that the Story of the Grail, which was dedicated to Count Philip of Flanders, was written sometime before 1190, when the count departed for the Holy Land: for he died there in the summer of 1191. According to Chrétien's own account, Philip had given him a book which contained the greatest story ever told in a royal court; but this is apocryphal and, in any case, Philip, who was a notorious heresy-hunter, would have had no tolerance of apparently heterodox elements in Chrétien's work (had he lived to read the work of his court poet).

But Chrétien, like all great poets, was a creator, not a philosopher or theologian and poetic creation, as Eliade has remarked (1972, 510–11), is "an act of perfect spiritual freedom." Thus we have no reason to assume that Chrétien was consciously an apostate, just because his works are capable of esoteric interpretation: It is the poetic impulse itself that resists the constraints of orthodoxy. While his patron was literally journeying to the East, Chrétien's Muse was re-orienting herself at a time when Christianity, in the wake of iconoclasm, was turning its back on the imaginal, on the noetic function of images, on the creative imagination as a *theophanic* power (the power to manifest the divine).

Disoriented by centuries of iconoclasm, the Muse of the western poetic imagination was encountering a powerful heretical movement (arguably influenced by a current from the East), which took the concept of spiritual freedom rather more literally.

An Excursion to the Languedoc

In 1167, at a village situated between Toulouse and Carcassonne, there was held a grand council of the Cathars, a Christian sect that was extremely popular in southern France and northern Italy; but which the Catholic Church considered heretical, though they themselves simply believed that they were "good Christians." They attempted to go back to the roots of their faith in the words of the Gospels and, in doing so, they came across the same problem that had led the ancient Gnostics into heresy: how could an all-wise, all-good, omnipotent God create a world so full of evil? For the Cathars, this question opened the door to a dangerously "dualistic" answer: the concept of two creations and two creators.

These dualist interpretations took hold especially in the Languedoc region near the Pyrenees, where a distinct language (those who say *oc* instead of *oui*, as in the mainstream French language) was the outward form of a distinct, Provençal culture; where the courtly love of the troubadours made odd bedfellows with the pure (*katharos*) lifestyle of those who had been "perfected" in their heresy. When the Gospel of John was translated into the Occitan language, one passage in particular could be read as though to justify the concept of two creations: "All things were made by Him; and without Him was not anything made that was made" (1.3). In the Occitan translation, this becomes: *Per luy tot es faict, et senes luy es faict neient*. This in turn could be understood to mean: "All things were made by Him and, without Him, there was made [the realm of] Nothingness," as if Occitan *neient* = modern French *le Néant* (Roquebert 1994, 125-6).

The visible world, for the Cathars, was the creation of a lesser god, who was opposed to the True God, the creator of all things invisible. Human souls had fallen from the invisible world and sought to return to it, escaping the history, politics and violence of *this* world. After the Council of 1167, the "Good Christians" appear to have become even more radical, perhaps under the influence of the heretical churches of Eastern Europe. But their rejection of the Roman Church as the Church of the Adversary of the True God, of its priesthood as fellow-travelers and of its sacraments as useless for salvation, brought the combined wrath of Church and State down upon the south of France in the cruel and vindictive Albigensian Crusade, launched by Pope Innocent III against the Cathars in 1208.

Like the ancient Gnostics (and more modern dissident Christians from

William Blake to the French philosopher Simone Weil), the Cathars could not accept that the cruel god of the Old Testament, the Jealous God of Exodus, could be the loving father invoked by Jesus. Ultimately, they may have felt that the forces of Church and State, who persecuted them in the name of that god, were living testimonial to the truth of their theology. In the event, history and politics brought not peace, but a sword to those who tried to step outside them.

The Cathars found their last refuge in the mountain fastness of Montségur, destroyed in 1244, at the hands of the French crown. What can we make, though, of the idea that the Cathars were the guardians of the Holy Grail and that it was smuggled out of the fortress, along with their other "treasures," just before the final surrender of the garrison?

A Poisoned Chalice

The most notorious exponent of the idea that the Cathars were the original Company of the Grail was Otto Rahn (1904–1939) who pursued his researches in the Languedoc between 1930 and 1932. In 1933 he published his first book, *Kreuzzuge gegen den Graal* ("Crusade against the Grail"). In this work, Rahn claims that the Cathars were the heirs of the Celtic Druids of the region, who had been converted to Gnostic Christianity in the fourth century. He goes on to build up a case for the identification of key characters in the *Parzival* of Wolfram von Eschenbach with historical Cathars and to claim that Muntsalvaesche (Wagner's Mont Salvat), the secret castle of the Grail Stone, was in reality Montségur!

For Rahn, the progressive Christianization of the Grail by Robert de Boron and the later romances was a distortion of the original meaning of the primary texts, the poems of Chrétien and Wolfram: "The Grail was a heretical symbol. Those who venerated the Christian cross cursed it and a crusade pursued it. The Cross undertook a holy war against the Grail" (Rahn 2006, 115). But Rahn's eccentric theories would almost certainly not have attained their current notoriety if it were not for the subsequent fate of the author.

Shortly after his return to Germany, Rahn discovered that a new government had been elected: the Third Reich had begun. The twelve years of Hitler's reign were to match the twelve years that Montségur was the capital of the Cathar resistance,[7] but Rahn did not live long enough to ponder the meaning of this curious synchronicity. His first book had found favor with Heinrich Himmler, who was himself undertaking a holy war against Judeo-Christianity and who could never be accused of being excessively scrupulous about accurate scholarship. As a consequence, Rahn soon found himself promoted to the Ancestral Heritage Division of the SS (the infamous Ahnenerbe) as a staff officer and commissioned to write another work.

Luzifers Hofgesind ("Lucifer's Court," first published in 1937) is a very different work to its predecessor, a travelogue littered with nationalist and racist sentiments (perhaps intended to curry favor with the regime rather than to reflect any deeply held convictions), which extend the Gnostic Christian rejection of the Old Testament and its "Jewish God of intolerance" (2007, 125) to the Jews themselves.

Rahn may have felt that he had sold his soul to the Devil: he is believed to have committed suicide on March 13, 1939, three days before the anniversary of the burning of the *parfaits* of Montségur, while out walking in the snowbound Wilder Kaiser (his own fatal Wildenberg, or Mount Savage). He may have died praying that the poisoned chalice from which he had allowed himself to drink, the Aryan Sangreal, would pass from him.

The Temple of the Grail

The fate of Otto Rahn must give all Grail seekers pause: it reveals perhaps the dangers of the disordered imagination, cut loose from reason (for Rahn was more of a poet than an accurate researcher); but also of unbalanced reason, cut off from the true or spiritual imagination—*fixing many a Science*, in Blake's phrase, by distorting archaeology, history and theology to fit a racist ideology.

The Cathars were Docetists (a heresy that also infects the apocryphal Acts of John, as we have seen) for whom the body of Jesus was purely spiritual. He was sent from Heaven by the True God to awaken us to the reality of our real home; He did not suffer physically on the cross of wood; His flesh was not such as could be pierced by an ordinary spear and the blood that flowed from His side was not the physical blood of a material being. The Cathar Jesus is an "apparitional reality" and they would have had no more interest in the relics of the Passion (the Bleeding Lance and the vessel of the Sangreal) than they did in the mainstream Church's sacraments or its doctrine of the Real Presence.[8]

The contemporary disputes about the Trinity and the Eucharist—and the redemptive nature of the Crucifixion—provided such powerful images for the Grail writers that it is not surprising that people have sought elements of Cathar ritual and doctrine in the work of Chrétien and his successors. But, as the French medieval historian Michel Roquebert has shown, the Grail stories show a progressive reaction *against* the beliefs of the heretics and not an attraction *to* them. By the time we reach the later prose romances, the main theological influence appears to be that of the Cistercian order, whose White Monks appear at strategic intervals throughout the Quest and who preached against the Cathars.

As I have discussed in an earlier work (Dixon 2012, 30–3) the twelfth century was also a time of the development of a rationalistic philosophy and the gulf between this movement on one hand and extreme religious movements such as that of the Cathars, on the other, was so great that western culture was threatening to come apart at the seams. To hold the tension of the opposites, a middle ground needed to be found. And so it was that, between the Cathar Council of 1167 and the massacre at Montségur in 1244, the western imagination created an alternative solution to the dilemma posed by the challenge of heresy: a new literature emerged into public consciousness, from the Celtic fringe to the central axis of Germany and Italy, with at its heart a numinous symbol.

Whatever else the Grail may have been, in the twelfth and thirteenth centuries it constituted a symbol of wholeness in a fractured society and, in the stories that flowed around the image of the sacred vessel, pagan and gnostic elements resurfaced in stories full of orthodox piety and the mysticism of divine grace. In creative literature, if nowhere else in western culture, these strands could all be woven together harmoniously: in the form of stories, rather than in the form of heretical theories or forbidden rituals. The lost continent of the *mundus imaginalis* was to become actualized in the location of the Grail stories. Arthur's Promised Land was to become a place of epiphany, an adventurous kingdom in which wonders never ceased, or rather, in which they would only cease with the coming of the Chosen One.

In the Grail legends time and space are relativized: we slip imperceptibly from the history and geography of this island to a counter-history and an imaginal landscape, from Camelot to Corbenic. In the early poems, above all, the pagan Celtic Otherworld finds a new existence, after centuries of Christian iconoclasm, as a part of Britain which is always just beyond the fields we know. The perilous forests and fords, the magical castles and royal cities, even on the rare occasions when we can identify them with places on the map, really belong to what Corbin calls the *intermonde*, that intermediate or in-between world where we can resolve the conflict between knowing and believing, between symbol and history (1986a, 297–8).

But believing and history turned out to have the biggest armies. Later, at a time when the creative force of the composition of the romances was becoming diluted and the violence of the crusaders against heresy was reaching its inexorable climax, an Italian Cathar would provide another theoretical underpinning for heresy: the idea of a second or "heavenly" Earth in which the miraculous events of the Bible took place: a parallel universe in which Jesus married Mary Magdalene, for example. John of Lugio, writing around 1240, appeared to believe that the Incarnation, Crucifixion and Resurrection did not literally take place on this earth, as Rome taught; but in another world, the Land of the Living, which was an exact mirror image of this world (Barber 2000, 92–3).

We are really not far here from the Otherworld of Celtic mythology; or from the alternate realities of modern fantasy and science fiction, however debased they might seem in comparison with the spiritual products of the medieval imagination. As Margaret Atwood has argued, both medieval legends and modern tales of the "marvelous and uncanny" are drawn from "the same deep well: those imagined other worlds located somewhere apart from our everyday one: in another time, in another dimension, through a doorway into the spirit world, or on the other side of the threshold that divides the known from the unknown" (8). In the 1960s, the editors of superhero comics would create an Earth-Two[9] and a Marvel Universe, like, but strangely unlike, our own, in which we could swiftly pass from a familiar New York to an unfamiliar Metropolis, where the laws of physics could be stretched indefinitely. The '60s, like the twelfth century, was a time of cultural renaissance in which Eastern religion and Western heresy flowered in the shadow of a mainstream "disjunctive" knowledge[10] that could create both the Inquisition and the atomic bomb...

But the comics creators were only doing what Wolfram von Eschenbach had done, in an exemplary form of verse storytelling, when he created an alternate world in which the Knights Templar were the guardians of the Grail and in which the sacred symbol itself was a Stone rather than a Chalice, kept in a temple on Mount Savage. A hundred years after the launching of the Albigensian Crusade, the Templars, having already lost the Holy Land that they were created to defend, were destroyed by a combination of political greed and theological dogmatism. But in the *mundus imaginalis*, where are also situated the cities of Corbenic and Sarras, the Temple of the Grail still stands and the Grail Templars guard its secrets eternally.

Twelve

An End to Adventures?

> "Don't adventures ever have an end? I suppose not. Someone else always has to carry on the story."[1]
>
> —J.R.R. Tolkien

We have seen that the most numinous image of western medieval literature, the Grail Procession witnessed by Perceval in the court of the Fisher King, has been emptied of all its spiritual potency as the scene is rewritten in the Post-Vulgate. It has become an unimportant prelude to the Galahad Quest, in which Perceval is relegated to second-place and Gawain cast as a villain.

The Post-Vulgate Cycle, in effect, gives us a much-expanded reworking of the Vulgate Grail Quest, in which some of the confusing elements of that romance are clarified. However, it also introduces new elements, such as the story of the Questing Beast which, as we saw in Chapter Nine, is considered to be one of the adventures of the Holy Grail but about which no one except Merlin (who is now incommunicado) seems to know anything else. In the Post-Vulgate *Merlin Continuation* the bizarre beast, which sounds as if it has thirty baying hounds inside it, is pursued by King Pellinor but, after the king's death at the hands of Gawain, the pursuit is taken up by Palomides the Saracen.

A Beautiful and Marvelous Adventure

Palomides is the son of a pagan warrior from Galilee, Esclabor, who was drawn to Britain by the rumors of Arthur's fame. Despite being a Saracen and marrying the daughter of a giant, Esclabor is welcomed in the Court of Adventures.

Esclabor and the giantess have twelve sons, all of whom, apart from Palomides, the eldest, are killed when one of them pierces the Questing

Beast with his lance while it is drinking from a lake. As a result of striking the creature, Esclabor and his sons are all rendered unconscious. The father survives, but his sons do not. Due to this and other incidents in which he witnesses pagans being struck by divine vengeance, Esclabor converts to Christianity; but his only surviving son takes up the pursuit of the Questing Beast, adamantly refusing to be baptized until he can uncover the truth about the bizarre creature—to the great sorrow of his father, who sees only harm befalling those who involve themselves with it.

The pursuit of the Beast continues throughout the Post-Vulgate Grail Quest, to which it appears as a kind of anti-quest, a pagan quest contrasting with the Christian Grail Quest; for it is possible to see this bizarre creature with the sound of thirty hounds as an image of the cult of the moon goddess that was established in Britain by Brutus the Trojan.

This association is reinforced in the text when, shortly after Galahad first encounters the "beautiful and marvelous adventure" of the Questing Beast (*LG* V, 136), he and Bors come to a castle which was founded by Brutus and which is currently ruled by a king who is named after its founder. King Brutus makes them welcome and puts them up for the night, for he loves chivalry; but his teenage daughter goes further, becoming so infatuated with the young Sir Galahad that she climbs into his bed. She is very disappointed when she discovers that he is wearing a hair shirt, indicating that he is not a lover, but one who finds joy only in penitence, so that God will reward him in the other world and forgive him for any offenses he may have committed in this one. Nevertheless, unable to overcome her feelings, the princess threatens to kill herself if the knight will not have sex with her.

But—like Bors in the Vulgate Quest (see Chapter Five), who would rather watch young women kill themselves than abandon his hard-won chastity—Galahad is committed to that "unhuman realm" in which earthly beauty is only a deception leading to the soul's death. In this case, it also leads to the physical death of the young girl, who stabs herself through the breast with Galahad's sword, the very weapon which he drew from the Floating Stone to indicate that he had been chosen by God to bring to an end the adventures of Logres.

The next day the knights encounter Palomides, who tells them that the pursuit of the Questing Beast is not for them. They also learn from Esclabor of the doom attached to the bizarre creature: that anyone who involves himself with it comes to harm in the end. And so, indeed, it will prove. Meantime, Galahad occupies himself with the quest which is undoubtedly his own, along the way healing the mad and the leprous and exposing the devilish origins of the magical powers of pagans, whose demonic powers disappear in the presence of the Good Knight.

Galahad clears up another loose end when he encounters Caiaphas, the Jewish high priest who was instrumental in having Jesus executed for sedition and who, in the *Estoire del Saint Graal*, is set adrift in a ship by Vespasian, acting as an agent of God's vengeance or mercy. Caiaphas, who was already at that point an old man, drifts for a couple of hundred years before becoming marooned on a narrow spit of land. He has been there at least another couple of centuries when Galahad, Bors, Perceval and his sister arrive there on the Ship of Faith. But, having heard his story, they realize that there is no way they can invite him aboard a ship that will not tolerate unbelievers and Galahad pronounces that Our Lord wants Caiaphas to stay lost. They leave him to his fate.

But Galahad is more merciful when he encounters another sinner from the days of the conversion of Britain, Simeon, whom he saves from endless fiery torment in an episode that is also recounted in the Vulgate (see Chapter Five). Moreover Simeon's son Moses, who so presumptuously sat in the Seat of Danger at the Table of the Grail and who was carried off to a ruined castle in a forest (see Chapter Seven), is found there by Galahad and also saved from hellfire.

Having dealt with these Jewish unbelievers, Galahad turns his attention to pockets of pagan resistance. His first triumph is over what will become known as the Castle of Treachery: an impregnable fortress built by a relative of King Priam of Troy in the days when Albion was first settled by Brutus and his followers—like the aforementioned Castle Brutus but which, unlike the latter, has never been converted to Christianity, despite the best efforts of Joseph of Arimathea and the Company of the Grail. The pagans have even preserved the ancient Trojan language as well as their old gods, but that does not prevent them from writing inscriptions on marble stones that can be understood by passers-by, inviting them to seek adventures at the castle—adventures which, it turns out, invariably end in the death of Christian knights and the imprisonment of Christian women. One such female prisoner, however, a saintly princess, prophesied before her death the coming of the Very Good Knight who would put an end to the castle and its evil customs, as well as to the adventures of the Grail. Her prophecy is fulfilled when Galahad arrives, is imprisoned, but then freed by a miracle: he kills the pagans while a God-sent storm destroys the buildings.

There is still one outstanding pagan warrior in Logres, however: that is Palomides, who has steadfastly refused baptism and doggedly pursued his quest for the Questing Beast; but who eventually comes to despair of achieving it. Challenged to combat by Galahad and fearing for his life, he is eventually persuaded by his father to become a Christian and trust to Our Lord's mercy. He is right to do so, as it transpires, for, after defeating him in battle, Galahad spares Palomides on condition that he receives baptism. As soon as he enters the holy water, Palomides is miraculously cured of all his wounds. He now goes to Camelot to become a Knight of the Round Table, a necessary preliminary to joining the Grail Quest.

But before the adventures of Logres can be brought to an end, another quest must be concluded: that of the Questing Beast. For this Palomides teams up with Galahad and Perceval, both members of the family of King Pellinor, for whom (the late monarch had declared) its accomplishment was vouchsafed. The three knights pursue the beast to a lake where Palomides spears it to death: the Lake of the Beast, as it is henceforth known, starts boiling and will never stop.

The trio next makes its way to Corbenic, entering the Palace of Adventures. Here they are joined by nine other knights, including Bors of Ganis and Arthur the Less, an illegitimate son of King Arthur.[2] Galahad is led to a room where he sees the Grail on its silver table and the Holy Lance, which he immediately recognizes as the one that pierced the side of Jesus on the Cross—*La Lance Aventureuse, celle meemes dont li filz Deu soufri mort*—and which is dripping blood into a silver basin. A voice tells him to take the basin and, as he does so, the Lance is carried up to Heaven. It will never again be seen in Britain (*PV* III, 320), although it will have an extended continental career in the literalist fantasies of conspiracy theorists.[3]

Galahad takes the basin into a chamber where King Pellehan lies, unable to stand since he was struck a blow by that very Lance of Vengeance, wielded by Balin the Savage (as we saw in Chapter Nine). Tipping up the basin, Galahad sees three drops of blood fall onto the Maimed King's thighs, whereupon the basin also flies heavenwards. The much lamented Pellehan—*que touz li monz pleignoit si durement* (321)—is immediately cured of the effects of the Dolorous Blow, leading him to praise Galahad as a holy creature, clean of sensuality.

After receiving the grace of the Grail in the form of a consecrated Host served from the Holy Vessel by a man whose face is too bright for the knights to gaze upon, the twelve go their separate ways. Shortly after leaving Corbenic, Palomides is treacherously slain by Gawain, "without reason" (*LG* V, 282). He dies with his arms in the shape of a cross on his breast.

Visiting Pellehan, who is now a hermit, Galahad at last finds out the origin of the Questing Beast. It transpires that its mother was a woman who, like Morgan and Ninienne, was led astray by book-learning. The most beautiful of all the princesses in Logres, she also has the best masters in the world teach her the seven arts.

> When she reached the age of twenty, she was so wise and intelligent that everyone marvelled at her knowledge, and they could ask her nothing about church matters

to which she could not reply comprehensively, but she studied no other discipline so gladly as necromancy [283].

Despite these accomplishments she loves two things to excess: the world and her only brother. But when the God-fearing young man rejects her sexual advances, she decides to end it all. In that moment of despair brought on by her own unnatural lust, it is perhaps only natural that the Devil should appear to her, seducing her as he did Merlin's mother and encouraging her to accuse her brother of rape.

The hapless young man is thrown to the dogs, but not before prophesying that her child will be so monstrous that no-one could believe that he was the father: "You carry a devil, and a devil will come forth in the semblance of the most grotesque beast anyone ever saw. Because you're having me thrown to the dogs, that beast will have inside it dogs who will bark constantly in remembrance of and reference to the dogs to which you're having me given" (284–5).

Gawain, when he first came upon the Questing Beast, had earlier commented to Palomides that it was precisely because the creature was "so strange and bizarre" that he was seized by the desire to pursue it and never leave doing so until he caught it (269). The bizarreness of the beast connects it with the *poétique de l'étrangeté* that is characteristic of the early Grail poems; but in the Post-Vulgate there is no room for the sort of poetic strangeness that risks leading us to the Mountains of Heresy. King Pellehan, himself the product of a distinctly unorthodox apostolic succession, is the voice of moral judgment when he takes all the poetry out of the strangeness: the beast is demonic, the child of the Devil, conceived in the shadow of incestuous lust and first manifesting when brother-sister incest is consummated (that is, in the union of Arthur and Morgause). The Beast is, symbolically, Mordred's animal shadow and, insofar as that shadow is pagan (for Mordred will certainly ally himself with pagans in his attempt to overthrow his father/uncle), it is his own former paganism that Palomides is destroying when he kills the beast after being baptized.

The cult of the moon goddess, the Huntress, the Lady of Wild Animals, has not just been superseded in what was once Diana's Promised Land: It has been demonized, tainted with accusations of necromancy, Devil worship and incest. When another Bizarre Beast emerges, in the story of Nascien the Hermit (in the Prologue to the *Estoire del Saint Graal* which we can also see as a prologue to the whole Post-Vulgate Cycle), its role is to lead the narrator and the reader into a confrontation with that free flow of images and fluidity of imagination which leads both to sexual transgression and to doctrinal heresy—and to lead us back to orthodoxy.

The Adventure of the Questing Beast turns out not to be very beautiful after all, except insofar as physical beauty, like that of the incestuous necromancer princess, veils an ugly soul. If it retains an element of the marvelous, the marvels are subordinate to those of Holy Church, which is the true goal of the Grail Quest, according to one of the ubiquitous hermits who counsels Bors. And when Helain the White (the son of Bors, the product of that knight's one lapse from life-long chastity) sees visions in an ancient chapel, his companion Gawain tells him that these are "beautiful marvels … signs from Our Lord, high marvels of the Holy Grail, and great secrets of Holy Church" (*LG* V, 153).

But "the signs and lessons of the Holy Grail" will not appear to Gawain himself, as a hermit who is explicating a dream the knight has had explains, because he is a "treacherous sinner" who is "wrapped up in earthly pleasures." The adventures that are befalling the knights on the Quest are not about chivalric battles: they are "the signs of the Holy Grail … things that show to good men the meaning of other things, for heavenly things are hidden, so that the mortal heart will never be able to know them except through the Holy Spirit" (158).

In other words, the adventures are allegories.

The Signs of the Holy Grail

The Post-Vulgate Cycle has brought us a long way from the poetic strangeness of the early Grail poems and, with the destruction of the Questing Beast, it seems to have effectively destroyed the pagan legacy of that moon goddess who once bequeathed Albion to Brutus and his descendants in exchange for a promise that she would be worshipped here eternally. When the marvelous adventures of the Perilous Kingdom are reduced to allegories of Holy Church, then we know that the Very Good Knight has accomplished his destined task of bringing them to an end.

But even in this most "ecclesiasticized" of Grail romances, much remains which reveals the Otherworld (neither heavenly nor hellish, but imaginative) that still lingers, poised between earthly life and the afterlife; which reveals the *mundus imaginalis* that, for Henry Corbin, is the repository of the esoteric lost Word of God.

Corbin draws our attention back to the extraordinary Prologue to the Post-Vulgate Cycle, in which Christ gives to Nascien the Book of the Grail, written in His own hand in the letters of Heaven, on the morning of Good Friday. The text must be translated into Latin by the hermit before the Feast of Ascension, because on that day the original will be taken up to Heaven, as Christ Himself was. These lost writings of Christ, like the empty tomb at the Resurrection, are for Corbin images of the lost inner meaning of a religion that has declined into literalism and legalism (1983, 202).

But what of the text bequeathed to us by Nascien, the Latin translation of the Book that Came Down from Heaven which, we are assured, has been translated into French by Robert de Boron and now into English as the Post-Vulgate Cycle?

It is clear that much has been lost in translation. For example, in the Prose *Joseph of Arimathea*, which constitutes the first part of the De Boron Cycle, the resurrected Christ comes to his disciple in prison, entrusts to his keeping "the precious vessel with the most holy blood that Joseph had gathered from His precious body when he washed Him" (*MG* 21) and gives Joseph an orthodox account of doctrines such as the Incarnation, the Virgin Birth and the Trinity. But He does not stop there, referring also to "other words" which Jesus spoke to Joseph, words contained in a "high book" he possesses (22).

As the De Boron Cycle continues, these divine words are transmitted by Joseph to Bron and finally to Perceval but, in the Post-Vulgate Cycle, although it purports to be the very "high book" on which de Boron drew, there are no other words spoken by the resurrected Christ, only those of comfort for Joseph in prison and of vengeance against those who have injured him—such as Caiaphas, whose ultimate fate we now know. They have become the lost Word of God and if, as Waite inferred, "these words were a formula of Eucharistic consecration" (257) or an unknown invocation to the Holy Spirit at the moment of transubstantiation, their loss would suggest that no Mass has been *truly* celebrated since the disappearance of the Grail (Corbin 1983, 203). If this was indeed the intention of de Boron, it is not surprising that the author of the Post-Vulgate, usually so eager to invoke de Boron's authority, has removed all such references from his cycle, which is committed to promoting the marvels of Holy Church.

Elements that appear to derive from an earlier paganism do survive into the Post-Vulgate, but they seem to be as emasculated as the Maimed King himself. Thus Philippe Walter sees in the peregrinations of the Ship of Faith and other maritime adventures in the archipelago of the Grail an echo, however distant, of the voyages to supernatural islands found in medieval Irish literature; a literature which stretches back to the archaic foundations of western culture (62) and which enables us to encounter remnants of ancient Celtic mythology (63). These voyages are initiatory visits to the Otherworld (66) but, as part of the process of Christianization, Faerie becomes transformed into sorcery (74): what cannot be reclaimed by Holy Church must be abandoned to the Devil (75).

This process of reclamation may even apply to the most sacred site of Grail Christianity, if we accept the argument of R.S. Loomis (235) that Corbenic, the Place of the Holy Vessel, may originally have been the Castle of the Sacred Horn. For this horn, one of the Thirteen Treasures of Britain, belongs to Brân the Blessed—whose near-namesake, Bron, is the father of the first Fisher King. It is interesting that Bron plays a much larger role in the earlier De Boron Cycle than he does in the Post-Vulgate. Again, we must ask whether it is the very closeness of Bron to a figure from Celtic paganism, "a euhemerized deity" who was only belatedly hailed as the king who brought Christianity to Britain (*TYP* 290–1), which has led to his sidelining in the later cycle?

Another pagan treasure reclaimed for Christianity is the Broken Sword, which is an image of divine sovereignty in Norse mythology, whence it was adopted by Wagner in his operatic Ring Cycle and transformed by Tolkien in the twentieth century into the Sword of Red-and-White Flame. Broken in battle at the moment of victory, the sword can only be re-forged when the true King of the West, who was lost, is found. The theme of the sword-that-will-break is introduced into the Grail romances by Chrétien and developed by his continuators, in whose poems its re-soldering becomes a test of prowess and chivalric election. But in the Vulgate *Queste* the Broken Sword becomes a sign of spiritual election. The sword has been used by a pagan to wound Joseph of Arimathea in the Castle of the Rock and is later carried from there by Eliezer (the son of King Pelles), who is on a quest to find the best knight in the world. Gawain, of course, fails the test; but Galahad, as soon as he arrives in Corbenic, is met by Eliezer and presented with the Broken Sword, which he has no trouble in rejoining.

For the Vulgate author, the breaking of the sword illustrates the conflict between the old Saracenic astral religion and the new gospel taught by the Company of the Grail. For Henry Corbin, the Broken Sword takes on a further symbolic importance, becoming an image of the disjunction between the exoteric and esoteric aspects of divine revelation which developed *within* Christianity. Milestones in this process, as we have seen, were the abandonment of the threefold model of being and with it the middle ground of the soul—and the attack on images (which is an attack on the imagination), leading to the reduction of their function to that of servicing allegories. It is "the mystical Sword of the Word" which is broken when the exoteric and esoteric aspects of religion cease to be contraries, to use Blake's phrase, without which there is no progression—and become instead opposites which negate each other.

I referred in the last chapter to how the development of a rationalistic religious philosophy in the twelfth century was negated by extreme heretical movements such as that of the Cathars in the West, culminating in the adoption of radical dualism. The appearance of the Grail at this historical moment can be seen as the attempt of the soul at self-healing, producing an image of wholeness out of *spiritus mundi*. For Corbin, the Galahad Quest is needed to reunite the broken Word.

How extraordinary then, that in the Post-Vulgate *Quest*, which is considerably expanded from the earlier Vulgate version, there is no mention of the joining asunder of the Broken Sword. For, if the Word remains split between the exoteric and the esoteric, this effects "an irreparable scission between the sensory and the spiritual," which is a catastrophe for the soul. Cut off from exoteric faith, esotericism "degenerates into a purely abstract knowledge, that of the forces of nature, for example, or else succumbs to spiritual libertinage"; while the exoteric religion degenerates into "a hollow cortex," merely a covering for an empty creed: "Everything, then, becomes institutionalized; dogmas are formulated; legalistic religion triumphs; the science of Nature becomes the conquest and possession of Nature..." (1995, 107).

Deprived of its "theophanic function," its power to reveal the sacred, Nature becomes a Waste Land. Institutionalized religion, no longer able to connect us to the sacred, becomes the theology of the Waste Land and "fixed" science creates the technology that perpetuates it.

The *Estoire del Saint Graal* describes the creating of the Waste Land when one of the Fisher Kings is killed with the Sword of David—and the *Merlin* Continuation describes the destruction of Corbenic, at the heart of the wasted kingdom, when another Grail guardian is maimed by the Dolorous Blow. But neither the Vulgate nor the Post-Vulgate versions of the Grail Quest refer either to the reconstruction of Corbenic or to the restoration of the Waste Land, though this must be implicated in the healing of the Maimed King by the blood from the Lance that struck him.

The First Continuation to the Story of the Grail does describe a partial restoration of the Waste Land, when Gawain asks the Grail King how the Lance bleeds; which, in an earlier work,[4] I interpreted as a challenge to the literal interpretation of the Incarnation. But the early Grail poems inhabit an imaginative world at loggerheads with that of the Post-Vulgate, both in their flirting with heterodox themes and in their exaltation to heroic status of the womanizing and "pagan" Gawain, the Knight of the Goddess, who very nearly succeeds in re-soldering the Broken Sword. By contrast, the Post-Vulgate Galahad apparently leaves the Sword broken and the Land wasted.[5]

If he is neither able to make whole the Sword of the Word nor restore the Waste Land, what are the positive consequences of healing the Maimed King, which has been such an important leitmotif binding together the romances that constitute the Post-Vulgate Cycle? The king himself, now healthy, retires to a hermitage whence he is able to clear up some of the mysteries of the Quest, including that of the bizarre creature; the Bleeding Lance is taken up to Heaven, nevermore to be seen in Britain; while the Grail goes East, pursued by Galahad, Perceval and Bors.

The final chapters of the Post-Vulgate *Quest* follow the Vulgate version very closely. Our three heroes pursue the Holy Vessel overseas to Sarras, whither it had been brought by the Company of the Grail on its outward journey from the Holy Land. After the departure of the Company, Sarras had reverted to paganism and its current monarch is so brutal and treacherous that he throws them into prison. Galahad prays only that he will die with "the marvels of the Holy Grail" before his eyes (*LG* V, 286). He will have his wish soon enough.

Fed by the sacred vessel, Galahad and his companions survive the rigors of a Middle Eastern prison and are released on the death of the pagan king. The Saracens heed a divine voice and make Galahad their new king but, on the anniversary of his coronation, he witnesses the Mass of Our Lady celebrated by the spirit of Josephus in the Spiritual Palace, with the Holy Grail used as the Eucharistic chalice. When Josephus lifts the paten from the sacred vessel, Galahad looks inside it, as he has always desired to do, praising God that he has at last been enabled to see openly "what mortal tongue could not tell nor heart imagine … the cause of the great marvels" (287).

He is now ready to pass from terrestrial to celestial life. Angels carry his soul up to Heaven and a hand reaches down from the sky and carries off the Holy Vessel, which is never again seen on Earth. His companions bury his body in the Spiritual Palace. Perceval and Bors retire to a hermitage but, when Perceval also dies, Bors has him buried next to his sister and Galahad. Bors then leaves for Logres, the only quester to return from Sarras.

Back in Arthur's kingdom, Bors inevitably gets caught up in the civil war that breaks out between Lancelot's kin and that of Gawain when Guenevere's adultery with the Leopard of Benoic is found out. The end is well-known: Mordred, the child of Arthur's incestuous relationship with his sister, revolts while Arthur is on the continent fighting the Romans. Arthur the Less, Gawain and most of the other Knights of the Round Table are killed. Arthur kills Mordred and Mordred mortally wounds his father. King Arthur bids Girflet cast Excalibur into a lake near the sea (presumably the Lake of Fays from which the king originally received it) and, when Girflet reluctantly does so, he sees a hand emerge to grasp the weapon and take it back into the waters.

A barque now arrives in which are many ladies, among them Morgan the Fay, Arthur's enchantress sister. She entreats him to come aboard and the barque heads out to sea. Later Girflet visits a chapel where a tomb purports to contain Arthur's body, apparently brought there by weeping ladies but, when he looks inside the tomb, Girflet finds it empty.

The king's ending, the knight reflects, is as mysterious as his beginning. This uncertainty is welcomed by Arthur himself, who, in his last great speech, tells Girflet, "just as I became king here by adventure, so shall I pass from this kingdom by adventure, and after this, no one will be able to boast that he knows for certain what has become of me ... if they ask news of me, answer them that King Arthur came through God's adventure, and by God's adventure he departed, and he alone was the King of Adventures" (306).

The Post-Vulgate seems to be telling us that with the achieving of the Grail Quest and the passing of Arthur, Britain is no longer the Kingdom of Adventures. But uncertainty remains.

For a start, it is intriguing that the last two people to see Arthur alive are both figures with an ancient pedigree, rooted in paganism. Girflet is described as the son of Doon, a woodsman; but it has long been recognized that Girflet is derived from Gilfaethwy, the son of Dôn in Welsh literature— and Dôn is not a man but a goddess who may have given her name to the River Dee (*TYP* 330). Morgan, as we have seen, is one of the Fatal Sisters who have descended from the threefold moon goddess and it is striking that there is at the end no longer any suggestion of the fratricidal hatred which Morgan has shown throughout the Post-Vulgate Cycle.

Lucy Allen Paton may have been right all along, when she suggested that Morgan's hatred was thwarted love and that all she had ever wanted was to have Arthur to herself in her Otherworldly realm, reigning together as King and Queen of Faerie. How curious, then, that there is no mention of the Isle of Avalon anywhere in the Post-Vulgate Cycle, as though this island of supernatural women had to be written out of the story in the same way that the fays themselves have been reduced to dangerously learned ladies.

If Avalon has disappeared, so has the Grail, taken away from Britain to the East and thence to Heaven. But does this mean the definitive end, as both the Vulgate and the Post-Vulgate cycles assert, of the marvels of the Adventurous Kingdom?

As we saw in the last chapter, Henry Corbin, reading these prose cycles in the light of the alternative German Grail tradition, finds powerful images which point beyond this world, not just to the other world of orthodox faith, but to the Otherworld of the Imagination, the *mundus imaginalis*; images which present us with an order of reality that is not merely "marvelous" or "imaginary" (1971, 186–7) but which can better be described as "spiritual realism" (190). In this reading, the journey of the Grail to Sarras—on the borders of Egypt (the Biblical place of exile)—and thence on to Britain in the Far West, represents the descent of the soul into incarnation. It is not a journey that can be traced on a map (160).

And so with the return of the Grail to Sarras at the end of the Quest, we see the re-ascent of the soul to the realm of light; for Sarras is the gateway to the East, a place of diverse (and sometimes conflicting) spiritual traditions—pagan, Christian and Islamic—like the soul itself. But all historical and doctrinal conflicts are resolved in the Spiritual Palace, which marks the threshold between the lower and the higher reaches of the soul. It was here that Josephus was consecrated by angels as the first Christian bishop (inaugurating an alternative apostolic succession which ignores the exoteric institutions of the Church) and, although Josephus has long since quit this Earth, we should not be surprised that the Grail Questers encounter him there, for they are no longer in the world we know (183).

Equally, the burials of Galahad and Perceval in the Spiritual Palace are not comparable to earthly burials: the heroes rather experience an *occultation mystique* like that of the Grail Hallows (177). For, whether we imagine this occultation as a heavenly hand taking up the Grail and rendering it thenceforth invisible to human eyes (as the French prose cycles do) or as the return of the Grail to the Orient (as the German tradition does), we are visualizing an encounter with the reality of the soul world, which cannot really be expressed by a theoretical exposition but only experienced (184). That experience can best be conveyed in a narrative, a mystical recital (188–9).

Where Is the Grail?

If the Grail has gone into hiding, then the story of its seeking continues: the Quest goes on, but on a different level. The Kingdom of Adventures is still all around us, though we cannot see it with earthly eyes; for we carry our heavens with us.

The Post-Vulgate Cycle represents the fullest and final development in the French language of the story of the Grail, some fifty years after Chrétien started it; while the poem by Albrecht, in which the Grail is transported to India, continued the work of Wolfram von Eschenbach some decades later, bringing a final variation to the medieval mythos. From now on the Grail Quest would take different forms.

Henry Corbin stresses the significance of the Grail Cycle for our whole spiritual culture and singles out Wolfram in particular as a precursor of the Christian Hermeticists of the Renaissance (1971, 152n243). Hermeticism along with alchemy (which is increasingly being recognized as a spiritual science in its own right and not merely as a misguided precursor of materialist chemistry) represents an important alternative intellectual current that was carried into the modern era by Protestant mystics such as Boehme and Swedenborg, both of whom had a formative influence on the young Blake.

Interest in the Grail legend itself revived among nineteenth century scholars, who were particularly interested in its Celtic origins, as we saw in the last chapter. But as the twentieth century dawned, eccentric scholars such as Jessie Weston, the occultist A.E. Waite and the "spiritual scientist" Rudolf Steiner were more interested in inner meanings than literary pedigree. The quest was taken up by the analytical psychologist Carl Jung, for whom the Grail was a symbol of psychic wholeness; although detailed work on the legend was left to his wife Emma and their colleague Marie-Louise von Franz. The Jungs and von Franz saw the alchemists as continuing a task that the Grail writers had left unfinished for, although the healing of the Maimed King is described, the Waste Land is only ever partially restored.

From a Jungian perspective, the Grail legend expresses the central dilemma of the second half of the Christian aeon: the need to re-balance the overly spiritualized Christ image and at the same time to counter the materialist reaction to this excessive spirituality. What the Grail writers at the beginning of the second Christian millennium were unable to accomplish, must be attempted at the end of that millennium with the new tools of analytical psychology, which (unlike Freudianism) does not deny the reality of spirit but puts soul back at the center of the human being.

According to Jung and von Franz, the Grail Quest remains unachieved because the sacred vessel remains in occultation rather than being brought back to the world. The Grail Hero, they argue, "should have brought the Grail to the Round Table, so that instead of the Spirit being divorced from the world, the world would have been impregnated with the Spirit." The Post-Vulgate describes the disastrous consequences of the loss of the vessel, although it characteristically blames it on people's sinfulness: a famine descends on the land, which lasts for three years and is so severe that the Britons are nearly reduced to eating each other. Meanwhile the Siege Perilous remains empty. For Jung and von Franz the Grail Hero, "who strives only upward, turns into an ideal figure or into one half of a pair of opposites and is unable to fill the empty place." The coming of the Paraclete, which followers of the mystic Joachim of Flora saw as the establishment of the Third Kingdom, the reign of the Holy Spirit on Earth, "likewise remains an unfulfilled ideal ... because of a renunciation of the world and of life" (389).

From a Jungian perspective, the attempt to fulfil the unachieved ideal of the Grail Quest was taken up by the alchemists, whose *opus* can be simplified to produce a schema of three principal stages: the "blackening" (*nigredo*), the "whitening" (*albedo*) and finally the "reddening" (*rubedo*). Black and white symbolize psychic death and spiritual rebirth: thus far, we have an image of the Galahad Quest or of the transfer of the Grail to the East. In the alchemical opus, red symbolizes the return of the spiritually reborn soul to manifestation (Burckhardt, 182–3). But in the medieval Grail romances there is no "reddening," for Bors returns to Logres empty-handed and there is no longer anyone to sit in the Siege Perilous. In fact, a coda to the Post-Vulgate describes the destruction of the Round Table by a vengeful King Mark of Cornwall. The Kingdom of Adventures ends in blackening because the Grail Quest ends in whitening and the Holy Vessel itself remains hidden.

In the Thirties, when western culture was undergoing a new *nigredo*, Jung's alchemical work inspired the founding of the Eranos conferences at which experts in the fields of comparative religion and mythology along with other scholars in the humanities and sciences meet annually to exchange the fruits of their researches—and sometimes to provide field notes from their own quests, for the purpose of Eranos has always been to bring into manifestation (*rubedo*) the fruits of spiritual enlightenment (*albedo*). The story of Eranos constitutes "an alternative history of the twentieth century" which, like the Grail itself, has remained hidden for too long. From its inauguration in 1933 it has provided a theoretical underpinning to the renaissance of the imagination that occurred in popular fiction in the same decade: in the birth of heroic fantasy in the work of Robert E. Howard and Tolkien, along with the appearance "up in the sky" of the American Messiah, Superman.

After Jung himself, who attended his last conference in 1952, two of the most important Grail Questers associated with Eranos were Henry Corbin (who gave his first lecture in 1949) and Mircea Eliade (who began attending the following year).[6] It was in Eliade's inaugural lecture, on the symbolism of the center, that he argued that in order to "regenerate the whole of Nature" it suffices to ask the question, Where is the Grail?

In that instant, everything is transformed: the King rises from his bed of suffering, the rivers and fountains flow once more, vegetation grows again, and the castle is miraculously restored. Those few words ... propound the central question, the one question that can arouse not only the Fisher King but the whole Cosmos: Where is the supreme reality, the sacred, the Centre of Life and the source of immortality...?

The Post-Vulgate tried to bring an end to questioning, but the occultation of the Grail raises a new question for our post-medieval world, which is perishing from "metaphysical and religious indifference," from "lack of imagination and absence of desire for reality." For Eliade, that "great European myth" which is the Grail story reveals to us that, for the life of the cosmos to be renewed, *it is enough only to raise the question of salvation* (1991, 56).

For us in the twenty-first century, faced with the twin threats of environmental destruction and terrorism in the name of fundamentalist religion, it is perhaps even more urgent than it was for the pioneers of Eranos to raise the salvific question, to ask the whereabouts of the sacred center where the Grail is hidden. For the Jungians, that sacred center is the soul, which holds the tension of the opposites of spirit and matter; while for Corbin, it is more particularly that region on the threshold of the soul which can only be accessed by that very imagination whose lack is causing the world to perish.

In a later work, based on a series of lectures he gave in 1956, Eliade argued that the Grail romances preserved initiatory patterns which, deprived of their spiritual context, became literary motifs; but that the very popularity of the Arthurian cycle proves "that such adventures provided the answer to a profound need in medieval man. It was only his imagination which was fed by these initiatory scenarios; but the life of the imagination, like the life of a dream, is as important for the whole psyche of the human being as is daily life" (1975, 125-6). Even today, popular fiction reworks mythical and initiatory scenarios (1958, 431). Indeed Eliade himself, in his own short stories and novels, tried to do just this. For, as he argued, initiatory themes, having lost their spiritual reality, "remain alive chiefly in modern man's unconscious" (1975, 134) and, as literary motifs, "they now deliver their spiritual message on a different plane of human experience, by addressing themselves directly to the imagination" (126).

In a lecture he gave at Eranos in 1971, Corbin follows Eliade in arguing that, for the contemporary Parsifal, the only important question is that concerning the whereabouts of the Grail, since on it depends the rejuvenation of the world (Corbin 1983, 260). But, unlike Eliade, he also points us in the direction of a particular work of popular fiction which he feels continued the Grail Quest into the twentieth century.

The Faring Forth

The work that Corbin refers to is one that was published in the mid–1950s, when he and Eliade were giving their first Eranos lectures (inaugurating a "silver age" that followed the "golden age" which ended when Jung was no longer able to attend). But this work only achieved mass popularity in the sixties, when a cheap but unauthorized paperback edition was published in the U.S., prompting much publicity and a great deal of interest in the authorized paperback that soon followed.

I refer, of course, to *The Lord of the Rings* by the Oxford philologist and expert in Old and Middle English, J.R.R. Tolkien. A sequel to *The Hobbit*, a children's "fairy" story which Tolkien published in 1937, *The Lord of the Rings* greatly outgrew its predecessor both in length and in grandeur, turning into a heroic romance aimed at older children and adults, which had to be published in three volumes. But unlike most of its imitators (and the commercial success of Tolkien's epic spawned a host of fantasy trilogies compared frequently, but invariably erroneously, by their publishers to "Tolkien at his best") the Rings trilogy was rooted in ancient languages and pre-existent mythology.

One of the aspects of *The Lord of the Rings* which sets it apart from other heroic fantasies is the frequent references to other stories and earlier events which constitute the history of Middle-earth and which provide a vast backdrop to the trilogy, a framework of mythology, topography and language that Tolkien felt he was discovering rather than merely "inventing."[7] Tolkien's conscious intention was to provide England with its lost mythology. But, although he was familiar with English-language Arthurian epics such as those of Layamon and Malory (and was an expert in the alliterative poetry which had been such an important element in early English literature from *Beowulf* to *Sir Gawain and the Green Knight*, both of which he translated), he was also aware that the stories of Arthur were rooted in Celtic rather than Anglo-Saxon language and culture—despite the fact that Arthur had, by the nineteenth century, become a very *English* king (regardless of historical theories which make of Arthur a Romano-British warlord who held at bay the Anglo-Saxon incursions).

For this among other reasons Tolkien abandoned an early attempt to write an Arthurian poem; but an exploration of the relation of his fictional *legendarium* to Britain's greatest legendary cycle would take us too far from our theme, so I refer the reader who is interested in Tolkien's Arthurian inspiration to the Appendix. What interested Corbin more particularly was the less-obvious relationship of *The Lord of the Rings* to the Grail Quest. Given the low esteem in which popular writers such as Tolkien are held by the custodians of "serious," "literary" fiction, it is worth quoting Corbin at length: "I think that this is the first time since the conclusion of the Grail cycle that there has appeared in the West an epic at once heroic, mystic and gnostic," he writes.[8]

It is the story of a "maleficent ring" which has been lost in Middle-earth (an intermediate realm, the domain of Men and Elves, between the worlds of Light and Shadow) and which exerts a powerful temptation for even "the best among the beings of Light," who must resist the compulsion "to put the evil desire for power at the service of the Light." For, as Corbin puts it, "it is not in the Darkness that the temptation of the Darkness can become virulent, but in the realm of Light. It is in the world of Light that the drama, which for all gnoses initiates the cosmogony, has its origin."

Here Corbin is referring to the mythical drama that, in the esoteric gnosis of the Abrahamic faiths (Valentinian Christianity, Ismaili Islam and Kabbalistic Judaism) is the prelude to creation: a war in heaven which, of necessity, precedes the human Fall on Earth, such as is also found in the gnostic mythology of Blake. In the work of Tolkien, a committed Catholic, this becomes the story of the fallen archangel Melkor, whose servant Sauron the Necromancer creates the Ring of Power.

However tempting it may be, the agents of Light cannot use the power of the Ring to defeat evil, for to succumb to the lust for power "would be to ensure the triumph of the Darkness." Instead, the Light must compel the Darkness to destroy its own weapon by equipping a hero to return the Ring to the fire in which it was forged: "What the hero performs in this epic appears as a Quest in the reverse direction to that for the Holy Grail. But at the same time this Quest seems to be a necessary prelude, a Quest without which the Quest for the Grail cannot succeed" (Corbin 1980, 217).

So Tolkien has provided us with a quest that corresponds to what Weston called "a test of fitness for an initiation" (1920, 182) which, for the medieval writers, took place in the Chapel Perilous but which Tolkien has transported to Mount Doom, where the Ring must be destroyed even though that means the hero's giving up the possibility of possessing absolute power—a peculiarly contemporary quest, as Tom Shippey has pointed out (169–70).

Small wonder that Tolkien should describe himself as an anarchist in the philosophical sense—"meaning abolition of control not whiskered men with bombs" (1981, 63)—and appeal to those gentle anarchists of the hippie counter-culture who would take their own test of fitness by renouncing the Ring of Power before setting off on the new quest for the hidden Grail. The search would take them to initiatory adventures *in contrayes straunge*[9] (as the Gawain poet puts it): some would go overland to the Far East, to India (where indeed it was claimed that the Grail is occulted); others would journey into inner space, conducting alchemical experiments on their own consciousness.

All were in search of marvels—and it is significant that this was precisely the name of the comics company which re-invented the superhero for the '60s generation, adding to the roster of mythical Supermen a Norse god and a Master of the Mystic Arts. Marvel Comics would also bring the work of Robert E. Howard renewed popularity through its graphic adaptations of his stories.

So the Post-Vulgate Cycle was wrong: the marvels did not end with the death of Galahad, nor are the adventures finished. As Tolkien's first Hobbit hero Bilbo Baggins puts it, in the quote with which I head this chapter, adventures do not end if there is someone to carry on the story; or, as Corbin and Eliade put it, if there is someone prepared to ask, Where Is the Grail?

The medieval romancers chronicled their Grail Quest in all its variations, until the stifling hand of religious orthodoxy blocked the free flow of images, so that the waters of the imagination once more dried up and the Waste Land returned. As writers such as Jung, Corbin and Eliade championed the true imagination in their theoretical works, so Tolkien gave it free reign in his fiction, becoming a channel for what he called mythopoeia, or "sub-creation": storytelling as the continuation of divine creation through the mind of Man. But, as Corbin points out, Tolkien only gives us the prelude to the contemporary Grail Quest and has left us with mere hints and fragments of what would come next.

Since Tolkien's death, many of his unfinished writings and much of his notes for his ever growing mythology have been arranged and edited by his son and literary heir Christopher; so that we now know that he began but abandoned a sequel to *The Lord of the Rings*; but to what extent this would have shown a contemporary initiation following the test of fitness, we will never know.[10] However, in his earliest writings, J.R.R. Tolkien introduced the theme, also later abandoned, of a special place for the island of Britain and of England in particular in the end times. Here we find the idea of Britain as the Lonely Isle, mid-way between the Blessed Realm of the gods and Middle-earth, where Men and Elves once lived in harmony in a country called Luthany. The heirs to this Kingdom of Friendship are the English, who alone have preserved the true fairy lore (*HME* II, 293).

Although the remnants of this conception are fragmentary and contradictory, we find one striking theme that Tolkien found it hard to let go of since it was clearly of importance to his sub-creation of English mythology: this is the idea that from England there was, or will be, the great Faring

Forth of Elves and Men to finally destroy Melkor and all his works. Insofar as the Faring Forth is set in the past, it is seen as unsuccessful: Britain is drawn eastwards, to become permanently a part of Middle-earth and the Elves of England fade, becoming the diminutive, gossamer creatures of children's fairy tales, no longer visible to most humans (285).

But insofar as the Faring Forth is not merely a tragic event in Elvish history, it remains a prophecy and a hope (303). As such, it can be compared with earlier conceptions such as the messianic belief that Arthur will return from Avalon to save the English, which we find in Layamon; or Blake's vision of the Last Judgment, in which Albion is awakened by his aged wife Britannia and re-united with his daughter, or Emanation, Jerusalem.

So when we fare forth to find the hidden Grail, we modern questers will no longer need to restrict our imaginations to the search for a Christian vessel. For the goddess of Britannia—the goddess who guided our ancestors to the isle that they would henceforth dedicate to her worship—is the pagan moon goddess. It is she who is tasked with waking the Sleeping Lord Albion, as Morgan is tasked with healing the wounded King Arthur. It is no longer a Perceval, let alone a saintly Galahad, who will heal the Maimed King, but the divine feminine, restored to her place at Albion's side, from which she has been too long exiled, since her Promised Land was usurped by the Company of the Grail and it became a Waste Land.

If the Post-Vulgate and its English translator Malory left us confused as to why Morgan, apparently Arthur's bitter enemy, should be restored to her earlier role as his healer, it is Blake who shows us in his prophetic poetry how the Emanations, who were lost, are found—and how the Shadowy Female can become once more beautiful in the light of vision. So it is with Blake that we shall end, as we began.

Epilogue—
From Albion to Avalon

> *... the other world already exists in this world; it exists in every moment, in relation to every being.*[1]
> —Henry Corbin

The Matter of Britain presents us with heroic images of man: of warrior kings and knights, of prophets, of lovers and of spiritual questers. Its heroes are powerful, archetypal figures: flawed yet deeply human. It also presents us with female figures whose power is distrusted, perhaps because it emanates from an older world than the one in which the stories are set. That world is still present, not wholly forgotten, existing alongside Arthur's Kingdom of Adventures and it is presented as pre-eminently the domain of the queens and enchantresses with whom the Arthurian heroes interact in love and conflict. Though they are excluded from the highest spiritual undertaking of Christian Logres, the Quest of the Holy Grail, they represent an alternative path to wisdom, one that is touched by magic, fated. They embody a separate reality and, if they appear treacherous, it may be because theirs is a deeper truth.

Truth and reality are the goals of every spiritual quest; but in the modern West they have been appropriated by an agnostic "ideology of science," or "scientism" (what Blake calls "fixed" science). The prevailing ideological model is that there is only one reality—*material* reality—the physical world perceived by the senses (or by the instruments created by the scientific mind, itself a material by-product or "epiphenomenon") and that the only truth is what can be ascertained by scientific experiment or "demonstration."

Against this (unverifiable) assertion is the statement of Jesus: "I am the way, the truth, and the life" (John 14.6).This statement in its turn can only be verified by personal experience, although it can be believed in by those who trust to the truth of revelation.

But the way of faith, when it is disconnected from *gnosis* (that knowledge that can only be found *within* the soul or the tradition), leads all too easily to a religious fundamentalism based on a purely literal understanding of sacred scripture. Equally, the way of gnosis, when it is disconnected from faith, can lead to what Henry Corbin has called "spiritual libertinage": the abandonment of all traditional values in exchange for a chimerical "enlightenment" and, ultimately, to the abandonment of the inner spiritual sense altogether—in short, to nihilism.

There is another way, shown to us by prophets such as Blake: the way of vision that leads to the truth of the imagination and transforms human life on earth, thus exemplifying the threefold means by which Jesus announces that he can bring us to the experience of a separate reality. This reality he calls, in the language of his Jewish culture, the Father: whose kingdom is *within* or *amongst* us (Lk 17.21) but is also *outside* for it has already arrived, it is spread out over the Earth, but people do not see it (*NHL* 138).

Blake, a visual artist for whom spiritual forms must always be clearly delineated, laments the inner blindness that denies the vision of the kingdom on Earth and leads to the ideologies which we now call scientism and religious fundamentalism. For between the forked paths of blind faith and blind materialism there is a middle path, one that balances faith and gnosis. This is the path of the creative imagination, which for Blake *is* Jesus, who is *the* way.

John Lennon asked us to imagine there's no heaven; Blake, to re-imagine Heaven and Earth.

Another Better World within Your Heart

In his prophetic poems, Blake has provided us with an epic psychodrama in which the Arthurian legends take their place as episodes in a much vaster mythic cycle, which begins in the time beyond time that precedes creation. Albion, the Universal Man, dwells in harmony with his Emanation, Jerusalem, in Eden; but falls into a death-like sleep, which is the chaos in which creation begins. The component parts of the Universal Man, the Four Zoas, become separated from their own female aspects and produce distorted mirror-images of themselves, called Spectres. All these split-off fragments of the Eternal Man (or, more accurately, the Human Being or Anthropos) fight among themselves, vying for supremacy. There is war in Heaven, reflected on Earth in the oppression of Church and State and in the violence of revolutionary upheavals against that oppression.

To break that cycle of violence, Blake believed, we need the power of the creative imagination. He saw himself as a prophet of that power, "sub-creating" in words and pictures, presenting us with mythopoeic images both of spiritual conflict and of imaginative resolution. The drama of Albion will be described through various poetic metaphors and on various levels of being in the later illuminated books. They are hard to read and even harder to summarize or explain, because they eschew chronological narrative or even consistent symbolism.

Blake's mythological poems are like a recurring dream in which archetypal images form and reform in changing shapes and patterns, or like a set of musical variations in which the basic theme is only hinted at, never clearly stated. To read them is like entering someone else's dream world; to attempt to explain them must be akin to practicing psychoanalysis. However, as with dreams, certain lines or phrases stand out and remain in the memory, taking on a greater significance for the meaning of the whole than their position in the overall structure seems to merit.

One such line is that stated by one of the Zoas, who says: "Attempting to be more than Man we become less" (*BCW* 376). Albion is the Ancient or Eternal Man; but the Eternal Great Humanity Divine is God (Damon, 191). To seek to be more than Man is the hubris of the being who wishes to identify their limited self with the unlimited. Such pride must come before a fall. Man becomes less: divided against himself, losing touch with the divine and thereby lessening his humanity. For Blake, this dehumanizing is the epic of creation and the task of the poet is to imagine how we can become human again.

The key to this process of re-humanizing lies primarily with three mythological figures seen in his visions: Los and his Emanation—whom Blake identified with himself and his wife (124)—and the Spectre that appears when man and wife are separated. Los is the Eternal Prophet who, while Albion sleeps, keeps alive the divine vision in time; Los' Emanation is Enitharmon, whose emblem is the Moon and who represents Spiritual Beauty; while the Spectre, who has become "horrible & Ghastly" to Los' eyes, ends up "buried beneath/ The ruins of the Universe."

Prophet, Emanation and Spectre are Blake's fallen Trinity, personifications of the three worlds of the ancient harmony, now shattered—and it is the one who has fallen the furthest who must begin the re-ascent. In a passage that anticipates twentieth century psychology, the Spectre describes himself as a Jungian Shadow or a Freudian (or even Frankensteinian) Monster of the Id ("ravening hungering & thirsting cruel lust & murder"), a thing of darkness which Los once subdued by his Immortal Strength but which he now must acknowledge as his own. For, if the Shadow knows what evil lurks in the hearts of men, he also knows the way back to the vision of Eternity.

Los must embrace his Shadow, "first as a brother,/ Then as another Self"; he must annihilate his separate self in order to return to "life Eternal" by *re*membering what has been *dis*membered: that the divided soul was once whole. In the "humanizing" words of the Spectre: "Unbar the Gates of Memory: look upon me/ Not as another, but as thy real Self."

The Spectre is the "medium" between male and female; he has come into being precisely because of their separation and it is only when he is accepted that Los and Enitharmon can "unite again in bliss." Moreover it is only when the Eternal Prophet is reunited with his Spectre and his Emanation that they can together in wholeness "repass" the Gates of Eternal Life: "If we unite in one," the inspired Spectre declares to Los, "another better world will be/ Open'd within your heart.... Threefold, as it was in Eternity."

Here the Spectre shows himself to be the key to restoring that threefold harmony whose loss is the metaphysical tragedy that produces the Waste Land—the ruins of the universe of soul. Though buried, like Merlin, the Spectre's cry must still be heard; for its tomb is the stone which the builders rejected, now become the cornerstone of the rebuilding of Eden. To this cry Los can only answer: "Even I already feel a World within/ Opening its gates..." (*BCW* 327–30). Through those gates will descend the Savior, to manifest on Earth. Because of this act of mercy Albion, the Fallen Man, will cease to shrink and, having reached the Limit of Contraction, he will begin to wake upon the Couch of Death (341).

The Eternal Man's ancient bliss is reassumed amid scenes that are literally apocalyptic. It begins with Los and Enitharmon having a vision of the Last Judgment. This occurs, not at the end of linear time, but whenever Imagination, the gift of the Holy Spirit, is "look'd upon as of no use" (604); but it is precisely at this lowest point that the Human Imagination appears "in the divine body of the Savior" (606).

Like the evangelist in the apocryphal Acts of John (see Chapter Eleven), Los and Enitharmon, seeing only with Phantom Eyes, think that Jesus has died on the Cross of Wood (357); but what dies is the phantom, not the reality. The place of that phantom death, Jerusalem—"a City, yet a Woman" (362)—is a gateway to both incarnation into time and resurrection into Eternity.

When Jesus stands beside them in spirit, Heaven and Earth are shaken; the Eternal Man wakes up and his Emanation Jerusalem returns from exile. The second coming is at hand: the Zoa of Reason can at last abandon the will to power and walk side by side with the once fallen, now regenerate

Albion, crying: "Times are Ended!" (372) For it is neither an ancient Golden Age nor the future establishment of the Kingdom of Heaven on Earth that the Expanding Eyes of Albion sees, but the freshness of an Earth made new in the time of the Imagination, which is Eternity.

So it is that when Los reunites with his Spectre and his Emanation, the Zoa of the Imagination arises in all its "regenerate power" (378). Times are ended: "The dark Religions are departed & sweet Science reigns" (379).

Break on Through to the Other Side

In the twenty-first century, when dark religion has returned with a vengeance and aspects of science have been fixed into an ideology of Rational Power, Blake's prophecy might seem unduly optimistic. But true prophecy is not fortune-telling: it is the unregenerate Zoa of Reason who is obsessed with futurity and has to learn that it is really "in this moment" (361–2) so that he can *be* in the moment. For the Eternal Prophet proclaims not what is to come in linear time but what is always present in all times. His task is not to predict the future outcome of events, but to imagine the way to truth and life.

So it is that, at the end of Chapter Three of Blake's *Jerusalem*, Jesus breaks through the zones of Death and Hell, which separate the limited from the unlimited, in order to open a doorway to Eternity. Through His mercy, Albion will be brought again into the light of "eternal day" (716). But we are not dealing here with conventional piety because, for Blake, the Divine Body of Jesus is the Imagination. Thus He can say that, by dying and resurrecting, He passes "the limits of possibility as it appears/ To individual perception" (696).

Blake's Jesus cleanses the doors of individual perception and shows us how, in the words of a Sixties song, to *break on through to the other side*. We too, through Imagination, can pass the limits of what appears to be possible and discover, beyond the doors of Time and Space, a separate reality. What prevents us from doing so is our shrunken vision: for we are types of the fallen Eternal Man, who once stretched out across the whole world, but has since "shrunk to a narrow rock in the midst of the sea," as his Emanation laments, while she now finds herself "clos'd out" from the "wonders of God" (720f).

In a series of increasingly powerful statements, Blake makes it clear that it is the rending apart of what should dwell in harmony and the building of "walls of separation," which results in the loss of Eternity. Los expresses the metaphysical tragedy in terms of spiritual hubris: It is blasphemous for any individual to appropriate to their limited self, the universal characteristics that are God's (736). In attempting to become more than human, we end up becoming less: males become Spectres; females, shadows of their former selves.

This is precisely the hubris that we can see in the life of Arthur, who achieves his greatest successes early in his career, according to the legendary chroniclers and the Welsh poets, defending Romano-British civilization against barbarian invaders from abroad and against giants and other supernatural threats at home. But, emboldened by his successes, he embarks upon a campaign of conquest on the continent, ending up as master of most of Northern and Western Europe. Although he even defeats the Roman Empire, he loses some of his most valued warriors in the process. Weakened, he is unable to put down a final revolt against his rule except at the cost of his own life and the destruction of his Round Table, the Arthurian symbol of fellowship—and it is precisely these qualities of Friendship and Brotherhood that Blake considers essential to humanity: without them, Man Is Not (743).

By attempting to conquer the known world, Arthur is imitating Albion, who "overspread all Nations ... in Ancient Time" (744); but Arthur is for Blake an historical individual for whom it is blasphemous to appropriate the universal characteristics of the Eternal Man. Only by dying to this world—changing his life, as Malory puts it—can he become once more at one with the archetypal Sleeping Lord: the universal appropriating the individual and not vice versa. He is betrayed by Guenevere, whom Blake sees as one of the Daughters of Albion, aspects of the Shadowy Female who is created by the exile of Jerusalem; but she cannot help serving a higher purpose. For the death of Jesus has shown that the cutting off of the vegetated body allows the spiritual body to be revealed—and so it is with Arthur and Merlin, who "appear" as a prince and his prophet in the Dark Ages, but who are "really" the spectral forms of the Eternal Man (Albion) and his Immortal Imagination.

The king and his magician must die, in order that they can be restored to their archetypal reality in that Last Judgment which is the awakening of the Sleeping Lord and his reunion with his daughter Jerusalem, in whom the beautiful but lost Emanations at last become one.

In the figure of Jerusalem are transcended the dualisms, not just of East and West, or of myth and history, but of Christianity and paganism: for the Emanations that she re-absorbs are the originals of the goddesses of the heathens, Fairies of Albion. Thus, in Blake's Christian mythology, Enitharmon, although her emblem is the Moon, is not simply the pagan moon goddess, migrating from Troy to Albion in the worship of the first

Britons; for the gods of Priam are "destructive to humanity" if un-subdued (571). Enitharmon is, rather, the spiritual archetype of the moon goddess, for the beings worshipped as goddesses are really "eternal principles" which appear in visions to poets throughout the ages. They are "divine names" (571) which manifest (emanate) as if they are separate from their source. But, reunited with their source, their name is Jerusalem (747).

Albion's Ancient Druid Rocky Shore

In Blake's mythos there is no mention of the Grail Quest, of the Lady of the Lake and Morgan the Fay, or of Arthur's passing to Avalon. What Blake gives us is a prequel and a sequel to the Matter of Britain: he gives it a framework which provides it with a spiritual meaning more relevant to the twenty first century than the allegorical sermons of the Grail hermits. For Blake, the Maimed King is Arthur; Arthur *is* the stricken Albion.

The Fall of Albion creates the time and space in which the medieval legends of Arthur and the Grail stories have their place: While Albion sleeps, his island is transformed through time; for the Trojans, guided by their moon goddess, create a British civilization from the primeval energy of the antediluvian giants; then the Romans in turn conquer the island and create the province of Britannia. With the arrival of the Company of the Grail, Christianity dethrones Diana/Tervagant and the other Saracen deities. Ultimately paganism is outlawed in the Roman Empire and the cult of the moon goddess is suppressed; but the island had been dedicated to her for eternity and so she returns in other forms, particularly as Fate and as those Fatal Sisters, the fays, who present such a challenge to Merlin and Arthur. We are left in no doubt that, when the feminine aspect of the godhead is denied, it strikes back with a vengeance (the return of the Goddess as the return of the repressed).

It is the Christian King Arthur who holds at bay the invading Anglo-Saxons, preserving what is left of the Romano-Celtic civilization of Britannia. But, when he at last goes to Avalon to be healed by Morgan the Fay, we can imagine, as Lucy Paton argued, that he is returning to his fairy lover, to dwell forever (or until recalled) in that Otherworld where paganism and Christianity can be progressive contraries rather than negations.

Meanwhile, Britannia has become England as first the Anglo-Saxons and then the Normans conquer what was once King Arthur's Logres. But England also sleeps, until her sister Jerusalem calls on her to awake—and it is here, where Jerusalem is built, that Goddess and Grail are at last united. For the Mighty Goddess who guided Brutus to Albion is one of the divine names of his Emanation; while Albion's daughter, the bride of the Lamb, is also Sophia, that Aeon of Wisdom whose symbol and receptacle is the Grail.

In Blake's vision of Heaven and Earth, the Emanation of Albion becomes the bride of the divinely embodied Imagination. Male and female souls "mingle & join" not just with each other (733), but with Tree, Metal, Earth and Stone (747); for Blake's Fairy has shown the poet that the material world is not dead but "all alive" (237)—and whatever lives is holy.

Blake's vision is of a web of imaginative sympathy that links the material, human and spiritual worlds in a way that neither the Net of Religion nor the "fixed" rationalism of science can. At its heart is the human, embodied in the Eternal Man whose Spectre, fallen in time and space, is Arthur. "All things Begin & End in Albion's Ancient Druid Rocky Shore," Blake wrote at the beginning of *Jerusalem*; but, when Albion, the Eternal Man in whose fall into the sleep of chaos all earthly things begin, is transformed in the material creation into Arthur, his ending is in Avalon.

That healing realm where Arthur lies sleeping until Albion awakes is that Otherworld of the fays, the goddesses of the heathen; that fairy realm between the earthly Kingdom of Logres and the spiritual Kingdom of the Grail; that intermediate world which holds the tension of the opposites. Here Arthur, wounded in Avalon, reveals his hidden identity with the Maimed King in Corbenic, but their archetype is the stricken Albion.

As Albion sleeps, suspended between Eden and Non-Existence, so Arthur sleeps in Avalon, suspended between heavenly and earthly existence; as though the Rock into which the Anthropos has shrunk is, when viewed with the Imaginative Eye, that fairy isle where Arthur dwells with the fairest of elves, the wise healer Morgan.

Whether we understand it as Heaven, or Faerie, another world is all around us, though we cannot see it through "This Life's dim Windows," when the soul sleeps. But when Britannia's cry awakens Albion, the soul too awakes and sees *through*, not *with*, "the Eye/That was born in a night to perish in a night" (753); sees that Avalon *is* Albion, as the place of awakening of the exiled Sleeping Lord and that the Otherworld *is* Britain, seen in the light of eternal day.

For what is Britain but a green and pleasant Island of Apples, the Promised Land of both Goddess and Grail? The voyage from Albion to Avalon is not a journey in time and space, but an eternal awakening, for the Otherworld is all about us.

Appendix—
Tolkien's Lonely Isle

> ... I believe that legends and myths are largely made of "truth," and indeed present aspects of it that can only be received in this mode....[1]
> —J.R.R. Tolkien

When J.R.R. Tolkien, convalescing at the end of the First World War, first began working on the stories that would make up what he called his *legendarium*, his fictional mythology of Middle-earth, he could not have known that he would eventually write what modern readers have hailed as the "book of the millennium,"[2] despite the fact that it was only published in the second half of the last century of that millennium, the twentieth of the Christian era. The Arthurian romances date from much closer to the beginning of the second millennium, but there is a direct line of continuity from them to the author who would, in the Twenties, co-edit what is arguably the greatest Arthurian poem in Middle English (*Sir Gawain and the Green Knight*) and who would, later on in life, produce a verse translation that attempted to emulate the medieval poet's alliterative style.

What is less well-known is that, in the early thirties, before he began work on *The Lord of the Rings*, Tolkien wrote the beginning of a long narrative poem in a modern alliterative style, entitled "The Fall of Arthur," which was published for the first time in 2013 in the wake of the successful Hollywood franchise which brought the hobbits Bilbo and Frodo Baggins, Gandalf the Wizard and various elves to Western multiplexes. Tolkien's Arthurian poem, however, presents the legendary king as a Romano-British warlord (which, if indeed he ever had a historical existence, is almost certainly what he was) and there are only faint echoes of the fairy mythology (or Elven lore, as he preferred to call it), with which he would soon become indelibly associated.

Arthur's domain is seen to stretch from its easternmost "margin," the

Mirkwood Forest (imagined as somewhere in central Europe), to its westernmost, the Isle of Avalon, so that the legions he levies can be "fay or mortal" (*FA* 25); while his bride, Guinevere, is described as, or compared to, a "fay-woman" who can be "fair" but also "ruthless" and "fell-minded" (37). This ambiguity about Elves, at least in the way they are perceived by the other races of Middle-earth, would also be a marked characteristic of their presentation in *The Lord of the Rings*.

Also of interest in this early fragment is Tolkien's presentation of Gawain, whose close association with fays arguably led to his denigration in the "ecclesiasticized" Grail cycles: Gawain is for Tolkien, as he was in all the English poems before Malory, Arthur's foremost warrior[3]:

> Greatest was Gawain, whose glory waxed
> as times darkened, true and dauntless,
> among knights peerless ever anew proven,
> defense and fortress of a falling world [19].

If he is a bulwark against the darkness, there are also more direct echoes of his association (whether metaphorical or mythological) with the sun: he is "gold as sunlight"; his glory,

> golden riding
> as the westering sun that the world kindles
> ere he red sinketh by the rim of ocean,
> before Arthur blazed, while the East darkened [42].

A "golden flaming" griffin is the emblem of "valiant-hearted" Gawain on his ship's banner (51) and these poetic associations reveal to what extent Tolkien was aware of "the Sunlike mythical figure that looms behind the courteous Gawain" (2006, 73).

The name of Gawain's sword, Galuth, Tolkien has borrowed from another Middle English alliterative poem, the *Morte Arthure*: "grim" Galuth is

> his sword renowned—smiths enchanted
> ere Rome was built with runes marked it
> and its steel tempered strong and deadly [*FA* 53].

These smiths may be elves, like the *aluisc smið* who makes Arthur's woven-steel corselet in Layamon's *Brut* (ll.10543–4). For, in developing his mythology of the elves, Tolkien makes of them master-craftsman and, of himself, the twentieth century successor to Layamon, who describes the *aluen* enchanting Arthur at his birth with strong spells (ll.9608–9) and who tells of the king's going to dwell with the fairest of the *aluen* in Avalon after the Last Battle (l.14291).

Avalon itself, in Tolkien's legendary, becomes Avallónë, an Elf haven that is on the Lonely Isle which "looks both west and east" (*S* 306). It is the nearest island to Elvenhome (on the eastern shore of the Blessed Realm that the High Elves share with the gods or archangels, the Holy Ones) and it is, at the same time, the closest part of the Undying Lands to Middle-earth, the world of mortals. Avallónë is, therefore, an *intermonde* where dwell only Elves, an "intermediate" race who are neither the earthly humans beyond the Sundering Sea, nor the spiritual "powers" of the West.

Tolkien's Elves are the firstborn of the One God, rising from His sleep by the Water of Awakening under the light of the first stars in the northeast of the world. The People of the Stars are all but immortal, dying not "till the world dies, unless they are slain or waste in grief"; but even then "they may in time return" from the halls of death (48).

They are hated, however, by the fallen archangel Melkor. It is their battle against him and his minions—a battle in which they are aided at first by the Blessed Ones (including the wizard Gandalf) and later by humans—Men (the Big People) and Hobbits (the Little People)—that constitutes the great overarching narrative of Tolkien's mythology, which unfolds over three great ages of prehistory.

The Blessed Ones create the sun and the moon to illumine the Earth and drive Melkor into the shadows. Under these new lights human beings (the younger children of the One) awaken in the East. In the first days humans are "companions and disciples" of the elves, learning their wisdom (123); but it will be the great triumph of Melkor to bring about their estrangement. Men are the Children of the Sun while Elves wander in "the lonely places of the great lands and the isles," taking to "the moonlight and the starlight, and to the woods and caves, becoming as shadows and memories" (124). Here we have the beginnings of the separation of *this* world and that *other* world, the world of Faerie that lies just beyond the fields we know.

One stage in this separation is literally recorded in the re-shaping of Middle-earth that occurs when the Blessed Ones come to the aid of the Elves and their allies among Men, the Elf-friends, in the Great Battle. Melkor is overthrown but Beleriand, the country in the west of Middle-earth where once played out the love affair between Beren and Lúthien, Man and Elf (whom Tolkien identified with himself and his wife, just as Blake before him had identified himself and his wife with his own mythological creations), is drowned beneath the sea. All that remains above the waves is Lindon, the Land of Song; but, when we learn that, in Tolkien's early writings, Beleriand, "that wide land of beech and elm and oak and flowering mead" is named *Broseliand* (*HME* IV, 103), it suggests the possibility that the Forest of Broceliande, where Viviane beguiles Merlin, is all that remains of the woodland where Lúthien beguiled Beren in the Elder Days.

By the second half of the twelfth century of *our* days, the process of demythologizing Broceliande was well under way. Wace, the author of the legendary chronicle of Britain that inspired so many French poets, also wrote a history of the Normans in which he describes visiting the Breton Forest of Paimpont, believed to be the Arthurian Broceliande, in search of marvels; but, in finding none, leaves himself feeling foolish (Le Saux, 100–1).

But we may feel that what was foolish was for Wace to seek for marvels in so literal a fashion: the mythic Broceliande cannot be found on any map, unless it is the map of Beleriand that Tolkien provided for his fictional Middle-earth.

Shining Kingdoms

The overthrowing of Melkor marks the end of Tolkien's First Age. The humans who allied themselves with the Elves and the Blessed Ones to break the power of the Enemy are rewarded by the creation of a haven in the Sundering Sea, an island which is neither part of the Undying Lands nor of Middle-earth, seeded by flowers from the Lonely Isle to the west. Those who set sail for Westernesse, the Land of Gift, are Kings among Men with eyes like starlight (S 313).

In the midst of their island is the Pillar of Heaven, a mountain hallowed to the One. From its height, on a clear day when the sun is in the east, the keenest-sighted can descry the tower of the white-shining city of Avallónë, which is the first thing that a seafarer would see if he approached the Undying Lands (312). But such closeness to the Blessed Realm is forbidden to the Sea-kings of Westernesse, who can sail only eastwards—bringing culture to the Men of Middle-earth, who later called them gods—though their hearts yearn for the West, for the undying city and everlasting life (316–7).

At last, grown proud, the Westlanders allow themselves to be seduced by the Necromancer, a servant of the Dark Lord who has survived his master's overthrow. They begin to perform human sacrifices to Melkor as the Giver of Freedom, who they believe will release them from death. When this proves ineffectual, they launch an expedition to conquer the deathless realm itself. But as soon as their king sets foot on the shores of the Blessed Realm the hills fall on him and his warriors. It is said that they lie imprisoned there, awaiting the Last Judgment (335).

The island of Westernesse is buried forever beneath the waves of the Great Sea: In the tongue of the High Elves it is remembered as Atalantë, "the Downfallen." The Earth is once more transformed by cataclysmic upheavals.

Some of the Westlanders who have not been seduced by the Necromancer escape the catastrophe and come to the eastern shores of Middle-earth, whence they renew the battle against the Abhorred One; but he has forged a Ring of Power through which he hopes to rule Elves, Dwarves and Men alike. Nevertheless the Necromancer is defeated by the Last Alliance of the peoples of Middle-earth and the Ring of Power is cut from his finger. It falls into a river, whence it is swept away.

So ends the Second Age of Middle-earth and, with it, the mythological background to Tolkien's most famous stories, contained in *The Hobbit* and its sequel, *The Lord of the Rings*, both of which have been made into feature films. Here we learn of the discovery of the Ring of Power by one of the Little People, the hobbit Bilbo Baggins, who then passes it on to his nephew Frodo. It becomes Frodo's task to take the Ring into the very heart of darkness in order to destroy it for, despite the desire of some to use the Ring against its creator, its greatest power is to seduce into doing evil those who would do good.

Nor can those who have once possessed it easily let it go; as Frodo discovers when he encounters his uncle again in an Elven refuge in a hidden valley in the foothills of the Misty Mountains, where Bilbo is writing poetry and studying the lore of the Firstborn. To Frodo's horror, his uncle is seized by a jealous rage when he is denied a sight of the Ring. But Bilbo recovers himself and, ashamed at his momentary lapse, asks if adventures will never end—adding, in answer to his own question, that someone will always carry on the story.

The story is indeed carried on by Frodo and the Fellowship of the Ring: which includes the King in Exile—heir to the Westlanders, he who carries the Broken Sword (in a nod to Arthurian and Norse mythology)—and Gandalf the Wizard who, we learn, is in origin an angel sent to aid the opponents of the Necromancer to resist his reviving power. Gandalf's angelic name is Olórin, derived from an Elvish word meaning "dream" but signifying both the power of the active imagination to perceive what cannot be seen with the physical eyes and the power of the creative imagination to clothe inner images "in particular form and detail" (*UT* 396). In other words Olórin is, like Blakes's Merlin, Immortal Imagination personified.

As Gandalf himself tells Frodo, "those who have dwelt in the Blessed Realm live at once in both worlds, and against both the Seen and the Unseen they have great power" (*LR* Book Two, Chapter I). But when Gandalf and the greatest of the Elves set sail for the Blessed Realm at the end of the Third Age, it represents a loss to Middle-earth of a living connection with the *mundus imaginalis*, between the *sensible* (the Seen) and the *intelligible* (the Unseen).

The Age of the Elves gives way to the Age of Men, but myth does not yet give way to history: for Tolkien's Fourth Age corresponds to that undreamt-of time between the fall of Atlantis and the rise of the Sons of Aryas, *when shining kingdoms lay spread across the world like blue mantles beneath the stars* (REH 7). Pulp writers such as Robert E. Howard would carry on the story, creating a forgotten history for the Sons of Aryas, the mythical ancestors of the early Indo-European peoples.

But with the foundation of the great western civilizations, the gods and goddesses would become objects of worship, no longer living presences; while with the triumph of monotheism over the old polytheistic religions, the goddesses themselves were exiled from the Kingdom of Heaven, reduced to fays and banshees, Elven women who would in time fade into the gossamer-winged sprites of fairy tales. After the Anglo-Saxon conquest, much of the surviving fairy lore was preserved only in the Celtic fringes of the British Isles; to the extent that, after the Norman Conquest, England was in danger of losing its mythology, despite attempts to preserve the power and importance of the Fairies of Albion by poets such as Layamon, Spenser and Blake.[4]

The Fairies Fade

It was the great task of J.R.R. Tolkien to attempt to provide England with its lost mythology by reconstructing one from his study of languages and, in so doing, to rescue the fairies from the insufferable tweeness to which they had been subjugated by Victorian writers. His Elves, both male and female, are tall and powerful, deathless and deadly, but wise and artistically creative. The Blessed Ones whom they revere are living powers whom later pagans would worship as gods and goddesses but whom the followers of One God call angels, so that the dualism of polytheism and monotheism is overcome, reduced to a problem of perspective.

Among the greatest of these powers, the High-ones, three are female—and it is easy to see in them the three aspects of the pre–Roman Britannia, the foundational goddess of Albion's lovely land, that Mighty Goddess described by Geoffrey of Monmouth. Thus Varda the Exalted corresponds to ethereal Selene, traveler through the celestial halls; Yavanna, maker of trees (and at whose prayer the tree wardens, or Ents, are created by the One) corresponds to Diana as goddess of the forests; while Nienna, the Lady of Mourning, corresponds to Proserpina or Persephone as traveler through the halls of death.

Further, we can see that Varda as Elbereth the Star-kindler corresponds to the Gnostic Sophia as creator of the stars—and this is perhaps as close as a Catholic writer could get to that numinous figure without risking falling into heresy. But whatever the vagaries of the Goddess in religious history, Tolkien was concerned to preserve a true memory of the race who revered Her above all other Powers—the Elves, who awoke in the light kindled by Her stars—and to establish a close relation between them and the English.

Thus in the early development of Tolkien's legendary—as we now know thanks to the editing of his drafts by his son Christopher—England had a very special role in the history of Middle-earth. It was the first land on which the Blessed Ones dwelled: it is they who hallowed it and made of it an island in the Western Sea (*HME* IV, 238).

After their first ordering of the world, the Powers withdraw to the Blessed Realm in the Far West and the Lonely Isle, after the defeat of Melkor at the end of the First Age, is dragged near to the Great Lands of the East, occupying the geographical position of modern Britain (II, 282–3). At first it is the exclusive homeland of the Elves; but in time Men come there "and ever as Men wax more powerful and numerous so the fairies fade and grow small and tenuous, filmy and transparent" until they are invisible to most mortals (283).

Thus the history of the Elves merges with the pre-history of Britain; but they will have a special relationship with the later English conquerors of the island. For a wandering mariner comes there from Anglia (the Angeln region of the Danish peninsula), seeking a fabled "unknown island" in the West (I, 24). The wanderer learns much of the lore of the Elves, equating the Powers that they revere with his own gods and becoming known as Ælfwine ("Elf-friend"). His sons, Hengest and Horsa, will later conquer much of the island from the Men who dwell there and their descendants will inherit a more authentic fairy-lore than their Celtic neighbors (II, 290).

So it is that, though the fairies are scattered throughout the world and for the most part the Men who dwell here "have no interest in "its ancient days," yet still some of the Elves of old linger on in the island of Britain "and their songs are heard about the shores of the land that once was the fairest dwelling of the immortal folk" (289).

Even when Tolkien's conception of Middle-earth changed and Britain was no longer identified with the Lonely Isle, it would still have a special relationship with the Elves. It would become Luthany, the Isle of Friendship (a remnant of Beleriand that survived the breaking of the world at the end of the First Age) and remains in our day the last dwelling-place of the Holy Fairies (IV, 199). Thence from time to time they still set sail at evening, abandoning Luthany before they fade away completely (39); heading beyond human ken to the Lonely Island or to the Bay of Faëry "that washes the western shores of the kingdom of the Gods."

It is therefore in Luthany alone that can still be found much of the Fading Companies, the Holy Fairies that have not yet left the world. For this reason Britain is still "a holy land, and a magic that is not otherwise lingers still in many places of that isle" (II, 312–3). Old English becomes "the sole mortal language" which Elves will speak with Men (304) and Tolkien therefore accords a special place to the Middle English poetry of Layamon, which he sees as the last authentic preserver of the traditions of Faerie and the Elven Isle of Avalon, from which Arthur will return to aid the English, the Elf-friends.

As his legendary developed, Tolkien even identified Avalon with Westernesse (VI, 215). But it eventually became another name for the Lonely Isle as an Elf haven, "within sight of the Blessed Realm" (IX, 332); before being reduced, in its definitive form in *The Silmarillion*, to a harbor port for those who set sail for the Undying Lands in the West. Nevertheless we can see these changing conceptions of the mythical islands of Atlantis and Avalon as a series of variations around the theme of Britain as a Holy Land, like Blake's Albion.

Tolkien's Lonely Isle in the West is an imaginal Britain, the closest place on Earth to the Blessed Realm.

Chapter Notes

Introduction
1. Loomis, 5.

Prologue
1. *BCW* 577–8.

Part 1
1. Brown 1943, 453–4.

Chapter One
1. *DGB* 18–20.
2. To be precise, Diana tells Brutus that giants *used* to live there, but that the island is now deserted and awaiting his people; a statement which turns out to be untrue. Thus Geoffrey can be seen as "undermining any real faith that the reader might have in pagan prophecy" (Gibson, 14). When he translated this passage into Norman-French, Wace stressed that Diana is a deceitful devil who uses *enchantement* (*RB* ll. 637–8).
3. Bridgman, 101: The idea was popularized by the poet Robert Graves in *The White Goddess*, 135, 276–7.
4. The appropriateness of talking about *the* Goddess, as though there were a direct female equivalent of *the* God of patriarchal monotheism in prehistory, remains a subject of controversy (see Hutton 2013, 72–6). But, in the Preface to their monumental work, Baring and Cashford point out that "in all the goddess myths of apparently unrelated cultures" there is a constant underlying vision of life as a "sacred whole ... where all orders of manifest and unmanifest life are related, because all share in the sanctity of the original source" (xi). I will therefore in this book refer to both God and the Goddess with a capital "G" to refer to the archetypal One (of either gender) as opposed to the many gods and goddesses of polytheism, without thereby implying a preference for one over the other or making any assumptions about prehistoric belief systems.
5. Baring and Cashford (80–2) follow the controversial archaeologist Marija Gimbutas in arguing that the cultures of Old Europe were swept away by invading hordes of nomadic warriors from the eastern steppes, who imposed patriarchy at the point of a sword.
6. For Baring and Cashford (118) the bee is an image of the Great Goddess of Regeneration.
7. Although the eagle is traditionally associated with the sky deity, grains belong to Mother Earth; the wolf, the cat and the sow herself can be seen as lunar creatures (Graves, 216).
8. Or names, since one Roman deity was frequently paired with several Celtic names; but whether these names indicate different attributes of the same deity (something also found in classical mythology) or an intense localism in religious worship, we cannot now know. The Welsh Arianrhod—whose name has been taken to mean "the Lady of the Silver Wheel"—was believed to have been a moon goddess by some early scholars (Loomis, 287), an identification that has been supported more recently by Miranda Aldhouse-Green (1995, 59).
9. The worship of Diana in imperial Britannia is attested along with that of Jupiter, Mars, Mercury, Venus (Hutton 2013, 235) and, of course, Minerva, who was associated with the Celtic goddess Sulis at Bath (244). There is also evidence of the cult of Hercules, a classical prototype of Arthur as slayer of giants and other monsters.
10. This is usually located in Brittany, but in the Arthurian legends it is frequently described as contiguous with the British mainland.
11. According to the text, the Saracens also worship a fourth deity: none other than the Prophet Mohammed, making an anachronistic appearance some five hundred years too early!

12. The suggestion was originally made by the nineteenth century philologist Walter W. Skeat who, in the entry for "Termagant" in his *Concise Dictionary of English Etymology* of 1884, wrote that *Trivagante* was "the moon, wandering under the three names of Selene (or Luna) in heaven, Artemis (Diana) in earth, Persephone (Proserpina) in the lower world" (499).

13. Baring and Cashford, 550-1: In a more secular age, the pagan moon goddess Artemis has been reincarnated as the superhero Wonder Woman (Atwood, 249).

Chapter Two

1. Paton, 4-5.

2. The connection between the moon and the waters is explored by the Romanian historian of religions and Eranos lecturer, Mircea Eliade: "Both because they are subject to rhythms (rain and tides)," he writes, "and because they sponsor the growth of living things, waters are subject to the moon.... All the moon divinities preserve more or less obvious water attributes or functions." Both the Greeks and the Celts observed the link between the moon and tides (1958, 159).

3. What is sometimes known as the noncyclic Prose *Lancelot* may have started off as an independent romance telling of his early exploits (scholars are divided on this) but, if so, it was soon continued by the addition of the story of the knight's rescue of Guenevere from the Otherworld (an adaptation in prose of Chrétien's poem) and (what is wholly original to this cycle) his begetting of the Grail hero, Galahad. This in turn leads to the Grail Quest and the civil war that brings about the death of Arthur and the fall of Logres. The addition of "histories" of the Grail and Merlin, acting as prequels to the other romances, completes the cycle which became known as the Vulgate "since it was the standard, common ('vulgar') source for all subsequent Arthurian literature" (Kibler, 1). When the Cycle is read in the chronological order of the events it recounts (rather than in the order of composition of the individual segments) the *Lancelot* constitutes the heart of the whole—an enormous central romance with two prequels (the *Estoire del Saint Graal* and the *Estoire de Merlin*) and two sequels (the *Queste del Saint Graal* and the *Mort Artu*)—suggesting the overall guidance of an "anonymous architect" (3).

4. *LdL* 54: While we can understand that the Christian author of the tale would want to dismiss the pagan beliefs of the Augustan era, when Virgil lived, it is not at all clear why a lake on the border between Gaul and Brittany would be named after a Sicilian monarch; whereas the cult of the goddess Diana, albeit assimilated to that of local deities, would have been widespread throughout the Roman Empire. Perhaps *la fole genz mescreanz* were not so daft, after all!

5. Quoted in Larrington, 164.

6. *The Byrth, Lyf, and Actes of Kyng Arthur* (London, 1817): Vol. I, xliii-xlviii.

7. In "Merlin and Vivien" (*PT* 1593-1620), "the wily Vivien" (l.5) wears a "twist of gold" in her hair (l.219), which becomes a "snake of gold" (l.886) after Merlin mocks her desire to read his book of charms (ll.665-88). As Larrington notes, "Vivien embodies the danger of the educated woman, distracted from the duties of home and family and seeking to possess equal knowledge with men" (153).

8. "It was a small ring with a flat, grey-brown stone that had the power to end a magic spell as soon as the wearer glanced at it" (*LG* II, 315). Later it is described as an emerald (323), the stone of Venus and hence appropriate as a love token.

Chapter Three

1. Brown 1943, 325.

2. Euhemerization is the process of reducing a mythical being to a historical one, named after the Greek mythographer Euhemerus (late fourth century BC), although such rationalizations are also found in Herodotus.

3. The feast is remembered by Ovid in his *Fasti* (Book Three, ll.263-4, 267-72): "In the valley of Aricia is a lake encircled by a dark wood. / Ancient awe has made it holy / ... / Threads hang veiling the long hedge where many a tablet/has been put up in thanks for the goddess' help. / Often a woman whose prayer has been answered garlands her forehead/ and carries burning torches from the city/ The 'king of the grove' is a powerful runaway slave, who kills/ his predecessor and later meets the same fate" (*OF* 88). The King of the Grove makes his appearance in the Romance of Yvain, as we will see in Chapter Ten.

4. This "castle on the sea" is frequently identified with, and often translated as, Carlisle, but John Darrah (1994, 201-3) more plausibly locates it in South West Wales. He also translates it as the Fortress of Dôn (1981, 125-6), suggesting that it is sacred to the Welsh mother goddess (whose daughter, Arianrhod, may originally have been a moon goddess).

5. This detail is provided by the *Estoire de Merlin*, which was written after the Prose *Lancelot*; and which tells us bluntly that "in the end, everything on earth rotted. And the land and the kingdom were under edict for nearly

three years, when no man's or woman's body was buried in consecrated ground except secretly and under threat of communication" (*LG* I, 339).

6. Rhys, 305–6: More recently this view has been championed by Caitlín Matthews, an arch-priestess of the modern cult of the Great Goddess, who hails Arthur's journey to the Otherworld as the oldest Grail Quest.

7. Malory's Dame Brusen, *one of the grettyst enchaunters that was that tyme in the worlde* (*MCW* 479). Lancelot believes that she has deceived him with *her wycchecrauftys*; Elaine claims she has been fulfilling a prophecy (481). The story is told in the first three chapters of Book Eleven of *Le Morte Darthur*.

Chapter Four

1. Brown 1903, 98.
2. *The Parchas sustren sponne so his fate*: *FP* 910. Lydgate presents Arthur after his passing as a king crowned in Faerie, who will return to Britain *as lord and souereyne* to *regne ageyn*.
3. Shakespeare is here drawing on Nordic traditions, where the three Fates are called the Norns and the eldest is called Urd, a name that becomes, in English, *wyrd* or *weird*, meaning "destiny."
4. Text with modern French translation in *MdF* 26–71; English translation in *LMF* 43–55.
5. Text with modern French translation in *LF* 63–103; English translation in *GLTB* 5–25.
6. In Malory's version, Morgan upbraids Arthur for tarrying too long. Similarly, Guingamor is criticized for disobeying his fay's command.
7. Text in *LMF* 139–55; translation in 73–81.
8. In fact, there is one story in which she is described as a fay, the late thirteenth century Romance of Escanor by Girart d'Amiens, but this may have come about simply through assimilation with Morgan.

Chapter Five

1. *BCW* 348
2. In Chrétien de Troyes' *Conte du Graal*, Perceval's father was "wounded through the thigh and physically maimed" (*AR* 380). The Fisher King was also maimed by being struck "through both thighs" (420).
3. Nutt sees the spirit in which the Quest is prosecuted as being "wholly outside the sphere of human action or interest," as indicated by the "glorification of physical chastity" and its unremitting misogyny: "Fully one-half of the romance is one long exemplification of the essential vileness of the sex-relation" (243). Writing a few years later, at the turn of the twentieth century, Nutt's friend Jessie L. Weston (1901, 113) was equally scathing about "the false and wholly sickly pseudo-morality" of the Vulgate Grail Quest, which, she claimed, "cannot but be utterly distasteful to any healthy mind."

4. "So little," Nutt comments (239), "had the Christian writer apprehended the signification of Christ's most profound saying." By contrast (as noted in the *New York Times* for 24 May, 1910), Nutt himself drowned trying to rescue his disabled teenage son, who had been swept into the sea in a riding accident. Greater love hath no man...

5. Nutt continues: "A shadowy perfection at the outset, he remains a shadowy perfection throughout, a bloodless and unreal creature, as fit when he first appears upon the scene as when he quits it, to accomplish a quest, purposeless, inasmuch as it only removes him from a world in which he has neither part nor share" (239).

6. It is difficult not to concur with the conclusion of Janina P. Traxler about the true significance of the fate of Perceval's sister: "In the world of the Grail Quest, not only is the best woman a dead woman, but the best woman is a dead virgin" (273–4).

7. Philippe Walter has explored the beliefs about the dangers of female blood in "La Femme Contaminée," Chapter Five of his *Galaad: Le Pommier et le Graal*. Only through her virginity can Perceval's sister, like the Blessed Mary, redeem the "contaminated" blood.

8. The identification of Jerusalem with Wisdom is also found in the philosophical system of Boehme, which inspired Blake (Damon, 41) and in Jung's late study of the Book of Job, where he describes Sophia as "the feminine numen of the 'metropolis' par excellence, of Jerusalem the mother-city" (41). "The city is Sophia, who was with God before time began, and at the end of time will be reunited with God through the sacred marriage" (141).

Chapter Six

1. Paton, 5.
2. In Romano-Celtic iconography, Fortuna is sometimes linked with the *Three Mothers* (the *Deae Matres* or *Matronae*, as they are named in inscriptions) and the *Three Fates* (Aldhouse-Green 2004, 78).
3. Unlike Weston, Paton does not merit her own Wikipedia entry, although her name is still remembered at Harvard by winners of the prize in the Humanities and Fine Arts established by her will. Her book on fairy mythology, based on the thesis she submitted for her PhD at what was then the all-women's Rad-

cliffe College, was re-edited in 1960 but has been out-of-print for decades. In 2012 the original 1903 edition was digitally scanned and reissued by a house whose name speaks volumes: Forgotten Books!

4. The complicated history of the Post-Vulgate Cycle has been brilliantly elucidated by Fanni Bogdanow (2006); what follows is my own summary of her findings.

Interlude

1. Eliade 1982, 338.
2. The opening of the Vulgate *Estoire de Merlin* closely follows the earlier Prose *Merlin*, itself based on a verse fragment by Robert de Boron.
3. Jean-Paul Ponceau, the modern editor of the text, dates it to the third decade of the thirteenth century (*ESG* xi–xiv).
4. Murray's most famous work is *The Witch-Cult in Western Europe* (1921), but she also produced two sequels, in 1931 and 1954.
5. We are talking here not about the historical (sixth century) bard Taliesin, but about his "mythical or semi-divine" namesake, to whom is ascribed esoteric poems such as "The Spoils of Annwfn," in which he accompanies Arthur on a proto–Grail Quest. Thomas Green (54–6) argues for a mid- late eighth to ninth century date for this poem, which would place its emergence in the period between Nicaea II and Constantinople IV.
6. The Eighth Ecumenical Council is not recognized by the Orthodox Church and in fact contributed to the eventual split between the eastern and western branches of Christianity. The full text of the council is available online at http://www.papalencyclicals.net/Councils/ecum08.htm.
7. The *Estoire* presents a somewhat garbled account of the subjugation of rebellious Judaea by Vespasian and his son Titus (here strangely made to be his father!) which was completed by Titus after Vespasian was made emperor in AD 69.
8. The *Estoire* here follows Robert de Boron (*RG* ll. 2653–78) in making the *graal* that which is most a*gree*able; a dreadful pun that is of interest only insofar as it illustrates the medieval penchant for false etymology.
9. King Pellehan, the Maimed King of the Post-Vulgate Cycle, is a descendant of Joseph's sister.
10. In this and other passages the *Estoire*, which gives otherwise a largely faithful copy of the account of the legend in the Vulgate *Queste del Saint Graal*, exaggerates and extends the description of the wife's evil nature, which has no basis in the Bible—although some Jewish traditions make Solomon's wife (the daughter of an unspecified Egyptian Pharaoh) an idolater who subverts his worship of the One God (D'Arcy, 261*n*37).
11. The phrase is from the Platonist Thomas Taylor's 1792 translation of the Orphic Hymns (available online at http://www.sacred-texts.com/cla/hoo). Taylor (1758–1835) was an almost exact contemporary of William Blake and an important influence on the poet: "Blake adopted eagerly Taylor's insistence that the ancients wrote obscurely, veiling their deeper meanings in symbols" (Damon, 397). For a discussion of the Orphic Hymns, see Guthrie, 256–61.
12. "You should know that they were natural colours, not painted, for they had not been put there by any mortal man or woman. And because some people who heard about it might be doubtful and consider themselves deceived if they knew nothing more, the story turns aside from the straight road of its material in order to reveal the truth and put doubt to rest" (*LG* I, 78). As Carol Chase points out, the possibility that the audience might be deceived "makes the ambiguous narrator into a possible source of trickery" (132). But any doubts that the public may have, like those of both Nasciens, "will be effaced by the text itself, which is likened to an article of faith" (134).
13. Perhaps mercifully, the author spares us the details of what the lady looks like when she is *muee en forme d'Enemi, come cele qui veraiement estoit deable* (*ESG* 401).

Part Two

1. Eliade 1991, 19–20.

Chapter Seven

1. Spenser, *The Faerie Queene* Book Two, Canto X, Stanza 53.
2. His name (*li rois Crudex*) is a bit of a giveaway. His parents must have somehow known that he would grow up to be *li plus fels et li plus delloiaus paiens del monde* (*ESG* 454), or else it is an instance of nominative determinism.
3. The origin of this silver table is recounted in de Boron's poem, but not repeated in the *Estoire*: Joseph of Arimathea had it made at God's command while the company was still in the Holy Land and it will allow no sinners in its presence. It will later serve as the model for the Round Table.
4. Ponceau suggests that the Grail mission is operative in Britain towards the end of the first century (*ESG* 628).
5. The country is actually named after him (*de Galaaz, Gales*): it was formerly the pagan

Kingdom of Hoselice, but it will forever after (*tant come li siecles durera*) be known as Wales (*ESG* 551). Here again the *Estoire* pulls rank over Wace, who attributes the name to a certain Duke Gualo or to Queen Galaes, who reigned over a thousand years earlier (*RB* ll.14855-8).

Chapter Eight

1. Spenser, *The Faerie Queene* Book Three, Canto III, Stanzas 11, 13.
2. Although we now think of the Picts as indigenous to northern Britain, native legend insists that they are invaders from Scythia (*TYP* 93).
3. See *RMP* 190-3&*n*89.
4. Wace tells us that the wise men have *deviné e sorti* (*RB* l.7347). According to Robert de Boron, they practice *un art qui est apielee astronomie* (*RMP* 204), one of the seven liberal arts but which included what we would classify as *astrology* (the sacred science of interpreting the movements of the stars) and also *l'autre art es elemens* (236), magic based on manipulation of the four elements.
5. Merlin adds that Perceval will be "conceived of a virgin mother and born of a virgin woman" (*LG* IV, 171), a detail that is never referred to again and may have been dropped because it verges on blasphemy in suggesting that Perceval will have a miraculous virgin birth, a characteristic of other mythical beings but one that Christians usually reserve for Jesus.
6. Hutton 1996, 225: Throughout the ancient British Isles this day marked the beginning of summer and, at this turning-point of the year, malign powers, both natural and supernatural, were believed to be especially active. In medieval Welsh literature May Day has "an especially arcane quality" (219).
7. Gilles Roussineau, the modern editor of the *Merlin Continuation*, does not think that Morgan can be assimilated to this Lady of the Isle of Avalon, since the former has not yet been initiated by Merlin into magical practices (*SRM* 647). If we accept this reading then perhaps the Ladyship of Avalon is a title that more than one person holds during Arthur's lifetime.

Chapter Nine

1. Weston 1909, 210.
2. *Chaliburne*, according to Wace, *En l'isle d'Avalun fu faite, / Ki la tient nue mult se haite* (*RB* ll.9281-2); but, if Excalibur brings joy to whoever unsheathes it, Balin's sword brings him nothing but sorrow, sheathed or not.
3. This number matches the prophecy of the Angel of the Bleeding Lance who, in the *Estoire del Saint Graal*, announces that the marvelous adventures of the Promised Land of the Grail will last as many years as the number of days in which Josephus carried the tip of the lance in his thigh, i.e., twenty-two.
4. There is some confusion about the geography of the Grail Kingdom. We know that the Land Beyond, where the castle of Corbenic is situated, has already been turned into a Waste Land by the blow that killed Lambor, King Pellehan's father. We must now imagine Listenois as a smaller territory within the Land Beyond, one which, perhaps because it contains the Grail Castle, survived the first Dolorous Blow unscathed; but which, with the maiming of its king, is also now devastated. In other words, the Waste Land has now penetrated to the very heart of the Grail Kingdom and has spilt out into Logres.
5. This does not tally with the origin given in the Vulgate, where her father is a vavasour. Further confusion ensues when we are told that she is from Northumberland, a kingdom that borders on...Brittany! It seems that Ninienne's true home cannot be found on any map....
6. Our sources do not agree as to whether Morgan is the daughter of the Duke of Tintagel (the version of the Vulgate Cycle)—and therefore Arthur's half-sister—or of Uther Pendragon (the version of the Post-Vulgate and Tristan Cycles), but her mother is always Igerna.
7. "The induction to the story," writes Paton, "resembles many another that recounts the entrance of a mortal into fairyland." Here the stag is a fairy messenger in disguise, who would originally have been sent by her "fairy mistress" to summon the hero she loves to the Otherworld (15); but "we are dealing with material that has been distorted from its original form" (19).

Chapter Ten

1. Weston 1906, 335-6.
2. The text of "The Weddyng of Syr Gawen and Dame Ragnell for the Helpyng of Kyng Arthoure," to give it its full title, is edited with useful critical material in *MER* 243-67.
3. Weston developed this theme in later works: Gawain as "a purely mythical hero" was increasingly "out of place" in what had become "a distinctively Christian legend" (1906, 335). As "he was a non-Christian hero," with a "close connection" not just to the Otherworld Queen but to "countless maiden dwellers," then "we have no cause to seek further for the grounds ... for the peculiar transformation which his character underwent" (1909, 305). More recently John Darrah has argued that Gawain has "strong links with paganism" (1981, 129).

4. Hutton 2013, 370: Unlike Weston and Loomis, who tended to be too free with their speculative theories, Hutton has all the caution of a professional historian but nevertheless admits that he is "inclined to think" that the Otherworld of medieval Irish and Welsh literature is not just *a* survival but "one of the most important survivals from the old religions to the world of the new, never theologically assimilated but apparently accepted without strain as long as the stories that involved it conformed to Christian values or were set in vaguely pre–Christian times."

5. For the role of Tolkien, Howard and the creators of Superman in the birth of modern fantasy literature and film, see Parsons 2014.

Chapter Eleven

1. Quoted in Cheetham, 26.

2. Carey has earlier argued that "the apocryphal Taliesin poetry" with its "arcane lore" and "scornful references to the ignorance of the clergy" marks an important transmission point from Ireland to Wales: "This anticlerical poetic tradition, preoccupied with the mastery of native esoterica, seems a favorable milieu for the transmission of any mythical material which might have survived into the early medieval period" (1991, 37).

3. *CA* 38: Disappointingly, the *Chanson de la Croisade Albigeoise* does not refer to the Grail, although mention is made of *las meravilhas que recomta Merlis* (416) who is described as *bos devinaire*, a good fortune-teller (234).

4. For English-language readers, a series of studies by Thomas Cheetham have become an invaluable guide to Corbin's thought and most of Corbin's major works are now available in English translation. In 2010 John Carey presented a lecture on "The Role of the Grail in Henry Corbin's Thought" to the Temenos Academy in London and Oxford, which has been printed in the *Temenos Academy Review* (No.14, 2011) as "Henry Corbin and the Secret of the Grail." An audio version of this talk is available at: http://temenos.thelincolncentre.co.uk/20100902/

5. "It is true to say that the Grail is not a single concept whose meaning has been lost," writes Richard Barber (2005, 255), "but a literary symbol which has developed over the years ... Poets and writers are creators; the Grail is the creation, not of mysticism, not of pagan religion, not even of Christian tradition, nor of the scholars themselves, but of the poetic imagination working on and with all these materials."

6. It was in 1095 that Pope Urban II called on all Christians to wrest control of the land of the Holy Sepulcher from the Moslem Turks, who were busily dismantling what was left of the Byzantine Empire. His call was answered beyond all expectation and, by the summer of 1099, Jerusalem was in Christian hands, for the first time in over four hundred and fifty years. The Christian kingdom of Jerusalem lasted less than a hundred years, however: in 1187, it was re-conquered by Saladin, triggering the third, but this time unsuccessful, crusade. It was during the Third Crusade that Philip of Flanders, the man who commissioned the Story of the Grail, died.

7. Roquebert 1994, 102: The citadel of Montségur was rebuilt in the early thirteenth century and pulled down after its capture by the French army. The present ruins, the object of pilgrimages by Grail seekers, treasure hunters and reincarnated Cathars, are of a later citadel.

8. As Richard Barber (2005, 313) puts it, "the Grail represents exactly those aspects of Christianity which they rejected" and therefore "could mean nothing to them."

9. One of the denizens of this other world is Wonder Woman, whose Amazonian powers and secret identity (Diana Prince) show her to be an avatar of the moon goddess for a secular age (Atwood, 19–20).

10. The historian F. Edward Cranz used the term "disjunctive" to describe the dichotomy between "the knower and the known" and between "meanings and things" which, he argued, emerged in the twelfth century. This "fundamental reorientation of the ancient categories of thought and the nature of experience itself," comments his student Tom Cheetham (38–9), "is the foundation of the modern sense of a self alienated in the world and trapped in a system of merely human meanings."

Chapter Twelve

1. *LR* Book Two, Chapter I.

2. King Arthur is hunting a stag through the forest when he comes across a lone maiden by a spring. She is so beautiful that he mistakes her for a fay; but that does not stop him from raping her! As a result she bears a child whom she names after the father. Here it seems to be beauty (rather than dangerous book-learning, as with Morgan and Ninienne) which can lead a man to sin and which leads women to be mistaken for fays.

3. See, for example, that extraordinary farrago of misinformation about Nazi occultism, Trevor Ravenscroft's sensationalist but entertaining *The Spear of Destiny* (Boston: Weiser, 1982), along with the sober response by Nicholas Goodrick-Clarke in the Appendix to his *The Occult Roots of Nazism* (2nd ed. New York: I.B. Taurus, 1992).

4. See Chapter Six, 'How Does the Lance Bleed?' in Dixon 2012, 89–103.

5. There is in fact a rather perfunctory account of the mending of the Broken Sword in the thirteenth century Prose *Tristan*, which Richard Barber considers to have developed "side by side" with the Post-Vulgate (2005, 204). The sword apparently goes on to work many miracles. There is also a somewhat redundant version of the Grail Question: after healing the Maimed King, Galahad asks him what the Grail and Lance are, although, as the king points out, he already knows—but "no one knows it perfectly" (202). Since the king is already healed, the Question has no salvific function and there is no mention of the Waste Land's being restored.

6. Hans Thomas Hakl has recently produced the definitive study of the early years of this symposium up to 1989, when it fragmented into competing factions.

7. Tolkien 1981, 145: But as a philologist Tolkien would of course have known that "to invent is to discover, and comes from the Latin *invenire*, 'to come upon.' It was only in the sixteenth century, with the appearance of the modern experience of subjectivity, that 'invent' came to mean 'make something up,' and only then could the imagination lose its rightful place as a feature of the objective world" (Cheetham, 168).

8. Quotations are from Henry Corbin, "The Dramatic Element Common to the Gnostic Cosmogonies of the Religions of the Book," originally published in the French-language journal *Cahiers de l'Université Saint Jean de Jérusalem* no.5, pp. 141–173. The English translation was first published in the journal *Studies in Comparative Religion* and is now available online at: http://www.studiesincomparativereligion.com/Public/articles/The_Dramatic_Element_Common_to_the_Gnostic_Cosmogonies_of_the_Religions_of_the_Book-by_Henry_Corbin.aspx.

9. "...pathways strange ... in countries unknown" (*GK* 42).

10. The fragment that remains involves "secret societies practising dark cults" and was abandoned when it proved "both sinister and depressing" (*HME* XII, 410).

Epilogue

1. Corbin 1998a, 207.

Appendix

1. Tolkien 1981, 147.

2. http://www.salon.com/2001/06/04/tolkien_3/.

3. In his translation of *Sir Gawain and the Green Knight*, Tolkien renders the anonymous poet's paean to the hero's qualities: "Gawain as good was acknowledged and as gold refined, / devoid of every vice and with virtues adorned" (*GK* 40–41). In the same poem, Tolkien translates *wodwos*, just one of the menaces Gawain has to brave in the wilderness, as "wood-trolls" (43); creatures (from the Anglo-Saxon *wudu—wása*) which must be understood as the descendants of the Woses, the primitive Wild Men of the Woods, of Tolkien's own stories (*UT* 387n14).

4. I have explored this theme further in *The Glory of Arthur* (Dixon 2014).

Bibliography

The primary sources are ordered by their abbreviations

Primary Sources

ANT—Elliott, J.K., trans. *The Apocryphal New Testament: A Collection of Apocryphal Christian Literature*. Oxford, England: Oxford University Press, 2005.

AR—Owen, D.D.R., trans. Chrétien de Troyes, *Arthurian Romances*. London: J.M. Dent, 1987.

BCW—Keynes, Geoffrey, ed. *Blake: Complete Writings*. 2nd ed. Oxford, England: Oxford University Press, 1979.

Brut—Allen, Rosamund, trans. *Lawman's Brut*. London: J.M. Dent, 1992.

CA—Martin-Chabot, Eugène, ed. and Henri Gougaud, trans. into modern French. *Chanson de la Croisade Albigeoise*. Paris: LGF, 1989.

CC—Méla, Charles, ed. and trans. into modern French. Chrétien de Troyes, *Le Chevalier de la Charrette*. Paris: LGF, 1992.

CG—Méla, Charles, ed. and trans. into modern French. Chrétien de Troyes, *Le Conte du Graal ou le Roman de Perceval*. Paris: LGF, 1990.

CL—Hult, David F., ed. and trans. into modern French. Chrétien de Troyes, *Le Chevalier au Lion*. Paris: LGF, 1990.

DGB—Reeve, Michael D., ed., and Neil Wright, trans. Geoffrey of Monmouth, *The History of the Kings of Britain: An Edition and Translation of* De Gestis Britonum [Historia Regum Britanniae]. Woodbridge, England: Boydell, 2007.

DKA—Cable, James, trans. *The Death of King Arthur*. Harmondsworth, England: Penguin, 1971.

EE—Foerster, Wendelin, ed., and Michel Rousse, trans. into modern French. Chrétien de Troyes, *Erec et Enide*. Paris: Flammarion, 1994.

ESG—Ponceau, Jean-Paul, ed. *L'Estoire del Saint Graal*. 2 vols. Paris: Champion, 1997.

FA—Tolkien, Christopher, ed. J.R.R. Tolkien, *The Fall of Arthur*. London: HarperCollins, 2013.

FP—Bergen, Henry, ed. *Lydgate's Fall of Princes*, Part Three. London: Oxford University Press, 1924.

GK—Tolkien, J.R.R., trans. *Sir Gawain and the Green Knight, Pearl* and *Sir Orfeo*. London: Allen & Unwin, 1975.

GLTB—Weston, Jessie L., trans. *Guingamor, Lanval, Tyolet, Le Bisclaveret: Four Lais Rendered into English Prose from the French of Marie de France and Others*. London: David Nutt, 1900.

GS—Layton, Bentley, trans. *The Gnostic Scriptures*. London: SCM, 1987.

HBG—Bryant, Nigel, trans. *The High Book of the Grail: A Translation of the Thirteenth-Century Romance of Perlesvaus*. Cambridge, England: D.S. Brewer, 1978.

HH—Holland, Tom, trans. Herodotus, *The Histories*. London: Penguin, 2013.

HKB—Thorpe, Lewis, trans. Geoffrey of Monmouth, *The History of the Kings of Britain*. Harmondsworth, England: Penguin, 1966.

HME—Tolkien, Christopher, ed. J.R.R. Tolkien, *The History of Middle-earth*. 12 vols. London: HarperCollins, 1983–1992.

HT—Wender, Dorothea, trans. *Hesiod and Theognis*. Harmondsworth, England: Penguin, 1973.

HvA—Tobin, Frank, Kim Vivian, and

Richard H. Lawson, trans. *Arthurian Romances, Tales and Lyric Poetry: The Complete Works of Hartmann von Aue*. University Park: Pennsylvania State University Press, 2001.

LA—Barron, W.R.J., and S.C. Weinberg, eds. and trans. *Layamon's Arthur: The Arthurian Section of Layamon's Brut*. 2nd ed. Exeter, England: University of Exeter Press, 2001.

LdL—Kennedy, Elspeth, ed., and François Mosès, trans. into modern French. *Lancelot du Lac: Roman français du XIIIe siècle*. 2nd ed. Paris: LGF, 1991.

LF—Tobin, Prudence, ed., and Alexandre Micha, trans. into modern French. *Lais Féeriques des XIIe et XIIIe siècles*. Paris: Flammarion, 1992.

LG—Lacy, Norris J., ed. *Lancelot-Grail: The Old French Arthurian Vulgate and Post-Vulgate in Translation*. 5 vols. New York: Garland, 1993–6.

LMF—Burgess, Glyn S., and Keith Busby, trans. *The Lais of Marie de France*. 2nd ed. London: Penguin, 1999.

LR— Tolkien, J.R.R. *The Lord of the Rings*. 3rd ed. London: HarperCollins, 2005.

MCW—Vinaver, Eugène, ed. *Malory: Complete Works*. 2nd ed. Oxford, England: Oxford University Press, 1971.

MdF—Warnke, Karl, ed., and Laurence Harf-Lancner, trans. into modern French. *Lais de Marie de France*. Paris: LGF, 1990.

MER—Shepherd, Stephen A., ed. *Middle English Romances*. New York: Norton, 1995.

MG—Bryant, Nigel, trans. *Merlin and the Grail. Joseph of Arimathea, Merlin, Perceval: The Trilogy of Arthurian Romances Attributed to Robert de Boron*. Cambridge, England: D.S. Brewer, 2001.

MO—Innes, Mary, trans. *The Metamorphoses of Ovid*. Harmondsworth, England: Penguin, 1955.

MRA—Baumgartner, Emmanuèle, and Marie-Thérèse de Madeiros, eds. and trans. into modern French. *La Mort du Roi Arthur*. Paris: Honoré Champion, 2007.

NHL –Robinson, James M., ed. *The Nag Hammadi Library in English*. 3rd ed. Leiden, The Netherlands: Brill, 1988.

OF—Nagle, Betty Rose, ed. and trans. *Ovid's* Fasti: *Roman Holidays*. Bloomington: Indiana University Press, 1995.

PSG—Bryant, Nigel, trans. Chrétien de Troyes, *Perceval: The Story of the Grail*. Cambridge, England: D.S. Brewer, 1992.

PT—Ricks, Christopher, ed. *The Poems of Tennyson*. London: Longman, 1969.

PV—Bogdanow, Fanni, ed. *La Version Post-Vulgate de la* Queste del Saint Graal *et de la* Mort Artu: *Troisième Partie du* Roman du Graal. Vol. 3. Paris: Société des Anciens Textes Français, 2000.

QHG—Matarasso, P.M., trans. *The Quest of the Holy Grail*. Harmondsworth, England: Penguin, 1969.

RB—Weiss, Judith, ed. and trans. *Wace's Roman de Brut: A History of the British*. 2nd ed. Exeter, England: University of Exeter Press, 2002.

REH—Louinet, Patrice, ed. Robert E. Howard, *The Coming of Conan the Cimmerian*. New York: Ballantine, 2003.

RG—Nitze, William A., ed. Robert de Boron, *Le Roman de l'Estoire du Graal*. Paris: Honoré Champion, 1971.

RMP—Füg-Pierreville, Corinne, ed. and trans. into modern French. *Le Roman de Merlin en Prose*. Paris: Honoré Champion, 2014.

S—Tolkien, Christopher, ed. J.R.R. Tolkien, *The Silmarillion*. London: Allen & Unwin, 1977.

SRM—Roussineau, Gilles, ed. *La Suite du Roman de Merlin*. 2nd ed. Geneva: Droz, 2006.

TL—Graves, Robert, trans. Lucius Apuleius, *The Transformations of Lucius, otherwise known as The Golden Ass*. Harmondsworth, England: Penguin, 1950.

TYP—Bromwich, Rachel, ed. and trans. *Trioedd Ynys Prydain: The Triads of the Island of Britain*. 3rd ed. Cardiff: University of Wales Press, 2006.

UT—Tolkien, Christopher, ed. J.R.R. Tolkien, *Unfinished Tales of Númenor and Middle-earth*. London: Allen & Unwin, 1980.

UZL—Kerth, Thomas, trans. Ulrich von Zatzikhoven, *Lanzelet*. New York: Columbia University Press, 2005.

VM—Clarke, Basil, ed. and trans. Geoffrey of Monmouth, Vita Merlini: *Life of Merlin*. Cardiff: University of Wales Press, 1973.

Secondary Sources

Aldhouse-Green, Miranda. *Celtic Goddesses: Warriors, Virgins, and Mothers*. London: British Museum Press, 1995.
_____. *The Gods of the Celts*. 2nd ed. Stroud, England: Sutton, 2004.
Atwood, Margaret. *In Other Worlds: Science Fiction and the Human Imagination*. London: Virago, 2011.
Barber, Malcolm. *The Cathars: Dualist Heretics in Languedoc in the High Middle Ages*. Harlow, England: Longman, 2000.
Barber, Richard. *Myths and Legends of the British Isles*. Woodbridge, England: Boydell, 1999.
_____. "Chivalry, Cistercianism and the Grail." In *A Companion to the Lancelot-Grail Cycle*, ed. Carol Dover, 2003. 3–12.
_____. *The Holy Grail: The History of a Legend*. London: Penguin, 2005.
Baring, Anne, and Jules Cashford. *The Myth of the Goddess: Evolution of an Image*. London: Penguin, 1991.
Bogdanow, Fanni. "The *Vulgate Cycle* and the *Post-Vulgate Roman du Graal*." In *A Companion to the Lancelot-Grail Cycle*, ed. Carol Dover, 2003. 33–51.
_____. "Rewriting Prose Romance: The Post-Vulgate *Roman du Graal*." In *The Arthur of the French*, eds. Burgess and Pratt, 2006. 342–52.
Bridgman, Timothy. *Hyperboreans: Myth and History in Celtic-Hellenic Contacts*. New York: Routledge, 2005.
Broek, Roelef van den, and Wouter J. Hanegraaff, eds. *Gnosis and Hermeticism from Antiquity to Modern Times*. Albany: State University of New York Press, 1998.
Brown, Arthur C. L. *Iwain: A Study in the Origins of Arthurian Romance*. Boston: Ginn, 1903.
_____. *The Origin of the Grail Legend*. Cambridge, MA: Harvard University Press, 1943.
Burckhardt, Titus. *Alchemy: Science of the Cosmos, Science of Soul*. Trans. William Stoddart. Dorset, England: Element, 1968.
Burgess, Glyn S., and Karen Pratt, eds. *The Arthur of the French: The Arthurian Legend in Medieval French and Occitan Literature*. Cardiff: University of Wales Press, 2006.
Busby, Keith. "Perceval and the Grail: The Continuations." In *The Arthur of the French*, eds. Burgess and Pratt. 222–247.
Carey, John. "A British Myth of Origins?" *History of Religions* Vol. 31, No. 1, August 1991. 24–38.
_____. *Ireland and the Grail*. Aberystwyth, Wales: Celtic Studies Publications, 2007.
_____. "Henry Corbin and the Secret of the Grail." *Temenos Academy Review* No.14, 2011. 159–178.
Chase, Carol. "*Or dist li contes*: Narrative Interventions and the Implied Audience in the *Estoire del Saint Graal*." In *The Lancelot-Grail Cycle: Text and Transformations*, ed. William W. Kibler. 117–138.
Cheetham, Tom. *Imaginal Love: The Meanings of Imagination in Henry Corbin and James Hillman*. Thompson, CT: Spring, 2015.
Corbin, Henry. *En Islam Iranien: Aspects Spirituels et Philosophiques* Vol. 2: *Sohrawardî et les Platoniciens de Perse*. Paris: Gallimard, 1971.
_____. "The Dramatic Element Common to the Gnostic Cosmogonies of the Religions of the Book." *Studies in Comparative Religion* 14.3 and 14.4 (1980): 199–221.
_____. *L'Homme et son Ange: Initiation et Chevalerie Spirituelle*. Paris: Fayard, 1983.
_____. *Histoire de la Philosophie Islamique*. Paris: Gallimard, 1986a.
_____. *Temple and Contemplation*. Trans. Philip Sherrard. London: KPI, 1986b.
_____. *Swedenborg and Esoteric Islam*. Trans. Leonard Fox. Pennsylvania: Swedenborg Foundation, 1995.
_____. *Alone with the Alone: Creative Imagination in the Sūfism of Ibn 'Arabī*. Trans. Ralph Manheim. Princeton, NJ: Princeton University Press, 1998a.
_____. *The Voyage and the Messenger: Iran and Philosophy*. Trans. Joseph Rowe. Berkeley, California: North Atlantic, 1998b.
Damon, S. Foster. *A Blake Dictionary: The Ideas and Symbols of William Blake*. Rev. ed. Hanover, NH: University Press of New England, 1988.
D'Arcy, Anne Marie. *Wisdom and the Grail: The Image of the Vessel in the Queste del Saint Graal and Malory's Tale of the Sankgreal*. Portland, OR: Four Courts, 2000.

Darrah, John. *The Real Camelot: Paganism and the Arthurian Romances*. London: Thames & Hudson, 1981.
_____. *Paganism in Arthurian Romance*. Woodbridge, England: Boydell, 1994.
Dixon, Jeffrey John. *Gawain and the Grail Quest: Healing the Waste Land in our Time*. Edinburgh, Scotland: Floris, 2012.
_____. *The Glory of Arthur: The Legendary King in Epic Poems of Layamon, Spenser and Blake*. Jefferson, NC: McFarland, 2014.
Dover, Carol, ed. *A Companion to the Lancelot-Grail Cycle*. Cambridge, England: D.S. Brewer, 2003.
Dubost, Francis. *Le Conte du Graal ou l'Art de Faire Signe*. Paris: Honoré Champion, 1998.
Eliade, Mircea. *Patterns in Comparative Religion*. Trans. Rosemary Sheed. New York: Sheed & Ward, 1958.
_____. *Myths, Dreams and Mysteries: The Encounter between Contemporary Faiths and Archaic Realities*. Trans. Philip Mairet. New York: Harper & Row, 1960.
_____. *Shamanism: Archaic Techniques of Ecstasy*. Trans. Willard R. Trask. Princenton, NJ: Princeton University Press, 1972.
_____. *Rites and Symbols of Initiation: The Mysteries of Birth and Rebirth*. Trans. Willard R. Trask. New York: Harper & Row, 1975.
_____. *A History of Religious Ideas* Vol. 2: *From Gautama Buddha to the Triumph of Christianity*. Trans. Willard R. Trask. Chicago: University of Chicago Press, 1982.
_____. *Images and Symbols: Studies in Religious Symbolism*. Trans. Philip Mairet. Princeton, NJ: Princeton University Press, 1991.
Franz, Marie-Louise von. *C.G. Jung: His Myth in Our Time*. Trans. William H. Kennedy. New York: Putnam, 1975.
Gallais, Pierre. *Perceval et l'Initiation*. 2nd ed. Orléans, France: Paradigme, 1998a.
_____. "La «maison» du Roi-Pêcheur." Rpt. in *Polyphonie du Graal*, ed. Denis Hüe, 1998b. 45–58.
Gibson, Marion. *Imagining the Pagan Past: Gods and Goddesses in Literature and History since the Dark Ages*. New York: Routledge, 2013.

Graves, Robert. *The White Goddess: A Historical Grammar of Poetic Myth*. 1948. Ed. Grevel Lindop. Rev. ed. Manchester, England: Carcanet, 1997.
Green, Thomas. *Concepts of Arthur*. Stroud, England: Tempus, 2007.
Guthrie, W.K.C. *Orpheus and Greek Religion: A Study of the Orphic Movement*. 1952. Princeton, NJ: Princeton University Press, 1993.
Hakl, Hans Thomas. *Eranos: An Alternative Intellectual History of the Twentieth Century*. Trans. Christopher McIntosh. Sheffield, England: Equinox, 2013.
_____. "Eranos: A Counter Current to the Common Intellectual History of the 20th Century?" *Spring: A Journal of Archetype and Culture* 92 (2015): 57–78.
Harris, Wilson. *Merlin & Parsifal: Adversarial Twins*. London: Temenos Academy, 1997.
Hillman, James *Loose Ends: Primary Papers in Archetypal Psychology*. Dallas, TX: Spring Publications, 1975.
_____. "Peaks and Vales: The Soul/Spirit Distinction as Basis for the Differences between Psychotherapy and Spiritual Discipline." In *Puer Papers*, ed. Cynthia Giles. Dallas, TX: Spring Publications, 1976. 54–74.
_____. *Healing Fiction*. New York: Station Hill, 1983.
Hüe, Denis, ed. *Polyphonie du Graal*. Orléans, France: Paradigme, 1998.
_____, and Christine Ferlampin-Acher, eds. *Le Monde et l'Autre Monde*. Orléans, France: Paradigme, 2002.
Hutton, Ronald. *The Pagan Religions of the Ancient British Isles: Their Nature and Legacy*. Oxford, England: Blackwell, 1993.
_____. *The Stations of the Sun: A History of the Ritual Year in Britain*. New York: Oxford University Press, 1996.
_____. *Witches, Druids and King Arthur*. New York: Hambledon, 2003.
_____. *Pagan Britain*. New Haven, CT: Yale University Press, 2013.
Jung, Carl. *Answer to Job*. Trans. R.F.C. Hull. London: RKP, 1984.
Jung, Emma, and Marie-Louise von Franz. *The Grail Legend*. Trans. Andrea Dykes. 2nd ed. London: Coventure, 1986.
Kahane, Henry, and Renée Kahane, in collaboration with Angelina Pietrangeli.

The Krater and the Grail: Hermetic Sources of the Parzival. Urbana: University of Illinois Press, 1965.

Kerényi, Carl. *The Gods of the Greeks*. Trans. Norman Cameron. London: Thames & Hudson, 1951.

Kibler, William W., ed. *The Lancelot-Grail Cycle: Text and Transformations* Austin: University of Texas Press, 1994.

Larrington, Carolyne. *King Arthur's Enchantresses: Morgan and Her Sisters in Arthurian Tradition*. London: I.B. Taurus, 2006.

Le Saux, Françoise. "The Arthur of the Chronicles: Wace." In *The Arthur of the French*, eds. Burgess and Pratt. 96–101.

Loomis, Roger Sherman. *Celtic Myth and Arthurian Romance*. 1926. London: Constable, 1993.

Mac Cana, Proinsias. *Celtic Mythology*. 2nd ed. Middlesex, England: Newnes, 1983.

Matthews, Caitlín, with paintings by Meg Falconer. *King Arthur's Raid on the Underworld: The Oldest Grail Quest*. Somerset, England: Gothic Image, 2008.

Matthews, John. *Gawain, Knight of the Goddess: Restoring an Archetype*. London: Aquarian Press, 1990.

Nasr, Seyyed Hossein. *The Spiritual and Religious Dimensions of the Environmental Crisis*. London: Temenos, 1999.

Nutt, Alfred. *Studies on the Legend of the Holy Grail with Especial Reference to the Hypothesis of its Celtic Origin*. London: David Nutt, 1888.

Parsons, Deke. *J.R.R. Tolkien, Robert E. Howard and the Birth of Modern Fantasy*. Jefferson, NC: McFarland, 2014.

Paton, Lucy Allen. *Studies in the Fairy Mythology of Arthurian Romance*. Boston, MA: Ginn, 1903.

Rahn, Otto. *Crusade against the Grail: The Struggle between the Cathars, the Templars, and the Church of Rome*. Trans. Christopher Jones. Rochester, VT: Inner Traditions, 2006.

_____. *Lucifer's Court: A Heretic's Journey in Search of the Light Bringers*. Trans. Christopher Jones. Rochester, VT: Inner Traditions, 2007.

Rhys, John. *Studies in the Arthurian Legend*. Oxford, England: Clarendon, 1891.

Roquebert, Michel. *Les Cathares et le Graal*. Toulouse, France: Privat, 1994.

_____. *La Religion Cathare: Le Bien, le Mal et le Salut dans l'Hérésie*. Paris: Tempus, 2013.

Shippey, Tom, *The Road to Middle-Earth: How J.R.R. Tolkien Created a New Mythology*. 2nd, rev. ed. London: HarperCollins, 2005.

Sims-Williams, Patrick. "The Early Welsh Arthurian Poems." In Rachel Bromwich, A.O.H. Jarman and Brynley F. Roberts, eds. *The Arthur of the Welsh: The Arthurian Legend in Medieval Welsh Literature*. Cardiff: University of Wales Press, 1991. 33–71.

Skeat, Walter W. *The Concise Dictionary of English Etymology*. Oxford, England: Clarendon, 1884.

_____. "Lancelot With or Without the Grail: *L'Estoire del Saint Graal*." In *The Arthur of the French*, eds. Burgess and Pratt, 2006. 278–284.

Southey, Robert. Preface. *The Byrth, Lyf, and Actes of Kyng Arthur*. London: Longman, 1817. i–lxiii.

Stein, W.J. *The Ninth Century and the Holy Grail*. Trans. Irene Groves and John M. Wood. 2nd ed. London: Temple Lodge, 2001.

Steiner, Rudolf. *The Knights Templar: The Mystery of the Warrior Monks*. Trans. Christian von Arnim. Ed. Margaret Jonas. East Sussex, England: Rudolf Steiner Press, 2007.

Szkilnik, Michelle. *L'Archipel du Graal: Étude de L'Estoire del Saint Graal*. Geneva, Switzerland: Droz, 1991.

Taylor, Thomas. *The Hymns of Orpheus, Translated from the Original Greek*. London: N.p., 1792.

Tolkien, J.R.R. *The Letters of JRR Tolkien: A Selection*. Ed. Humphrey Carpenter. London: Allen & Unwin, 1981.

_____. *The Monsters and the Critics and Other Essays*. Ed. Christopher Tolkien. London: HarperCollins, 2006.

Traxler, Janina P. "Dying to Get to Sarras: Perceval's Sister and the Grail Quest." In *The Grail: A Casebook*, ed. Dhira B. Mahoney. New York: Garland, 2000. 261–78.

Waite, Arthur Edward. *The Hidden Church of the Holy Graal: Its Legends and Symbolism considered in their affinity with certain mysteries of initiation and other traces of a secret tradition in Christian times.* London: Rebman, 1909.

Walter, Philippe. *Galaad: Le Pommier et le Graal.* Paris: Imago, 2004.

Weston, Jessie L. *The Legend of Sir Gawain: Studies upon its Original Scope and Significance.* London: David Nutt, 1897.

_____. *The Legend of Sir Lancelot du Lac: Studies upon its Origin, Development, and Position in the Arthurian Romantic Cycle.* London: David Nutt, 1901.

_____. *The Legend of Sir Perceval: Studies upon its Origin, Development, and Position in the Arthurian Cycle.* Vol.1. London: David Nutt, 1906.

_____. *The Legend of Sir Perceval.* Vol. 2. London: David Nutt, 1909.

_____. *The Quest of the Holy Grail.* 1913. New York: Dover, 2001.

_____. *From Ritual to Romance.* 1920. Princeton, NJ: Princeton University Press, 1993.

Williams, Andrea M. L. "Perceval and the Grail: *Perlesvaus*." In *The Arthur of the French*, eds. Burgess and Pratt. 260–4.

Zimmer, Heinrich. *The King and the Corpse: Tales of the Soul's Conquest of Evil.* Ed. Joseph Campbell. 2nd ed. Princeton, NJ: Princeton University Press, 1956.

Index

Abel 76
Accalon of Gaul 165–9
Achamoth 84; *see also* Sophia; Wisdom
Acts of John 194–5, 200, 226; *see also* apocrypha
Adam 6, 75–6, 81, 85, 114, 115, 137
Adonis 189; *see also* Dying-and-Resurrected Gods
Aeneas, Prince of Troy 6, 20, 68
aeons 84, 86, 215, 230; *see also* Sophia
Afallach (god) 149
Agrestes, King of Camelot 128
Ahnenerbe 200; *see also* Himmler, Heinrich; Nazism
Alan the Fat (Grail companion) 129, 130, 134, 135, 141; *see also* Rich Fishers
Albion 5, 12–3, 15–8, 27, 48, 78, 79, 116–7, 125, 154, 176–7, 205, 208, 221, 224–30, 236, 238; Daughters of 16–8, 221, 228, 230
Albrecht (poet) 191, 214
alchemy 106, 188, 192, 215, 216, 220
allegory 6, 13, 72, 78, 79, 90, 105–7, 110, 117, 177, 194–5, 208, 210, 229
Alphasan, King of the Land Beyond 134–5
Aminadap 135, 137; *see also* Fisher Kings
Amite *see* Helizabel
anarchists 219
angels 7, 10–1, 33, 76, 83, 100, 103, 110–2, 187, 212, 214, 219, 233, 235–6
Annwfn 8, 10, 46, 47, 52, 53, 59, 149; *see also* Faerie; Otherworld
Anthropos 224, 230
Antichrist 98, 104, 153
Antor (knight) 66, 145
apocrypha 10, 84–5, 114, 194–7, 200, 226; *see also* Acts of John
Apollo (god) 21, 27–8, 110, 130; *see also* Phoebus
archetypes 16–7, 22, 37, 49, 84, 102, 106, 142, 163, 174, 223, 225, 228–30
Arcturus 24
Argante 92–3; *see also* Avalon; Fairy Queens
Argon 28, 130–1; *see also* Saracens
Ariosto, Ludovico 6

Arroy (forest) 172
Artemis (goddess) 21, 24–5, 28, 160, 163–4; *see also* Diana
Arthur, King of Britain 5–8, 10, 13, 16–7, 25–6, 29, 38, 41, 44–50, 51, 53, 58, 59, 61, 65–7, 70, 88, 89–93, 95, 116, 145–7, 149–52, 155–6, 158, 165–9, 178, 212–3, 228; as Albion 17, 229–30; as bear 24, 25; as god 7; as King of Adventures 146, 213; as King of Faerie 21–23; as Maimed King 229–30; as Spectre 17, 230
Arthur the Less (knight) 206, 212
Arviragus, King of Britain 129
astral plane 178
astrology 59, 62, 143, 145, 189
Atalantë 234; *see also* Westernesse
Atlantis 236, 238
Attis 189; *see also* Dying-and-Resurrected Gods
Atwood, Margaret 179, 202
Aurelius Ambrosius, King of Britain 29, 139, 143–4
Avallónë 232–4
Avalon 8, 46, 52, 58–60, 65, 89, 92, 116, 156, 163, 168, 180–1, 191, 213, 221, 229–30, 232, 238; Lady of 65–6, 92–3, 151–4, 163, 183; Lord of 65, 149
Avenging Lance 156, 187; *see also* Bleeding Lance; Holy Lance; Lance of Vengeance

Bademagu, King of Gorre 52, 176
Balin the Savage 136, 151–2, 154, 156–8, 163, 171–2, 183–5, 206
banshee 10, 45–6, 236
Baring, Anne 21–2, 24
"The Beguiling of Merlin" (painting) 36; *see also* Burne-Jones, Edward
Beleriand (kingdom) 233–4, 237
Beli 10
Beltane (feast) 150
Benoic (kingdom) 33, 161, 170
Beren 233–4
Berthelay the Old 50–1
Bilbo Baggins 220, 231, 235; *see also* Hobbits

253

Index

Bizarre Beast 101, 104, 207
Bladud, King of Britain 52
Blaise (hermit) 98, 104, 141–4
Blake, William 6, 9, 13, 15–8, 24, 46, 78–9, 83–5, 100, 116–7, 175–7, 179–81, 199–200, 210, 215, 219, 221, 223–5, 227–30, 233, 235–6, 238; see also Jerusalem (poem); "The Marriage of Heaven and Hell"
Blancheflor 192
Bleeding Lance 112, 186, 195, 200, 212; see also Avenging Lance; Holy Lance; Lance of Vengeance
Blessed Realm 220, 233–5, 237–8
Boehme, Jacob 215
Book of the Grail 97, 195, 208
Bors (knight) 72–4, 86–9, 104, 111, 204–6, 208, 212, 216
Bran (Irish hero) 71
Brân (Welsh giant) 10, 210
Briar-Rose (Sleeping Beauty) 61, 63
Briosque (forest) 35
Brisane 56, 70
Britannia 17, 221, 229–30, 236
Broceliande (forest) 27, 36, 130, 140, 182, 233–4
Bromwich, Rachel 45, 64, 149
Bron (Grail companion) 127–9, 134, 154, 209–10
Brutus the Trojan 5, 17–8, 20–1, 27, 79, 124–5, 131, 204–5, 208, 229; see also Castle Brutus
Burne-Jones, Edward 36–7; see also "The Beguiling of Merlin"; Pre-Raphaelites

Caer Sidi 10, 46, 60; see also Annwfn
Caer Vedwit 47; see also Castle of Carousal
Caer Wydyr 46, 52; see also Annwfn
Cahus (squire) 178
Caiaphas, Jewish High Priest 109, 205, 209
Cain 76
Caledonian Forest 181
Callisto 25
Cameliard (kingdom) 44, 47–8, 50, 63
Camelot 8, 48, 69–71, 96, 128, 134, 151, 158–63, 184, 201; forest of 165, 184
Canaan (Grail companion) 127, 132–3
Canaan (land) 15, 17, 18
Caradog of Llancarfan 52
Carcelois 135; see also Fisher Kings
Carduel (city) 49, 66, 144–5, 147–8, 159, 185
Carey, John 187–8, 196
Cashford, Jules 21–2, 24
Castle Brutus 204–5; see also Brutus the Trojan
Castle of Carousal 47, 159; see also Caer Vedwit
Castle of Enchantments 50
Castle of the Rock 28, 131–2, 210
Castle of Treachery 205
Cathars 103, 108, 189–91, 198–201, 211
cauldrons 10, 46–7, 53, 59

Cei see Kay
Celice (river) 132
Celidoine, King of North Wales 113, 118–20, 125–7, 134
Chapel of St Augustine 178
Charlemagne 6–7
Le Chevalier au Lion 59
Le Chevalier de la Charrette 31
Chrétien de Troyes 11–13, 31–2, 40, 52–3, 55, 59–60, 62, 65, 94, 104–5, 174, 184, 186–7, 189, 192, 193–5, 197, 199–200, 210, 214; see also Le Chevalier au Lion; Le Chevalier de la Charrette; Erec et Enide; Perceval ou le Conte du Graal
Cistercians 71, 201; see also White Monks
Coilus, King of Britain see Old King Cole
Coll the Enchanter 25
comics 7, 180, 202, 220; see also graphic novels; Superman
Company of the Grail 12, 27–8, 83, 94–5, 112, 116, 120–1, 124, 126, 129, 131–2, 137, 143, 145, 154, 191, 199, 205, 210, 212, 221, 229
Conan the Barbarian 180; see also Howard, Robert E.
Constans II, Western Roman Emperor 138–9
Constantine the Great 99, 106, 138
Constantine III, Western Roman Emperor 29, 138–9, 165
Constantine V, Eastern Roman Emperor 105–6
Constantius Chlorus, Western Roman Emperor 138
Conte du Graal see Perceval ou le Conte du Graal
Corbenic 8, 55, 69–72, 81–2, 86, 95, 135, 137, 142, 156–7, 191, 201–2, 206, 210–1, 230
Corbin, Henry 9, 11, 16, 89, 102, 142, 175–7, 179–81, 190–7, 201, 208–11, 213, 215–20, 224
Corpus Hermeticum 190; see also hermeticism
Crater (constellation) 190
Crusade Against the Grail 199; see also Rahn, Otto
crusades 103, 121, 127, 190–1, 197–9, 201–2

Damsel of the Lake 180; see also Nimue
Dante (poet) 8, 88
D'Arcy, Anne Marie 85–6, 116–7
Darnantes (forest) 34, 132
David, King of Israel 53–4, 56, 71, 113; Sword of 56, 76–7, 82, 113–4, 119, 135, 156, 211
De Boron Cycle 62, 99, 142, 209; see also Prose Joseph of Arimathea; Prose Merlin; Robert de Boron
deities 9, 27–9, 35, 45, 78–9, 110, 124, 130, 149, 164, 210; Romano-Celtic 10, 27, 188
Demiurge 78, 84, 116
demons 7, 11, 26, 33–4, 53, 55, 60, 72, 81, 87–8, 93, 98, 101–7, 110–1, 132, 134, 137, 139–41, 143, 153, 167, 204, 207
Devil Cat 26, 29, 34–5; see also Palug

Index

devils 7, 9–10, 33, 35, 74–5, 98, 102, 104, 106, 110, 120–1, 126, 131, 140–1, 143–4, 148, 153, 165–7, 169, 172, 177, 200, 204, 207, 209
Diana (goddess) 12, 20–1, 24, 27–30, 32–5, 48, 60, 79–80, 124–5, 130, 162–4, 182, 207, 229, 236; Lake of 33, 162–4; Temple of 20, 29–30, 35, 124; *see also* Artemis
divination 33, 143, 169
Docetism 195, 200; *see also* heresy
Dolorous Blow 56, 75, 82, 96, 112, 135–6, 147, 153–4, 158–9, 171, 183, 185, 187, 206, 211
Domas, Lord of the Tower of Ambush 166
Dôn (goddess) 213
dragons 8, 30, 40, 56, 60, 143, 172
Druids 189, 199, 230
dualism 9, 11, 16, 108, 190–1, 193, 196, 198, 211, 228, 236
Dubost, Francis 193
Dying-and-Resurrected Gods 53, 107, 109, 137, 182, 189, 227; *see also* Adonis; Attis; Osiris

Earth-Two 202; *see also* comics
Ecumenical Councils 106–7, 195
Eden 15–7, 53, 75, 77, 85–6, 114–7, 224, 226, 230
Egypt 18, 25, 110, 126, 134, 214
Elaine, Princess of Corbenic 53, 55–6, 70, 184; *see also* Helizabel
Elaine, Queen of Benoic 71, 161
elementals 16, 79
Elen of the Hosts, Empress of Britain 138–9
Eliade, Mircea 63, 195, 197, 216–8, 220
Eliezer, Prince of Corbenic 210
Elvenhome 61, 233; *see also* Faerie
elves 8, 13, 46, 60–1, 65, 181, 219–21, 230–8
Elysium 71, 93, 115
emanations 16, 79, 84–6, 117, 221, 223–30; *see also* Enitharmon; Jerusalem
enchantment 13, 17, 31, 33, 38–41, 43, 46, 49, 60–61, 65, 96–7, 119, 145, 148, 153, 158, 161–2, 166, 169, 175, 180, 185, 213, 223, 232; *see also* Castle of Enchantments
Endymion 34
Enitharmon (emanation) 225–6, 228–9
Eranos 11, 102, 216–8
Erec et Enide 59; *see also* Chrétien de Troyes
Esclabor 203–4; *see also* Saracens
esotericism 142, 179, 188, 190–1, 197, 208, 210–1, 219
Estoire de Lancelot 94–5; *see also* Vulgate Cycle
Estoire de Merlin 26, 34, 62, 95–6, 98, 137, 140, 142, 146; *see also* Vulgate Cycle
Estoire del Saint Graal 27, 77, 94–6, 98, 100, 105, 117, 137, 146, 177, 205, 207, 211; *see also* Vulgate Cycle
Eve 75–77, 85–6, 114–6
Evelach the Unknown, King of Sarras 110; *see also* Mordrain

Excalibur 44, 58, 92, 151–2, 154, 163, 166, 168–9, 212
Ezekiel (prophet) 78

Faerie 8, 24, 43, 61, 175, 177, 181–3, 197, 209, 230, 233, 238; *see also* Elvenhome; fairyland
Faerie Queene 6; *see also* Spenser, Sir Edmund
fairies 16, 92, 181, 236–8; of Albion 79, 228, 236; *see also* fays
Fairies' Fountain 55
fairy godmother 38, 95, 170
Fairy Queens 65, 213; *see also* Argante
fairyland 61, 87; *see also* Faerie
fairytales 61, 65, 80
False Female 16, 84
fantasy 60, 64, 102–4, 179–81, 192–3, 202, 206, 216, 218
Fatal Sisters 62, 66, 148–9, 213, 229; *see also* Fates; Weird Sisters
Fate (goddess) 35, 61–2, 91, 158, 178, 229
Fates 61, 63, 92; *see also* Parcae
Faunus 162, 164
fays (fairy women) 8–9, 13, 24, 30–1, 35, 43, 45, 53, 55, 60–2, 64–6, 80, 86–8, 90–3, 97, 120, 150, 155, 163–4, 173, 175, 180, 183, 213, 229–30, 232, 236; Lake of 151, 154, 156, 158, 163–4, 169, 183, 212
Felix 162–3
Findabhair 45–6; *see also* Gwenhwyfar
Fisher Kings 8, 10, 51, 53, 73, 77, 90, 94, 118, 135, 153, 185–7, 192–4, 203, 210–1, 217; *see also* Aminadap; Carcelois; Joshua; Lambor; Manuel; Pellehan; Pelles
Flegetanis (astrologer) 189–90
Flualis, King of Jerusalem 29–30
Fortunate Isle 52, 58, 116; *see also* Avalon
Fortune (goddess) 89–92; Wheel of 87, 90
Franz, Marie-Louise von 215–6
Frazer, Sir James 182
Frea (goddess) 139; *see also* Venus
Freudianism 215, 225
Frodo Baggins 231, 235; *see also* Hobbits

Gaheriet (knight) 66, 89–90, 176, 184
Gaia (goddess) 115–6
Galafort (city) 125–6, 133–4; *see also* Ganor
Galahad (knight) 5, 54–7, 70–2, 74–5, 77–8, 80, 82–3, 94, 112, 127, 132, 134, 158, 183–4, 193, 204–6, 210–12, 221
Galahad, King of Wales 53, 56, 133–4, 148
Galehaut (knight) 39, 51, 88
Gallais, Pierre 192–3
Galuth (sword) 232
Gandalf the Wizard 231, 233, 235; *see also* Olórin
Ganor, Lord of Galafort 125–6
Gareth (knight) *see* Gaheriet
Garlon the Red 156, 172
Garlot (kingdom) 62, 148, 169
Gawain 13, 48, 51–2, 72, 89–91, 154, 156, 158,

160, 169, 171-5, 183-5, 203, 206-8, 210-2, 232; and paganism 174-5, 211, 232
Geoffrey of Monmouth 10-1, 27, 45-6, 52, 58-60, 62, 93-4, 138, 148, 151-2, 181-2, 236; *see also* Historia Regum Britanniae; *Vita Merlini*
giants 6, 8, 12, 17-18, 21, 47-8, 118, 154, 159, 182, 203, 228-9; *see also* Albion; Brân; Rion of the Isles
Giant's Knoll 128
Gilead 71
Gingalin (knight) 175
Girflet (knight) 92, 212-3; and paganism 213
glamour 7, 97, 120, 175
Glass Island 46, 52-3
Glastonbury 46, 52
gnosis 7, 83-4, 116, 188-90, 193, 196, 219, 224
Gnostics 78, 83-5, 107, 116, 188-90, 192, 195, 198
God 11, 28, 35, 115; Hidden 84; as Monad 190; as One 117, 130-1, 233-4, 236; as Three-in-One 110; True 198, 200; *see also* Trinity
Goddess 12, 17, 18, 21, 22, 23, 24 124, 148, 153, 158, 160, 163, 173, 174, 175, 183, 193, 229, 230, 237
goddesses 9, 12, 20, 23, 24, 32, 33, 35, 45, 46, 47, 51, 60, 87, 118, 119, 121, 149, 229, 230, 236; *see also* Artemis; Diana; Dôn; Fate; Fortune; Frea; Gaia; Great Mother; Inanna; Ishtar; Matrona; Moira; moon goddess; Mother Earth; Night; Persephone; Proserpina; Rhea; Rosmerta; Selene; Sovereignty; Tervagant; Venus
godhead 85-6, 100, 117, 229
gods 5, 7, 9, 10, 11, 13, 23, 28, 29, 30, 46, 78, 79, 84, 111, 113, 115, 116, 118, 124, 130, 131, 149, 181, 198, 199, 200, 205, 220, 229, 233, 236, 237; *see also* Afallach; Apollo; Hermes; Jupiter; Lugh; Maponos; Mars; Mercury; Osiris; Phoebus; Saturn; Woden; Yahweh; Zeus
Golden Age 115-6, 181, 218, 227
Golden Ass see Lucius Apuleius
Golden Bough see Frazer, Sir James
Gorlois, Duke of Tintagel 66
Gorre (kingdom) 31, 42, 51-2, 54, 67, 134, 148, 184
Grail: adventures of 54, 68, 81, 104, 128, 144, 205; bearer 56, 69, 190-1; as bowl 109; as Cross of Light 193-4; as dish 109; Hallows 157, 214; as Hermetic Krater 190; Question 12, 177, 185-7, 216-7; as Stone 189, 202; as symbol 7, 12, 62, 85, 125, 188-9, 199-202, 215, 230
Grail Castle 8, 90, 135, 142, 192, 195; *see also* Corbenic
graphic novels 6; *see also* comics
Graves, Robert 107, 182
Great Mother (goddess) 149
Guenevere (false) 44-5, 48, 50-1; *see also* Lady of Cameliard

Guenevere, Queen of Britain 8, 38-53, 55-8, 63, 65-9, 71, 77, 80-1, 87-9, 91, 120, 158-9; as Daughter of Albion16, 228
Guigemar, Prince of Brittany 63
Gui(g)omar, Lord of the Isle of Avalon 59-60, 63, 67, 88, 165
Guingamor (knight) 63-5
Gwenhwyfar 45, 47; *see also* Findabhair; Guenevere

Harris, Wilson 179
Harrowing of Hell 141; of pagan Britain 137
Hartmann von Aue 60, 148
heathenism 16, 30, 45, 79, 106, 228, 230
Helain the White 208
Helena of Britain 138
Helizabel 55; *see also* Elaine, Princess of Corbenic
Hengest (Saxon leader) 139-40, 143, 237
heresy 7, 84, 103, 106, 108, 189, 195, 197-8, 200-2, 207, 237; *see also* Docetism
Hermes (god) 164; Trismegistus 190; *see also* Mercury
Hermeticism 80, 189-91, 196, 215
Herodotus 25
Hesiod 61
Hillman, James 102-3, 106-8, 110, 197
Himmler, Heinrich 199; *see also* Ahnenerbe; Nazism
Historia Regum Britanniae 10-1, 58, 94; *see also* Geoffrey of Monmouth
The Hobbit 180, 218, 235; *see also* Tolkien, J.R.R.
Hobbits 220, 231, 233, 235; *see also* Bilbo Baggins; Frodo Baggins
Holy Blood 12, 62, 109, 124, 209; *see also* Sangreal
Holy Lance 82, 112, 157, 185, 187, 206; *see also* Avenging Lance; Bleeding Lance; Lance of Vengeance; Longinus
Holy Land 12, 15, 17, 54, 84, 94, 103, 109, 111, 113, 119, 121, 191, 197, 202, 212, 238
Holy Vessel 12, 56, 69-70, 81-3, 85, 96, 99, 125-7, 129, 134-5, 137, 206, 210, 212, 216; *see also* Grail
Holy War 7, 199
Howard, Robert E. 216, 220, 236; *see also* Conan the Barbarian
Hutton, Ronald 174, 196
Hyperboreans 21

iconoclasm 99, 103, 105-7, 113, 117, 124, 131, 197, 201
icons 85, 105-6
idols 105, 110, 112, 126, 128, 130-1, 134
Idylls of the King 6; *see also* Tennyson, Alfred Lord
Igerna, Queen of Britain 62, 66, 145, 148
imagery 9-10, 17, 21-4, 28, 49, 61, 79, 83, 85, 89, 91, 100, 102-7, 109-11, 113, 117-8, 121, 124,

130–1, 173, 177, 179–80, 192–7, 200–4, 207, 209–11, 213–6, 220, 225, 235
imaginal 9, 11, 21, 89, 93, 175–7, 190, 192, 195, 197, 201–2, 208, 214, 236, 238; *see also* mundus imaginalis
imagination 9, 13, 16–7, 102, 106, 108, 175–7, 179–81, 192–3, 195–7, 200–2, 207, 210, 214, 216–7, 220, 224, 227, 230, 235; as Jesus 117, 224, 226–7; as Zoa 16, 79, 227
Imaginative Eye 9, 16, 79, 175, 192, 230
Inanna (goddess) 51
incest 66, 92, 96, 147, 165, 207–8, 212
incubus 140–1; *see also* demons; devils
India 181, 191, 214, 219
initiation 23, 178, 188, 192–3, 196, 219–20
Ishtar (goddess) 51
Islam 105, 130, 179, 197, 214, 219; *see also* Moslems; mosques
Island of Apples 58; Britain as 230; *see also* Avalon
Island of Maidens 31
Isle of Joy 70
Isles of the Blest 115
Ismailism 192, 219

Jerusalem (emanation) 16–17, 84, 116–7, 221, 224, 226, 228–9
Jerusalem (poem) 227, 230; *see also* Blake, William
Jews 73, 103, 109, 112, 200, 205
Joachim of Flora 103, 108, 216
John of Lugio 202; *see also* Cathars
Joseph of Arimathea 8, 12, 27, 53–4, 56, 71, 82, 94, 99–100, 105, 109, 112, 119, 124, 126, 129–30, 133–4, 139, 141, 144, 187, 205, 210
Josephus (Grail companion) 28, 82, 94, 109–13, 124–30, 132–4, 212, 214
Joshua 135; *see also* Fisher Kings
Judaism 78, 85–6, 103, 200, 224; *see also* Kabbalism
Judas 144
Jung, C.G. 84, 195, 215–8, 220; Jungian 21, 215–7, 225
Jung, Emma 215–6
Jupiter (god) 27–8, 34, 115–6, 118, 130, 139; *see also* Zeus

Kabbalism 85, 219; *see also* Judaism
Kahane, Henry, and Renée 189–90, 196; *see also The Krater and the Grail*
Kay (knight) 26, 66, 146
Kerényi, Carl 25, 61, 164
King of the Wood *see* Lake Nemi
Kingdom of Adventures 146, 157, 213–4, 216, 223; *see also* Logres
Kingdom of No Return 52; *see also* Gorre
Kingdom of the Grail 8–9, 53, 73, 87, 230; *see also* Listenois
The Krater and the Grail 189; *see also* Kahane, Henry, and Renée

Krypton (planet) 180; *see also* Superman
Kyot 189–90

Lady of Cameliard 50–1, 58; *see also* Guenevere (false)
Lady of the Enchanted Isle 170; *see also* Morgan the Fay
Lady of the Fountain 182–3
Lady of the Lake 24, 30–2, 34, 36–40, 42–3, 53–4, 56–9, 69, 72, 80–1, 87, 90, 92, 94–6, 153, 162, 164–5, 168, 170, 229, 252; *see also* Nenyve; Nimue; Ninienne; Viviane
Lady of the Wild Animals 22, 24, 60, 207; *see also* Artemis
Lake Nemi 182
Lake of Fays 151, 154, 156, 158, 163–4, 169, 183, 212
Lake of the Moon 163
Lambor 75, 82, 135–6, 147; *see also* Fisher Kings
Lance of Vengeance 157, 206; *see also* Avenging Lance
Lancelot (king) 104, 120
Lancelot of the Lake 8, 31, 33–4, 38–43, 49, 51–7, 67–71, 81, 88–92, 120, 133, 158, 161, 170, 184, 212; *see also* Lanzelet
Land Beyond 55–6, 69, 134–7, 142, 156; *see also* Listenois
Land of Maidens 31–2, 71
Land of Women 46, 58, 71
Lanval (knight) 65
Lanzelet (knight) 32, 58
Lanzelet (poem) *see* Ulrich von Zatzikhoven
Larrington, Carolyne 33, 38
Last Judgment 13, 17, 157, 187, 221, 226, 228, 234
Lateran Council, Fourth 100, 103, 105, 108, 121
Layamon 29, 60–1, 91–3, 218, 221, 232, 236, 238
lays, Breton 12
legendarium 218, 231
legends 7, 10, 11, 15, 103, 114–7, 129, 137–8, 144, 162, 174, 191–6, 201–2, 215, 232, 237–8; Arthurian 5, 7, 13, 18, 179, 196, 224, 229
Lennon, John 224
Leo III, Eastern Roman Emperor 105
Leodagan, King of Cameliard 44–5, 47
Leogetia (island) 20
Lionel (knight) 73–4
Listenois (kingdom) 55, 156–7; *see also* Land Beyond
literalism 11, 13, 89, 91, 100, 105, 110, 118, 131, 177–9, 194, 198, 202, 206, 209, 211, 224, 234
Lludd Silver Hand 10
Loathly Damsel 175
Logres (kingdom) 8, 9, 13; Adventures of 53, 96, 112, 159–60, 204, 206; Sovereignty of 47–9, 51, 55; *see also* Kingdom of Adventures
Longinus (knight) 187
Loomis, Roger Sherman 174, 182, 188, 210

258　Index

Lord of the Dance 194
The Lord of the Rings 218, 220, 231–2, 235; see also Tolkien, J.R.R.
Los, the Eternal Prophet 225–7
Loth, King of Orkney 62–3, 66–7, 133, 145, 148, 150, 154–5, 160, 184
Lucifer's Court 200; see also Rahn, Otto
Lucius, King of Britain 22–3, 29, 94, 133, 135, 137, 191
Lucius Apuleius 23
Lugh (god) 188
Lunete 174
Luthany 220, 237–8
Lúthien 233–4
Lydgate, John 61

Mab 45, 47; see also Fairy Queens
Mabon see Maponos
Mac Cana, Proinsias 71, 188
Maeve, Queen of Connacht 45–7
magic 6, 10, 23, 31–43, 52–3, 61, 64, 69, 72, 87, 89, 92, 96, 121, 144, 148, 150–3, 155–6, 158, 161, 163–70, 173, 175–6, 180, 183, 201, 204, 223, 238
Magnus Maximus, Western Roman Emperor 138
Maheloas, Lord of the Isle of Glass 52
Mahomet 130–1
Maimed King 16, 51, 72, 75, 81–2, 115–6, 127, 136, 157, 172, 185–6, 206, 209, 211–2, 215, 221, 229–30
Malory, Sir Thomas 6, 13, 37, 43, 55, 59, 66, 89, 92–3, 136, 145, 147, 162, 173, 180, 218, 221, 228, 232; see also Morte Darthur
Manessier (poet) 104–5
Manuel 135; see also Fisher Kings
Maponos (god) 149
Margue(l) 59–60; see also Morgan the Fay
Marie de France 63, 65
"The Marriage of Heaven and Hell" 78; see also Blake, William
Marvel Universe 202, 220; see also comics
Mary, Blessed Virgin 7, 28, 48, 79, 114
Mary Magdalene 202
Matagran 28, 131; see also Saracens
Matarasso, Pauline 85
materialism 83, 176, 179, 194, 215, 224
Matrona (goddess) 149
Matter of Britain 6–8, 11, 13, 15, 17, 20, 27, 29, 94, 97, 137, 139, 223, 229
Matter of France 6
Matter of Rome 6–7, 20
Matthews, John 174
Meleagant, Prince of Gorre 31, 42, 52
Melkor 219, 221, 233–4, 237
Melwas 52
Mercury (god) 139, 188; see also Hermes; Woden
Merlin 13, 17, 26, 29–30, 33–7, 40, 44, 47, 54, 59, 62, 67, 72, 91, 115, 120–1, 141, 143, 145–7,

149–51, 153–69, 175–7, 180–1, 207, 226, 229, 233; as Immortal Imagination 17, 176, 179, 181, 228, 235; as Lord of the Animals 182–3; as Prophet of the Grail 13, 95–6, 98, 104, 141–4, 148, 153–4, 156–7, 159, 171, 183, 203
mermaids 31–2
metaphor 21, 36, 142, 174, 181, 225, 232
Metropolis 202; see also Superman
Middle-earth 218, 220–1, 231–5, 237; see also Tolkien, J.R.R.
Milton, John 6, 15, 180
Mirkwood (forest) 232
Modron see Matrona
Moira (goddess) 61; see also Fate
Montségur 199–201
Monty Python 162
moon goddess 12, 21–2, 27, 34–5, 63, 78–9, 120, 125, 153, 160, 164, 173, 182, 193, 204, 207–8, 213, 221, 228–9; as cat 25, 28–9, 131
Morcadés 66; see also Morgause
Mordrain (Grail companion) 110–1, 113, 119, 126–7, 134; see also Evalach
Mordred (knight) 57, 67, 90–1, 150–1, 154, 169, 207, 212
Morgan the Fay 7, 40–3, 57–9, 62–3, 65–9, 77, 87–9, 91–7, 120–1, 145, 148–9, 154–5, 159, 165–70, 183, 206, 213, 221, 229–30
Morgause, Queen of Orkney 66–7, 92, 147, 151, 154, 159, 184, 207
Morgen the Healer 59, 93, 152, 181
Morgue 59; see also Morgan the Fay
Morholt 171–3, 175–6
Morris, William 36–7; see also Pre-Raphaelites
Mort Artu 174; see also Vulgate Cycle
Morte Darthur 6, 13, 36–7, 51; see also Malory, Sir Thomas
Moses (Grail companion) 125, 127–9, 132, 144, 205
Moslems 27, 105, 131
mosques 128, 130–1; see also Islam
Mother Earth (goddess) 25, 115; see also Gaia
Mount Doom 219
mundus imaginalis 89, 176, 192, 195, 201–2, 208, 214, 236; see also imaginal
Muntsalvæsche 189, 191, 199; see also Wildenberg
Murray, Margaret 107
mystery religions 22–3, 61, 93, 178, 188–9; see also Orphism
mysticism 13, 23, 61, 85, 103, 142, 177, 181, 187–92, 196, 201, 210, 214–6, 219–20
mythology 45, 47, 60, 101, 180, 188, 218, 220; Blakean 15–6, 84, 219, 225, 228; Celtic 7, 11, 27, 45, 49, 58, 149, 202, 209; classical 6–7, 11, 21–2, 34, 103, 121, 163; Egyptian 25; English 220; fairy 6, 13, 16, 34, 93, 220, 231, 236; Gnostic 219; Irish 45, 58, 60; medieval 11; of Middle-earth 231, 233; Norse 210, 220, 235
mythopoeia 220

mythos 16, 62, 65, 155, 215, 229
myths 6–7, 11, 15–7, 20–2, 24–5, 51, 58, 65, 93, 103, 120, 148, 163–4, 174, 180, 182, 184, 191, 196, 228, 234, 236

Naassenes 189; *see also* Gnostics
Nascien, Duke of Orberica 110–13, 117–21, 125–6, 135
Nascien the Grail Hermit 72, 101–4, 106–7, 109, 117, 142, 191, 195, 207–9
Nasr, Seyyed Hossein 179
Nazism 180
necromancy 33, 62, 155, 164, 169, 207–8
Nemoralia (feast) 48; *see also* Lake Nemi
Nenyve 37, 92; *see also* Nimue
Nicene Councils 106–8, 110, 118, 131, 195
Nicene Creed 27, 99
Nienna, the Lady of Mourning 236
Night (goddess) 61
Nimue 37; *see also* Damsel of the Lake
Nimuë (poem) 37; *see also* Tennyson, Alfred Lord
Ninienne 33–5, 39, 57, 87, 92, 95–6, 120–1, 160–5, 167–8, 170, 181, 206; *see also* Nenyve; Nimue; Viviane
North Wales (kingdom) 126–7, 172
Northumberland (kingdom) 126, 141, 143–4, 151–2, 161, 163, 178
Nutt, Alfred 74, 104

Old King Cole 138
Olórin (angel) 235; *see also* Gandalf the Wizard
Orcaut (city) 111
Orkney 133, 150, 184
Orpheus 61
Osiris (god) 189
Otherworld 10–1, 24, 43, 46–7, 51–3, 55, 59–60, 64, 69, 71, 80, 87, 89, 93, 105, 107, 174–5, 177, 179, 183, 188, 191–2, 197, 201–2, 208–9, 213–4, 229–30
Owein (Welsh hero) 148–9, 182; *see also* Yvain

paganism 7, 9, 10, 27, 29, 35, 46, 49, 53–4, 60, 62, 79–80, 93, 111, 119, 128, 130–1, 134, 174, 177–8, 182, 187–8, 196–7, 201, 204, 207–10, 212–4, 221, 228–9
pagans 12, 29–30, 75, 78, 111, 120–1, 126–8, 130–3, 135, 137, 139, 153, 189, 203–5, 207, 212, 236
Palace of Adventures 70, 206
Palomides (knight) 148, 203–7; *see also* Saracens
Palug 25; *see also* Devil Cat
Paradise, Earthly 18, 116
Parcae (goddesses) 35, 61; *see also* Fates
Parsifal 217
Parzival (knight) 190–1, 199
Parzival (poem) 189–90; *see also* Wolfram von Eschenbach

Paton, Lucy Allen 34–5, 93, 155, 213, 229
Pellehan 75, 136, 147, 156–8, 185, 206–7; *see also* Fisher Kings
Pelles 53–6, 70–1, 81, 210; *see also* Fisher Kings
Pellinor, King of the Isles 147, 149, 154, 156, 160–1, 184–5, 203, 206
Pentecost (feast) 51, 71, 134, 145–6
Perceval 49, 53, 71–5, 83, 87–8, 94, 104–5, 147–8, 177, 185–6, 188, 192–5, 203, 205–6, 209, 212, 214, 221; sister of 74, 77–8, 80–2, 86, 113, 116, 183–5
Perceval ou le Conte du Graal (poem) 49, 53, 135, 192, 195, 197; continuations 104, 195; First Continuation 195, 211; Second Continuation 61; *see also* Chrétien de Troyes
Perilous Forest 34, 82, 167, 176
Perlesvaus 177–8
Persephone (goddess) 23, 51, 236; *see also* Proserpina
Peter (Grail companion) 127–9, 132–5, 141, 145, 154
Philip, Count of Flanders 197
Phoebe (Titaness of the Moon) 163–4
Phoebus (god) 139
Pleroma 84, 86
Plutarch 115
Post-Vulgate Cycle 43, 77, 93, 98, 136, 146–7, 151, 163, 173, 175, 203, 207–9, 212–4, 220
Post-Vulgate Grail Quest 194, 211–2
Post-Vulgate *Merlin Continuation* 147, 149, 203; *see also* Suite du Roman de Merlin
Pre-Raphaelites 6, 180; *see also* Burne-Jones, Edward; Morris, William; Rossetti, Dante Gabriel
Prester John 191
Priam, King of Troy 79, 205, 229
Pridwen (ship) 46
Promised Land 15, 17, 29, 97, 112, 119–21, 125, 146, 153, 157, 201, 207, 221, 230
prophecy 54, 77, 79, 82, 154, 176, 188, 205, 221, 227
Prose *Joseph of Arimathea* 142, 209; *see also* De Boron Cycle
Prose *Lancelot* 31, 55, 94–6
Prose *Merlin* 62, 142; *see also* De Boron Cycle
Proserpina (goddess) 23, 236; *see also* Persephone

Queste del Saint Graal 85, 136, 177, 210; *see also* Vulgate Cycle
Questing Beast 147–8, 154, 160, 203–8

Rahn, Otto 189, 191, 199–200; *see also* Crusade Against the Grail; Lucifer's Court
rationalism 176, 201, 210, 230
Reason 108, 200; as Zoa16–7, 226–7
Red Cross Shield 110, 134
Red Knight 49

Rhea (goddess) 115–6
Rhys, Sir John 104
Rich Fishers 130, 134–5, 185
Ring of Power 219, 235
Rion of the Isles 44–5, 48–9, 154; *see also* giants
Robert de Boron 62, 94–5, 99, 104, 109, 113, 142, 199, 209
Roman de Brut 139; *see also* Wace
Roquebert, Michel 200
Rosmerta (goddess) 188
Rossetti, Dante Gabriel 36
Round Table 8, 47–51, 56–7, 72, 87, 92, 101, 144, 146, 159–60, 181, 185, 206, 212, 215–6, 228; and superheroes 180

St. Philip (apostle) 109; Church of 133
St. Stephen's Church, Camelot 48, 128, 160
Salisbury Plain 91, 140, 143
Sangreal (Royal Blood) 13, 135, 200; *see also* Holy Blood
Saracens 27–9, 103, 110, 113, 118, 125–7, 130, 134, 212
Sarras (city) 8, 27, 56, 80, 82–3, 86, 94, 109, 111–3, 116, 118–20, 124–6, 134–6, 139, 142, 191, 202, 212, 214
Saturn (god) 115–6, 118, 139
Sauron the Necromancer 219, 234–5
science fiction 179, 181, 202
scientism 223–4; *see also* materialism
Seat of Danger 128, 132, 144, 205; *see also* Table of the Grail
Selene (goddess) 236
Seth 85, 116–7
Shadowy Female 77, 221, 228
Shakespeare, William 6, 45–6, 62
shamans 11
Shekinah 85; *see also* Wisdom
Shelley, Percy Bysshe 45
Ship of Faith 75, 80, 83, 85–6, 93–4, 113, 117, 120, 135, 147, 205, 209
Siege Perilous 53–4, 56, 71–2, 144, 159, 185, 216; *see also* Round Table
Silmarillion 238; *see also* Tolkien, J.R.R.
Simeon (Grail companion) 54, 82, 125, 127–8, 132–4, 205
Sir Gawain and the Green Knight 218, 231; *see also* Tolkien, J.R.R.
Sleeping Beauty *see* Briar-Rose
Sleeping Lord 17, 221, 228, 230
Solomon, King of Israel 76–7, 81, 114–5, 135, 189; ship of 77, 82, 113, 118–20; wife of 76–7, 80, 82, 85–6, 114, 121
Sophia (aeon) 84–6, 116–7, 230, 237; *see also* Wisdom
sorcery 33, 40–1, 49, 58, 96, 155, 161–2, 167, 175, 209; *see also* enchantment
Southey, Robert 6, 37–8, 180
Sovereignty (goddess) 46–47, 49, 138, 158, 173, 175, 183, 188, 210

Spectres 16–7, 224–7
Spenser, Sir Edmund 6, 8, 13, 236; *see also* Faerie Queene
Spiritual Palace 80, 82–3, 86–7, 212, 214
spiritus mundi 196
"The Spoils of Annwfn" (poem) 46–7, 197
Stein, W.J. 191
Steiner, Rudolf 189, 191, 215
Stone of the Stag 172, 176
Stonehenge 144, 153
Sufis 192
Suite du Roman de Merlin 96; *see also* Post-Vulgate *Merlin Continuation*
Superman 180; as American Messiah 216; *see also* Krypton; Metropolis
Swedenborg, Emanuel 215
Sword: Broken 82, 119, 187, 210–1, 235; Ill-Fated 152, 156, 158, 163; in the Floating Stone 72; in the Stone 67, 95, 158; of David 77, 82, 113–4, 118–9, 135, 156, 211
Sword Bridge 42, 52–3
symbolism 7, 11–12, 27–8, 32, 38, 49, 62, 73–4, 79, 85–7, 96, 100, 103, 116–9, 125, 152, 158, 173, 177–9, 182, 188, 191–3, 195–6, 199–201, 207, 210, 216, 225, 228
synchronicity 199
Synod of Constantinople 106

Table of the Grail 8, 72, 128–9, 144, 157; *see also* Seat of Danger
Table of the Last Supper 56, 71–2, 144
Taliesin (bard) 10, 59, 107, 148, 181
Templars 189, 202
temples 27, 29, 111, 128, 134; of Diana 20, 29–30, 35, 124; of the Grail 202; of Solomon 189; of the Sun 109–10
Tennyson, Alfred Lord 6, 37, 136, 162
Tervagant (goddess) 12, 27–9, 130, 229
Tetramorph 78–9
Theodosius, Roman Emperor 27
Tintagel 8, 145, 177; Duke of 62, 66
Tolkien, Christopher 220, 237
Tolkien, J.R.R. 60–1, 177, 180, 210, 216, 218–20, 231–8
Tree of Knowledge 75–6, 80, 85, 114
Tree of Life 76–7, 80, 85–6, 113–5, 117
Trevrizent (hermit) 190
Trinity 7, 9, 98–100, 105–6, 108–10, 113–4, 116–7, 130, 144, 200, 209, 225
Trojans 5, 12, 17–8, 20, 27, 79, 115, 119, 124–5, 204–5, 229
Troy 6, 18, 20–1, 68, 205, 228
Turning Isle 118

Ulrich von Zatzikhoven 31; *see also* Lanzelet (poem)
Urien, King of Gorre 134, 148–9, 165, 168–9, 172, 178
Uther Pendragon 29, 44, 47, 62, 66–7, 139, 143–5, 147–8, 159

Valentinus 84, 219; *see also* Gnostics
Valley of False Lovers 67
Valley of No Return 40
Varda the Exalted 236-7
Varlan (Welsh king) 75, 135-6, 156
Venus (goddess) 20, 23, 115, 139; *see also* Frea
Veronica, veil of 109
Vespasian 109, 205
Virgil (poet) 33, 162
Vita Merlini 58, 60, 180; *see also* Geoffrey of Monmouth
Viviane 35, 95, 233; *see also* Lady of the Lake; Ninienne
Vivien 37; *see also* Nimue
Vortigern, King of Britain 29, 139-41, 143
Vulgate Cycle 27, 29, 31, 33, 48, 53, 55, 57, 62, 65-7, 80, 83, 85, 94-5, 120, 134, 137, 146-7, 153, 159, 171, 184; *see also Estoire de Lancelot*; *Estoire de Merlin*; *Estoire del Saint Graal*; *Mort Artu*; *Queste del Saint Graal*
Vulgate *Lancelot* 40, 99, 146; *see also* Prose *Lancelot*

Wace (poet) 11, 62, 94, 138-40, 145, 234; *see also* Roman de Brut
Wagner, Richard 6, 199, 210
Waite, Arthur Edward 142, 188, 209, 215
Walter, Philippe 80, 209
Waste Forest 75, 78, 81, 147
Waste Land 51, 56, 75, 82, 85, 129, 136, 142, 156, 171-2, 191, 211-2, 215, 220-1, 226; Queen of 72
Water Bridge 52
Water Fay 31-2, 34, 58-9, 71
Weil, Simone 199
Weird Sisters 46, 62; *see also* Fatal Sisters
Welsh Triads 25, 45, 64, 138, 149
Westernesse 234, 238; *see also* Atlantis
Weston, Jessie L. 93, 103-4, 107, 174, 178, 182, 188-9, 196, 215, 219
White Forest 178
White Monks 201; *see also* Cistercians
Widow Lady 115
Wildenberg 189, 200; *see also* Muntsalvæsche
William of Tudela 190
Wisdom 16, 83-6, 107, 116, 230; as Jerusalem 84, 116-7; *see also* Achamoth; Sophia
Woden (god) 139; *see also* Mercury
Wolfram von Eschenbach 189-90, 199, 202, 214-5; *see also* Parzival

Yahweh (god) 18
Yavanna 236
Yeats, William Butler 9, 196
Yvain (knight) 92, 95, 104, 134, 148-9, 155, 165, 169, 171-2, 176, 182-4

Zeus (god) 25; *see also* Jupiter
Zimmer, Heinrich 181-3
Zoas 16, 78-9, 224-7

www.ingramcontent.com/pod-product-compliance
Ingram Content Group UK Ltd.
Pitfield, Milton Keynes, MK11 3LW, UK
UKHW041932140426
5217IPUK00014B/440